Possessed by the Virgin

Possessed by the Virgin

Hinduism, Roman Catholicism, and Marian Possession in South India

Kristin C. Bloomer

OXFORD
UNIVERSITY PRESS

OXFORD
UNIVERSITY PRESS

Oxford University Press is a department of the University of Oxford. It furthers the University's objective of excellence in research, scholarship, and education by publishing worldwide. Oxford is a registered trade mark of Oxford University Press in the UK and certain other countries.

Published in the United States of America by Oxford University Press
198 Madison Avenue, New York, NY 10016, United States of America.

First issued as an Oxford University Press paperback, 2019

Library of Congress Cataloging-in-Publication Data
Names: Bloomer, Kristin C., author.
Title: Possessed by the Virgin : Hinduism, Roman Catholicism, and Marian possession in South India / Kristin C. Bloomer.
Description: New York : Oxford University Press, 2018. |
Includes bibliographical references and index.
Identifiers: LCCN 2017006768 (print) | LCCN 2017039303 (ebook) |
ISBN 9780190615109 (updf) | ISBN 9780190615116 (epub) |
ISBN 9780190615123 (oso) | ISBN 9780190615093 (cloth) |
ISBN 9780190067809 (paper)
Subjects: LCSH: Mary, Blessed Virgin, Saint—Cult—India—Tamil Nadu. |
Christianity—India—Tamil Nadu. | Mariyamman (Hindu deity)—
Cult—India—Tamil Nadu. | Tamil Nadu (India)—Religious life and customs.
Classification: LCC BT652.I4 (ebook) | LCC BT652.I4 B56 2017 (print) |
DDC 200.954/82—dc23
LC record available at https://lccn.loc.gov/2017006768

For my parents and sisters

CONTENTS

Acknowledgments *ix*
Dramatis Personae *xiii*
Note on Transliteration *xv*
Maps of India *xvii*

Introduction *1*

1. Rosalind *32*

2. The Place, the People, the Practices: Our Lady Jecintho and the Quest for Embodied Wholeness *56*

3. Authenticity and Double Trouble: The Case of Nancy-as-Jecintho *84*

4. Possession, Processions, and Authority *109*

Interlude *130*

5. Return to Mātāpuram *133*

6. Women's Work: Gendered Space and the Dangerous Labor of (Virgin) Birth *156*

7. Memory, Mimesis, and Healing *187*

8. Conclusion: Departures and Homecomings *209*

Epilogue *234*

Notes *247*
Glossary *289*
Bibliography *295*
Index *309*

ACKNOWLEDGMENTS

To have worked on a project for more than a dozen years means that I have lots of people to thank—more than can possibly be listed here. But I will try.

First, to the Tamil women about whom this book is written, I owe a debt I can never repay. They opened their lives to me with immeasurable grace, hospitality, and patience—for reasons I may never be able to understand. To "Dhanam," her extended family, and to all the people of "Mātāpuram;" to S. Nancy Browna and family; and last, but certainly not least, to C. Rosalind and family—to M. Charles, Lawrence, Robert, Benjamin, M. Paul, Celina, Ruby Mary, their spouses and children, Julie, Alex, and the entire extended family of Our Lady Jecintho Prayer House—*mikka anbudan*. I will never be able to communicate the depth of my gratitude.

For the kindness of strangers. To the guard at Chennai International Airport who hailed my first auto-rickshaw on my first night in India; to the driver of that auto, who dropped me in the middle of that night in the middle of a dark highway amidst a group of day-and-night-laborers; to those same kind strangers, who pushed me backpack and all onto the bus that would take me to Pondicherry: thank you. To the myriad people who helped pave my way—the coffee-*karars*, sari-tiers, restaurant servers, hotel owners, night watchmen, slum dwellers, house holders, fish sellers, kadai-*karars*, farmers, relief workers, painters, dancers, doctors, business people, children, and civil servants, especially the immigration official who tried to kick me out of the country (resulting in my stumbling upon the subject of this book): thank you.

To my teachers. To Annie Dillard, whose friendship and early mentorship changed my life. To my two dissertation advisers: Wendy Doniger, One Amazing Woman, and Kathryn Tanner, whose brilliance and bravery inspired me from the start. To the two outside members of my doctoral committee: Kalpana Ram, whose first book catalyzed my interest in this topic, and Corinne Dempsey, whose warm friendship, sense of humor, commitment to intellectual community, and thirst for adventure lift my heart. To Dan Baum and Margaret Knox, working writers and great lovers of life, who have mentored me from my first years as a journalist through today and who—along with Rosa Knox-Baum—gave me a place to live in Boulder, Colorado, when I came back broke from India. Thank you.

To my Tamil instructors. At the University of Chicago, the late Norman Cutler introduced me to the romance of bhakti poetry through *Hymns for the Drowning* while helping me discern the difference between adverbial and adjectival participles. John Bernard "Barney" Bate's high spirits, big heart, and famous fluency kept me from giving up. James Lindholm, who wrote the best textbook on Tamil yet to be written, supported me morally and generously in our tutorials; Jonathan Ripley and Benjamin Schonthal modeled what it meant to be a good student of Tamil; and David Shulman passed on his patient teaching and love for the language. In India, the Summer Tamil Language Program at the French Institute of Pondicherry enabled my first Tamil "field interview" with the family of a boy possessed by St. Anthony; and in Madurai, Dr. S. Bharati at the American Institute of Indian Studies, now at the University of California–Berkeley, showered us with learning like the goddess Saraswati.

To academic institutions and scholars in India. S. Anandhi, Padmini Swaminathan, and A.R. Venkatachalapathy took me under their wings at the Madras Institute of Development Studies and shepherded me through particularly difficult times. In Palayamkottai, the Folklore Resources and Research Center at St. Xavier's College shared their holdings, and Peter Arokiaraj in particular labored to procure copies of texts and films that gave me early insights into Marian possession in rural Tamil Nadu.

In Chennai, the generous hospitality and intellectual companionship of Dr. Nirmal Selvamony, his wife Dr. Ruckmani, and their daughters Madhini and Padini enriched my experience more than I can express. Sitting around their dining table late into the night discussing everything from *Tolkāppiyam* to contemporary Tamil politics, they lost much sleep while feeding my mind, soul, and body. The completion of this book and many of its insights are very much indebted to our conversations.

To my research assistants. S. Padma Balaji of Chennai helped me tirelessly from 2005 to 2006, through floods and hot, dry spells, while sharing hearty laughter and hardwork. Her interviewing techniques were impeccable. M. Thavamani of Gingee lent me invaluable assistance from 2005 to the end of this book and beyond, traveling many miles away from his farm and his family to help me navigate difficult interviews and painstakingly transcribe recordings. Some of my favorite memories include sitting in his own house in beautiful Pasumalaithangal, coffee by my side, as we worked on these translations together. To his wife, Jothi, and to his children, Anna and Les: *mikka anbu*.

To the many priests and nuns who extended their generosity: Rev. Fr. Bernard Lawrence of Annai Velankanni, Besant Nagar; Rev. Fr. Vincent Chinnadurai and Rev. Fr. Gaspar of Chennai; Rev. Fr. Ananthan of Sacred Heart Seminary, Poonamalee; Rev. Sr. Dr. Mother Annamma Philip and Sr.

Florine Monis of Stella Maris College; Rev. Fr. Pictaimuuthu, the wandering priest of the people; the priests at the Basilica of Our Lady Velankannni, Nagapattinam; Rev. Fr. Aasir Vatham of Sivagangai Diocese; the Most Rev. M. Devadass Ambrose, Bishop of Thanjavur; Rev. Fr. Arul Selvam of Sivagangai; Rev. Fr. R. K. Sami of the Liturgical, Biblical and Catechismal Institute, Bangalore; Rev. Dr. G. Patrick of the University of Madras; and Rev. Fr. S. P. Xavier, now of Kolkata, who first helped me to understand the rosary in Tamil. *Nandri.*

To the many people who helped me navigate the aftermath of the 2004 Asian Tsunami, opening their hearts, homes, and stories to me, and to the Sisters of the Sacred Heart of Jesus Convent in Nagercoil, who housed and fed me: thank you.

To my many colleagues and friends throughout the United States who sustained me through various stages of this book, even before it began, I owe thanks beyond words. I list you non-alphabetically and in no particular order, but in groupings you may recognize: Lee Siegel, Elizabeth Blalock, Monica Ghosh, Paul Lyons, Sai Bhatawadekar, Chad Bauman, Steven Hopkins, Selva Raj, Joyce Flueckiger, Kaori Hatsumi, Gemma Betros, Anne Braude, Judith Casselberry, Hauwa Ibrahim, Zilka Spahić Ŝiljak, Francis X. Clooney, Chinnappan Devaraj, Sarah Feldman, Gabriel Robinson, Gabi Marcus, Eliza Kent, Elaine Craddock, Gillian Goslinga, Kristen Rudisill, Katherine Ulrich, C. Maheswari, Gardner Harris, Venkatesh Chakravarty, Francis Cody, Davesh Soneji, Shiladitya Sarkar, Martha Selby, James Laine, Erik Davis, Pam Percy, Sigrid Austin, Venkateshwaran Ravichandran, Dietrix Jon Ulukoa Duhaylonsod, J. Michelle Molina, and Wendy Boxer. My colleagues at Carleton College kept me afloat with ongoing good cheer and intellectual companionship, most belovedly: Amna Khalid, Paul Petzschmann, Meera Sehgal, Brendan LaRoque, Noah Salomon, Roger Jackson, Lori Pearson, Michael McNally, Louis Newman, Asuka Sango, Kevin Wolfe, Sonja Anderson, Sandy Saari, Bardwell Smith, Eleanor Zelliot, Annette Nierobisz, Jane McDonnell, Paula Lackie, Liz Coville, Van Dusenbery, Amel Gorani, Anita Chikkatur, Laurel Bradley, Sam Demas, Peter Balaam, and Laska Jimsen. Many of my former graduate students at the University of Hawaii-Manoa, now dear friends—Deeksha Sivakumar, Juston Stein, and Jessica Freedman, in particular—gave me helpful feedback and emotional support. At Carleton College, the ongoing curiously, insight, and open minds of my students, especially in "Many Marys," the "Sacred Body," and "Spirit Possession," gave me innumerable insights and kept me on my toes.

This research was generously funded by the National Endowment for the Humanities, the American College of Learned Societies, the Women's Studies in Religion Program at Harvard University, the Center for the Study of World Religions at Harvard University, Carleton College, the University of Hawaii Research Relations Fund, the American Institute of Indian Studies, the

Fulbright-Hays Doctoral Dissertation Research Abroad Fellowship, and, at the University of Chicago, the Committee on South Asian Studies, the Martin Marty Center, the Center for Gender Studies, and the Harper Dissertation Writing Fellowship. Carleton College granted me four terms of leave for research and writing.

To editors, to my two anonymous outside readers, whose comments and suggestions helped me focus and pare down a manuscript that threatened to outweigh *Moby Dick.* To Cynthia Read, my editor at Oxford University Press whose early faith in this project gave me hope; to Drew Anderla, the editorial assistant who answered my emails swiftly and with much appreciated exclamation points; and to Ginny Faber, a terrific copy editor. To Tracy Thompson and Jerri Hurlbutt, who helped me edit early versions of this manuscript, and to Katherine Ulrich (again), indexer and Indologist editor extraordinaire. Thank you.

To Brian Welch, whose patience, emotional support, fastidious proofreading, and level-headedness helped me especially through later stages of this project.

Last but not least, to my family. To my cousin John J. Bloomer, who took me salsa dancing in Cambridge when I desperately needed it, and to the Bruce and Sandy Bloomers who housed and cheered me on cross-country treks from Minnesota to Massachusetts and back. To my nieces Izzy and Addy Bloomer-Duffy, the lights of my life who delight me both in person and over Face Time, Instagram, and Musical.ly. To my grandparents, whose spirits inform this work. And, most deeply: to my parents, John and Patricia Bloomer, and to my sisters, Karin and Joanna Bloomer—without whose support and love this book would never have been possible, let alone conceivable. There is no word for "thank you."

DRAMATIS PERSONAE (IN ORDER OF APPEARANCE, ORGANIZED BY PLACE)

OUR LADY JECINTHO PRAYER HOUSE

Alex: M. Paul's son, Rosalind's youngest cousin, who first fell ill; had visions of Mary; and later became possessed

Rosalind: Charles's daughter, the eldest child in the family, and only girl

Fredy: Rosalind's son

M. Charles: Rosalind's father

Lawrence: Charles's eldest son, Rosalind's brother

Maria Auxilia: Lawrence's wife

Benjamin: Charles's second son

Robert: Charles's third son and Rosalind's youngest brother, to whom she is closest

M. Paul: Charles's younger brother, Rosalind's uncle

Celina: M. Paul's wife, a Hindu

Ruby Mary: M. Paul's eldest daughter

Julie: M. Paul's youngest daughter

Francina: Rosalind's attendant, confidante, and best friend

Lata: possessed by *pēy*, and a prayer house member

Anna Francis: prayer house member

Rex: lay preacher and prayer house member

Rev. Dr. Lawrence Pius: Auxiliary Bishop of Madras-Mylapore Archdiocese

Rev. Fr. Vincent Chinnadurai: parish priest of St. Patrick Church at Saint Thomas Mount, Chennai; first told me about Rosalind

Sr. Florine Monis: Director of Administration at Stella Maris College, Chennai

Rev. Sr. Dr. Mother Annamma Philip: Principal of Stella Maris, Chennai

Rev. Fr. Pitchaimuuthu: priest supporting Our Lady Jecintho Prayer House

Most Rev. Dr. A. M. Chinnappa: Archbishop of Madras-Mylapore Archdiocese

Rev. Fr. A. Thomas: parish priest of Muthamizh Nagar, in which Our Lady Jecintho Prayer House is located

KODAMBAKKAM, CHENNAI

Nancy: S. Nancy Browna, the second woman to get possessed by Jecintho Mātā, after Rosalind
Maatavan Shanthakumar: Nancy's father
Leela: Nancy's mother
Antony: Nancy's brother (younger)
S. Padma Balaji: field assistant, from Chennai
Vadivambal: Nancy's paternal grandmother
Rev. Fr. Ambrose: parish priest of Our Lady of Fatima Church, Kodambakkam

MĀTĀPURAM (ALIAS NAMES)

Dhanam: possessed by Mātā
Rev. Fr. Arlappan: guide back to Mātāpuram; Aarokkiyam's brother
Aarokkiyam: Arlappan's brother and Sahaya Mary's husband
Sahaya Mary: Dhanam's neighbor, a woman possessed by Pandi Muni
Sebastiammal: Aarokkiyam and Arlappan's mother
Ubakaram: Aarokkiyam and Arlappan's grandmother
Sebastian Samy: Dhanam's husband
Sofia Mary: Dhanam's daughter
Peter Raj: Dhanam's son-in-law, husband of Sofia Mary
Adaikkala Raj: Dhanam's eldest son
Aananthan: Dhanam's second eldest son; ordained priest
Dhanam's youngest son: unnamed seminarian in Agra
M. Thavamani: field assistant, from Gingee
Arokkiya Mary: Dhanam's daughter and eldest child
Rev. Fr. Michael Antony: Dhanam's brother, living in Agra
Rev. Fr. Aasir Vatham: parish priest of Sahaya Mary Church, Devakotai

NOTE ON TRANSLITERATION

Tamil words were transliterated following the University of Madras Tamil Lexicon. According to this system, "c" is pronounced "s," and "ḻ" is the unique Tamil letter linguists refer to as the voiced retroflex approximate, which is pronounced somewhere between "l" and retroflex "r." For reading ease, Tamil personal, caste, and place names are given with diacritics at first mention if at all and then without diacritics using the most widely recognized Anglicized forms. Also for easier reading, I have generally transliterated the Sanskrit "ś" as it sounds: "sh." Most non-Tamil Indian words have been transliterated without diacritics, using the standard Anglicized forms when possible.

MAPS OF INDIA

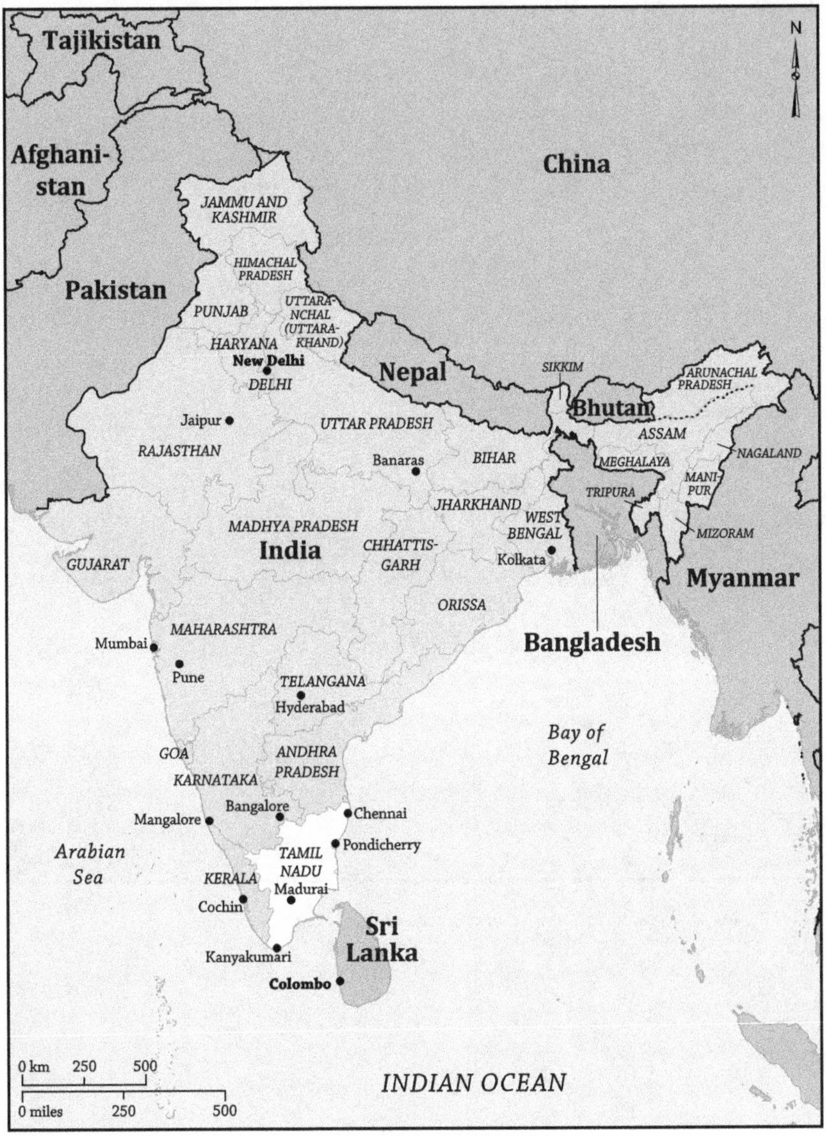

Map 1: India and its states, with Tamil Nadu highlighted.

Map 2: Tamil Nadu, with Chennai and Sivagangai Districts highlighted.

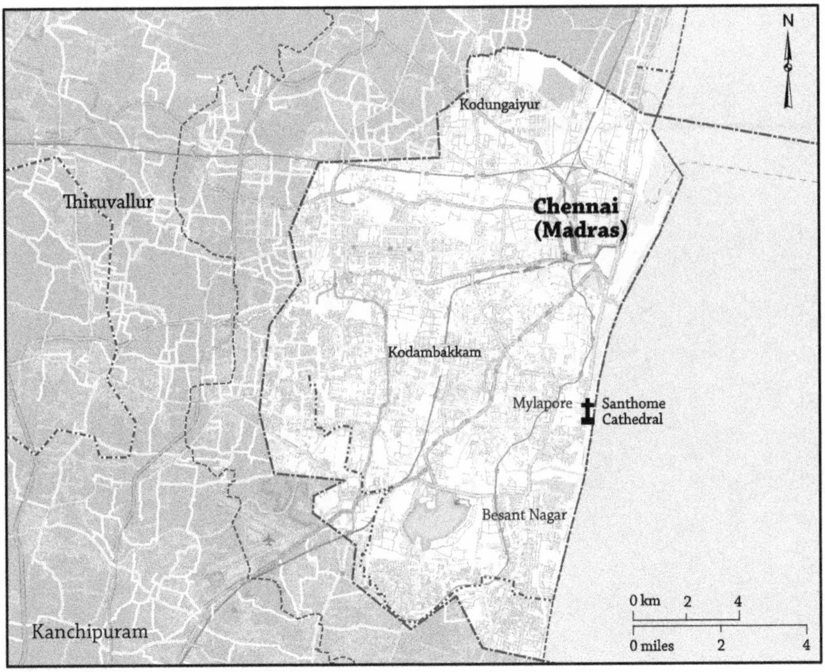

Map 3: Chennai, with neighborhoods of Kodungaiyur, Kodambakkam, Mylapore, and Besant Nagar.

Possessed by the Virgin

Introduction

It all started with the deaths of five men. That's how Dhanam saw it, anyway.

The year was 1979. The victims were five Hindu Untouchables—now known as Dalits, which means "ground down" or "oppressed."[1] Their village was Chinna Unjanai, which lay in the parched, red-soil countryside of southern Tamil Nadu, India. Dhanam, a graceful tenant farmer with sleek black hair and a voice like velvet, was also a Dalit. Unlike the murdered men, she was Roman Catholic, and lived in Mātāpuram, the Roman Catholic village next to theirs. Both Dalit villages had been in the service of higher castes who had oppressed them for centuries.

It was a time of mounting tensions, especially on those rare occasions when high- and low-caste[2] people came together—usually on important religious festivals. In June of 1979, some members of the Pallar clan from Chinna, also Dalits, had been barred by the higher-caste Kallars[3] from participating in two annual religious processions—one at a huge Shiva temple in the nearby village of Kandadevi, and another to a lesser god named Aiyanar.[4] The Pallars, denied the honor both of pulling the huge chariot carrying Shiva around town and also of carrying the terra-cotta horses for Aiyanar,[5] cooked up a plan to hold their own Aiyanar festival. Somehow the Kallars learned of it, and hired some fifteen hundred low-caste people from another district to attack the men from Chinna.[6] At dawn on June 29, the hired thugs set off fireworks in the fields outside the village, luring people outside.[7] Then they attacked. They set fire to the village, and—armed with knives and hatchets—hacked five men to death, nearly killing a sixth and injuring about thirty more. The five dead men were buried between Chinna Unjanai and Mātāpuram.[8] No Dalit—either in what remained of Chinna Unjanai or in the next-door village of Dalits, Dhanam's village of Mātāpuram—slept well those nights.

Dhanam was eighteen at the time of the murders, two years married and nursing a six-month-old daughter. News traveled quickly to Dhanam's village: its residents were of the Paraiyar clan—from which the English word "pariah" comes. Paraiyar men historically went from village to village, shirtless, beating their *parai* drums, announcing upcoming festivities and funerals.[9] Before the attack, Dhanam had seen the murdered Chinna men in passing. She knew their faces, and she had seen the white body bags in which they were brought back for burial after the postmortem. Now, collecting firewood or walking to the fields for water or work, she would sometimes pass by their headstones. In South India, many people believe that the spirits of the untimely dead—*pēy*—can "catch" women, especially newly married women, and cause illness or domestic havoc, even blocking their ability to conceive.[10] Dhanam and her husband longed for a son—and Dhanam came to suspect that the *pēy* of the murdered Hindu men were preventing her from getting pregnant again. The minute she flicked off the single light bulb of their clay home, or extinguished a lamp, they would be standing there, dead, one holding his own head, the others' faces swollen and blue. She feared she would never conceive. But when she was twenty-one, she felt a child stirring in her belly. She and her husband thought it might be a boy, which made them even happier.[11]

In the seventh month of Dhanam's pregnancy, the rains refused to come. The naked sun raked the fields until the paddy withered and the dirt rose in puffs to the sky. Pregnant women were not supposed to fish, particularly not in Hindu territory—or so many local Hindus and Christians believed. But Dhanam was bold, the heat was unbearable, and the villagers' stomachs were near empty—so she joined her husband and a crowd of villagers, and walked past the graves to catch fish on the other side of Chinna. The water level in the lake then had fallen so low, it was said, that people were catching fish with their bare hands.

Villagers' spirits were high as they set out with the prospect of cooling off and catching fish. They took the path along the shore through low-lying scrub and bramble, passing Aiyanar's temple. The warrior god's immense terra-cotta horse guarded the edge of Hindu terrain. His divine peons, lesser gods, animated the black stone icons housed there, all smeared with ghee, *vibhuti*, and *kumkum*[12] in dark, cave-like shelters. Dhanam hardly noticed them, eager as she was to reach the boisterous activity at the lake.

The trip was a success: she and her husband caught several mackerel and catfish. But the way out was slippery, and she fell, belly-down, toward the bank. She thought little of it—she felt fine—and returned home with fellow villagers, relaxed and contented. Dhanam cleaned and cooked the fish, fed her husband and daughter, ate after they did, as is custom for women in South India, and went to sleep full and happy. But later in the night, Dhanam awoke in terrible pain. Her stomach ached and torqued; she couldn't hold down her food. Her husband carried her to the nearest health clinic in Aravaiyil, a village one-and-a-half-kilometers away, where a nurse gave her an injection.[13] When the relief proved only temporary, Dhanam's parents arrived to take her home to her natal village of Manapunjai, about twenty kilometers away.[14] In the center of their village, as in Dhanam's, was a chapel to Mary. Sick people often sought refuge there for healing—her father, a staunch devotee, sometimes said mantras over the sick in her name.

Dhanam's parents brought her to the chapel, and her mother attended to her. She lay on the cool cement floor while her mother tried to feed her curd rice and gruel. She even tried to tempt her with *murukku*, the savory, crunchy twists of rice and chickpea flour usually reserved for South Indian holidays, but Dhanam wouldn't eat. When it was clear that she was not improving, her parents took her to the Christian hospital in Puliyal, a few kilometers away. A medically trained nun gave Dhanam another injection, telling her that she was anemic and that her blood pressure was low. She should stay at least ten days and eat well, the nun said.

The pain only increased. Ten days later, Dhanam's parents brought her back to the Mary chapel in her natal village.

It was there, lying on the cool stone floor of the chapel in Manapunjai, that Dhanam heard a *madduk-madduck* in her stomach and felt a shudder and shake in her womb: the death throes of the fetus. She felt faint, then drowsy. "Take me back to the hospital," she said. The sisters in Puliyal gave her another injection, causing contractions.

The child, a boy, was stillborn.

Dhanam and her husband cried inconsolably. About ten other babies were born in the clinic that day. Dhanam's was the only stillbirth.

They buried the small body in the cemetery outside the hospital and returned home to Mātāpuram, empty-handed.

Back home, the pain in Dhanam's stomach remained; it became an ache that would not release her. She could barely breathe when the cramps came, and she thought she would suffocate, feeling at times as if several people were sitting on her chest.[15] At night in her dreams, the five Dalit men returned in their gory lineup. She now knew her mistake—to pass the burial ground of the murdered men as a bride and new mother, with the fragrance of jasmine in her hair and the smell of sex on her skin, and to wade into a lake guarded by Hindu gods while pregnant. She had been too loyal to her Christianity to appeal to Hindu rites for protection. Now, it didn't help that some people thought they would have saved her baby.

One night, as Dhanam lay in pain, bleeding, cramping, and mourning, Mary—whom the people of Dhanam's village, like most Tamils, called *Mātā* (mother)—came to Dhanam's pallet, took her by the hand, and led her to a little chapel made of brick and cement which stood in a clearing at the center of Mātāpuram. Dressed in a sari, Mātā told Dhanam to hold a lighted candle and repeat her name, Mātā. Then she beat Dhanam with a broom, and Dhanam started dancing, arms akimbo, head rocking back and forth so violently that her hair loosened from its knot and flew around her face. She fell to the ground: her body rolled and resisted. Out flew the spirits of the five dead men.[16] Out also came, for that matter, a *muni*,[17] one of the seven fierce incarnations of Shiva—and a *pēy*, the ghost of a neighboring Hindu woman who had died in pregnancy. As Dhanam writhed on the cool, dark floor of the chapel, damp with sweat, her body throbbing, people watched while something else, something terribly alien, seemed to be speaking through her mouth. Was it Mātā? Some other demon or spirit? "*Chi! Pō!* (Chi! Go!)," Mātā threatened, wielding the broom. "*Illai!* (No!)," another voice cried.

For three months, Dhanam's body remained a battleground. The *muni*, one of Aiyanar's peons, refused to leave her—so Mātā would return, periodically and unannounced, to engage in a violent struggle with him. Over time, Dhanam came to understand that Mātā was warring with the fierce god who had caused her first boy to die. Mātā was revealing to the entire village, and to anyone else who came to see, her power to win over a powerful Hindu god, and to heal.

OTHER BEGINNINGS, AND THE BEGINNING OF AN "OTHER"

I first heard about Dhanam in the summer of 1999, during a trip to Madurai, an inland temple town known for its elaborate, colorful, multitowered temple to the Hindu goddess Meenakshi. There, at the guest house of the American Institute of Indian Studies, I met Gillian Goslinga, a young scholar with a thick red braid down her back, accomplished in Tamil, and quite advanced in her own pre-dissertation fieldwork on the Hindu god Pandi Muni, whom we had separately seen possess busloads of women. Gillian and I sat on the cool stoop of the institute's veranda, picking pomegranate seeds out of their hive-like shells, when I told her about my interest in Marian devotion. "I know a village you need to visit," she said. The village, only a few hours away, was entirely Roman Catholic and Dalit—and in it lived a woman who healed people while possessed by Mary. On top of that, one of Gillian's informants—one of the Pandi-possessed women she had interviewed—was a Catholic from this same village. A *Catholic* possessed by a *Hindu* god! It was the Marian-possessed woman, Gillian said, who diagnosed such afflictions in her healing and exorcism rituals. I knew I had to find her, this Dhanam.

I had come to India ostensibly to study the Tamil language, but my motivations also had to do with fantasy and upbringing: I grew up in a Charismatic

Roman Catholic family with parents who prayed in tongues and participated in faith healing—a manner of worship that to many of my friends in our wealthy Connecticut suburb may have seemed as exotic and foreign as India at the time did to me. I wanted to understand my own natal beliefs because I was determined (or so I thought) to escape their confines. I was particularly troubled by patriarchal constructs in Roman Catholicism, and by the problem of Mary in relation to those constructs. The pantheon of Hindu goddesses—and the idea of female divinities who were equal in power to their male counterparts—intrigued me. I wondered if female divinities translated into a more egalitarian world for women and men.[18]

India made sense as a focus for my research in that it was the geographic origin of the wide variety of discourses and practices that early missionaries and colonial administrators had grouped under the umbrella-term "Hinduism."[19] In particular, I was drawn to Tamil Nadu because it was the home of politically oppressed Dravidian people, whose language and culture was notably different from those of North India, and comparatively understudied. There was also my attraction to classical Tamil poetry, called *Caṅkam*, meaning "an academy or society," for the societies of poets who wrote it. This poetry, dating back to as early as 100 BCE, is divided into two groups: *akam* (pronounced "aham"), poetry of the "inner world," and *puṟam*, poetry of the "outer world." Whereas *puṟam* poetry celebrates kings, laments heroes, and describes war and politics, *akam* poems are love poems. This two-thousand-year-old literature speaks in an almost modernist and certainly symbolic way of the complex feelings between men and women, among women, between women and their mothers, and between mothers and their sons. It is a view clearly infused with religious as well as erotic feeling, and many subtle sorts of love. It is also intimately connected to nature, and to a complex symbolic system that reflects a deep human connection to the earth.[20]

Roman Catholics are a historically oppressed, minority population in India.[21] In 2011, Christians of all stripes made up a small percentage of India's total population of 1.21 billion—anywhere between 2.3 and 6 percent—with Hindus and Muslims as the far greater majority.[22] Of these Christians, the Catholic Church in India was the largest portion, and divided into three rites: Syro-Malabar, Syro-Malankara, and Latin (Roman Catholic). Together, these rites represented only 1.6 percent of the country's total population—but India is so big that this works out to be about 19.4 million people. About two-thirds of all Christians were Roman Catholic, and about 40 percent lived in the southern states of Tamil Nadu and Kerala.[23] In Tamil Nadu, which the Portuguese began colonizing in the sixteenth century, the percentage of Christians (6.12 percent) was three times higher than the official, 2.3 percentage rate for all India. Most Tamil Roman Catholics lived on the east coast, but early Roman Catholic missions had also extended inland to Madurai in the early seventeenth century, and to Palayamkottai, spreading the Christian population inland.[24]

I was struck by the similarities and differences between Tamil Christianity and the Christianity with which I was familiar—in particular by the devotion to Mary among both Catholics *and* Hindus. Early Portuguese missionaries were clever to fashion local Catholic festivals in ways that would attract local non-Christians. At coastal Velankanni, one of India's largest Marian pilgrimage sites, and elsewhere, devotees flocked in the hundreds of thousands to "car festivals," or *tēr bavaṉi*, the grand chariot processions of Mary and saints that occurred especially at festival times. These Marian chariot processions, which had originated in different incarnations in Rome and Europe as vibrant processions in their own right, were modeled here on the local Hindu ones.

I was also impressed by people's intense outward signs of devotion, no matter what their religion. Even in the bustling metropolis of Chennai, Tamil Nadu's state capital, businessmen could be seen stopping their motorcycles outside roadside shrines on their way to work, crossing their hands to opposite earlobes, and bobbing up and down from squatting to standing positions. Shopkeepers at set times stopped everything, even in the middle of an exchange, to light incense and ring bells in front of small shrines to Lakshmi, the goddess of prosperity. At daybreak, women stepped outside their homes in bright saris to sweep the area outside their front doors—whether those doors opened onto packed-dirt lanes or high-rise apartments—and bent to draw intricate *kolams*, geometric designs made of rice powder, also to welcome the goddess.

South India also has a strong history of *bhakti*, or personal religious devotion to a god or goddess. The term *bhakti* is derived from the Sanskrit root *bhaj*, "to divide, apportion, share." *Bhaktas* (devotees) are linked with their personal deity and with one another by a bond of shared love and grace.[25] The *bhakti* movement exploded in popularity in South India in the twelfth through eighteenth centuries CE, mostly as a reaction to Brahmanical Hinduism. In this form of Hinduism, brahmin priests sit at the top of the caste hierarchy and most rituals are only for people in the top three *varnas*, or categories, of society—leaving out the vast majority of the population. *Bhakti*, on the other hand, holds as two of its basic principles the unimportance of ritual purity for the attainment of divine grace, and the idea that love is the way to freedom—love that is boundless, love that is common and accessible to all.[26] *Bhakti* is the great leveler of status. People who by virtue of their low or untouchable caste do not have access to ritual purity can claim to have access to a different sort of purity—purity of the heart. In fact, it is the suffering experienced by those at the bottom of the social ladder which makes room for a god (or goddess) in their hearts.[27] Much *bhakti* poetry alludes to states of possession by the deity, and at times it can invoke states of possession in its devotees.

I was emotionally and intellectually interested in the notion of a deity's power entering a person, having seen such beliefs fleshed out in my own family: my parents prayed in tongues, prophesied, and—during certain prayer services—would fall back into a catcher's arms, "slain" by the Holy Spirit. I was also fascinated by the question of whether or not, and in what contexts, this divine power connected to worldly power. That Mary would be the divine power acting through people fascinated me for a number of reasons, also personal. My maternal grandmother had been an ardent devotee of Mary, my maternal grandfather had had a vision of Mary while lying on a hospital bed during World War II, and my maternal uncle had also had visions. My mother had taught me how to pray to Mary; a small statue of Mary stood in the backyard; and as a child, I prayed every night to her with the rosary beads and book of novenas I kept in an empty chocolates box by my bed.

In India, that Hindus *and* Roman Catholics alike worshipped Mary was notable in itself, but on top of that, what struck me was the materiality of their exchanges with her. Devotees touched her statue, leaving their hands on her feet for several seconds if not minutes, and then touched their own eyes and hearts; they decked her with garlands of flowers; they donated elaborate saris with which women dressed her. The silk, "touched," as it were, by Mary, was thought to confer blessings upon whoever wore it next. Another time, I joined the millions who flock annually to Our Lady of Velankanni Church in the coastal town of Nagapattinam. Many people walk hundreds of miles to pay their respects to this incarnation of Mary, also known as Our Lady of Good Health, or in Tamil, *Ārōkkiya Aṉṉai* (also known as *Ārōkkiya Mātā*). The transnationally popular pilgrimage site of Velankanni, with origins dating back at least to the sixteenth century, is like Lourdes, Fatima, Medjugorje, Guadalupe, and countless other shrines to Mary around the world famous for miracles. Velankanni, too, was known for healing all sorts of ailments—especially for women, and especially those ailments related to fertility. In exchange for health and other boons, people made vows (*nērccai*) to *Ārōkkiya Mātā*, such as walking on their knees for miles in exchange for the granting of a life-changing wish. At the Grand Tonsure Hall beside the church, barbers shaved the heads of men, women, and children who offered their hair to Mary. (Some of this hair, barbers told me, would soon become wigs in the United States.) Women rolled down the street toward the church like tubes of dusty gift-wrap, while female friends ran beside them, tucking in their friends' saris so they would not unravel.

BEING "DANCED" AND GETTING "PLUCKED": THE SOMATIC SEMANTICS OF POSSESSION

It was on these early, heady language-study trips to India that I heard, directly and indirectly, about local belief in possession by Mary and by saints, and witnessed forms of Hindu deity and spirit possession that seemed to serve as an important backdrop for—and influence on—local, Catholic phenomena. I conducted a few informal interviews: I interviewed, for example, a Tamil Christian family in Pondicherry whose members believed that St. Anthony had possessed and healed their young son. The twelve-year-old boy, head shaved and wide-eyed, seemed stunned. Their home had become a local shrine: Visitors from various religious traditions gathered in its inner courtyard to hear St. Anthony give messages (*kuri*, lit. "signs") that might help them through difficult times. I also witnessed possession practices among low-caste Hindus. On more than one Tuesday or Friday (auspicious days for temple visits) I boarded the crowded number 42 bus from downtown Madurai toward the temple to Pandi Muni, which stood in the forest (*kāṭu*, "uncultivated area") at the edge of the city where women would regularly get possessed. On the women's side of the bus, I breathed in the smell of fresh jasmine that the women wore in their hair and took in the view of colorful saris, babies (their faces decorated with the black kohl dots that ward off the evil eye), and men across the aisle—husbands and brothers also dressed in neatly ironed shirts, looking slightly nervous.[28] The chatter got louder as we careened together through the Lotus City, under the Vaigai Bridge, and around the large city reservoir toward the temple to the god Pandi Munisvarar.[29] Not long into our journey, as we neared the temple's boundary stone, women started belching and yawning, and the looks on their faces started to change. Some women stiffened and tilted backward, as if they had stuck a finger in an electric socket. Others started to swoon or shake. Soon, more women were ululating and shrieking; the spirit was contagious. I thought of my mother, who had sometimes trilled "alleluias" off her tongue while she washed clothes, and of both my parents, who "sang in tongues" as the Holy Spirit moved through their Friday-night prayer group—causing some to fall over backwards, "slain in the Spirit." Here in India on the number 42 bus, these women loosened their otherwise tightly bound hair and, when the bus stopped outside the temple, ran toward it, still ululating. There, Muni would make them dance—or in Tamil, *āṭuvaṅkaḷ*, from the Tamil root *āṭu*, to sway to and fro, dance, or shake.

But being "possessed" by a spirit or deity in a South Asian context is different than getting "slain in the spirit" (being filled by the Holy Spirit) among American, Charismatic Christians—which raises the question of whether the term is even useful in a South Asian context, Christian or non-Christian. For one, most Americans filled by the Holy Spirit are not believed to lose their identity—they don't *become* the Holy Spirit—whereas people possessed by a god or goddess in India are generally understood to *be* that deity as long as they show the signs of possession. A woman possessed by Mariamman *is* Mariamman while possessed. Second, in English-speaking Europe and North America at least, the term "spirit possession" is largely understood in the Protestant and orthodox Roman Catholic context of Satan and evil: to "be possessed" often refers to the entrance of an evil spirit entity into the body. (Think of the film *The Exorcist.*) The exorcisms I saw growing up in a Charismatic community sometimes included the exorcist—a priest or a lay person—casting out "the spirit of sloth," "the spirit of addiction," or other troubling "spirits" from a person's body. Notably, in these and other European and American contexts, the "self" (organized around the notion of a soul, a conscience, and an autonomous will, which also carries a particularly Christian past[30]) is generally understood to be a fairly bounded entity. Comparatively, India's long tradition of deities and spirits coming into bodies, and the notion of a "self" that has more permeable boundaries with the spirit world (as well as with the social body) makes it more akin to beliefs and practices of many indigenous peoples before European conquest—people whose life worlds also involved permeability between human bodies, natural bodies, and gods, goddesses, and other spirits.

Certainly, some forms of spirit and deity possession among South Indians share characteristics with certain outward forms of Charismatic "gifts of the Spirit" in North America and elsewhere. Cross-culturally, men and women who are "possessed" (for lack of a better word)[31] by a deity or spirit move or speak in "odd" ways—that is, in ways considered to be outside the realm of proper daily behavior. In India, the bodily signs of "dancing" or "shaking," as well as loss of memory and personal identity during the possession period, are some of the authenticating marks of spirit possession.

In Tamil Nadu, there are many kinds of "god-dancing," many kinds of gods and spirits that can "dance" a person, and many terms that differentiate the type of possession. In one category of possession—and of beings who "possess"—one can dance or "be danced" by a god (a *cāmi*, such as Aiyanar), a *muni* (such as Pandi Muni), or an *ammaṉ*, a goddess (such as Kali Amman, Icakki Amman, or Mariamman). The same god or goddess can both heal and afflict. Within this form of possession are other differentiating terms: benevolent deities and spirits can "descend" (*iṟaṅku*), "come" (*varu*), or "come onto" (*varu mēl*) a person. A second category of "lesser spirits" include those of deceased humans: *pēy* (the spirit of a person who has died an untimely death, as in accident, suicide, or murder, as we saw in Dhanam's story), *āvi* (spirit of a dead person or ancestor), or *picācu* (ghost). *Pēy* and *picācu* are almost uniformly mischievous and havoc wreaking; and though *āvi* can be called upon for blessings and guidance—they, too, can "come onto" a person—they can also be troubling. Possession by these lesser spirits is often expressed with the verb *piṭi* (to be caught, grabbed, or plucked).[32] The language is key in indicating the benevolent inclination of the spirit or deity.

THE THREE "MARYS": DHANAM, ROSALIND, AND NANCY

And so, this book isn't just about Dhanam. It is about the larger phenomenon of Marian spirit possession in Tamil Nadu, and about the even larger question of whether Mary, in this context, challenges or confirms patriarchy and other forms of hegemony. It is also about the problematic categories of "universal" religious practices, symbols, and beliefs (possession, devotion to a deity, doctrinal Roman Catholicism) versus "local" ones ("being danced" by *pēy*, Mary "descending" on someone, devotion to Mary in particular forms, Tamil forms of Roman Catholicism). It is about the boundedness (or lack thereof) of religious "traditions." It is about gender, power, and agency. Most specifically, it is about three women who were repeatedly possessed by Mary over a period of many years; Dhanam was just one of them.

These three women came from different class, caste, and geographic backgrounds and drew hundreds—and in one case, thousands—of Christian and Hindu (and a few Muslim) devotees, also from a range of class, caste, and geographic categories. All three were Roman Catholic, and all were familiar with the widespread practice of deity and spirit possession in popular Hinduism. Beyond that, they had little in common. Rosalind, whom I met in 2003, was a college-educated single mother of thirty-eight, who regularly drew hundreds of people to her prayer house in Kodungaiyur, a northernmost neighborhood of sprawling Chennai. She was possessed every Wednesday and Saturday by a form of Mary who revealed herself as "Jecintho." The family with whom Rosalind lived was lower middle class and upwardly mobile.

Nancy—twenty-one, unmarried, and living with her parents and younger brother in a dense, mid-Chennai neighborhood of Kodambakkam when I met her later, in 2004—started getting possessed by Mary about a month after attending Rosalind's shrine. She seemed to act just like Rosalind while possessed by "Jecintho"—with one key difference: Nancy presented stigmata. Blood sometimes ran from her eyes, hands, and feet. Her family, from a Scheduled Caste,[33] was low or lower middle class.

Nancy knew Rosalind, and Rosalind came to know of Nancy, but neither knew Dhanam, and vice versa. Dhanam, unlike the other two, was illiterate.

These women were part of a larger phenomenon. While Marian possession may not be so widespread as to be much talked about or known among the general Indian public, it is recurrent enough to be worthy of attention. Some scholarly attention has already been paid, briefly. Most notably, Kalpana Ram, in two chapters of her book on Mukkuvar women—outcaste women from a coastal fishing caste in Tamil Nadu—wrote about Marian possession based on fieldwork she conducted in the early 1980s.[34] In a collection of essays about Christianity in India, one chapter by Richard MacPhail features a Tamil woman in Coimbatore, a central city in the state, whose Marian possession, exorcism, and healing practices drew crowds in the early 1990s.[35] Very little scholarly work, moreover, has touched on Marian churches and shrines as centers of exorcism.[36]

Despite the dearth of literature on the subject, there seemed to be no lack of anecdotal accounts about Marian possession and exorcism in India during my travels there. For example, I heard about a "Sister Alphonsa Mary" in Tanjore (Thanjur/Thanjavore) District who claimed to be possessed by Mary and gave messages in that state;[37] I watched raw footage, at a folklore research center, of an elderly woman who claimed to heal sick cattle while possessed by Mary;[38] I heard about a woman in the Besant Nagar neighborhood of Chennai where I lived for two years, who conducted healings through Mary.[39]

Marian possession also occurs in neighboring Sri Lanka,[40] where there are large populations of Tamils. In Madagascar, in the 1990s, Maurice Bloch wrote an article about Mary then possessing members of a community of ex-slaves.[41] Practitioners of Haitian Vodoun also arguably practice Marian possession, depending on the extent to which one associates Mary with the goddess Ezili.[42] In Tanzania, from the late 1980s to at least 2009, members of the Marian Faith Healing Ministry in Dar es Salaam believed that four mediums, embodying Mary, gave messages to the congregations and helped heal people.[43] North America has hosted at least one case of Marian possession in recent years that upset the Vatican: in 2007, it excommunicated an eighty-six-year-old Canadian nun claiming to be possessed by the Virgin and the six Catholic nuns living in Arkansas who followed her.[44] Marian possession may well be happening in other places around the globe as well—but if so, news of it does not seem to have reached the English-speaking world. In no other place than in South India am I aware of so common a phenomenon.

WHY IS MARY POSSESSING PEOPLE IN SOUTH INDIA TODAY?

South India is a relatively fecund place for Marian possession practices, in part because of its rich history of possession and healing across religious lines.[45] This historical context sets the stage for adoption of "new" forms of possession—by a "new" goddess, Mary, who fits somewhat easily into already-existing local notions of female divinity.

Spirit possession practices in India date back more than three thousand years, at least to the period of the *Rig Veda*, the earliest Indian sacred text, a collection of hymns composed in Sanskrit over a period of several hundred years, beginning as early as 1500 BCE.[46] Possession is a literary motif in the epic Mahabharata, a highly influential Indian text probably completed between the second and fourth centuries CE.[47] In very old non-Sanskritic South Indian texts, in particular, spirit possession also figures prominently—from the earliest extant Tamil grammatical text, the *Tolkāppiyam* (meaning "Old Composition," written sometime between the first and sixth centuries CE), and the poetry it describes, through the later poetry of *bhakti*.

A visit to any number of Hindu temple sites today, however, shows that despite the effects of globalization and modernity, possession and exorcism rituals are in full swing. Even cinema reflects this—from Satyajit Ray's famous 1960 art film *Devi*, in which a woman believes she is possessed by the goddess Kali, to the 2005 Bollywood movie *Paheli*, about a ghost who takes on the body of an ignored new bride's absent husband (played in double by Shah Rukh Khan). The 2015 romantic thriller *Anegan* (a classical word taken from the ninth-century Shaivite *bhakti* poem *Tiruvācakam* that means "multiple single person," or "one with many personalities"), focuses on the past lives of programmers in a gaming company; it features a scene in which sexual predator *pēy* and *picācu* haunt and try to grab one of the unmarried female programmers. She jumps from a high-rise office window and dies. (The two main characters, however, realize they have been in love in a past life, and eventually—spoiler alert!—reunite as lovers.)

THE DIVINE LANDSCAPE: DIVINITIES OF BLOOD AND POWER

Historical evidence suggests that fierce goddess possession and healing practices were prevalent in the precolonial Tamil-speaking region as well. These states of possession were sometimes *invited*, in the case, for example, of *cāmiyāṭis* (god dancers) who used ecstatic trance dancing to induce the deity, and sometimes *uninvited*, becoming a source of torment and debilitation which could only be relieved through exorcism.

The "divinities of blood and power" of this precolonial period can be categorized into two groups: *ammaṉ* goddesses—understood as divine power activated, or *shakti*, the visible energy of divine essence symbolized as a female—and warrior gods. Also common in this landscape were *nagas*, snake gods of the underworld, and *pēys* and *picācus*, who fed on human blood and on the passions of their victims. Each household and patrilineal clan, moreover, had its own *kulatēvam* (family deity), "usually a goddess who protected the ancestral domain and whose shrine would be a place of power and pilgrimage for the group even if its members had migrated far outside its original homeland."[48] The goddess was a source of stability, a sort of representation of home, even in periods of rapid change.

This long and vibrant history of possession and fierce goddess traditions in South India provided fertile soil in which local forms of Marian devotion could spring up once it came into contact with Christianity. One characteristic of this fecundity was (and still is) inclusivity. While Hinduism, like many religions, contains right-wing, purifying factions that claim Hinduism only for certain castes or types of "pure" Indians, it can also be a particularly inclusive, open tradition. The great number of gods and goddesses in Hinduism (some say there are 330 million[49]) expresses the basic notion that the divine can be found anywhere. In this sense, some Hindus see even Jesus and the Buddha as manifestations of Hindu gods—and Mary as another manifestation of *shakti*. Devotees at Marian pilgrimage sites who self-identified as Hindu often told me, referring to Mary, "Mātā is *shakti*." Roman Catholics said this too.

Early Jesuit missions worked hard to map Mary onto this inclusive, preexisting goddess landscape in order to lure new converts to the fold. But even as they wanted to capitalize on similarities to Hindu goddesses, they also wanted to stress how different Mary was from indigenous goddesses. (They wanted, in other words, to have their cake and to eat it too.) From the eighteenth to the mid-twentieth century, priests brutally punished converts who "attend[ed] pagan worship and secure[d] things offered to the devil."[50] On the other hand, eighteenth-century Jesuit letters describing South Indian mission fields show that some priests actually worked hard to turn the Virgin Mary into a manifestation of the goddess, and vice versa.[51] The historian Ines Županov tells us that "Jesuit Marian devotional practices were . . . easily fused with the older system of propitiation of this vengeful, merciful, and thaumaturgic goddess, regarded as both inflicting illness and curing it. . . . Their intention was not to fuse the two, but neither could they separate them altogether."[52] *Shakti* grew easily and quickly over (or with) Mary, despite some Jesuit attempts to stop it.

CHRISTIANITY IN INDIA: A BRIEF HISTORY

Mary has had a long time—far from European centers of Christianity and from the gaze of the Vatican—to develop into a spectrum of particular local Indian identities. Indian Christianity is almost as old as the historical Jesus himself. Legend tells us that it was about 50 CE when St. Thomas—the "doubting Thomas" of the Gospels—sailed to the west coast of India, to present-day Kerala. Having cast lots along with the other disciples and winning India, as we are told in the Acts of Thomas, he traveled to the Malabar Coast to convert the Jews who had moved there in the diaspora. He later traveled east to Mylapore, one of the oldest parts of current-day Chennai. Mylapore abuts the beach on the Bay of Bengal where St. Thomas is said to have met his bloody end, in 72 CE, and where his supposed remains are entombed in Santhome Cathedral.[53] Some historians promote the idea that Christianity in India may have started even sooner than Thomas. Mathias Mundadan, for example, notes that Indian philosophy and myth may have found its way via trade routes into the Gospels and teachings of Jesus, and perhaps back again via those same trade routes—even before St. Thomas arrived.[54]

Whatever the case, we know that an East Syrian Chaldean Christian community was established by at least the fourth century, "reinforced by continuous waves of Syrian immigrants involved in Kerala's thriving spice trade."[55] The historian of religion Corinne Dempsey tells us that not much is known about this early Christian community "except that it had become, by the time of the Portuguese arrival in the late fifteenth century, highly integrated into Hindu society."[56] It had also achieved high status.

Roman Catholicism arrived in India a good fourteen hundred years after St. Thomas Christianity and its various Syrian sects had become well established. Not long after Vasco de Gama and his Portuguese expedition reached the west coast of India in 1498, the Portuguese Estado da Índia—the overseas state of the Portuguese empire[57]—recognized its competition. European Roman Catholic missionaries began to strategize how to outdo the Syrian Christians, and quickly managed not only to block the Arab trade routes but also to cut off Syrian Christian ecclesial ties to east Syria. In the sixteenth century, the flow of foreign bishops on which Kerala's Syrian Christian community depended slowed to a standstill.[58]

Establishing the importance of Mary in this landscape was part of another Roman Catholic scheme to convert the heathens, and to make Catholicism translatable into Indian terms. One can trace the development of Marian shrines and feasts rapidly in Tamil country from 1543, the time of official Portuguese occupation of Mylapore.[59] In 1558, the Estado initiated the feast of the Exaltation of Our Lady. In 1582, Jesuits imported a statue of Our Lady of the Snows from Manila to Tuticorin, also on the Coromandel Coast, establishing a cult of the Virgin that became a focal point of caste identity among fishing people.[60] Around that same time, near the port of Nagapattinam, two young boys from fishing communities reportedly saw two separate (though similar) apparitions of Mary, and locals built her a thatched hut as a chapel. By the early seventeenth century, Portuguese sailors who were saved from a storm attributed their survival to Mary—and turned that hut into a solid construction overseen by Portuguese Franciscans.[61] They dedicated the chapel to the Portuguese Nossa Senhora da Saude (Our Lady of Health). Tamils, meanwhile, called her either *Ārōkkiya Mātā* (*ārōkkiya* means "health") or *Veḷaṅkanni Mātā* (*veḷai* means "white"; *kaṉṉi* means "maiden")—and the place came to be known as Velankanni. It is no coincidence that the annual Velankanni festival, which celebrates the birth of the Virgin Mary on September 8, replicates Hindu Navarāttiri festivals at goddess temples with nine-night, ten-day celebrations and a climactic event on the final day. By 1908, Velankanni had become known as the "Lourdes of India";[62] in 1962, Pope John XXIII bestowed on it the title of Basilica Minor. It is now the most prominent Marian shrine in India. Masses are celebrated daily in five languages, bringing in tens of millions of dollars and people annually.[63] To many Indians, Velankanni has also become a national symbol, and Mary is venerated as Mother India.[64]

At the time of my writing, there were at least eight other churches named Velankanni in Chennai alone, including one in Besant Nagar, the south Chennai neighborhood where I lived. Those eight did not include dozens if not hundreds of other churches and chapels also dedicated to the Virgin Mary in the city. Her image was ubiquitous, from huge murals on the sides of buildings, to popular calendar art, to pop-up shrines on street corners, to car dashboards and the sides of auto-rickshaws and trucks. In each of these cases, she appeared with a particular local name and visual form.

WILL THE "REAL" MARY PLEASE STAND UP? POSSESSION, AUTHENTICITY, POWER, AND GENDER

Spirit possession in South India is about as common as Starbucks or fantasy football in the United States. Walk into any Internet café in Tamil Nadu (of which there are thousands), ask if anyone has seen or heard about someone who has been possessed by a deity, ancestral spirit, or a *pēy*, and you will get not only a yes, but a long story involving someone's uncle, grandma, cousin, or neighbor. It is in part such widespread social acceptance of spirit possession that has created the conditions for Marian possession to be understood as authentic by many Hindus, Christians, and Muslims living there. At Fatima, Lourdes, Medjugorje, and Guadalupe, Mary was experienced as an apparition; in India today, she is embodying and being embodied by real women. If people can be possessed by a Hindu goddess, then why not by Mary?

Whatever one believes about goddesses or Mary, there is no denying that she has very real effects on people in South India, and that people have very real effects on her. I treat Mary in this book the way many Hindus and Christians in India regard her—as a goddess, a female deity with supernatural powers.[65] Goddess and devotee depend on one another for their existence; they shape one another's identities. Mary has many local incarnations—both in orthodox Roman Catholic representations and in women's bodies. Furthermore, Mary is never the same twice.

The phenomenon of Marian spirit possession raises questions about its relationship to gender, as well as to different forms of social power. As we shall see, men rarely seem to get possessed by Mary—though there are many men who claim to channel her. This can be explained in part because globally, more women than men experience spirit possession.[66] My study likewise suggests that women are more likely to get possessed by Mary than men. Women who engage in these possession practices—and who typically suffer from forms of low social standing owing to caste and to being female (especially if they are unmarried and childless)—enjoy elevated social status, both in their families and in their larger community. People pay more attention to them. They may benefit economically as a result of their possession, and they may help other people to feel better off. They also risk derogation should their practices be read as inauthentic. Authenticity, then, becomes one of the core themes of this book. Each of the three women I write about has been judged as authentic by some people and inauthentic by others. Each has performed their type of Marian possession with varying degrees of success. This book explores the meaning of authenticity—of what is required in order for something to be understood as authentic, and how context makes all the difference.

The "real" Mary—Miriam of Nazareth, the mother of Jesus—is very hard to pin down historically, and I have not pursued her. We know very little about her other than that she was Jewish. However, what we do know is that she is mentioned surprisingly little in the New Testament,[67] and that early Church Fathers grappled over the problem of her body and her sexuality for centuries. The eventual negation of her body by these early Church leaders is important to my argument.

From just about the same time that St. Thomas may have traveled to India, despite popular stories and legends that made Mary sound somewhat human, ecclesial leaders started to control those stories and to build increasingly more doctrine around Mary that simultaneously desexed her, put her on a pedestal, and made her otherworldly. In European and Middle Eastern popular imaginations, she became many different Marys: daughter of Zion, model of chastity, Theotokos, Second Eve, heroine in the Qur'an, mater dolorosa, foil to Mary Magdalene (the penitent whore whose identification with Mary of Magdala is a fiction—another story in itself), vanguard for war, source of apparition, regal Queen, Bride of Christ, symbol of the Church itself, and a sign of the Apocalypse.[68] Popular imagination has not always pictured Mary as without a fertile body—one only has to look at an early Coptic image of her nursing Jesus from Egypt in 893 CE,[69] or Joos van Cleve's voluptuous *Virgin and Child* (ca. 1525), to see that.

But by the early fourth century, Mary had become a site for establishing an orthodoxy set by the imperial state. Church councils debated her. Bishops gathered from all over the empire to figure out the exact nature of Christ: was he human, divine, or some of both? Connected to this question, of course, was the nature of his mother. At the root of the debate was a grand structural and theological problem: how can a divine man, perfect and devoid of sin (including the sin of sex), be born from a human woman? The answer: she must be without sin—that is to say, sexless and virginal.[70] The Council of Trent (which began in 1545, two years after the Portuguese had formally taken Madras), upheld the doctrine of Mary's virginity before *and after* Jesus's birth. In 1854, Pope Pius IX promulgated the doctrine of Mary's Immaculate Conception (that Mary had been conceived by her mother, Ann, without sin); and in 1950, Pope Pius XII declared Mary's Assumption into Heaven—the doctrine that she did not die but was raised, bodily. By this time, she had been dehumanized and desexed, but not deified. Mary, *both* a virgin *and* a mother (a human impossibility), was blocked from dying or decaying (that is, she was deprived a body); and simultaneously denied the status of deity or goddess. As a model for women, she held out an impossible standard.[71]

And yet. As long as the Church has tried to contain women, women have refused to be contained. Church Fathers evacuated Mary of so much bodily integrity that the lacuna begged to be filled. Popular imagination has long exceeded the limits of Church canon and doctrine, spilling out of orthodox control to fill in Mary's life. No matter how hard the Church may try, Mary cannot be contained. In fact, the more it tries to contain her, the more she "bleeds out" (like stigmata and other forms of blood over which women have no control) to exceed its control. Volatile bodies that escape the Church's control become activated by Mary, in ways and for reasons they themselves may or may not understand. The masses love her, sometimes to "excess" (according to policing Church Fathers), in ways that the Church cannot master.

Places particularly ripe for this "excess" are colonized places—places where Christianity has come into contact with other, indigenous forms of spirituality, places often far out of reach from the Vatican. We have seen this in Haiti, where the practices of slaves and ex-slaves from West Africa mixed their indigenous traditions with Catholicism and the traditions of the indigenous Taino people to create the Ezilis of Haitian Vodoun. We have seen this in Guadalupe, where a peasant named Juan Diego saw a maiden on the Hill of Tepeyac who told him in his native Nahuatl language to gather flowers in his *tilma* (cloak). And we have seen this in Velankanni, where a beautiful white lady appeared to two poor Tamil boys, separately (one buttermilk-selling and one lame), and, in another instance, saved Portuguese sailors from a storm. In each case, Mary became a site for contestation between precolonial, indigenous forms of divinity and colonial Roman Catholicism. Such places have offered particularly productive spaces for local people to invent new versions of her—versions that challenge the status quo of colonial powers, of church orthodoxy, and of local hegemonic orders. This "localization" or "indigenization" of Mary serves as a fecund process of negotiation with hegemony, always threatening to upset its status quo.

The process reveals the agency of postcolonized people who produce their own ways of negotiating oppression through adopting fluid, hybrid identities—that is, through mixing preexisting, indigenous forms of religiosity with colonial and postcolonial ones. Devotion to Mary offers significant spaces for resistance and moments of escape from the social and personal suffering brought on through oppressive regimes. In the case of South India, these oppressive regimes include Brahmanical Hinduism, which for thousands of years has categorized a vast majority of the Indian subcontinent's population as outcastes; the Indian nation-state, which has categorized Christians and other non-Hindus as "Other Backward Castes"; orthodox Roman Catholicism, which has kept women from joining the priesthood and has tried to control their sexuality; and local forms of patriarchy, which runs through all these systems, including indigenous ones. Marian possession is just one of many "weapons of the weak," as James C. Scott called such everyday forms of resistance to dominance among subalterns.[72] Like Scott, I found that Tamil women and men struggling under various forms of hegemonic oppression do not fully consent to dominance; rather, they often use and manipulate the very tools of their oppressors to resist it. Such manipulation also requires collusion. The coexistence of resistance and collusion do not necessarily negate each other; nor do they necessarily result in a lack of change to institutionalized structures of dominance. Change can occur in all sorts of directions. People's daily negotiations with power involve micromovements of resistance and collusion that help them survive, and may, over time, undermine the effects of structural and institutionalized forms of hegemony.

HEGEMONY, AGENCY, POWER

The phenomenon of Marian possession in Tamil Nadu can be viewed from a number of angles. One approach is historical: Contemporary Marian possession is the result of a long-term encounter between Syrian Christians, Roman Catholics, Pentecostals, and people and practices indigenous to the Indian subcontinent, including deity and spirit possession. Marian possession can also be viewed from various theoretical perspectives. Among those that this book takes up are subaltern religious practices and their interaction with hegemony.[73]

"Hegemony" means something akin to "dominant ideology." It implies complex relations of power between people and a dominant class with an ideology that claims prominence over others. There are different forms of hegemony. One could say, for example, that the United States enjoys a capitalist hegemony; or the Vatican, a patriarchal one. Key to the notion of any hegemony, however, is the manner in which it is maintained. Hegemony not only suggests a moral and intellectual class that dominates others (such as subalterns); it suggests that subalterns *participate* in their own domination. This happens because the dominating class maintains its hegemony by convincingly incorporating into its ideology the interests and beliefs of the classes it dominates, in a sort of depressing feedback loop.

But as Indian liberation theologian Santhianathan Clarke notes, hegemony is never complete; it is an evolving process that requires the participation of the dominated masses, within which can emerge possibilities for change. I argue that the very repetition of symbols, actions, and words within any hegemonic order create opportunities for resistance, for variation, and for meaning that *is not the same* as that which members of the dominating class may intend. Some say that the master's tools will never dismantle the master's house.[74] Others say that *only* the master's tools will dismantle the master's house.[75] This book is about Tamil women who each dipped into different toolboxes, repeating and reiterating certain preexisting symbolic, ritual, and discursive systems, resulting in new meanings. In so doing, each built *and* dismantled things—for themselves and for others.

All three women—Dhanam, Rosalind, and Nancy—repeated and re-embodied orthodox versions of Mary along with their own, notably personal, Tamil ones. By becoming sorts of priestesses of the goddess (like many *bhakti* poets preceding them), they turned things upside down. To some extent, they participated in their own domination: they never completely escaped its confines as they used patriarchal concepts and symbolic systems that at times relegated women (including themselves) to lower status than men. But they also enjoyed raised status, working with the limited tools they had to counter their own and others' suffering. Some of these tools were disruptive; spirit possession is disruptive. And the forms of Mary that they expressed through their possession were likewise disruptive: to orthodox ideas about Mary; to the patriarchal hierarchy of the Roman Catholic church that has shaped Mary's institutionalized character and doctrine over the ages; and to notions that low-caste or Dalit people, particularly women, should remain contained, disempowered, and voiceless.

My main argument is that Dhanam, Rosalind, and Nancy engaged in antihegemonic practices that challenged the status quo while also colluding in some of the very same hegemonic structures that their practices threatened. Theirs are not easy stories of resistance but of struggle within complicated webs of power and meaning. This complexity leaves open the vexing question of whether their possession practices are actually liberating. As an American feminist—someone schooled in the late 1980s at an East Coast liberal arts college where, as an undergraduate, I became increasingly politicized and later, as a journalist and graduate student, further sensitized to the patriarchal conditions that constrain both women and men—I struggled during my fieldwork with a yes or no answer to this question. Perhaps in a desire to resuscitate Mary and to honor the women with whom I worked (and to honor so many women around the world who venerate Mary, including my mother, my grandmother, and my younger self), I wanted to argue that Mary could indeed be liberating. Perhaps this was part of a deeper psychological desire to liberate myself from the guilt I felt for having "left" Mary—for no longer praying to her, for being angry at Church Fathers who had contorted her into an impossible standard for women, for the Church's oppressive system of discourse and practice, which began its long march through misogyny with early decisions about Marian scripture and doctrine. Aware of this bias, I wanted to confront it squarely while critically interrogating the Marian phenomena I encountered. I needed to face the possibility that women claiming to be possessed by Mary were merely charlatans "impersonating" her. I also needed to face the possibility that even as they claimed that their experiences of Marian possession were authentic and redemptive, these women were actually participating in their own continued domination, and in the domination of other women and men, by perpetuating a symbolic system that remained antifeminist.

I am not suggesting that Dhanam, Rosalind, and Nancy lacked critical consciousness. Quite the contrary—though they did not always engage it on my terms. While they did not use the words "hegemony" or "agency" (though they did use "power"), I found these terms useful for understanding their practices in relation to the academic questions that concerned me. Furthermore, while forms of hybridity or double identity (such as Christian-Hindu, Tamil-Catholic, human-divine) were operating in each case, I wanted to avoid reference to split consciousness, which has been rampant in analyses of spirit possession.[76] Rather, I wanted to understand the *embodied* nature of consciousness—the ways in which action and thought roll into one another. A number of variables can affect this embodied consciousness. A person's daily actions (e.g., praying, dressing, moving, or talking in a certain way, with specific vocabularies and within particular linguistic and symbolic formations) repeated within shifting social and environmental relations enable the very *conditions* for that person's thoughts and dispositions. Likewise, a person's thoughts and dispositions enable the conditions for their actions. Here, I borrow from the concept of "habitus"—an old Aristotelian and Thomist term, subsequently developed by Pierre Bourdieu and Catherine Bell, whose influences can be seen later in the book.

To recognize embodied ways of knowing—the manner in which action and thought roll into one another to create different subjective realities—is also to recognize different forms of agency (the capacity to act) that are not fully autonomous but rather social, instrumental, and reciprocal, both with other people and with deities and spirits. This book will investigate some of these forms of agency. Furthermore, it will consider how Dhanam, Rosalind, and Nancy actively developed their own subjectivities—meaning the range of thoughts, perceptions, beliefs, emotions, and sensations that constitute a "subject"—through a process of engaging hegemonic symbols and practices while creatively constructing their own counterhegemonic symbols and practices. The power they gave and received through their possession and healing practices enabled them not only to survive but also to buttress communal ties, find support in community, find wholeness in a situation that sought to grind them down, advance their social status, lead people to a sense of redemption, and escape totalizing control by dominant classes.[77]

So what does patriarchy have to do with it, and what does patriarchy mean in this context? In Tamil Nadu, it includes expectations that a woman will marry, with a dowry, and have children; that she will probably not own property; that after marriage she will move to her husband's native place; that she will generally follow much more restrained sexual norms compared to men; that her movements will be relatively constrained compared to men's (even more so during her menstrual period); and that she will cover more of her body than men do. Having made such a sweeping statement, I must add that patriarchy means different things in different contexts throughout Tamil Nadu, from city to city, town to town, village to village, and family to family. The details of these particular differences can only be examined in specific instances—another goal of this book.

It could be said, then, that I explore at least three sorts of hegemonies in this book. The first hegemony is the largest and most all-encompassing: patriarchy itself, which permeates not only India today but also many parts of the world, including the United States. All three women with whom I worked, I argue, would have been more vulnerable to their local forms of patriarchy had they not been possessed by Mary. The second hegemony is orthodox Roman Catholicism, as imported and promulgated by colonizers and missionaries who rationalized and promoted conquest. Though Roman Catholicism has offered outcaste converts a way to reassert their humanity and escape caste hierarchy, it remains heavily patriarchal and caste-ist. The third hegemony is Brahmanical Hinduism—now also appropriated politically by the Hindu right as *Hindutva*, a particular strain of Indian nationalism—which promotes not just certain normative ways of approaching divinity (i.e., through brahmin priests and Sanskritic discourses and rituals), but also certain normative ways of approaching other human beings. It does so in part through the caste system, which seeks to keep Dalits and low-caste people outside certain rituals and access to power, both human and divine.[78]

Dhanam, Rosalind, and Nancy all, in various ways, bucked these three forms of hegemony while also borrowing from the very symbols and practices that constituted those forms. Each used tools from both Brahmanical ("high," Sanskritic) Hinduism and non-Brahmanical ("low," non-Sanskritic) Hinduism—a tool-box that includes gods and goddesses, deity and spirit possession practices, and healing practices and exorcism rituals associated with gurus, *mantravādi*s, and priests. They also deployed tools from Roman Catholicism—a pantheon that includes Mary and the saints, Catholic prayers, and exorcism rituals that are also associated with priests.

The women are not the only ones with agency here. Deities, spirits, and Mary have agency, too. There is a material and kinetic reality to these deities and spirits, as materialized agents who have real effects on real people's lives. One need not talk about a god "out there" beyond the social realm (except that people may be believe that to be so) in order to talk about the reality of a god "right here" as a real, social, and material force. Gods, goddesses, and other spirits accumulate real force from the accrued weight of repeated human practice, a force that builds and gathers momentum and perceived density—even materiality—through discourses and practices that treat those deities and spirits as real. These discourses and practices include acts of exchange between those humans and the deity or spirit. The god creates the person as the person creates the god. Each depends on the other for existence.

MARIAN POSSESSION AND MODERNITY

Historians in particular will want to know about the extent to which Marian possession is a modern phenomenon. To some extent, I will fail them. It is certainly possible that when news of Mary reached the Malabar Coast, by about 50 CE, people started to invoke her in goddess and spirit possession practices that were already popular. Certainly, apparitions of Mary are believed to have started almost immediately upon the news of her reaching that southwest coast, within the first or second centuries CE.[79] It is equally possible that Marian possession practices occurred in the 1700s, when the Jesuits accelerated their attempts to strengthen devotion in Tamil country. Priests' records from the 1800s tell us about women coming to confession "struck with frenzy," seeing beings who threatened to stab or kill them, and of people flocking to the site of the martyrdom of St. John de Britto, in Oriyur, to be exorcised by a particularly charismatic priest who whipped them.[80] However, I have not as yet come across evidence of Marian possession prior to the 1970s—and it could take years of combing through archives in the United States, India, and Rome to do so. (One problem is that the early Jesuits in India would likely not have wanted to mention Mary as a "possessor," and if Indian Christians had reported that it was Mary who entered them, the Jesuits would have wanted either to dissimulate this or not to report it in their letters, because that would have landed them into trouble with their superiors in Rome.)[81]

What I can say with certainty is that Marian possession has been occurring in South India from the 1970s through today. Depending on when we decide modernity began there, I can also say with some certainty that it is a modern phenomenon, perhaps a late modern one if it did not occur during the periods of Portuguese and British conquests, and that the modern moment may be a particularly ripe time for Marian possession to occur in South India.

Here's why: India's fairly recent, rapid economic and social change has on the one hand created a quickly growing middle class with a greater "capacity to aspire,"[82] and on the other hand put increasing stress on traditional gender roles and family dynamics. The pressures of globalization have challenged long-held notions about tradition—causing some to turn to more "Western" modes of worship such as Pentecostalism, and others, in response to perceived, incoming threats by such "non-Indian" forces and an old colonial order, to cling more intensely to "Indian tradition." Throughout my fieldwork and at the time of my writing, Hindu nationalism (and its supporting ideology of *Hindutva*) had mobilized into a powerful political force. Christianity, in relation, was arguably counterhegemonic. Some Indians, particularly non-dominant Indians, saw it as a way to negotiate oppressive circumstances.

To be sure, the problems that Rosalind and Nancy faced, along with their devotees, were particularly modern ones. Dhanam, on the other hand, faced more ancient problems—lack of proper access to medical care, water, and education, to name a few. But her village's ability to measure its poverty against the outside world made these problems modern, too. Also modern were the phenomena of middle-class people buying land and building houses on the village outskirts; the emergence of a local cotton mill, which changed economic relations and patterns of daily life; people moving back to the village after failing in the city; and the forces of global capitalism, which compelled Dhanam's husband and other village men to work far away, in places like Kerala, Singapore, and Malaysia, and for long stretches of time.

What struck me in the field in 2004, among certain differences, was a sense of a pattern. Rosalind, Nancy, and Dhanam all reportedly healed people who approached them for help. All three were located on the margins of society in a variety of ways—geographic, economic, and social. All three were Roman Catholic women either ignored or opposed by church authorities. All three narrated their experience of possession as having followed a period of illness or significant family problems. All three focused on healing illness and other problems related to the body: marital problems (including sexual problems), fertility and menstrual problems, problems in finding grooms or brides, economic and housing problems. All three understood Mātā in opposition to *pēy* and to various spirits believed to be malevolent. All three believed, as did their devotees, that when they were possessed, they were no longer themselves. All three spoke as Mātā while in this state, indicating a subjectivity that was multivocal and fluid.[83] All three described Mātā as compassionate and loving, and associated her with joy and happiness—and yet in all three cases Mātā made threats while possessing them and, when necessary, enacted physical violence. (In Rosalind's and Dhanam's cases, Mātā struck people to drive out *pēy*; in Nancy's case, she caused her to bleed.) All three women claimed not to ask for monetary offerings, and yet they did receive them. All acquired status from their position, although they also received criticism. Following their initial possession experiences, all three beckoned Mātā to come to them, and all narrated stories of gaining more control over Mātā's visitations, which first came unannounced and seemingly without invitation.

HOW I WILL WRITE ABOUT WHAT THEY SAID

A note about my writing methods. Any words in quotation marks are indeed direct quotations, either as I heard them, or as they were recalled to me by the original speaker. In the latter cases, I have wherever possible cross-checked such quotations (and events) with other people present at the time of the original speaking or event. Any scene depicting a situation in which I was not present is my rendition of a community's shared memory of what happened—not a direct, eyewitness report.

Meanwhile, I use certain conventions of the *Caṅkam* grammar and poetics written two thousand years ago in the chapter subtitles, and in other ways throughout the book. This earliest Tamil grammar of *Caṅkam* literature, *Tolkāppiyam*, tells us quite a bit about certain forms of possession, particularly in regard to its *akam* (inner) poetry, and about conventions to be used to describe it. First, the text mandates that when one is describing states of erotic love, names are neither proper nor necessary—whereas they are appropriate in *puṟam* poetry, which documents in poetic form some of the courts, politics, and wars of the era.[84] The dramatis personae for *akam* are idealized types: the hero, the heroine, the hero's friend(s) or messengers, the heroine's friend and foster-mother, the concubine, and passers-by. Poems are titled "What He Said," "What She Said," or "What Her Friend Said," for example. Take perhaps the most famous of the *akam* poems, "Kuruntokai 3":

What She Said
Bigger than earth, certainly,
Higher than the sky,
More fathomable than the waters
Is this love for this man
Of the mountain slopes
Where bees make rich honey
From the flowers of the *kuṟiñci*
That has such black stalks.

A. K. Ramanujan, *Interior Landscape*[85]

There is much more going on here than meets the average English-reading eye, for *akam* poetry works in a sort of code: layers upon layers of tropes and symbolic conventions. Personal names are not needed; we need no specific *place* names, either, for we have general landscapes (ecosystems specific to the Tamil-speaking region) signaling different emotional states. Five landscapes correspond to five different kinds of inner subjective states felt to be appropriate for love poetry—and by extension, five different *uri* (stages of love) and states of possession: union, separation, patient waiting/domesticity, anxiety in love/separation, and unfaithfulness/sulking.[86] These emotions are not something one *chooses*: they happen *to* a person. The body is attacked, as it were, by love and by landscape in its various manifestations. One can also see these states of union, longing, separation, and faithfulness/unfaithfulness as modes of relation to a god.

Somewhat in line with *puṟam* poetry, I have decided to follow the rules of ethnography as borrowed from the ethics of print journalism: I stick to real names and places in the cases of public officials (including priests and bishops), parishes, institutions, and individuals who have already volunteered themselves for public scrutiny by the press. This includes Rosalind, Nancy, and their families, who by now have appeared on television and in newsprint, and the devotees at Our Lady Jecintho Prayer House, who openly gave their names when they agreed to speak to me. As for the people of the villages of Sivagangai District, I feel that the political situation there is simply too unpredictable and potentially dangerous to risk exposing their identities. When writing about the recent controversy and political unrest among the predominantly Hindu communities in the area, I use real place names where relevant, since the issue has already received attention from local Tamil newspapers and from the local, internationally read English-language press. I also include such place names because I believe that caste discrimination and violence surrounding the nearby Hindu festival described at the start of this book is key to understanding some of the dynamics behind possession rituals in the Roman Catholic village where I spent time.[87]

These conventions and genres of storytelling, these voices that I narrate, facilitate another type of possession—one slightly different, but perhaps only slightly, from the topic of this book. As a writer I become, in a manner, possessed by the conventions, as well as by my memory of the people whose voices I represent. I become a medium as I try to invoke the spirits of these people and places. I try to make them come alive in your head.

MĀTĀPURAM

Mātāpuram is the fictional name, then, that I have given to stand for a real Tamil village. It is located in Sivagangai District, the real name of a south-central, largely agricultural inland district just east of Madurai District. To the general Indian tourist public, Sivagangai District is known, to the extent that it is, for its spicy Chettinad food and elegant, nineteenth-century houses in which, on occasion, Tamil and Bollywood films are shot. Some of these homes and their surrounding villages speak of a feudal era, now bygone, in which the wealthy elite of the Chettiar caste, mercantilists known for their business acumen, fueled the local economy. Many of these homes now lie vacant, in some cases decrepit, visited by their owners only for holidays, if at all. Green and lush in winter and spring, arid in summer and fall, Sivagangai is not frequented by foreign tourists as much as is, say, the famous temple town of Madurai, an hour away by bus, or the state's coastal regions. But it is equally if not more beautiful than those places in its own way.

Sivagangai District's landscape consists, significantly, of the *Caṅkam* landscapes of *pālai* and *marutam*. In this district, the cultivated fields are full mostly of rice paddy and cotton. During the monsoon season, the fields can literally teem with water as the rivers and streams burst their banks, flowing out into hard, dry fields that do not readily absorb it. Between such rains, Sivagangai is green, muddy, and fecund. Its paddies lie full. Wild peacocks strut and heron alight in fields rimmed with palm and coconut trees. In dry season, this same land can become brown and vacant looking. In areas that are particularly *pālai*, below the sparse trees, mostly thorn bushes grow. The milky *kaḷḷi* plant, which serves as a witness to murder and as a weapon of revenge in one of the central narratives to the fierce goddess Icakki Amman, also grows in abundance here. The *Puṟanāṉūru*, one of the three *puṟam* (outer) anthologies of *Caṅkam* poetry, speaks of the *kaḷḷi* as inhabited by a deity and as characteristic of the dry *pālai* landscape and the cremation grounds.[88]

Mātāpuram, a settlement of about thirty-five houses in 2001 (and about forty-five in 2015), lies off a narrow, potholed, asphalt road serviced by a local government bus that stops twice a day within walking distance from the village. It sits in the northeast corner of Sivagangai District, between the towns of Karaikkudi and Devakottai. Like many of its neighboring villages, Mātāpuram is agricultural; cotton is its main crop. This cotton, grown and picked by locals, fuels the mills that now supply the fabric industry in the big cities. There is one such mill just outside Mātāpuram, where several of its residents work as day laborers when they are not farming.

From the asphalt road that runs to Chinna Unjanai, where the murders occurred in 1979, and beyond that to Karaikkudi, another, narrower dirt road turns off through the prickly brush into the village. Several walking paths also run through uncultivated fields from the village to paved roads beyond, from which a person can determine the outlines of a few outer huts of the settlement. Villagers construct their homes with mud, thatch, cement, and, in some cases, brick. The roofs are thatch or clay tile, or both, with wooden supports. In the center of this hamlet, in a clearing near a well, stands a small, Portuguese-style church. More the size of a chapel, with a newly painted baby blue exterior, pink interior walls, and a pointed wooden-beamed roof, this church, or *kōyil*,[89] as residents call it, is a substation of the parish at Devakottai. The Devakottai parish priest celebrates Mass here once a month, if that. The chapel has two rooms: a front room—a sort of sitting room, or front hall—and an inner room, accessible also by side doors, which houses the altar. The altar, many tiered in the style of several churches in Tamil Nadu, holds no icon of Jesus or of God the Father. Two central statues of Mary, one of Our Lady of Fatima (a replica of the original in Portugal) and one of *Aṭaikkala Mātā* (a version of Our

Lady of Refuge—or *aṭaikkalam,* "shelter"—introduced to Tamil Nadu in 1734 by the Italian Jesuit Constantine Joseph Beschi),[90] stand flanked by smaller statues of the saints.

It was in this chapel, in 2001, that I first met Dhanam.

We sat cross-legged on the cement floor, empty of pews or chairs, surrounded by the village children, who wandered freely during the day, and some women. Dhanam, who then was forty-three, had dark brown skin, high, round cheekbones and unflinching, penetrating brown eyes. Her notably poised, almost regal countenance seemed to contrast with her manner of speech, which—though also direct—came through a soft, warm voice that at times could seem particularly calm, almost still. When Dhanam spoke of seeing Mary, or "Mātā," as she called her, the volume of her voice fell practically to a whisper. She was dressed in a cotton sari and blouse, and wore the sari's *pallu*, or loose end, tucked into the front of her skirt, local style. Also like many of her neighbor women, she wore round, gold earrings the size of small coins and two equally large gold nose ornaments, one on each nostril. Her ears protruded notably from her head; her black hair, which showed no signs of gray, was oiled and pulled back into a tight knot. She was married, she told me, to a farmer, her *māmā*, or uncle (he was actually her distant uncle, through relations' marriages on both sides). Together they had one daughter and three sons. One of the sons was studying to be a priest. Her daughter, who was married, had two small children of her own. Her family had been Roman Catholic for five generations. Both her parents had strong devotion to Mātā. Mātā had even "come on" (*iṟaṅku mēl*) her father, but Mātā did not possess him to the extent that she possessed her, Dhanam said.

When her periods of possession became known in the district, people started to come for healing, at the rate of maybe a dozen per month. Most were Hindu, she said. They came from all *jātis*, or communities—not only Dalits, but also "Chettiars, Pallars, Idaiyars, like that," she said.[91] Some of the people, the majority, had family problems; some had *pēy*; some had bodily problems (*uṭambu piraccinai*); some had seen a doctor but were not cured. "Everyone says they are scared and they are unable to do anything," she said.[92]

She told me that people camped out in the church for weeks or sometimes months—however long it took to be cured. One Hindu family, from Devakottai, who was staying in the church at the time of our visit had brought their grandmother, who suffered from "unstoppable bleeding," they told me. After seeing many other healers and finding no relief, they had brought her to Dhanam and stayed for two months—she was now cured, the family confirmed, and they were readying themselves to make the journey back.

Dhanam didn't take much money for her services—only a little, when people insisted. The mechanism of her healing was empathetic: she had the suffering person kneel behind her; she also knelt, veiling her head with the loose end of her sari, and prayed to Mātā. Mātā, she said, used her body so that she could feel the person's specific pain. It was in part through this feeling that Mātā diagnosed the problem.

"For example, let's say she is grabbed by *pēy*," Dhanam told me. "There, behind you, I will make her kneel down and light a candle. Then she and I look face to face. Then the *pēy* that is on her comes on me. If she has stomach pain, I will have stomach pain. If she has chest pain, I will have pain. If she has a headache, I will have that pain. Then I come to know about your *pēy*, its having come on me. Then if I drive out that *pēy*, I will drive it out immediately. Otherwise, I will make that person stay a week; anytime in that week you can catch a glimpse of Mātā. Any day during that week, I will come and drive out the *pēy* that is hiding there."

Sometimes the problem is a *pēy*, sometimes it's a *muni*, sometimes both, Dhanam said. Sometimes the person needs to go to the hospital. Often, Dhanam will apply turmeric and holy water to the person from a large, stainless steel pot she keeps on the altar.

Dhanam is not frightened.

"I'm not scared (lit. to me there is no fear)," she said. "Mātā is there. *Pēy* will also be there. If the *pēy* gives a fight, Mātā will say, 'Pick up a broomstick and beat them.' I will beat (the person/*pēy*) using the broomstick. 'I'm going! I'm going!' that *pēy* says and leaves."

Dhanam told all of this to me with a calm, even voice, though her tone signified reverence toward Mātā. The broom, I later found out, is a tool commonly used by women in Tamil Nadu to keep *pēy* and other mischievous or malevolent spirits at bay. As an *acuttamāṉa* or unclean item, it is thought to cause *pēy* to recoil from its filth. People sometimes lay it across the lintel of the doorway at night to keep the unruly spirits out of the house. Shoes (other dirty objects) are also used to block the entrance of *pēy*. Exorcists of both Christian and Hindu persuasions in Tamil Nadu will use brooms or shoes to beat or, more commonly, to tap (the word used either way, is *aṭi*, "to beat, hit, or strike") the *pēy* out of people. Even priests have told me that they have done this in village exorcisms.[93]

What seemed most remarkable to me, other than the possession itself, was the broomstick—and the *nature* of the Mary that possessed Dhanam. This was not the Mary of the stories with which I had grown up, a Mary of sweetness and light who gave birth to a god, all while somehow remaining a virgin. This was a fierce Mary more like Mariamman, Kali Amman, Icakki Amman, or other local goddesses of Tamil culture, than the poised queen of the heavens who evolved through European history.

And so I returned to India on a Fulbright Fellowship, in January 2004, intending to work with Dhanam, as part of a larger project about Marian devotion in Tamil Nadu. I wasn't planning to write an entire book on Marian possession: I didn't know at the time that Dhanam's story was part of a much larger one about Marian possession, and that there were two other women in

Chennai I would work with, and others. I planned on writing about Dhanam's village as one window—one important window—into various forms of popular Marian devotion in the area.

But within two weeks of my arrival, upon registering with the local immigration office, an officer handed me a single white sheet of paper:

LEAVE INDIA NOTICE

IN EXERCISE OF THE POWERS CONFERRED BY CLAUSE C OF SUB-SECTION 2 OF SECTION 3 OF FOREGINERS ACT, 1946 (CENTRAL ACT XXXI OF 1946) READ WITH NOTIFICATION OF GOVERNMENT OF INDIA IN THE MINISTRY OF HOME AFFAIRS F.NO.25022/96/F.I. DATED JULY 13, 2000, I, (name), CHIEF IMMIGRATION OFFICER AND CIVIL AUTHORITY HEREBY DIRECT THAT YOU, BLOOMER KRISTIN COOK, US, NATIONAL, PASSPORT No. X-XXXXXXX dated 11.06.2001 **Valid upto** [*sic*] **10.06.2011,** SHALL LEAVE INDIA WITHIN 15 DAYS OF RECEIPT OF THIS ORDER.

(signature)
CHIEF IMMIGRATION OFFICER
Bureau of Immigration
MHA, Govt. of India
Chennai–6

Following advice from the local Fulbright office, I appealed the order to the Central Government and stayed put.[94] The decision took seven months. Meanwhile, the chief immigration officer forbade me to leave Chennai or to conduct fieldwork. He checked on me by sending random notices to my mailbox commanding me to appear in his office within three days. Over one of many cups of tea we sipped during those meetings, he told me he had ordered me out of India because I was studying Christianity in "volatile areas." They did not seem particularly volatile to me—at least not in the way I suspect he understood the word.

HOW I HEARD ABOUT ROSALIND

It was under these conditions—city arrest, intense loneliness, growing anxiety, economic instability (the U.S. Fulbright Office in Washington had stopped my stipends), and a sense of failure before having even begun—that I first heard about the Marian shrine of Our Lady Jecintho in Kodungaiyur.

After several nights of lying awake on the cool tile floor of my apartment in Besant Nagar, staring up at the slowly revolving ceiling fan, I figured it couldn't hurt to get out, practice my Tamil, and talk to people. I was talking to a priest at St. Thomas Mount in Chennai when he got a phone call. It was from the father of a woman named Rosalind. When he got off the phone, he told me that this woman claimed to possessed by Mary, and that, having visited their prayer house, he believed that the possession was real. He handed me a small, triptych-like brochure: the front leaf, folded from the left, held an image of Mary dressed in blue, with the caption, "Vision Given to Rosalind"; the next, folded from the right, revealed an image of strewn rose petals with the caption, "The Image Left by Our Lady"; the back leaf featured an image of Our Lady of Velankanni. Inside was a small narrative in both Tamil and English:

OUR LADY JECINTHO PRAYER HOUSE
9, Venkateswara Nagar, (Opp. Bharat Gas Godown)
Kodungaiyur, Chennai-118. Ph: 25553755
Prayer Timings:
Saturdays, 4 p.m. Wednesdays: 8 p.m.
Visit: www.jecintho.com

In April of 2004, then, instead of talking to Dhanam and the villagers of Mātāpuram about possession by a form of Mary called *Adaikkala Mātā*—a research plan that had been approved by the Indian government before my arrival—I was talking with Rosalind about possession by a Mary named *Jecintho*. Instead of talking to Dhanam about how it felt to be possessed by Mary, the illness that predicated the possession, and the problems with which people would come to her seeking succor, I was talking to Rosalind about these things.

By Christmas of 2004, long released from my visa restrictions (the government had ruled in my favor), I had met Nancy, and had finished (or so I thought) my Chennai fieldwork. My plan was to head to Velankanni with Rosalind's family and join the thousands of pilgrims headed there for Christmas; from there I would head to Mātāpuram on my own. But a few days before Christmas, Rosalind's son Fredy (pronounced "Freddy") fell sick, and we canceled our plans. On December 26, I was safe in my apartment a few blocks from the beach[95] when the Asian Tsunami hit the coast of Tamil Nadu—including, among other places, Velankanni, which was hardest hit of all. In Tamil Nadu alone, more than eight thousand people, mostly women and children, lost their lives. I would have been there had Fredy not fallen ill. Rather than travel to Mātāpuram, then, I decided to help with the relief efforts—and spent two months visiting villages that had been almost entirely wiped out.[96]

My point here is that a course of events that lay outside my control helped to shape my developing perception of what was important. Not only my visa problems and the politics undergirding them but, more significantly, the tsunami and the stories that survivors told me about the importance of Mātā in protecting or not protecting them from the waves—all of this affected my questions, my stance as an ethnographer, my attentions and perceptions, as it affected Rosalind and Dhanam and their stance as healers. Also crucial to the shape of my inquiries in Chennai and in Kanyakumari District was the original 2001 interview with Dhanam.

Little did I know, sitting on the chapel floor with her, that it would be more than four years before I would see Dhanam again.

CHAPTER 1

Rosalind

WHAT THEY SAID

In May 1999, a seventeen-year-old boy named Alex came down with a fever. The fever had started suddenly while he was at the home of his *attai*—his father's sister—in Kodungaiyur, the same northern neighborhood of Chennai where Alex lived. The pain began in his head and moved down his body. It lasted a day. Then, slowly, horrifyingly, over a number of days his body started to bend increasingly to the right, little by little, until it listed so far that he could no longer walk straight. It wasn't exactly painful, this shrinking and tightening—it just happened silently, steadily, stealthily, in a manner that made Alex feel that the right side of his body had a mind of its own.

The family's big fear was polio. They were lower-middle-class Roman Catholics—a joint family of twelve in a two-bedroom rental house—who shared a strong faith and a combined income sufficient to sustain them. ("Joint family" generally means, in a patrilocal society such as this one, that a father's sons, their wives, and their children all live under his roof.)[1] Their belief in God the Father, Jesus, the Holy Spirit, Mary, and all the saints did not exclude or negate a belief in doctors. They prayed and took Alex to one hospital after another. Doctors submitted him to a battery of X-rays and MRIs, but they couldn't figure out the problem. In the "GH," or government hospital, near his home, Alex spent a month in traction. Doctors tightly bound his body in a full-body bandage, attached sand weights, and hung the weights so that they pulled his body to the left, toward straight. That, Alex says, is when the real pain began. The treatment was far worse than the ailment.

Alex lay like this—his limbs pulled exactly opposite the direction they seemed to want to go—for a month. When the doctors released him, his body still wasn't straight. Alex's family then took him to the Madras Institute of

Orthopaedics and Traumatology (MIOT), a private hospital known for doing organ transplants, so locally famous that a plethora of cottage industries had sprung up to service it. Private hotels housed long-term patients; poor people camping outside reportedly offered their organs for sale.[2] Several of MIOT's fancy doctors consulted with Alex and his family. He would require an operation, they said, in which a steel plate would be inserted next to his spine to straighten it. The surgery would probably work, they said, but it was dangerous. Best case: he would walk straight again. Worst case: he would end up in a coma.

The family was facing the end of a long list of options. Unwilling to risk the coma, they informed a nun at their church, who in turn told a priest, who in turn told the family that a foreign doctor was in town—an American. In January, more than six months after the fever had entered and left his body, Alex saw the American doctor, who told him that an operation might indeed be best. First, however, the doctor proposed another, less invasive option: to set Alex's body in a plaster of Paris cast for several days.

About a month later, in February, Alex was lying in a different hospital, St. Anthony's Hospital in Madhavaram, near his home, encased neck-to-thigh in plaster. His pain was so severe that he couldn't sleep. By about seven o'clock on the night of February 8, 2000, bathed in sweat, he was starting to blabber and lose his vision. He was unable to see any visitor who came to his bedside—except for one.

"After that, as soon as I start to go to sleep—I don't know what time it is—a cross descends, one cross," he said when we spoke, in 2005.[3] Tamil speakers often refer to past events in the present tense. "It is fully leaking blood. In that cross, Mātāmmā[4] (Mother Mary) is coming in that way itself. She is very tall—quite a fair height."

I asked where she had been standing, at which point Alex shifted from the present to past tense.

"I saw her on the hospital ceiling," Alex said. "'Alex. Get up and walk,' she said. 'I can't get up and walk.' Mātāmmā said, 'No, you[5] get up and walk,' she said like that. 'See how I am! Look, how can I get up and walk?' I said. After that, a rosary appeared on the bed. I took it, got down from the bed and started walking."

His father, M. Paul, who, after his shift as a chemistry lab custodian was finished, had come to visit his son earlier that night, had been half asleep as the apparition progressed. He heard Alex mumbling, opened his eyes, and watched his son walk the length of the hall and back, still in the full body cast.

A nun—a nurse—saw him, too. The memory of it, five years later, still made Alex smile wildly. "'Ai! That boy is walking!' the nun cried," Alex recounted. But Alex politely rebutted the nun, "'Mother Mary is going; I'll also go,' I said. 'No, no, no! Go to bed,' the sister said. She made me lie down and informed Mother Superior. She came and gave me a sleeping injection to put me to sleep." Later, when Alex awoke, he saw that the cast had loosened. "After that, the news spread all through the hospital that Mātāmmā had come," Alex said.

The next day, the doctors cut off the cast. Alex's body was straight. He appeared to be cured. The family was overjoyed. Both his Catholic aunt and his Hindu mother attributed the healing to Mātā. Eventually, his whole family did.

A month later, in thanks to Mātāmmā for the healing, Alex and his father walked to Velankanni. It took them about a week.

When Alex returned from Velankanni, Mātā started appearing to him regularly,[6] and he felt sure that the pilgrimage had strengthened their relationship. She appeared to him in the night, and this sometimes frightened him.

His family was dubious; or rather, some believed him more readily more than others. At night they kept a close watch on him, afraid that he might wander outside, whether merely disoriented or under the influence of Mātā. Meanwhile, they remained constant in their family devotions, continuing a long-held nightly practice of praying the rosary together[7]—and adding prayers for Mātā's guidance in the matter of Alex.

In those days Alex slept in the bedroom of his vigilant older cousins, Robert and Benjamin. But on the night of February 12, 2001, a year and four days after his cure, his thirty-year-old cousin, Rosalind, displaced him from that spot. She had been having trouble sleeping on the floor of the room she shared with her young son, Frederick; her mother; and her cousin Julie (Alex's sister). The fan had stopped working, and the heat was oppressive. Her mother urged her to switch places with Alex. So, wearing a long, cotton, dressing gown (akin to a *mumu*, and which most South Indian women wear at night), her black wavy hair braided down her back, Rosalind slipped into the boys' room, where the fan was still working. She found Alex with the sheets pulled up over his head.

"Hey. Alex. Get up," she said. He peeked at her from under the sheet, his nose and mouth covered.

"*Akka* (older sister)," he said in a whisper, "someone is standing outside."

"Stop your blabbering," she said. "Get up and come with me." It took some prodding but eventually Alex dragged himself out of bed and followed Rosalind back to her room. He tried the fan. No luck. "Okay," he said, agreeing to give up the spot to Rosalind and Fredy. He shuffled aside in his lungi and bare feet, resigned to sleeping in the hall.

The next morning, Tuesday, February 13, Rosalind's mother was one of the first in the household to get up, as usual. As she walked to the outhouse between her house and that of the neighbors, she found something unusual: hundreds of pink rose petals strewn on the cement path. In India, as throughout the world, rose petals are a symbol for Mary—and Rosalind's mother, a particularly avid devotee of Our Lady, shouted to family members: "Come! Come and see!" They were as astonished as she was—perhaps it was a miracle—and Alex felt vindicated. "Yes, last night Mātā came!" he told them. "You see, I told you but you didn't believe me!"

Alex's cousin Benjamin took a photograph.

The family notified the parish priest, who sent nuns to the house to serve as witnesses and recommended that the family tell no one else. The nuns, from the same hospital where Alex had been cured, questioned everyone within a close radius. Neither the family members nor the neighbors admitted to knowing anything about how the petals got there or to having anything to do with their appearance. The nuns noted that the type of rose petals strewn on the walk were not readily available for purchase in the area. They also exuded an unusually powerful rose scent. The nuns reported their findings to the parish priest, who reported them to the bishop.[8]

When Benjamin returned with the developed photo a few days later, he pointed out something that no one had yet noticed: if you turned the image a certain way, the petals seemed to form a clear image of Mary. *Āmām*! (Yes!)" "Aiyo! Aiyaiyo!" family members cried—there she was! The outline of her head, here; her crown and flowing gown, there; and here, the head and crown or halo of Jesus, whom she seemed to be holding. The form was that of the famous statue of Our Lady of Velankanni at the site to which Alex had walked only months before![9] Alex showed me the picture: one could indeed find the outline if one were inclined to do so.

Until she saw the image in the photo, Rosalind had been doubtful.[10] She had, after all, dismissed Alex's claim that Mātā was present—on the fateful night before the appearance of the rose petals—as "blabbering." But when Benjamin pointed to Mary's outline in the photograph, tears rolled down Rosalind's cheeks. "It must be true," she thought. "Mātā really must have come to our house."

Still, her mind wavered. She felt caught in a bind: so many people were asking about Alex's cure, and now the rose petals. What to tell them? She didn't want to be a "doubting Thomas"[11]—she wanted to believe. On the day that Benjamin showed her the photo, she had started praying intensely to Our Lady, seeking certainty—or at least guidance. "Somehow you have to reveal to me, Mā," she prayed. "I don't want to be like this. I want to believe in you completely, that *you* have come to our house." Intending to show Mary the intensity of her desire to believe, she went to a nearby flower shop to purchase offerings to take to church.

She chose mixed *kaṭambam* petals, the delicate, narrow, white and orange petals from the common cadamba tree. She also bought roses—whole roses, not merely petals. She filled her bag with both and went to worship, as usual, at Our Lady of Velankanni Church (named after the Nagapattinam church) in nearby Muthamizh Nagar. She approached the statue and, bowing her head, placed most of the petals and roses at the feet of Velankanni Mātā. She touched Our Lady's feet with her right hand, a traditional South Indian sign of respect and devotion, then touched her own head and heart. She turned to the adjacent statue of the Infant Jesus and, placing the remaining flowers near it, touched the statue's feet and continued to pray. Suddenly, the empty bag she was holding felt heavy. She looked inside.

To her astonishment, it was filled with flowers, not the kind that she had left at the feet of Our Lady, but orange *kanakāmbaram*, the blossoms of the Cassandra tree, which South Indian women often wear in their hair. How could this be? She was sure that she had emptied the bag. In any case, the flower shop where she had made her purchases had only carried *kaṭambam* and roses—not *kanakāmbaram*. She found herself praying, "Mā, somehow you have revealed to me that you have come to our house. Now you have revealed to me."

It is Rosalind (Figure 1.1) to whom the story now turns. For Rosalind believes that she is regularly "occupied" by Mary, that is, that she is possessed by Mary (though she prefers the word "occupation," *eṉṉai ākkiramittu koḷḷutal* in Tamil, lit. "occupying/possessing me and keeping me").[12] Her family and her substantial community of followers believe it, too. By the time I met her, three years after the Cassandra-tree blossoms appeared in her bag, Rosalind's prayer meetings and healing services were attracting hundreds, sometimes

Figure 1.1: Rosalind, 2004. Photo by author.

thousands of people—the size of a typical Chennai parish church—twice a week, at set hours, to a small white chapel, renovated from what had been the extended-family home. Most of Rosalind's followers were ailing—physically, economically, or in social and family relations—and they came to her for succor.

But why did Rosalind rise to prominence in the little white chapel in Kodungaiyur, and not Alex? He had also been "occupied" by Mary—and for a longer period than Rosalind, the family admitted; it still happened regularly, during family prayer meetings.

Robert explained that Alex cannot touch or physically bless people the way a woman can.

In Tamil Nadu, touching, especially between the sexes, remains, well, touchy. On the wall of the shrine were strict instructions not to touch Rosalind, specifying that only she could touch visitors. (I saw many people put a hand on her shoulder, for support, while she blessed them in a state of possession, but that seemed to be the extent of permissible touching.) In any case, the family did not publicize Alex's possession experiences, they claimed, because they felt the disclosure wouldn't have benefited anyone. Meanwhile, Alex, a young, single male, couldn't touch devotees in the all-body way that Rosalind could, because it might attract the wrong kind of attention. Alex's possession experiences would stay at home, where they continued occasionally to occur, even after Rosalind started to get possessed.

After her first onset, Rosalind shared her prayer and healing in the tiny front room of the house. When crowds became too unwieldy, the family moved to a different rental house, on a street within walking distance. They collected donations, formed a trust, and bought and renovated the old house as a proper shrine[13] to accommodate prayer meetings comfortably.

Rosalind, for her part, never expected—on that day when Mātā had revealed herself through the Cassandra-tree blossoms—that she would receive visitations. It certainly never occurred to her that Mātā would occupy her, as she had often occupied Alex. But soon, Mātā was indeed entering her body. Soon, Mātā was making her a "living vessel," she said, for her special work of "*aruḷ*" (roughly translated as "grace")—not just once or twice, but twice a week, regularly. And Rosalind increasingly welcomed the occupations: ever since that day Mātā had bestowed more petals on her, Rosalind had increased the intensity and frequency of her prayer.

WHAT THE PRAYER HOUSE SAID

Kodungaiyur, Chennai, April 2004. Repetitive, rhythmic chanting pours out of the whitewashed bungalow, and a pale scent of jasmine and rose infuses the thick, humid night. The round-faced flower seller outside Our Lady Jecintho

Figure 1.2: Our Lady Jecintho Prayer House, Kodungaiyur, Chennai, 2005. Charles sits with his back to the camera, beside a priest. Fredy stands right, leaning against the motorcycle. Photo by author.

Prayer House (Figure 1.2) cuts me a garland (*mālai*) of jasmine—for free—and pins it to my hair. The woman's touch is calming. Above our heads, a blue neon sign bears the image of a woman in blue-and-white robes—Mary. Red neon letters in Tamil script read, Aṉṉai Jecintō Jebavīṭu; below, smaller English letters translate: Our Lady Jecintho Prayer House. On the veranda, nuns wearing pale blue habits sit in white plastic chairs beside elderly and infirm people holding canes. The bungalow is brightly lit and packed to overflowing.

Hundreds of shoes are strewn on the packed dirt. The cement steps leading to the veranda are smooth and cool. A statue of a winged St. Michael spearing a dragon flanks the left side of the entrance; on the right, another saint, possibly Gabriel, stands above a small, garlanded statue of Mary. Visible through the rose-vined grille of the open window, a huge crowd, maybe two hundred people, sits on the floor, a sea of black heads and bright saris. Many women have draped their *pallu*—the sari's long, loose end—over their heads. Some saris are fancy, laced with gold thread; some are simple polyester. Many young women wear *churi dar*, pajama-bottom pants, long tunic, and front shawl; some wear the traditional half-saris of the prepubescent. Sprigs of fresh jasmine adorn the women's braids and buns. Men wear pressed shirts and pants, or *dhotis*, a traditional long piece of cloth wrapped around the waist like a skirt. Small children, faces pale with white powder, wear dime-sized black kohl dots on their cheeks to ward off the evil eye.[14]

As I am about to enter the prayer house, a tall man with a shock of white hair and a thick moustache approaches: Rosalind's father, Charles. He has been expecting me since my phone call, and extends his broad right hand to grasp mine in a firm handshake—a sign that he is no stranger to *farangi*, "foreigners."[15] His pressed pants, dress shirt, gold-wire-rimmed glasses, and excellent English bespeak at least middle-class status. He insists on taking me for "cool drinks" at a nearby shop. The Tamil hosting tradition demands it, he explains, and I would, he knows, reciprocate in my country. He orders me a Fanta at the window, and we settle into plastic chairs outside. He is trembling slightly, and passes on a beverage for himself: at fifty-nine, he suffers from hypertension and high blood sugar. Rosalind, too, is in rather poor health, he says, and had visited a doctor yesterday for stomach pain—the family thought it might be ulcers. The doctor told Rosalind to drink coconut milk and orange-and-lime juice; she's been fasting for forty days. She eats only one meal a day, at three in the afternoon, and even less on Wednesdays and Saturdays, the days of prayer meetings, perhaps just a bit of bread and a few biscuits.

Charles has worked in the chemical and petroleum business for years. His parents were both Roman Catholic, he says, and their marriage was arranged, his father hailing from the southern city of Madurai, and his mother from Bangalore, in the state of Karnataka, west of Tamil Nadu. Charles guesses that his family has been Roman Catholic for more than a century. His wife, also from Madurai, Roman Catholic, and an ardent devotee of Mary, died in 2003. Ever since, he has had heart problems and hypertension. By now, I am sucking air from the bottom of my Fanta bottle. It is time to return to the prayer house.

Charles offers me a plastic chair on the VIP veranda, with the nuns and the infirm, but I ask to go inside. He kindly requests that I enter through a side door so that I will not disrupt the prayers. My foreign presence—white-skinned, though I am *churi dar* clad—has already attracted notice through the back windows. As I walk clockwise around the house[16]—past open windows, around the back wall, and to the right side entrance—I bow my head, trying to disappear or, at least, to indicate modesty. As a woman in Tamil Nadu, I have learned the importance of indicating *kaṟpu* (loosely translated as "chastity" or "sexual modesty").[17] Despite my attempt to shrink, I note from the corner of my eye that I have become an object of attention. As I pass each window, heads turn my way. I slip in quickly, lowering myself into a seated half-lotus. Faces turn; necks crane; children suppress giggles; a few women sitting beside me offer smiles. But the crowd mostly continues to pray, lips moving, chanting Tamil. Even those I've distracted quickly return their gazes to the altar.

It is covered in roses, several tiers of them—most of them plastic and brightly colored (Figure 1.3). Statues rise out of the roses: among them a bearded Jesus, perhaps three feet tall, crowned and dressed in white, and a Mary, about the same height, in blue-and-white robes and crowned in a tiara, carrying a baby. Between them stands a smaller statue of Velankanni Mary and child, recognizable by their red-and-gold crowns; and on a lower tier, an even smaller Mary holds her hands clasped, no Jesus. Each drips in multiple garlands of fresh flowers and rosary beads—and, the two largest, in a single garland of gold paper and sandalwood.[18] A framed photo, about twelve by

Figure 1.3: Altar, Our Lady Jecintho Prayer House, 2005. Photo by author.

fourteen inches, leans against the lowest tier, showing the strewn rose petals featured in the brochure. None of this reminds me of the Catholic churches I know from home. If anything, it makes me think of Mexico.

On the yellow wall behind the altar a bleeding Christ, about the same size as the biggest statues, hangs on a crucifix. Below, a sign reads, "Word of Christ." To the right, a large poster shows Mary and Jesus superimposed on a map of India. The text at the bottom—in big roman letters, rather than modern Tamil script—reads, "Bhārat Mātā" (Mother India).[19]

The paint job is a confetti of pastels. Most of the walls are pink; the doorways, arches, and ceiling fans, trimmed white. On an archway above the altar, a blue-and-white dove spreads its wings, unfolding white rays.

The crowd chants Tamil prayers in a fast, fervent rhythm. The pulse of so many voices, a harmonic buzz, suffuses the house, suggesting to me a simultaneous fullness and longing, a full emptiness. Suddenly, the percussive, fricative syllables of the Tamil click into meaning. This is the rosary—a prayer I chanted thousands of times as a child. With the relief that can come after months of feeling lost in a new linguistic world, I note each decade—each ten recitations of "Hail Marys," separated by one "Our Father," one "Glory Be," and one "O My Jesus."[20] I ponder the Tamil words, knowing that the non-English valences may change the meaning of the prayer significantly. Before I get far, though, the crowd begins a Tamil verse that breaks the pattern.

"*O Jecintovē*!"
O most holy Virgin Mary!
O Jecintho, O Queen of Roses,
pray for us to the Holy Trinity
to shower his mercy on his most beloved mankind.
O Mother of our merciful Lord
make us a channel of peace,
so that we may spread the fragrance of
the Lord's merciful peace throughout the world.
O Jecintho, O Queen of Roses,
bind us in your wonderful love,
be with us in our times of need and
grant us our petitions.
protect us from all evil and
make us worthy to be the children of our Lord
for ever and ever. Amen.[21]

Who or what is a *Jecintho*? And what is a "fragrance" of the Lord's merciful peace? All I smell here is sweat; the scent of jasmine and rose has long faded.

The crowd resumes the traditional rosary. Between decades, someone initiates what seems a spontaneous song, and the crowd sings together, a capella.

New arrivals approach the altar, dramatically, in comportments of respect, from a red-tiled center aisle. The men walk somewhat stiffly, pants pressed (or *dhotis* long), hands clasped at the chest. The women take smaller steps, ankle bracelets jingling. Many people carry roses and place them on the altar. One man prostrates himself before the altar, face down on the floor, his arms and legs extended, then raises himself up, crosses himself, and melts into the crowd.[22] Some kneel in adoration or touch the feet of Mary's statue and stand before her for a while. Others touch Mary's feet quickly, and then their own heads, eyes, and chests. As the altar swarms with devotees, a boy of about twelve moves through the crowd with a plastic dishpan, distributing heads of pink roses.

The rosary surges to a gallop. A woman yells her Hail Marys. Some people pray as if in pain. One, on her hands and knees, squints her eyes shut, rosary beads trailing on the floor. Almost everyone is holding rosary beads.

People sing "*uṇmai aṉbu ceykiṉṟom*!" (We give real love!), the chant raw and sweet. Suddenly, I am about to cry. Fatigue, or maybe it's release of the anxiety caused by my city arrest, or simply the relief of recognition—of being, in some way, home? Three women sit cross-legged at the altar. The one in the center, with the long black braid, must be Rosalind.

She faces the photo of the strewn rose petals, wearing wire-rimmed glasses and a blue-and-white sari, her head slightly bowed. To her left sits a woman with big, sad eyes, perhaps in her thirties, wearing a dull-colored *churi dar*. To Rosalind's right sits a younger woman, quite thin, whose own braid hangs down her back, clear to the floor. All three sing and pray with the crowd.

As we chant the rosary's third decade, Rosalind removes her glasses and places them on the floor in front of her. She starts rocking gently, barely perceptibly at first, then with greater momentum, back and forth, bending at the waist, to and fro, more forward than back, slowly lowering her torso closer to the floor each time until her forehead is almost touching the tiles. Her hands extend in front of her, palms up, a few inches above the floor.

The singing crescendos. A man in the middle of the crowd, having seen Rosalind rocking, raises his right hand over his head, palm open toward the altar. "*Mariyē vāḻka! Mariyē vāḻka*" (Long live Mary!),[23] he sings. Other hands shoot up. I try to block out visions of Hitler's Germany, but then I am reminded of the upraised hands of Charismatic and Pentecostal worship—though here, the arms seem more rigid. Within seconds, all hands are raised, and the chapel fills with gentle Tamil voices lifting the tune of "Ave Maria" as composed by Schubert. Rosalind, still rocking, cocks her head slightly to the right and takes salt from a bag in front of her. The woman in the *churi dar* hands her a clear plastic bottle of water—it looks like an empty, screw-top Pepsi or Coke—and Rosalind pours the salt into the bottle and hands it to the thin woman with the exceptionally long braid. Still rocking, she reaches to both sides, grasps her assistants' hands, and leans on them hard as they help her to her feet. The "Ave Maria" swells.

The helper with the long braid holds the Coke bottle while the other supports Rosalind, who turns toward the crowd and totters down the center aisle like an old woman, her gait stiff and bent. The helper with the bottle pours salty water into Rosalind's cupped right hand, and Rosalind flicks it liberally into the crowd. It sounds and feels like a rain shower. Rosalind moves down the aisle, drenching one side of the crowd, then the other. The throng sings a new song, *Mātāvē caraṇam*, "O Mother of refuge!" as Rosalind arrives back at the altar. Then, from a bowl held by the woman with the long braid, she strews rose petals and whole blossoms over us. Women kneel, and hold out the long ends of their saris to catch them.

Now people are eating the rose petals, picking them off the floor and popping them into their mouths. I hesitate—but never, myself, having tasted a rose petal, I do so, too. It is bitter-sweet, and I chew it down as I see others doing. Some are stuffing the petals into bags they have brought with them for the occasion. People sing another "Ave Maria."

Someone in the crowd is hushing us. Overhead, the fan coasts to a stop. Rosalind stands by the altar, facing us, speaking in a whisper. The crowd stills.

"*Inshallah nama ashalla kashta . . .*" This is not Tamil. It sounds more like Arabic—certainly, *inshallah* is Arabic—with a few Tamil-sounding words thrown in. (It is neither Arabic, nor Tamil, nor Aramaic, nor Hebrew, a scholar of these languages later tells me.)[24] From my experience in American Charismatic groups, I realize that this is must be a local version—Rosalind's (or Jecintho's)—of "speaking in tongues." She talks in this babbling, glossolalic language for some time, occasionally moving into Tamil and English. The woman in the *churi dar* is seated at her feet, scribbling into a notebook. Rosalind places her right hand on the woman's head and leans. Then she takes a step and leans on the head of a man also seated, like most everyone else, on the floor. "When you want to . . . *be* proud," she says in English. "You should believe more," she says in Tamil.

The air is stifling. From the dargah a few blocks away comes a high-pitched Muslim call to prayer, the Arabic-speaking male voice overlaying Rosalind's whispers.

Possession is nothing new. I've seen women become possessed at Hindu temples and in Hindu goddess processions in Madurai. I've seen Charismatic deliverances of evil spirits, and what might be called possessions by the Holy Spirit, in Connecticut. The prayer here seems quite like what I heard as a kid. It seems clear to me that this sort of worship is influenced by Pentecostalism.[25] But I've never seen anyone possessed by Mary. Then I realize that I only recognize Rosalind as possessed by Mary because I've been *told* that is her practice. There is nothing particular in her bodily comportment to make me think: Now, there's Mary! Rosalind's old-lady bent stance and the tremor of her head indicate, in fact, quite the opposite of Mary. However, many other possessions in Tamil Nadu are aggressive ones, by demons—*pēy*—or by such fierce Hindu goddesses as Mariamman or Pandi Muni, who have shaken the bodies of the women possessed, causing them to "dance," causing their hair to loosen.[26] The contrast—the soft and gentle voice—then, might indicate Mary. That, and everything around her: the explosion of rose petals, the Mary statues, and the quiet that has fallen over the room.

But now, after a brief silence, Rosalind is speaking in lickety-split Tamil. Even with the fans off, people are leaning forward to hear. I make out "*bhakti*" (intense, personal devotion), "*aruḷ*" (grace) and "*an̲bu*" (love). Then Rosalind lists places from around the world, predicting disasters, telling us to pray for the affected people. "Colombo." "Cameroon." Abruptly, Rosalind stops speaking and turns to face the altar. She rocks, palms up again, toward the photo and statues.

When she turns back to us, the crowd splits in two, to either side of the red-tiled aisle, and people kneel. From Rosalind's posture, focus, and facial expression—and from the submissive, attentive behavior of the people around me—she appears still to be possessed. Standing at the head of the aisle, she turns stage left, places her right hand on the closest person—a middle-aged woman in a dusk-blue sari—and starts praying, touching the woman first on her head, then her shoulders, down her arms, and across her torso. The woman, eyes closed, seems to melt. With each touch, she sways. Her head rolls back. Rosalind pulls her down by the shoulders so that she bends at the waist, pressing her hands all over her back, and then raises her straight again. She motions for the woman to rise and then massages her legs, presses her feet, spends a little extra time around the knees. The woman kneels again and Rosalind leans on her shoulder to speak into her ear. The woman nods as if in assent. Rosalind pulls back, and their eyes meet. The woman shakes her head side-to-side, an Indian-style yes, and smiles. Rosalind starts to turn away, then turns halfway back, and seems to throw some sort of joke: the woman breaks into laughter, as do those around her. Rosalind, composed, turns shakily back and moves to the next kneeling person down the aisle.

The blessings will go on well into the night—perhaps till midnight, Charles has explained—and it is only 8:30 p.m. I am dripping with sweat. My fingertips are wrinkled as if I have just emerged from a long bath. Rosalind massages dozens more of the faithful as she works her way up and down the aisle on each side. The fans are still; the room, torpid and close.

Outside, the night is sultry but cooler than the packed prayer house. A puff of breeze rattles the palm leaves overhead. The red neon letters below the blue neon Mary seem to shout *Aṉṉai Jecintō Jebuvīṭu*. "Jecintho," apparently, is the name of the form in which Mary comes to Rosalind—"Our Lady Jecintho" is a local form of Mary, just like Our Lady of Lourdes or Our Lady of Fatima. In this case, however, the honorific is not attached to a place but to a proper name: *Jecintō*. (*Jecintō*, properly transliterated from the Tamil script, is not a Tamil word, but a name that means "queen of roses." Mary revealed it to Rosalind in a vision.) Now resuscitated by the night air, I spot Charles across the veranda and ask his permission to question people as they leave. He assents, and I approach several, telling them that I'm a researcher. None refuses me.

"Lots of power comes (*romba shakti varum*)," a thirty-eight-year-old woman who has been attending for three years says. "Lots of energy." *Shakti* (power or energy)—is the word people give most as a reason for coming. A Sanskrit word associated with Hindu gods and goddesses, *shakti* can mean many more precise things: the feminine divine principle, the creative force, the power that causes an effect, the Goddess herself.

Other Tamil words come up nearly as often as *shakti*. A diminutive, middle-aged woman in a bright pink sari speaks of the *nambikkai*, "faith," necessary to experience its *palaṉ*, meaning its "fruit" or "outcome." Mātā once sent a Jecintho statue from the shrine home with her, the woman says, and told her to dress and bathe it, pray to it regularly for a week, and then return it. Such dressing and bathing is classic Hindu devotional behavior toward an image, bringing it to life in domestic space.[27] It is also part of a regular ritual at Our Lady Jecintho Prayer House: someone new takes the statue home each week.

"Wherever the statue goes, we can feel something different," a soft-spoken woman in a pink sari says, "*nalla palaṉ vantatu, nēriya* 'gifts'"—a good outcome came, excellent gifts. The woman has born many hardships. Her father was hit by a motorcycle while he was walking, for example. In his pocket, he carried a slip of paper with the name and address of the shrine. An auto-rickshaw driver took pity on him, drove him fifteen kilometers to the nearest hospital for treatment, and returned him, naturally enough, to the prayer house. "Now Father is fine." A good outcome, thanks to Mātā's grace. Another example: her husband's partner stole the business, worth 80,000 rupees (at the time, about $1,800). But Jecintho Amma has given them a sense of peace, by promising to rid them of their troubles. "I am happy. Even though we don't have money, that happiness alone is enough."

A nun, Sister Solome, has come, with three other nuns, from the Cluny Order at Santhome, in the neighborhood of the city's cathedral. She comes three or four times a year. "Hindus and all are coming," she tells me in English. "Our Lady is a very powerful lady. She is doing things for all people." Sister Solome has seen many people healed after coming: one small boy had a lump that went away, despite the doctors' prognosis that it would not heal without an operation. "Doctors will say, 'No hope for this patient,' and then they will be healed. We need faith. If we have love—love and respect for each person—then God will do a miraculous thing." The four nuns are planning to head straight from the prayer house to Velankanni, on a double pilgrimage. "Our Lady came and inspired me," Sister Solome explains. "She said, 'You have to go.'"

A nun with chronic neck pain, Sister Veronica, says it is Mary's faith and humility that make her great: "She totally surrendered to God." Veronica is not troubled by the idea that Mary is entering the body of a simple woman in a Chennai suburb in a form called Jecintho. "She is revealing herself in many places, to many persons," Sister Veronica figures. She feels peace and relief under Rosalind's touch; already, her neck feels better. She will come to Our Lady Jecintho Prayer House whenever she has a chance.

Gerard, a round-faced Tamil in a navy-blue Adidas shirt, has been called to accompany me back into the stifling chapel. Gerard has big, bright, brown eyes and a quick smile, and he speaks good English. Charles has asked him to help me. Charles knows that I am doing research for a book, and he is happy to have me advertise the goings-on at the chapel. He also is a generous man, welcoming to strangers, and he recognizes that I am a foreigner in a foreign land but still part of a larger "church" family. Gerard leads me to the left side of the altar, and we sit cross-legged behind a group of middle-aged women who look over their shoulders and smile at me. Across the aisle, Rosalind prays over a woman in a bright yellow sari, who stands, weeping and breathing heavily, chest heaving, her hands held out from her sides, palms up.

Oh no, I suddenly think. I don't want to be prayed over. *What if Rosalind comes to me?* "Please God," I think, slipping into the language of my youth, "just let me watch." The idea of getting prayed over, for me, comes freighted with childhood memories of giving up control, of being touched by people I don't want to have touch me. *But what kind of a message will I send if I refuse the prayer?* And then, parasitically, *Maybe I should get prayed over, just to write about it.* Already, Gerard is pushing me to the front, and two women are parting to let me move in beside them. Rosalind is coming down the aisle, pressing her hands all over the young woman to my right, one of those who smiled at me. Tears roll in glistening trails down her dark cheeks. She crouches on all fours, heaving. Her body shakes. Rosalind eases her back to her knees, sprinkles water over her, and says something in her ear. The woman calms, and Rosalind turns to me.

Half bent over, she looks directly into my eyes. *Here we go.* She puts her right hand on my head and presses firmly, repeatedly, then runs her hands down my shoulders and arms, pressing and patting. She takes each of my hands, pressing my palm and each finger. She puts her hand on my left shoulder, leans over, and whispers into my ear in an unintelligible tongue—"*Inshama sahani, mihad . . . nisha shaha ni . . .*" Her voice is breathy, her breath delicately sweet and sour. *Does the smell have to do with her fasting?* In a clear English whisper, she croons, "I will always be with you. Do not worry. Relax. Reeeelaaax. I will bless your path so that everything you do will be a success. You have nothing to worry about. I will bless you with the Holy Spirit." She pulls me slightly forward, so that she can reach my back, and runs her hand down my left side. I relax, giving in to the touch, and rest my head lightly against her shoulder. She moves her hand to my right side. "I will bring you health. I will bring you happiness." She touches my chest, stomach, two hip bones. My purse is somewhere on the floor behind me, but I let the thought go. Rosalind pushes me down, mushes her hands down my spine—spending a lot of time on the left, where I have an old injury—and across the back of my hips. She raises me up, turns, and asks one of her female assistants for something—I can't hear what. The assistant motions to a young man, who, in a seeming chain of command, gestures to Alex, who has been sitting in back. Alex springs to action, disappearing briefly to return with a small plastic bag. He hands the bag to the assistant, who pulls out a tiny clear-plastic envelope, perhaps an inch square—the kind in which a jeweler might keep earrings. She hands it to Rosalind, and out of the bag, Rosalind pulls a miniscule, gray-white feather. She moves in close and holds the feather in front of my face.

"This," she says, "is a feather from the wing of the Holy Spirit."

What? I think. *You've got to be kidding me*.

She strokes my cheek with it. "I will take care of you. Good things will happen." She hands the feather to her assistant and turns to the next patient in line.

I tap her assistant's shoulder.

"Excuse me," I whisper. "May I ask a question?" The assistant tugs at Rosalind, who turns back to me and leans forward. I look into her attentive brown eyes. I haven't prepared any question.

"Why am I here?" I blurt.

There is a brief pause.

"Because," she says in a whisper. "You are a witness."

The attraction to me, now, is clear—much clearer than if I had not let Rosalind-as-Jecintho bless me. The intimacy, the assurance that all would be well, the personal attention—I, for one, was fairly desperate for it. And if I was desperate for it, then what about all the people living on of a tiny fraction of my stopped Fulbright stipend? What about all the people disconnected from their families because they had migrated from the village to the city, or because they were feeling their way through the labyrinthine, bureaucratic, neocapitalist world of the "New India"? Here, so many young adults—if they were lucky, like Rosalind's brother and cousin—might work at a call center or an outsourcing company. Older people who depended on children and extended family for support in this quickly changing world faced their own anxieties. Their children might be exposed to coworkers of the opposite sex or, worse, marry outside caste or community and abandon them, or leave them to ridicule. Mostly, it was the Indian elite who could make it to schools like IIT (Indian Institute of Technology—the dream of many an aspiring engineer or scientist) or to the great medical colleges, or to the United States, Canada, or England for graduate school, or who could, through brilliance and grinding hard work, get themselves American or Canadian work visas. If you were not one of those people, this teeming, quickly shifting world left little on which to depend. *Of course* so many people would find solace in this prayer house.

On top of all this was the matter of illness and access to medical care—or the lack of it, based on economic resources. I wanted to believe that Rosalind knew where to touch my formerly injured back, and to my lower abdomen. I took the latter to mean she was attending to my fertility, as she did with so many women my age or younger.

And then there was simply the physical touch. I cannot emphasize enough the comfort of the close contact—especially after such a long period of being alone. I felt like I would melt. And the words, whispered so intimately into my ear, "Relax . . . Do not worry . . . I will always be with you . . . You will be a success." It was exactly what I wanted to hear.

After the prayers, near midnight, when Rosalind-as-Jecintho has prayed over hundreds of people, she returns to the same kneeling and rocking that brought Mātā. "Mother is going out," Gerard whispers. Rosalind's rocking stills, and her forehead almost touches the ground. An assistant hands over the gold-rimmed glasses. She puts them on, sits back on her knees, and touches Jesus's and Mary's feet and garlands.

People stand and mill about, chatting, the way congregants do after a church service. Rosalind stands, too, and speaks to the visitors who approach. She is sitting in a white plastic chair beside her father, holding a cup of juice. Her face looks blotchy—dull and wan, dark under the eyes. She hasn't eaten, she says, since morning.

The assistant wearing the *churi dar,* Francina, with the sad puppy-dog eyes, says, "She won't eat." She speaks with scolding affection. "She'll only pray."

How does she stay on her feet for so long?

"She gives," Rosalind says, of Jecintho Mātā, and asks how I feel and whether Jecintho spoke to me.

I am slightly put off that Rosalind is acting as if she hadn't been there, touching me and speaking to me. But she is looking at me expectantly.

"Yes. She knew just what to say." I feel slightly duplicitous, unsure whether I stand behind my words. I ask Rosalind about the messages Jecintho whispers. Several people have told me that she seemed miraculously to know about their problems. How does she know? Do the people speak to her or to others ahead of time?

Sometimes, she says, people tell no one but Mātā, in their private prayers or during the service, so that "nobody knows their secrets—only the *right* person."

And how did she feel during the service?

"I won't feel anything," she says. "I won't know anything." On Saturday afternoons, she says, she fasts and can eat by perhaps nine at night or so, but for these evening services, she won't eat until about midnight or one the next morning. "That's eight or nine hours," she says. "But I won't feel anything, isn't it?"

"Isn't it?" is an Indian colloquialism, meaning variously, "you should know that" and, in the case of Rosalind, "isn't it remarkable?"

Again, hasn't she any memory of the service?

"I don't know anything."

God. I could feel my frustration mount. How much is "not knowing anything" a ruse, a mask that women wear—not just in Tamil Nadu but everywhere—when what they know threatens social equilibrium? In family contexts in which men are given the greatest permission to speak, and to rule, for women, "mum" is the word. Rosalind's intelligence, I suspected, was channeled by such strictures into this shrine. Perhaps *An̲n̲ai Jecintō Jebuvīṭu* was one of the few spaces where her pronouncements carried weight. Although Rosalind had run a tutorial service before her routine possessions began, her words and actions as Jecintho certainly had more widespread effects, winning her higher status than that of a tutor with no husband.

Charles breaks into my thoughts by mentioning that the local parish priest has created, or said, "some mischief" about Rosalind. "It is not fit for a priest to be saying such things," he says with indignation. But Rosalind brings the conversation back to the here and now, asking, for a second time since the service, how I feel.

Good, I say, and then, noting her blank expression, I amp it up: *very* good.

"*Very* good," she repeats in English, exaggerating the "r" and taking my hand in hers. The cold shocks me: her hands were warm when she lay them on me earlier.

"They say I can become very hot, it seems," she says.[28] "But she is taking care of everything . . . . How do you think it is possible that I can stand for so long? I am a low-BP patient only."

Rosalind often says these two things in tandem, I come to realize as I get to know her—that she stands long in the heat and has low blood pressure—as though while possessed, she defies the laws of science. And never once, in all my years of knowing Rosalind, will I hear her speak of herself while possessed without suggesting that she heard about it through a third party. Now, though, I merely note that she qualifies the statement about her hot, possessed body with "it seems." I am impressed that she can stand for so long. But I also keep pressing for an answer: what does it feel like to be Jecintho?

"I've told you; I won't recall anything. I won't be feeling anything at all."

PARTICIPANT OBSERVER, OR OBSERVED?

In April 2004, after that first trip to the shrine, I accepted the invitation of Rev. Fr. Vincent Chinnadurai—the bespectacled, compact priest in his fifties who had first told me about Rosalind (the man with whom I had been talking when Charles called)—to attend lunch at Our Lady Jecintho Prayer House with him and a fellow priest named Fr. Gaspar Raj. Rosalind's family had invited them for an informal Sunday meal, Chinnadurai said, and I would be more than welcome to join. Chinnadurai, whom I had first met at the foot of St. Thomas Mount at a church he was pastoring there, had just been named communications director for Santhome Cathedral, the center of the Madras-Mylapore Archdiocese. He had featured an image of Our Lady Jecintho on the back cover of a recent issue of the Archdiocese's weekly, *Nam Vazhvu.*

Now, we collected Gaspar in Chinnadurai's white, air-conditioned SUV. A Tamil native from Nagercoil, Gaspar, like Chinnadurai, had worked on interreligious dialogue and forms of worship. He was also a talented Karnatic singer. He spoke excitedly of his role in an orchestral,[29] based on poetry by the ninth-century Hindu *bhakti* poet Manikkavacakar, with the famous Tamil musician and film music composer Ilaya Raja. Central to the poem is the notion of *aruḷ*. Tamil Roman Catholic liturgies and discourses refer often to *aruḷ,* as does Rosalind when possessed by Jecintho. Gaspar waxed eloquent: in the *Tiruvācakam*, "*aruḷ* can come directly to you; you need not have priests . . . no mediation." The *Tiruvācakam* "is more Catholic than Catholicism sometimes!"

I wondered: Like Manikkavacakar, who had an intimate relationship with his Lord—no priests—might Rosalind and other women claiming to be possessed be understood as expressing a sort of hybrid, Catholic-Hindu *bhakti*—an intensely personal, direct devotion inflected by both traditions? Gaspar said he could certainly see the connection: he had visited Rosalind's shrine only once, but she had impressed him. What did the church hierarchy think?

"The church is watching," Gaspar said. "It neither condemns nor supports."

I asked him to elaborate, and he answered, "I am not supposed to say." Personally, though, the shrine triggered deep emotions in him, he said, and Rosalind, as Jecintho, had somehow seemed to know things that he held very private. Her messages—the depth to which she seemed to read his psyche—had shocked him.

Soon we were driving past an industrial area near Erukkanchery, a neighborhood next to Rosalind's Kodungaiyur and close to an oil refinery—a sprawl that Blake might have described as "dark satanic mills." But in the center of one residential area, instead of a smokestack rose a steeple. "Father was known to give a face-lift to this place," Gaspar said, speaking of how Chinnadurai had built a church and worked to clean up the neighborhood. "Before he came, this place was known only for its terrible smells." We crossed a bridge over bright green water from which rose a strong fecal stench. A young man walking on the bridge looked up with exhausted eyes. Gaspar shook his head. "When a country is under subjugation so long, the vibrancy goes out. It loses its spiritual vitality."

Soon we were in Kodungaiyur, pulling up to the shrine. The people milling around outside turned to look at the immense, white, air-conditioned SUV. A neatly dressed man with white hair stepped up to greet us: Charles. The heat was crushing. The shrine was crowded inside, and I suddenly suspected, in the pit of my stomach, that arriving in this grand style—and with priests!—was a mistake. We hadn't been invited to a simple Sunday lunch; we'd been invited to what local folk would call, in Tamil-accented English, a *function*, a formal event. Worse, our arrival, visit, and eating with the other guests *was* the event. Neutrality as an observer was, I knew, impossible, no matter my native tongue or the color of my skin. But to my own dismay, I was no longer even an informal observer—I was an associate of the priests—in this case, beloved priests, but still *priests*—the very elite I'd assumed Rosalind's sort of possession ritual to oppose fundamentally. I was on the receiving end of a "welcoming-the-two-priests-and-one-white-American-scholar" function. Crowds had been invited; it felt like a coronation. Forget any notion of approaching the devotees "on their level."

This was the sort of moment—the sort of reversal that has itself become a trope in postmodern ethnographic writing. It happens to fieldworkers all the time.[30] But I was not prepared for it. This site, which I had recently imagined as being crucial to my work—indeed, as the site most relevant to my work in a city that I was forbidden to leave—was reversing the lens: this community in which I'd imagined myself as a "participant observer" was setting things up to observe me. I was as much a curiosity to them as they were to me. If I was going to research their goings-on, I'd better pass muster. Furthermore, as a white foreigner from the wealthy and (in this community) lusted-after United States, I probably lent further status to the prayer house and validated their beliefs. They were now important.

The next several minutes are a blur. I must have removed my *chappals* (sandals) at the bottom of the entrance steps, as everyone did, and entered the house. The crowd seated on the floor must have shimmied aside, clearing a path.

I remember seeing three empty chairs in the center of the room: one for each priest, and one for me. To reject a chair, I feared, would be an egotistical rejection of hospitality. It was too late to back out gracefully.

I took my cues from the priests, who themselves accepted the seating arrangement with chagrin—but this, too, seemed part of the ceremony: to communicate modesty, one may say "no" a number of times before accepting an honor. But ultimately, one must accept the gift, so as not to embarrass the giver. And so, again as I had during the prayer service, I sat in the middle of the community I was intending to study, surrounded by a crowd of perhaps two hundred people—this time beside two priests, on seats that literally raised us heads and shoulders above others.

Someone introduced us, noting that Chinnadurai had supported the prayer house in spirit from the beginning. Just that March, he had been there at a *mālai aṇivittu varavērpu,* or "garland-adornment-welcoming," in which he had worn around his neck (I would later see in a photo) a gigantic garland made of roses and tulsi leaves that represent the consort of Vishnu, the goddess Tulsi. The garland was as thick as a large roll of paper towels, and it looped almost to his feet. He had cut the green ribbon at the newly renovated prayer house and concelebrated a Mass with four other priests—thus authorizing the space as sacred and properly Roman Catholic—and with more than five thousand people in attendance, many if not most of them Hindu.

Dozens of priests had lent the weight of their authority to various functions throughout the past few years. Photos of many appeared with captions in a small booklet that the community published as a sort of *sthala* purāna,[31] "ancient stories of a sacred site," of the prayer house. Rev. Fr. Ignatius, S.J., a professor of philosophy at Sathya Nillaiyam Seminary in Thiruvanmaiyur, Chennai; a popular preacher and a specialist in Charismatic Catholicism had said Mass and consecrated the Eucharist. Rev. Fr. Anandam, a theologian and the author of a popular book about Mary, *Aruḷ oru ōviyam* (*A Picture of God's Grace*), had said Mass and attended a flag-hoisting ceremony.[32] Several other prominent priests from the diocese had consecrated and distributed Eucharist at the shrine and had been present for festivals and ceremonies. They did this, I thought, both to authorize *themselves*—with their rituals of authority and authorizing, such as the Eucharist, which only they could perform—as well as to authorize the shrine. The two groups—elite and popular, priests and lay people—needed each other to exist. Remaining distant from Our Lady Jecintho Prayer House—an emerging site of devotion—priests would be left out of the loop. If they could not control and contain new expressions of faith among the people, it would be better to participate—both to keep an eye on things and to authorize them.

Suddenly, I was being introduced as a scholar of religion who had come all the way from the United States to study devotion to Mātā. I saw that Charles and other members of the prayer house held long sandalwood-bead and gold-laminated cardboard garlands, versions of the thick flower garland that I had seen in the photo of Chinnadurai and had associated with Hindu political ceremonies but never yet with Roman Catholicism. Both priests bowed their heads to be garlanded, and their palms pressed together at their chests. I did the same. I watched them remove the garlands a few seconds later and hang them over the backs of their chairs. I did the same. Such mimetic gesturing is, of course, the very beginning of human communication and social bonding. It is how babies learn. I was watching carefully in order to be accepted. I had been chagrinned by the association with priests, but now, like a toddler learning to talk, I was copying the patterns—adopting the assigned priestly parents and accepting the gifting gestures of Rosalind's family. I felt the weight of this first, formal impression.

Now Rosalind asked Chinnadurai to speak, and he did so, at length, in Tamil. Next, she asked Gaspar to speak. My heart was thumping in my ears. Gaspar sang. People clapped enthusiastically—and now, everyone was looking at me. Rosalind was asking me to say something.

"*Vaṇakkam,*" I said, putting my hands together in formal greeting, and embarked on an impromptu speech that was probably filled with errors. I remember saying "*eṉakku romba santōsham*" (I am very happy) and seeing little exclamations, smiles, and whispers rippling through the crowd. I spoke for no more than three minutes—which felt like an eternity—and ended with "*nandri*" (thank you). It was worse than a bad Tamil movie. The crowd broke into applause.

If Chinnadurai and Gaspar had merely been "rectory priests," the kind who confined themselves to the church or who were for various reasons seen as detached and elitist—my association with them could have been trouble. But had that been the case, they probably would not have come. As it turned out, my early association with them may have bought me some trust—a stamp of authenticity in the eyes of the shrine community. From that point on, however, I tried to be more careful about my alignments.

I could never escape being part of the act. It was always a balance between surrendering to the situation, giving up some control over my place in it, and trying to maintain a hold on my position as a separate "self," an outside observer. It was, perhaps at base, no different from any relationship. I felt, fairly constantly, the pull between identification and separation.

WHAT A WITNESS SAYS

What does it mean, to be a witness?

In Tamil, the word *cāṭci* comes from the Sanskrit *sākṣin*, which means something like "seeing with your own eyes." Many devotees used the word repeatedly in the context of the prayer house. They would "give *cāṭci*" (*cāṭci koṭu, cāṭci col*), meaning that they would give personal testimony about the blessings Mātā had worked in their lives. They would do this, publicly and orally in the packed prayer house (usually after Mātā had invited them to do so) or in writing, in the printed, soft-cover, prayer-house booklet that contained the history and description—the *sthala purāna*—of the place. Each person's story was printed in Tamil next to a thumbnail black-and-white, passport-like photo, under the heading *cāṭcikaḷ*, "eye-witnesses" or "testimonies," in Tamil script. One woman—a poor, twenty-nine-year-old mother of two named Lata who had migrated with her husband from Nagercoil District for work—witnessed in the pamphlet about how she had been possessed by *pēy* before Jecintho Mātā exorcised her. Another, lower-middle-class man witnessed that he had been unemployed and hopeless but then found a job; another, that he had been cured of cancer. Another, a man in his forties who had migrated to Chennai from a small village near Sivagangai District and who owned a small company that made detergent powder, witnessed that business had picked up after he had visited the shrine. He had named his marketing division Jecintho Trade Links. Another two businessmen called their car service Jecintho Madha Travels, and their cell phone business, Jecintho Madha Cell City. A lower-middle-class family with black magic on their house had brought a Jecintho statue home for one week—dressed it, bathed it, and prayed before it—and had been released of their suffering. A widow with three daughters had struggled to survive, but had found peace of mind—and her daughters had found jobs—through Jecintho.

The English word "witness" suggests not only stating a fact but also giving testimony in court. Its legal meaning emerges from the Christian notions of witness and of confessing one's sins. Such a meaning mixes Christian ideas of an inner self (which suggests distinction from an outer one) with legal testimony—which also contains the idea of being judged or watched.[33]

"I hereby swear to tell the truth, the whole truth, and nothing but the truth, so help me God." Is this what Rosalind-as-Jecintho was calling me to do when she brought out the little feather? Did she want me to offer some big megawitness to her prayer house, which had become a small but growing cottage industry? Was this meant to be some conversion/success story? The Christian language of witness informed not only the Western legal system but also the development of anthropology, which went hand-in-hand with colonization. Meanwhile, Augustine's *Confessions* gave witness to an experience of conversion while heralding a whole new literary genre. The *Confessions* evokes the entire tradition of memoir, of reporting, of travel writing, and of the sort of witnessing that began as a testimonial, "confessional" argument meant to convince through the authenticity of experience—and that later emerged, empiricized and sterilized, as ethnography.[34] To me, the genealogy of "witness" also resonated with the transformation of the "examination of conscience" and rites of confession to more general mass governmental and judicial techniques designed to direct human behavior.[35]

But just who was witnessing what, or whom, here at the shrine of Our Lady Jecintho? Is there ever any stable, reliable witness? To what extent is possession itself an act of witness? A person who is possessed, by Tamil standards, must have witnesses of the possession in order to know that it happened at all.

And yet, it was discomfiting to respond to a person who was unable (or refused) to witness her own spectacular performance. That Rosalind claimed not to know what happened while she was possessed—that she seemed to disavow consciousness—suggested that she gave up all claims to agency. Perhaps my reaction was steeped in American feminism's second wave and post-Freudian psychoanalysis. Aren't claims of all "unconscious" behavior suspicious? It seemed irresponsible, maddening, even frightening, that Rosalind willingly entered—or performed—such a state. On another level, I feared, Rosalind's willingness to "be possessed" by Mary made her a co-conspirator with patriarchy. Not only was she submitting to Mary; she was submitting to the images and tools of the oppressor—the patriarchal Roman Catholic Church—which had reduced the place of women and Mary to that of helpmate and vessel, and had helped Europe deploy its colonizing mission. Rosalind's claims of possession paralleled long-standing critiques of Mary, the church's manipulation of her life story, and its effects on the lives of real men and women—including some in my own family.

And yet. Rosalind was clearly gaining status in this venture. Thousands of people were flocking to the prayer house over which she presided, and priests at the highest levels of Archdiocesan power were coming to pay their respects. In May 2002, I later discovered, Auxiliary Bishop Rev. Dr. Lawrence Pius had formally approved the Jecintho Prayer in a letter that was circulated to churches throughout the city. As far as I could see, Rosalind was not only insinuating herself into the crucible of power at Santhome Cathedral; she was easing many people's very real pain. She was giving hundreds if not thousands of people—many of them migrant workers and recent implants—a sense of home, of community, and of respectability amid the industrial, postcolonial world that was Chennai.

CHAPTER 2

The Place, the People, the Practices

Our Lady Jecintho and the Quest for Embodied Wholeness

But this was not home. The early trips I made to Kodungaiyur were an assault to my senses. As the bus bounced northward from the Besant Nagar bus depot, my knees banging against the green steel seat in front of me, I tried to meditate on what, if anything, this discomfort said to me. Certainly, it spoke to my position as a white, corn-fed *farangi* in relation to the mystifying multiplicity of people and places that swarmed around me. But as I moved through the masses, I also reflected on what we had in common: a search for safety and love—a desire to move up in the world, escape confines, grab opportunities, survive. What I shared with the people on the bus—other than bruised knees—was that here, right at this moment in Chennai, we were all winding our way through peripheral urban modernity, at the crossroads of postcolonial neocapitalism and tradition (*Whoa, watch out for that truck! . . . No! The bullock cart, the bullock cart!*). We were all trying to make sense of things, searching for wholeness amid the forces of globalization and natural chaos that threatened to fragment us. We were all, in our own ways, seeking home.

Religion, for lack of a better word,[1] offers many people just that: a sense of wholeness, of connection, of being united with one another as a social body, and to something (a power, a presence, a oneness) larger than ourselves. Religious people might call this "something" God or divinity; others, *brahman*; others, *moksha* or *nirvāṇa*; others, any one of thousands of personal gods (*devas* or *devīs*) or *avatars* of divinity. The italicized words are all Sanskrit, though many of the local personal names for gods and goddesses in Tamil Nadu are not (and in Tamil transliteration, the words are *tēva* and *tēvi*). The oldest word for God in Tamil is *kaṭavuḷ*. Many native speakers say that the word is from *kaṭa*, "to transcend, go beyond, cross over."[2] God is a being who crosses over to us, or to whom we cross over. We are all "crossing over"—many of us hope—to one another, to a resting place, to a state of wholeness, to what some would call salvation (or Tamils would call *mīṭpu*—literally, "rescue"—an important word at Our Lady Jecintho Prayer House). Salvation, in many forms of Euro-American Christianity, is usually a conception about the next world maintained by those who live in this one. In Tamil Nadu, however, salvation and rescue (*mīṭpu*) were very much about this world. The quest for a state of wholeness and equilibrium was here and now, though one might have to engage with the world of spirits and gods to reach it.

I was particularly interested in what this quest for wholeness specifically meant at Our Lady Jecintho Prayer House—how it was expressed in people's discourses and practices, and how those discourses and practices translated into their bodily dispositions and subjective states.[3] More broadly, I was curious about how the world shaped the body and how the body shaped the world in the constantly entwined nature of outer and inner, practice and disposition, environment and subjectivity. I wanted to explore how a person's worldview, affect, and sense of reality comprises experiences of divinity, which are also wound up in competition over goods and resources. I wanted to investigate how the interplay of these two worlds—inner and outer—informed a sense of home. Specifically, I came to understand that Our Lady Jecintho Prayer House had become a kind of home for many people, that Rosalind and her family cultivated that home, and that Rosalind cultivated her own body as a "home" for Mātā.

That, at least, was the overarching mental map beginning to take shape in my mind—but the journey it delineated was circuitous, full of alternate paths and intermediate stops. One of the latter was the intersection of religion, social class, and different forms of capital.[4]

Notions of upward mobility and Roman Catholicism in Tamil land have gone hand in hand for centuries. The specifically Christian idea that all are equal under God and in the eyes of Jesus Christ, that "whatsoever you do to the least of my brothers, so you do unto me," had long been a tantalizing promise for low-caste and Dalit people, drawing many to the Church from various local forms of Hinduism.[5] The promise, however, did not always deliver. I had only to walk down the street on a Sunday from my apartment to Chinna Velankanni Church ("little Velankanni"), where I could see low-caste people flowing outside from the back rows to the hot pavement, and high-caste people sitting up front in the pews. Many priests talked openly to me about discrimination within clerical ranks.

However, there was more going on at the shrine than a quest for upward mobility. To its devotees, Our Lady Jecintho Prayer House was a path to salvation, literally. The title of its 2004 devotional book was *Turning toward the Dawn: In the Path of Salvation* (*Viḍiyalai nōkki: mīṭpin pātaiyilē*). Interestingly, Rosalind-as-Jecintho had translated *mīṭpu* ("salvation" or "rescue") as "resurrection." (Rosalind said that Jecintho gave her the Tamil words as well as the English ones for the translation, which was printed inside the cover.) But the resurrection that Jecintho taught to devotees seemed different than the one many Euro-American Christians imagined. Her use of the term *mīṭpu* stressed resurrection in *this* world, not the next. Moreover, her way of "crossing over"—or "turning toward the dawn"—was both spiritual and material. It was, in the most literal sense, incarnational. Devotees, likewise, were seeking redemption *now*, from fragmentation and from alienation to wholeness. To them, salvation in the next world meant a good home in this one. And the salvation that Jecintho Annai opened to people included a *way* of life—a way that would inculcate dispositions of respectability (*mariyātai*),[6] faith (*nambikkai*), and devotion (*bhakti*)—among others—that would lead one "across," and back home.

WHAT THE HEART/MIND (*MAṈACU*) SAID

Many scholars of religion, anthropology, and gender have noted that a person is not just a body acted upon by culture; a person participates in the culture that acts upon that person.[7] Practices shape persons' internal worlds, which in turn shape outer ones.[8] The model of "person" here isn't exactly dualistic; it's closer to a Möibus strip.[9] Bodies and minds are neither two distinct and separate substances nor two different attributes of a single substance, but something between the two.

Here is another mind-boggler to the English-wired brain: the notion of the "mind" as such does not exist in Tamil the way it does in English.[10] The closest word to "mind," perhaps, is *maṉam* or *maṉacu*, which means something more like "heart" than "mind." In some contexts, it can also be translated as "purpose," "intention," "desire," or "inclination"—but always with the emphasis on emotion rather than will. It is often understood as an emotive organ, an inner sense-perceptor and receiver. In Tamil, emotive states *come to* a person, as if taking possession of them. The Tamil language does not presume that a person has agency in regard to emotion; a person doesn't *have* a feeling; rather, the feeling has them. "I feel very happy" translates literally into Tamil as "to me much happiness has come" (*eṉakku romba santōsham vantatu*). Like spirits, feelings occupy people from the outside. Tamil notions of embodiment as something permeable and fluid have predated Western approaches to the body for centuries.

This notion of cultivating a *maṉacu*—the organ that senses, perceives, and emotes and that is affected by others—offered a framework for exploring how the context of the place, people, and practices of Our Lady Jecintho Prayer House affected (and effected) its devotees' sense of reality, of what was authentic, of what constituted "home"—and their willingness to believe in Jecintho. The same questions applied to me.

I came to see the bodily practices at the prayer house as blueprints for the cultivation of a particular kind of *maṉacu* that could hold Jecintho. What did that mean? It meant, among other things, that devotees would wade through the soundscape of prayer house songs, prayers, and sermons to learn how to be an "ethical self."[11] It meant that they would allow Jecintho to touch them. It meant that they would watch and listen to her and to one another in order to learn how to comport themselves and develop specific practices of virtue—practices that included propriety (including gendered propriety), effort, submission, sympathy, generosity/charity, selflessness, faith, and love. This path of virtue would help them live and thrive—find salvation—in urban, postcolonial South India.[12]

Countless devotees spoke about relief from real suffering (*cōkam, tukkam*), and Mātā helped them strategize how to deal with it through manners of praying, placing substances around their house or on their bodies, treating these substances in particular ways (e.g., taking a Jecintho statue home, bathing it, and dressing it), and making various sorts of material exchanges with Mātā. The goal was to establish good relations with Mātā, who would in turn grant good results (*palaṉ*), health (*ārōkkiyam*), and happiness (*santōsham*).

FARANGI ON A BUS

To the extent Kodungaiyur was known to outsiders at all, it was as home to one of the city's two garbage-dumping grounds, and as the place thought to have hatched the plot to assassinate prime minister Rajiv Gandhi. So much garbage burned in Kodungaiyur's four-hundred-acre dump that the rancid smell and smoke often made the front page of *The Hindu*, the city's main English-language newspaper, during 2004 and 2005. Kodungaiyur was so cloaked in suspicion that I had a difficult time finding field assistants willing to join me. I sought female assistants, and women who were otherwise eager to work, with good reputations as fieldworkers, would agree—and then back out, citing perceived danger or distaste. One assistant who failed to show up told me that she could not find an auto driver in Perambur willing to cross into Kodungaiyur. Another sent her brother in her stead, a guy on a motorcycle who wanted to sell me a leather jacket. I decided to work on my own.

I tried to understand my potential colleagues' concerns and looked up some stats. The suburbs of Tondiarpet, the name of the zone that encompassed the neighborhoods of East and West Kodungaiyur,[13] are among the most densely populated and industrial in Chennai. Of the approximately 5,000 permanent households in West Kodungaiyur recorded in the 2001 census, only 52 percent had access to water within the house (10 percent less than the city average); 65 percent had open or no drainage (compared to the city's 11 percent); and almost 50 percent had only one room.[14] The figures for East Kodungaiyur were comparable.

These figures did not include impermanent dwellings. Although it is possible to reach Kodungaiyur without passing the smoke stacks or teeming tenement houses of this district, it is difficult to avoid the slums of Perambur—the nearest bus stop and largest dot on the map within a ten-mile radius. Perambur includes both middle-class homes and acre upon acre of slums: from squeezed-together temporary and permanent dwellings of stucco or mud to plastic tarps and open areas. Chennai has the highest slum population of all the cities and towns in the state, as well as the highest percentage of slums—more than 25 percent—compared to the total population of 3.84 million.[15] I could easily imagine how people might seek respite from this sensorial assault in ordered, collective prayer, motherly healing, and promises of upward mobility.

Indeed, there had been a recent proliferation of roadside temples, murals, and shrines to Mary in Chennai.[16] I counted seven between Perambur and Kodungaiyur alone. Several of the roadside shrines or murals depicted Mary in the popular form of Velankanni Mātā: a white woman clothed in red and crowned with gold, standing on a crescent moon, holding a gold staff in her right hand and a child in her left, also crowned. Another mural, in nearby Madhavaram, depicted Mary as "Sahāya Mātā," or Our Lady of Succor. Here she was plump and Botticellian, garbed in flowing robes and holding an equally rotund, healthy-looking, white Jesus. At another roadside shrine in Moolakkadai, a statue of Mary and child stood in a glass case. From there I often caught an auto-rickshaw for the rest of the ride.

Moolakkadai—"corner store"—is a bustling commercial area with a particularly busy four-corner intersection. Negotiating the bullock carts, trucks, and motorbikes of Moolakkadai could be a tricky business. From the asphalt cross streets there, we turned down side streets into less congested and noisy residential areas. These tree-lined roads carried the feel of a quieter, more rural past, perhaps satisfying a nostalgic longing for home.[17] When the rickshaw driver didn't know the way, I directed us: right at a Kali Amman temple; right at the temple to Vinayagar, the elephant-headed god of auspicious beginnings; past the bust of MGR (locals' nickname for M.G. Ramachandran, the late film star, former Tamil Nadu chief minister, and to some a minor deity);[18] right at the bell tower of Good Shepherd Lutheran Church; left before a small auto mechanic's shop, and straight to the small white bust of Mahatma Gandhi outside a sweets store. Turning right at the display of gooey ladoos, we headed straight toward the shrine, in Eveready Colony. Leafy and green, this residential colony was so named because it was created to house employees of the Eveready Battery Company, the area's major local employer during the 1970s and 1980s. Past a small vegetable market, a Muslim *dargah*, and a Hindu *mandapam* (an open hall used for weddings and other large gatherings), we finally turned left down a nameless and unsigned side street. About three houses down on our left, the large sign, lit neon blue at night, bore the blue-and-white garbed image of Jecintho.

THE FAMILY

A few blocks from the prayer house, down yet more narrow side streets, stood the rental house where Rosalind and her extended family now lived. Charles and Rosalind's' faded yellow, single-story house stood behind an iron gate bearing the sign "Nancy Illam" (Nancy house), evidently the name of a former inhabitant. On the gate of the house beside it hung a red mask with huge eyes and black horns, a *tiruṣṭi bommai*, warding off the evil eye.[19] Outside Charles's house, two motorcycles stood parked beside Fredy's two-wheel blue bicycle with training wheels. Green palms, neem trees, and other tropical foliage hung over the roof and extended front porch. Inside the gate, Vikki, a mangy white lapdog, barked and yipped at the odd visitor. These were all middle-class signs.

"Kristine! *Vāṅkaḷ*! *Vāṅkaḷ*!" Charles always greeted me. Sometimes Rosalind came and pinched my cheek—I was her *taṅkaci*, her little sister. "Where have you been?" she said, as the scolding ensued. "We've been waiting for you!" I sat regularly on the couch in the busy front room, its robin's egg-blue walls soiled from the backs of people sitting against it and covered in children's crayon and pencil scribbles—including "Aswin" (Fredy's middle name), scrawled in pencil at just about his height. A large-screen TV was seemingly always tuned in to cricket, news, or Bollywood films. Fish swam in a tank in one corner; in another, a smorgasbord of Catholic religious statues, plastic flowers, and other devotional kitsch crammed a table and walls. Over the couch hung a large portrait of Charles's wife, Stella Rani, who had died in 2003.

Eleven people lived in this house of four rooms—two bedrooms, a living room/dining room area, a kitchen, and a bath. The prayer house's body of devotees comprised both nuclear and joint families, but Charles's family still lived largely according to the old Tamil ideal, every bread-winning member pooling his or her income for the good of the whole. Each of the family's seven workers handed his or her paycheck over to Charles, recently widowed and the dominant patriarch. The men—Charles's three sons and his brother M. Paul—made about $200 each a month. The women made less or did not work at all. From the pool, the joint family covered its expenses.

Charles's eldest son, Lawrence, was a thirty-three-year-old computer outsourcer with sleek, well-coiffed black hair, newly married, with one son. He held a master's degree in economics and entered data for American doctors as a medical transcriptionist for a Chennai-based company. His wife, Maria Auxilia, taught fourth and fifth standard students at a private secondary school, Velankanni Matriculation.

Charles's middle son, thirty-two-year-old Benjamin, had been in the business of buying and selling shirts until 2004 when, after the election of Manmohan Singh as prime minister, he worked for a local wing of the Congress party. He was married and had one daughter. His thirty-one-year-old brother Robert, bespectacled, with a soft, polite manner, worked as a lecturer in math at Loyola College and at Mar Gregorios College in Chennai, teaching day and night classes.

Rosalind, Charles's eldest child and only daughter, was thirty-four when I met her. She held a bachelor of science degree in chemistry from Stella Maris Women's College, a Roman Catholic college run by the order of the Franciscan Missionaries of Mary and one of the most prestigious women's colleges in South India. Her son, Fredrick Aswin ("Fredy"), was seven when we met—doe-eyed, pudgy-cheeked, mischievous, and lavished with attention.

Rosalind's family remained tight-lipped about the absence of Fredy's father. When I tried to bring the matter up with Charles, he clenched his jaw and looked away. When I asked Rosalind the reasons for their separation, she simply said he was a "bad man" who drank too much. "He had an affair and left" when she was pregnant with Fredy, she said—she didn't like to talk about it. "All that is behind me now; I'm very strong, see?" She pumped her bicep. I eventually found out from Alex and another prayer house member that her ex-husband still lived in Chennai and only very rarely saw Fredy. In any case, Rosalind seemed to have no regrets. "I have my brothers," she joked. "Why would I need a husband?"

Charles's brother's side of the family seemed to take a lower profile in the house. M. Paul, fifty-one, had entered a love marriage with Celina, a Hindu, and worked a low-level job as a lab assistant at Annamalai University. Celina did practically all the cooking and housework for the extended family (and made a mean sambar, a lentil and tamarind stew). Her daughters helped out, particularly the youngest, Julie, twenty-two, whose braid fell past her waist and who did not work outside the home. Her other daughter, Ruby Mary, was twenty-four and like Lawrence worked for an American outsourcing company. Alex, the youngest, was twenty. Thin, angular, and slightly gaunt, he was studying for his bachelor's degree in history at Annamalai University, where his father worked, and where he, too, would seek work when he finished, he said.

Eager and bright-faced as he was, there was something "not quite right" about Alex, I thought. His illness had left him slightly feeble compared to the brawnier men on Charles's side of the family. Given how central Alex's story was to the life of the prayer house, I was curious about why he did not play a more visible role in its rituals—especially since he continued to get possessed on occasion at home. It turns out that Alex's possession practices had "jumped onto" Rosalind, as if through benign contagion. The family believed his possession experiences were real, but they seemed to have relegated him to secondary status in the prayer house. Could part of the reason for this be that he appeared still slightly affected—not quite "whole"—from his earlier illness? Was it because his English was not as good as hers? Perhaps the charismatic, well-educated Rosalind better projected an aura of authenticity and respectability.

These characteristics—authenticity and respectability—were very important to people at the prayer house. Devotees yearned for both in their unmediated contact with divinity, and perhaps a sense of self-worth, honor, and distinction. This full experience depended not only on the successful performance of Mātā, but also on the successful performances of class, gender, and "being modern." The family's particular form of modernity was one that projected not only middle-class success and patrilineal unity but also the image of a strong woman, Rosalind, who had retained her dignity despite her separation from her husband. The prayer house had embraced an attractive, "new" form of Catholicism that included Marian spirit possession, popular Pentecostal practices, familiar tropes of Hinduism, and strong adherences to and dependence on orthodox Roman Catholic tradition. To many, the mélange was emblematic of upward mobility and modernity in India.

WHAT PEOPLE SAID AS WITNESSES

The devotional book, published in 2004, held more than twenty *cāṭcikaḷ*, or eyewitness testimonies. I interviewed the people who had given them, and at least fifty more. Several themes and key words repeated themselves: health (*ārōkkiyam*), peace (*ammaiti/nimmati*), happiness (*santōsham*), love/affection (*aṉbu*), stability (*nilaimai*), faith/belief (*nambikkai/vicuvācam*)—and their opposites: disease (*nōy*), sadness (*cōkam*), anger (*kōbam*), instability (*nilaiyāmai*), and uncertainty (*niccayamillaimai*). Other words exceedingly common in the discourse were "family" (*kuḍambam/kulam*), "body" (*uṭambu/uṭal*), "work" (*vēlai*), and "home" (*ūr* "place of origin," or *vīṭu*, "house").

Other patterns emerged along gender lines. While the majority of both men's and women's stories tended to revolve around illness, the men's narratives tended also to focus on jobs and salaries; employment or business problems; and the need, if the man was young (or in one rare case, divorced), to find a suitable marriage partner. Women's stories tended to revolve around marriage, children, domestic problems, lack of money, and separation from and worries about kin. Both men and women talked about the pain of dislocation, economic hardship, and domestic strain that migrating to Chennai brought with it. One such woman was Lata.

Lata

I sat with Lata and Charles one early evening on the steps of the prayer house. It was April 2004. Hers was the first short testimony in the prayer book. It had drawn me because of its ending: "Annai fully released us from all the evil works that the evil spirit (*acūta āvi*) that had grabbed (*piṭi*) me had done against our family. Since then my body has been completely fine. My family has remained (*nilaittu*) peaceful (*nimmati*) and happy (*santōsham*)."

The language of *āvi* and *piṭi* had grabbed me. It reminded me of Dhanam.

Someone had likely helped Lata write her story, as she was barely literate. Here on the steps, however, she spoke freely. Twenty-nine, small-boned, pretty, and with a husky voice, she elaborated on details that contained many local tropes of spirit possession. The more she elaborated, the darker they got.

Lata was from Nagercoil, India's deep South, and had married her husband Edward in 1996. Seven days after the wedding, the two had boarded a train for Chennai with what few possessions they had in search of work. They settled in Kolathur, a quickly growing district just north of Perambur, and lived with an extended family of twenty-two. Her husband eventually found a job in a Konica Color Lab, a photo-developing shop in Chennai, while Lata remained at home. Together they had two children: a boy and a girl.

Soon after their son was born, Lata had experienced wheezing problems for which she took all kinds of medicine. When her condition failed to improve, she went to one of the best private hospitals in Chennai, Apollo Hospital, where the doctors, fearing that she had a heart problem, sent her for medical tests. The tests came back normal. Still wheezing and feeling unwell, she returned to her natal *ūr* in Nagercoil.

"Suddenly I got very bad stomach pains," she said, her voice coarse as sandpaper. She returned to Chennai and was given "English medicine," but remained sick. "No one could recognize me, I had became so weak and thin."

Lata didn't know then about the prayer house. "But one day my husband's *aṇṇaṉ* (older brother) phoned and said, 'There's this church—you have to go there.'" Lata came here, to the steps of Our Lady of Jecintho Prayer House—but could not go inside.

"I felt that someone would not let me. It was like someone saying, 'You must not go into this church,'" she said. "I had such a terrible headache. 'Go home, go home,' it was saying." She went home but returned the following Wednesday. "I came to this place and sat," she said, gesturing again to the steps. It got to be late, and her family urged her to come home—but she had no desire to do so. "I sat there, thinking, 'Okay, let's see what happens and what that Amma says when she puts her hand on my head.'" She prayed, "'Amma, you know my illness, you know everything. You cure me.' I was worrying a lot. Time passed. Ten o'clock passed. As I was still sitting like that, Amma (Rosalind-as-Jecintho) came and blessed me. She blessed me and immediately I fell. I didn't know anything. When the second round (of blessings) came, I shouted, cried out and made a lot of noise." Again, Rosalind-as-Jecintho put her hands on her. "Straight away my two legs felt as if they were paralyzed. I couldn't walk; I couldn't move my feet." Her family carried her home.

Later that night, while Lata was lying in her room, three men seemed to be standing there, watching and taunting her. I again thought of Dhanam and her five *pēy*.

"'Why did you go to the church? Who took you to the church?' they said, and they took my two legs; they turned and screwed them. They were crushing my throat.[20] I felt as if they were pushing me into a hole. Two of them closed my eyes like this"—she closed her eyelids with her hands—"because if they were open, I would be able to identify them."

Lata rushed to her husband in the next room, and told him. "Then they laughed a lot," she said, referring to the three men. "They laughed and laughed, telling me that I was hiding from them with my husband."

She continued to tell about her next visit.

"It was really rough. Amma gave me twelve candles. She gave me milk. She told me to keep them in my house, gave me a garland (*mālai*) and said, 'I will come to your house at exactly twelve o'clock.' She put the garland around my neck. That day, at twelve o'clock, she came. Everyone saw. There was a strong rose fragrance. I asked Mātā whether I should move to another house. Amma said, 'You should not go from this house. In this house itself, only having washed everything, you can go to another house.' She gave me a prayer"—the Jecintho Prayer—"and said, 'I will come whenever you call me.' Thinking of this, I prayed and lay down. Then she came to me wearing a blue sari like she has in the church. Suddenly, a snake slithered up toward my head to bite me.[21] She saved me by putting her hand like this (in front, palm up) to block it."

Now Mātā wakes Lata up regularly at 4:40 in the morning to pray and leads her to the bathroom to wash her face, Lata said. "She will come to me, having stamped her feet (*avaṅkaḷōṭaiya kālāl mitittu*), saying, 'No one can do anything to you.'" She came to Lata like this for two weeks. The whole family started to pray to Our Lady Jecintho in front of her photo, as Mātā commanded them, and things had become much calmer. "After how many years of suffering!" Lata said. "Only after coming to this church I learned that it was black magic (*ceyviṉai*) and *pēy*. I'd been thinking, 'This is illness; this is disease (*nōy irukkum*),' and so I was taking medicine. No one had discovered this real cause.

Due to Amma I am cured. Now I am all right. I'm still exhausted—I have two children. But my whole family suffered so much due to me."

I was ready to turn off the tape recorder. But just when I thought the story was over, Lata pressed on about her suffering before Mātā's regular visitations. Some of the problems seemed to do with sex.

"For three weeks, I didn't know anything. I was like someone who is unconscious. 'These children, who are they? This husband, who is he? Who is in my house?' I didn't know anything." When she found it difficult to sleep with her husband, or even in the same room with him, sometimes she would lock the door, and he would cry behind it, lamenting why she didn't like him. She took it out on the children. "I hit my children a lot," she said, lowering her voice. "I didn't know what I was doing. So much anger would come to me."

My tape reached the end of side A. I flipped it, and Charles used the silence to offer an English interpretation.

"Possessed," he said. "She was possessed, actually."

At one point, the voices got terrible. "They said that if I hadn't come to this church . . . within 'one week' . . . *tūkku poṭṭu* . . . " She turned to Charles, still speaking in Tamil. "How do they say in English?"

"*Tūkku poṭṭu*," Charles said. "Hang yourself."

"Hang yourself." She continued in Tamil. "'You have to die,' they told me. 'You have to go somewhere, anywhere. You have to leave your children and go.'"

I had been quick to fly to the conclusion that Lata had been suffering from some sort of mental illness, triggered or exacerbated by a number of stressors. Like her, I was first thinking in Western terms of disease. I was also angry: what were the conditions that had led to such suffering, and how could we change them for good? But Lata had come to interpret her suffering differently—through the local idioms of being plucked (*piṭi*) by *pēy*, of black magic and the spirit world. Given no other obvious options, having chased down every other medical option and unable to return to her *ūr*, she had gone to a different sort of shelter: Our Lady Jecintho's house. Her repeated efforts took willpower—and in response, Jecintho had come to Lata's house. I interpreted Jecintho's command to "wash the house" as encouragement to Lata that she "own it," that she take some control, that she put effort (*muyaṟci*) into making it hers and ridding it of all ill feelings and spirits. She was inviting Lata to wash the slate clean. She was also calling her back into the "inner" world of family and domestic work.

There was another parallel with Dhanam's Mātā. This Jecintho was not always gentle. She could be somewhat fierce: stamping her feet, keeping snakes at bay.[22] I was jolted from my thoughts by Lata's conclusion.

"In my *ūr*," she continued, "everyone is so surprised that I am well. They are waiting for me in my *ūr*." Lata was a dislocated woman yearning for home.

SIMILARITY AND DIFFERENCE: WHAT ROSALIND SAID

Lata was not the only one whose actions carried dramatic local indicators of spirit possession. One young woman who refused to enter the prayer house had paced the veranda, grunting and stamping her feet like a beast with hooves. A man dropped to the floor when Jecintho touched him, hissing and coiling like a cobra. She threw salt on him—and he slithered up to the altar, arms behind his back, and lay there for about ten minutes until he regained consciousness.[23]

Such dramatic signs of what we would call possession, as recognizable in the villages outside Nagercoil as in urban Chennai, were not the only indicators of a South Indian healing site. Many people longed for a guru to show them a path to salvation,[24] and they recognized Rosalind's Jecintho as authentic in part because of their familiarity with, and perception of her similarity to, Our Lady of Velankanni, "the white virgin." Known for her miraculous healings, Annai Velankanni offered a prototype.

Once, sitting in the shade under a pipal tree outside the prayer house, Rosalind described the moment of recognition when Benjamin brought home the photo of the rose petals outside Alex's window. She had come rushing home from her tuition center just to see it. "I was holding the picture, and I turned it," she said. "And then I saw completely the picture of Our Lady of Velankanni. Tears were *running* from my eyes. 'See, it's Our Lady of Velankanni!' I was shouting. So everyone could see that."

"Everyone knows Our Lady of Velankanni very well," Rosalind said, lifting her silver-rimmed glasses higher on her nose toward well-coiffed eyebrows. "In Tamil Nadu, everyone is very close to Our Lady of Velankanni. It's Our Lady of Health, isn't it? Everyone goes to Our Lady of Velankanni . . . so many churches are here called Our Lady of Velankanni. So, it's very clear, you know? Our Lady of Velankanni. The image was clear. The whole family was crying, and we were praying. See, it's a very big thing, you know?"

About a month later, on March 25, 2001, before there was any formal prayer house, the family held a prayer meeting upstairs in their home to announce Alex's incident. That day, Rosalind had a vision of her own, markedly different from his. "She was wearing a white dress. But the crown was *very* different. She was holding Jesus in her hand. The crown was *quite* different—I hadn't ever seen such a type of crown. Then there was the blue heart (on her dress). I hadn't ever seen such a thing."

The next day—March 26, to be exact, as Rosalind was very careful to mention dates—Our Lady of Velankanni appeared to her, holding Jesus. "But Jesus was . . .," she faltered. "He didn't have a dress on that day. He was, you could say, three years old—a baby. So, I saw her. Our Lady of Velankanni, I was saying, with the golden dress . . . And from that day onward they started speaking to me. They were telling me many messages. They were showing me many faces. Daily they were appearing to me, in different costumes, wherever they have appeared. The same, but in different costumes they were appearing to me." In other words, Mary was appearing in slightly different garb or gesture, as associated with famous apparition sites around the world.

"On April 8, I saw Our Lady of Lourdes. Daily, I would be seeing her. Daily, they would be speaking to me, and giving me messages."

The type of Mary she saw depended on her audience.

"It depended on the people," she said. "See, I was telling people, 'I saw a lady, and she looked like this'—and I was asking each and every person whether they had ever seen such a type of Our Lady somewhere. Usually, they would say yes, and give me a particular name. But on March 26—for that one, there was no name." That was the first day that Mary had appeared with the blue heart and crown that eventually distinguished Jecintho.

Rosalind kept asking this differently dressed Mātā her name. It took a few weeks for her to reveal it. "She told me on April 11 only," Rosalind said. "'You call me *Jecintho*. And you pray. You have to say that only your prayers are giving you joy and happiness (*santōsham*).' That was the first message given to us . . . when we were doing our family prayer."

Sometime between March and early April 2001, however, something more than prayers and visions had started happening at these family prayer sessions: Alex had started getting possessed.

"Suddenly his body would be shaking," Rosalind said. "He would be going into ecstasy. We had an Our Lady of Lourdes statue [in the room], no? She was speaking through Alex, and she was calling; she used to call me 'Rosalie' only. . . . She was blessing through me."

Mary's attention was now shifting, through Alex's body, from Alex to Rosalind. *His body* was now Rosalind's conduit, her mediatrix to Mātā. This was a double or even triple gender bender: Mary, a woman, was the conduit for Jesus; Alex, a male, was a conduit for Mary, who blessed his female cousin, Rosalind. And on the night of May 11, 2001, a month after revealing her name to her, Jecintho possessed Rosalind.

"I went very close to the statue," Rosalind said. "Nearly fifty people were there on that day. It was midnight, about 12:30."

She was at her aunt's house, near theirs. Mary had indicated that they should bring the Our Lady of Lourdes statue to the aunt's house, so they did. Then, according to Rosalind and other family members who told her about what had happened, Mary occupied that statue, and then Rosalind.

"I lost my conscious[ness]," Rosalind said. "I went very close to her."

Had Rosalind been standing? Did she fall down?

"No," Rosalind said. "Through me she was blessing the people."

Meaning, she just started blessing people like she does at the prayer house?

"Yeah. The same thing, the same thing. She started blessing the people."

Rosalind had shifted from "I" to "she."

This regular occupation continued for nine months—until the night of February 25, 2002, when Mary appeared to Rosalind and gave her rose petals while she was asleep.

"She said, "*Vaittu kōḷ* (keep this)," Rosalind said. "And so I got up from bed. '*Mariyē vāḻka* (Hail Mary!),' I was shouting. I woke Daddy. He was sleeping."

"So," she said, now addressing me directly, "see from where she has come? From the start, first: rose petals. Next to Alex. Then, she came inside to see me, no? So there also, petals were there. And she put the petals in my hand. On that day only, she told us, "Jecintho means 'Queen of Roses.'" She also left a few petals near Alex, Rosalind added.

Alex was still included in the story—his original illness and miraculous narrative and experience were key—but Mātā's focus now was clearly on Rosalind. Petals, among other physical indicators, such as bodily comportment, linked the two.

But there was more to the story. During this visit, Jecintho Mātā told Rosalind to make a picture or a representation of her. Rosalind wasn't entirely sure how.

"I told her [Jecintho], 'I have seen you. But I don't know what was in your right hand that day—when you appeared to me on the first day. I didn't see. What was it?' She [Jecintho] said: 'The Lord's mercy is showered on the [*sic*] mankind.' She said it in English."

The family commissioned a designer to make the image. Just as designers and artisans make images of Ganesh and other Hindu gods and goddesses for mass consumption, thousands of artisans in India also make visual images of Our Lady. The first such artisan the family approached refused. "See, we cannot do this," Rosalind recounted the chief designer saying. "If we make it, then everyone will be worshipping." How could he promulgate a form of Mary that had not yet been verified as authentic? But Rosalind and her family were adamant. "It took them nearly fifty hours," she said. "I was the only person who had seen her (in this form), so I had to tell them how to do it. I told them everything. Then they were saying, 'It's God's work. We don't know how we have done this.' How they had made the crown and all, that is. I was with them when they were making all of it. Then, it came out clearly, and we showed Our Lady, and she said, 'Yes. Everything's perfect.'"

Then things really got rolling. Rev. Fr. Gregory, the rector of St. Joseph College of Engineering, Chennai, consecrated the image during a Mass on March 25, 2002. On May 21, 2002, the Auxiliary Bishop of the Madras-Mylapore Archdiocese, Rev. Dr. Lawrence Pius, approved the Our Lady Jecintho Prayer and issued the letter that the prayer house could circulate to all the area's Catholic churches. And on May 30, 2002, Rev. Fr. Tarcisius Rathnaswamy blessed and crowned the statue, along with Rev. Fr. A. Thomas, the parish priest of Our Lady of Health in Muthamizh Nagar, the parish in which the prayer house was located. Ironically, it was Fr. Thomas who would later contest the prayer house's authenticity.

SOCIAL AND CULTURAL CAPITAL: WHAT THE SISTERS SAID

Rosalind had attended better schools than Alex. At St. Joseph Girls Higher Secondary School in Vepery, the nuns taught her the prayer, "Jesus, Mary and Joseph, I love you. Save souls." The nuns told her that every time she said this prayer, a soul would go to heaven. She believed them.

After higher secondary school, she enrolled at Stella Maris College for Women, a prestigious Roman Catholic autonomous college affiliated to the University of Madras. When the Stella Maris sisters graced the prayer house with their presence, they conferred onto it their own social clout. At Stella Maris, Rosalind learned how to dress and how to speak and became extremely literate in Catholic theology. All this conferred more social and cultural capital[25] on the prayer house, which added to its credibility and attraction.

What Sister Florine Monis Said

Stella Maris College sits elegantly on Cathedral Road, a main thoroughfare in central Chennai. Its mission statement asserts liberal humanitarian values—among them justice, inclusiveness, and the pursuit of learning—and seeks "to form women of character, with sound moral principles." The college seeks to inculcate women with an appreciation of Indian traditions and cultures and to sensitize them to "all forms of oppression relating to class, caste and gender."

Through the gate, past the watchman, the green, leafy campus offers an oasis from the hot, noisy, dirty street. When school was in session in 2004, young women criss-crossed the campus in fancy, flowing *churi dar*s and, in some cases, jeans and short *kurta*s, strappy high-heels and bright pedicures.

Sr. Florine Monis, the light-skinned, fifty-one-year-old director of administration, sat at her desk in the college's main office, near the tennis courts. With her was the college bursar, Sr. Ann Mathew, fifty-four.

"This really is an act of divine intervention," Sr. Florine said of the prayer house. "One really must experience it in order to believe." She paused, smiled, and threw her right pointer finger down on the desk. "See my finger."

It was black at the end, from the top joint to the tip. The tip was cracked and looked as if it could fall off, or as if it had been burnt to a crisp. This was not the stubbing of leprosy, but something else altogether.

It had started with some tingling, and then horrible pain, she said. Specialists at Apollo Hospital diagnosed it as scleroderma, a chronic connective tissue disease. It had developed into a case of digital gangrene.

Sr. Florine said that ever since going to the shrine, she had been filled "with a tremendous sense of gratitude, and healing." "Even though I was in such pain, I never felt like I was uncared for," she said. "After only one visit to the prayer house, I would be smiling and going about, and everybody would be amazed."

The doctors caring for her at Apollo were also treating her successfully. They had controlled the disease so it would not spread. She credited the sudden decrease in pain to Jecintho. "So many of us from the convent have gone [to the shrine] and experienced healing and inner healing."

Sister Ann chimed in, "While in Sr. Florine, healing is most externally visible," others had experienced *internal* healing. She and Sr. Florine were the first two nuns from the college to visit to the shrine—"and then we spread the word." Since then, the nuns had been going by the busload.

What Sister Annamma Philip, FMM, M.Sc., PhD, Said

The college principal, Rev. Sr. Dr. Mother Annamma Philip, had once been an associate professor of chemistry, and Rosalind had been her student. Philip recalled Rosalind as a qualified but unexceptional undergraduate, who had had to travel very far by bus to get to the school, from north Chennai. Years later, in about 2002, Philip—who was now in her sixties—had heard through friends and colleagues that Rosalind was healing people, possessed by Mary. This news, plus that of Rosalind's mother's death, impelled Philip to accompany some of her fellow Franciscan Missionaries of Mary (FMM) sisters to the shrine. It was a festival day. Unlike the other nuns, Philip had been invited into the prayer house as a VIP, along with three priests, a handful of core volunteers, a prominent Hindu magistrate, and a local Muslim leader. Philip was blown away.

"I saw Rosalind getting into that form," Philip said, lowering her voice almost to a whisper. "And after the prayer, after the blessing, after everything, she came back. It looked very . . . you know, quite natural for that kind of a . . ." Philip seemed to lose her words. "I was just saying to myself when she became like that, 'How long has she been that way?' Because people were waiting outside, about four or five thousand people, for the Mass to begin. So I said to myself, 'Oh, she'll go into ecstasy.' That was the second or third time I went there. It was a very moving, heavenly experience." Later, she had asked her fellow nuns how they had felt sitting outside. "They had been waiting patiently half an hour, forty-five minutes," Philip said. "They said the sky was beautiful. Deep blue. A rare blue, which you normally don't see. And a star, they could see—very bright. They said the sky was very special, a different blue." It would have been about six o'clock in the evening. And they (Rosalind et al.) had predicted there would be manifestation in the skies.

"So within the room," Philip said, her voice becoming even breathier as she returned to describing what had happened inside the prayer house, "I felt really that we were *away from*. We were transported to a different plane. While we were in there, she blessed the three priests, individually. She washed their feet; she even kissed their feet. She *kissed* their feet. She dried their feet and she kissed them."

Rosalind-as-Jecintho was enacting the scene in the New Testament (John 13:1–17) when before the Last Supper, Jesus washed his disciples' feet. The act, performed around the world on Maundy Thursday, the Thursday before Easter, is generally understood to be a sign of Jesus's humility, servility, and love—to be modeled by each member of the church. The Vatican also mandates that it be done only by men, for men. While I had seen women's feet washed in Catholic churches in the United States, it was less common in India. Perhaps this is why, when I asked Philip whether Jecintho had washed and kissed her own feet, she looked so surprised. "No, no, no," she answered quickly. "Only the three priests. Because they were the main celebrants. She blessed me, just touched me like that, and gave me the special picture [of Our Lady]."

This strategic act of Rosalind-as-Jecintho was no simple act of humility[26]—it also lent her authority. Bucking Vatican mandates, she honored priests by paying them respect—and excluding the one nun present. "Then she gave them the vestments," Philip said. "And when she put the garment on them—pure white, it was—she gave each one some message: 'You are called to be great.' And finally, when they lit the lamp and gave it to them, she said, 'You are the light of the world.' . . . And at the end," Philip continued, her voice still soft, "she went. There toward the altar, she just gave her prostration, prayed one or two minutes, and her body came back. Like that."

By sequestering the visiting clergy and VIPs in the reserved space of the shrine while becoming possessed, Rosalind-as-Jecintho had created a sacred space of distinction—and a more powerful experience of *darshan* for the devotees outside. When Rosalind and the newly garlanded, fresh-footed priests emerged from the private space of the shrine into the out-of-doors, it was like throwing open the curtains of a temple's inner sanctum—an action which, in both Catholicism (in reference to the liturgy of the Eucharist) and in Brahmanical Hinduism, is generally reserved only for male priests. This sudden exposure of the sacred space, and the *murti* inside (the statue and presence of Our Lady Jecintho), offered the devoted public an opportunity for astonishment, for abrupt and even volatile exposure to the sacred.

"And then they [the priests] said Mass," Philips continued. "In fact, she sat near me for that Mass; she sat a little in front with her son. She was perfectly the same Rosalind, with specs. When she is becoming that [Mātā] she doesn't wear specs. One day somebody asked, 'You don't wear specs?' "

"Mother Mary doesn't wear specs," she recounted Rosalind saying. "But I also noticed: when she came back, she took her specs and put them back on."

Philip seemed to have no doubt that Rosalind was truly occupied by Jecintho. She also seemed confident about another matter raised during the conversation: the ordination of women.

"I feel we should go in favor of such things when there is a need," Philip said. "Maybe in Jesus's time, there was a reason to have only male disciples, but he had close aides who were women, too. In rural areas and places where you don't have priests, it would be nice if women could celebrate the Eucharist."

BEHIND THE SCENES: WHAT RITUAL MASTERY SAID

For all Rosalind's claims of "doing nothing" while Mātā did all the work, Rosalind actually worked hard to cultivate the sort of body that could receive her. Rosalind's quite active role involved submission.[27]

"I pray," she repeatedly said, in Tamil. This prayer practice, which she disciplined herself to follow throughout the day and night, gave her a particular sort of "ritualized body."[28] What enabled this type of body was the discipline itself, with its own Christian and South Indian histories.[29] Rosalind practiced it and personalized it, like a virtuoso pianist or sitar player training muscle memory, aesthetic sensitivity, and the ability to play concertos and ragas. And though she claimed to have no memory of the possession itself, she did have memory of what she needed to do to welcome Mātā. The memory became "embodied," giving tangible, visible form to her discipline.

Meanwhile, Rosalind's prayer schedule and her responsibilities to Mātā allowed her to escape the demands of home and domesticity otherwise demanded of her gender. She conducted her private prayer in the bedroom—the most inner part of the house. The double bed, blue metal bureau, and high shelf of boxes and plastic bags took up most of the space in the room—but the opposite corner housed a makeshift shrine decorated with laminated lithographs of Jesus and Mary and other religious memorabilia.

Her day began at around three o'clock in the morning. "I wake up and pray," she said. "Dawn prayer is a must." It was important to pray at three o'clock, because "Jesus died at that time—three in the afternoon," she said. She sat and prayed in the bedroom, usually leaning against the wall, while Julie and Fredy slept.

She usually woke up with an alarm, though "sometimes somebody will be tapping me," she said. "If I am very tired, I will keep an alarm." She would pray for at least a half hour: the Prayer of Divine Mercy, the Our Lady Jecintho Prayer, and the Rosary. During the Lenten season, she recited the Way of the Cross. Then she would fall back to sleep until seven or eight, before Fredy left for school at nine. Rosalind would then bathe and say more prayers, more again in the afternoon and evening, and finally, after dinner—at least until eleven at night and as late as one o'clock the next morning. The schedules were no different on Wednesdays and Saturdays before the prayer meetings, when she would dress in a sari, powder her face, and re-braid her hair. Otherwise, she said, she really did nothing before the gatherings.

"What's there to prepare?" Rosalind said of the meetings. "She [Jecintho] will do everything, so what is there to do? We are not doing *anything*."

FAMILY PRACTICE: HOW IT CHANGED ROSALIND'S HOME

Rosalind had felt very close to Our Lady since childhood. She credited much of this faith to her own mother, to whom she was very close and who also had great devotion to Mary.

For years, the family said the Rosary together on a nightly basis. But starting in about 1991, Rosalind said, shortly after one of her aunts got married, the family prayer sessions started to unravel. Women had begun to work outside the home, and domestic practices were changing. Instead, "we used to pray individually, and we'd go and do our work."

After Mātā's visits, however, things changed.

"Wherever we were, we'd come at that time," she said. "Exactly at 8:30 [p.m.] we'd be at home. After this [visitation by Mātā], everyone would *r-r-rush* and come. It would be exactly 8:30 and we would start the prayer at 8:30. From that day onward, we were increasing our prayers. We felt really very joyful when we said the prayers. So we know that we are much closer to the Lord. We are much closer to Our Lady. We are able to see her! So what else can be given? Nobody can give this, isn't it?"

But then, Rosalind's grandmother died, on August 8, 2003. Three months later, on November 8, 2003, Rosalind's mother also died.

"It was a *very* [*sic*] tragedy for us," she said. "Very big. Nobody can console us."

After her mother's death, Rosalind started to increase her fasting. Doctors became worried. She spoke of this time almost jokingly—which was her way when talking about herself. "The doctors were *shouting*," she said. "I was fasting and praying. Fasting is part of the thing, isn't it? Jesus fasted for forty days. For the past two or three months, I am eating only curd rice. I'm not taking anything." She smiled. "I am living by the power of God and by my prayer only . . . It is no easy joke to stand from four [in the afternoon] to eleven or twelve. See, normal human bodies can't do that. See, I am weak. You know? I am a low BP [blood pressure] patient."

This fasting added to her air of authenticity. People wondered how she was able to stand for so long, in such heat, on such little sustenance.[30] I asked Rosalind how it felt just before getting possessed.

"I can see her coming," Rosalind said. "Yeah! She will be walking and coming. And after that I won't be knowing anything."

And afterward?

"I won't be feeling any different. I won't be feeling tired. Yeah! See, how long she'll be bending the body."

Rosalind had never heard of anyone else in any other place becoming possessed or occupied by Mātā—until I told her. I told her about Dhanam—that I had once met a woman in Sivagangai District who claimed to be possessed by Mary—and that I had read about Mukkuvar women in the Kanyakumari District getting possessed by Mātā.

"No," she said, shrugging. "We don't know anything about that." She looked at me blankly.

What she seemed to care about was home: Chennai, keeping herself ready as a home for Jecintho, the prayer house, and its community. She was also happy to have news spread about it.

HOME IN THE WORLD

The prayer house's website announces, "Our Lady Jecintho insists us to pray for the whole world! She tells us about what is going to happen in this world, right from the road accidents to the air crashes." The prayer house book *Turning toward the Dawn* highlights the oracular component of Jecintho's appearances.[31] These predictions were a central element of the prayer meetings, and they became increasingly dire, even apocalyptic, after the Asian Tsunami on December 26, 2004. They filled about half the devotional book. Each page of that section had two columns; one listed Rosalind-as-Jecintho's predictions and the date she uttered them, and the other showed the disasters believed to correspond to those pronouncements and their dates. "Pray for Dubai, for London, for Hyderabad," she would say during her messages, people seeming to hang on her every word. "There will be a bomb blast in Iraq—pray for that," and so on. The oracles not only lent a sense of impending disaster to the meetings; they also impressed a sense of urgency on praying for the world outside, as well as the relative safety inside the prayer house.

Rosalind distinguished the difference between scientific prediction and the oracles: "We are not scientists," she said. "They can find out everything like, 'This place will have an earthquake.' But with a plane crash or other accidents like that, only the Lord knows. He wants us to avert everything. So he's asking us to pray, sending his mother."

For devotees already feeling overwhelmed by instability and uncertainty, the call to prayer around danger as an organizing principle simultaneously tapped into, stoked, and offered relief from fears. No wonder Jecintho appeared to be bent. I had assumed, like everyone else, that Jecintho was old. But Rosalind corrected me: she was bent because she was carrying the weight of the world on her shoulders.

WHAT ALEX SAID

Mātā's prophetic habit did not begin with Rosalind. With so much attention placed on her, though, it was easy to forget about Alex—sweet, smiling, slightly scraggly Alex—who himself still got possessed, but only during private family prayer meetings, never in public at the prayer house.

"Some messages, I get," he said as we sat on the tiled floor one evening after a prayer meeting. "Some, Mātā gives to Rosalind. Sometimes I hear only the voice. It comes here." He patted his chest. Sometimes, however, Mātā spoke to him from outside, "just like you are speaking to me now," he said, except that she would appear with rays of light behind her head.

Family members corroborated Alex's story. After his illness, before Rosalind started to get possessed, Mātā spoke through him during the family prayer meetings. As the family became immersed in a rosary, Alex would seem to fall asleep. Then he would launch into directives: "Read that chapter," he reportedly would say in Tamil, or "read this verse." When Alex came out of his trance, he would stretch and yawn like a cat, Robert said.

At first, just as before, the family didn't understand what was going on.

"Hai! What are you doing?" they would ask him. "Why aren't you saying the Rosary?"

"I *was* saying it," he'd say. "I just fell asleep."

"Hey, don't mess with us," they'd say.

"No, really," he'd say.

"Come on," they'd say. "You've just given some messages. Tell us what they were."

"What messages?"

First, the family joked about it. As it began happening repeatedly, however, they started to listen more closely. Then they started reading the Bible passages and looking at an atlas to find the places. After the message, Alex's body would suddenly bend, as if it were deflating. Later, someone in the family might hear something on the news that corroborated his pronouncements. They family decided that Mary was indeed speaking through him.[32]

Like Rosalind-as-Jecintho's later pronouncements, the content of Alex's messages usually had to do with disasters. Sometimes, she would reveal to Alex the place but not the disaster. However, if Mātā told Alex *both* the place and the catastrophe, she would forbid him from revealing both, he said. Why? Such a revelation would cause people to ask too many questions, he said; they might want to know why something hadn't happened exactly like Mātā had predicted, or they might stampede to the place in a rush, either to help or to evacuate. Mātā preferred simply to have people pray to destroy the danger, Alex said.

Didn't withholding this information feel like a tremendous burden?

"That's why I pray," he answered simply. "My heart remains peaceful (*ammaitiyā*)."

Meanwhile, the turning of Mātā's attention to Rosalind caused him no distress or jealousy.

"A lot of happiness came to me," he said. "Because in one place, she has appeared to two people, and has given messages."

Mātā's bifurcation—her appearing to two people in one place—had increased the power of that place, the family believed. Yet the family did not advertise Alex's possession. If anything, they seemed to hide it.

Robert explained that Mātā would be able to do more by working through the bodies of two people. Indeed, Mary was using Rosalind to do things she couldn't do through Alex, Robert said. "You know what I mean," he said.

I did not.

"The thing is," Robert said, "through Rosalind, she (Mātā) is using her (as an) instrument, and through her (Rosalind), she is blessing everyone. The problem is, Mātā cannot use Alex for those things. She can only use *her*. If he touches people, those who oppose us will take it in a different manner and they will exploit it in some different form. But since she is a lady, nobody can raise those sorts of questions. About touching."

"'You should not touch,'" Alex interjected, quoting what Mātā had told him.

Was that why people couldn't touch Rosalind's feet, either? Because she is a woman?

"That's not the only reason," Robert said. "Actually, it's because she is stamping down all the evil. If people touch her feet, they may get hurt."

WHAT GENDERED BODIES SAID IN THE QUEST FOR RESPECTABILITY

This gender-biased rationale for allowing only Rosalind to touch devotees was consistent with local, normative understandings of gender roles.[33] Because Rosalind was married (albeit separated) and had a son, she could be considered less sexually dangerous than an unmarried, post-pubescent single male, whose touching might be misinterpreted as sexual. Alex would not have been able to give the sort of direct touch that Rosalind included in her repertoire (on the afflicted area, including at times on women's breasts and lower abdomens) without committing a transgression.[34]

Moreover, Rosalind, by nature of her gender, was perhaps also more able to exemplify heroic female—and particularly Marian—virtues, such as fortitude (*vīṟam*), self-sacrifice (*tapas*), feeling (*uṇarcci*), love (*aṉbu*), softness (*meṉmai*), and endurance (*poṟumai*). Her possession practice at times *inverted* normative public female behavior, as well as her own daily physicality:[35] Although Mary is iconographically presented as ever young, Rosalind when possessed appeared as a bent, old woman.[36]

What enabled the efficacy of Rosalind's performative action in part, then, was *difference*: from single, abandoned woman to Queen of Roses, from young to old, from straight to bent. This difference was enabled both by the very perception of her "straightness" in real life—of being physically able-bodied and, despite her single-mother status, pious, educated, and conforming to norms of middle- to upper-middle-class femininity. Alex, by nature of his gender and with a body marked by his earlier illness, was less able to perform a convincing possession by Mary—a perfect, holy, whole woman.

Notably, however, the protection both of Rosalind and of the prayer house seemed to require strong, healthy male bodyguards. Mātā would regularly call on Robert to manage the crowd—to police the problem of people wanting to touch *her*. I watched with some discomfort one Saturday as Jecintho, usually calm and soft-spoken, started shouting. A man had tried to touch her feet—a common act of respect, among Tamil Hindus in particular. She called Robert.

"You go and inform!" she ordered. "You go and inform the people not to touch my feet! I am very much struck (taken aback)." The man, apologizing profusely and repeatedly, bowed and backed away deep into the crowd.

Jecintho also scolded people for loitering after they had been prayed over. She did this quietly but notably, turning to Francina in mid-blessing, head-bobbing, informing her to go tell Robert. Robert acted like a bouncer.

"You go! Go! Move!" he would command, even to core community members who would occasionally forget themselves and stand outside the prayer house door, talking.

The job of Jecintho was to try to keep prayer house members safe and ordered amid disorder. The job of the men was to support her.

WHAT MONEY SAID

Support also took the form of money—usually donated by men, who then also had the honors of distinction for their donations. And the money was growing: by the end of my fieldwork, the prayer house had been raised a second story.

On the one hand, Rosalind's family and the prayer house community prided itself on not soliciting money. "What do you notice here that is different from other places?" Charles asked after my first visit. I looked at him blankly. "Do you see a *dum* box?" He was referring to the *hundi*, the container, usually silver, standing at the entrance of most Hindu temples for taking donations, which were used for temple upkeep. The prayer house had none. Nor, unlike most Roman Catholic churches, was there ever a general collection taken in the many years that I frequented the shrine. Repeatedly, devotees and community leaders commented on how wonderful it was that the prayer house did not ask people for money. Solicited or not, people made contributions of all sizes—voluntarily, they said, and without social pressure.

After two years, Charles opened his financial books to me. The community had created a trust—the Our Lady Jecintho Welfare Trust, a certified, tax-exempt institution—which named Rosalind as its president. It had raised several hundred lakhs[37] for the running of a free Medical and Blood Donation Camp, for an essay contest on the subject of eradicating poverty and disease, and for various festivals to Our Lady Jecintho, usually on feast days. In order to raise money for the camp and the essay contest, the welfare trust had distributed a letter, printed on colored letterhead stationery, asking recipients to "donate liberally"—an obvious contradiction to claims that the prayer house did not solicit money.

The festivals were particularly costly. One required fifteen hundred chairs and served six thousand people. Charles named the line-up of VIPs who attended, including chief justice of Gujarat and the principal of Mar Gregorios College (where Robert lectured). The festival included a Mass, a raffle, a *Bharatanatyam* dance, and a dinner. Rosalind had given the welcome address. Mr. Francis George, a businessman, had given an interest-free loan of three lakhs for three months. He and other contributing devotees were building a generous and hospitable home.

HOW TO PRAY THE ROSARY: WHAT ONE LAY LEADER SAID

Despite all this fundraising, it was building a home in one's heart on which the prayer house discourse focused. Not only *what* one prayed but also *how* one prayed would affect one's disposition, one's *maṉacu*—the home made for Mātā. Jecintho devotees believed that the manner in which one prayed could also affect the way that prayer would be divinely received. As devotees cultivated dispositions that would open them up more or less to divinity, these dispositions, likewise, attracted divinity to them.

The Rosary—which Jesuits probably introduced to India in something resembling its current form in the sixteenth century[38]—can be understood as a "technology of the self."[39] At the prayer house, devotees imagined it as a *jeba mālai*—a flower garland of prayers—that helped them cultivate selves that were both Roman Catholic and Tamil. This was a hybrid self, in the words of postcolonial theorist Homi Bhabha, a "partial and double [self] . . . that disturbs the presence of the colonial presence and makes the recognition of its authority problematic."[40] The colonial authority—the hegemonic presence to be disturbed—in this case could be understood as the colonizing Roman Catholic Church, or as a fracturing neo-capitalist society, or simply as evil. On the one side, the authority of the Rosary, or some meaning of it, was maintained—but each time Jecintho devotees repeated the Rosary, they removed its original authority and replaced it with their own. Meanings shifted.

An example of this "performance of difference" in praying the Rosary with the Jecintho stanza could be seen in a message delivered by Rex, one of the core members of the prayer house. A tall, lithe, mustached man in his fifties, Rex gave the following extemporaneous address to the devotees at the prayer house before an evening service as Rosalind listened with seeming approval:

The Rosary (*jeba mālai*) that we read—how it should reach? With so much devotion/love (*bhakti*) this rosary must reach. With so much longing/pining (*ēkkam*), with *bhakti*, with impact (*tākkam*) we must read the Rosary. . . . Velayudha Arulappa has written a book about Mātā and the Rosary. In that, many flowers (*pūkkaḷ*) have gone and reached. Many garlands (*mālai*) are there. Within that, some garlands are made of dry/faded flowers. Some are fresh. Some garlands are beautiful. Some garlands contain glittering pearls.

What Mother (*tāy*) does is, she picks the garlands with happiness (*santōsham*) and gives them to the Father's son. When he takes that garland in his hand he takes it with happiness and hugs it to his chest. All these Rosaries (*jeba mālaikaḷ*) are in your Bibles (*vētankaḷil*). One should not read them carelessly.

Mary also takes the *jeba mālai* and wears it as a garland. Even the dry garlands have gone to heaven (*paralōkam*, "other world"); the fresh garlands and the garlands that glow with pearls have also gone. Whatever kind of garland our prayer is, that is the very kind of garland we have to give to the Lord Jesus. Keeping this as your base, if we say the Rosary, we have to read it with love (*aṉbu*), thinking that God (*āṇṭavar*) has to wear it as a flower garland, a pearl garland that glows. Shall we say an ordinary Rosary? . . . Every Rosary that we read with love (*aṉbu*) will change into a beautiful, glowing pearl. We have seen this with our eyes. We have seen how her (Mātā's) crown has glittered. All this is happy (*santōsham*). Our prayers are glowing in mother's crown.

Here, Rex was repeating the priest or catechist's act of teaching people to pray the Rosary—with a particularly Tamil difference. In Rex's teaching, prayers are not just words; they are physical substances—flowers. These flowers must be fresh with feeling, with living, emotive presence. Tamil *bhakti*, or devotional tradition, lent a specific physicality to the Rosary. Similarly, God's son doesn't just hear these prayers as one would hear words; he takes the flowers with happiness and hugs them to his chest. Likewise physical in her relation to the devotee, Mary wears these prayers of devotion as a garland, literally around her neck in *paralōkam*, Sanskrit for "other world" or "world of the gods." Rex's teaching called for the cultivation of an interior posture that reflected the outer Tamil physical world, in which devotees must have an interest in maintaining an *āṇṭavar* who looks good. He was calling for members to cultivate a particular habitus, or *paḻakkam*. Though he mentioned heaven, it was a place where the "three gods" and Mātā dwelt. Salvation could be experienced here in relation to them.

And from *paralōkam*, as well as here on earth, Jecintho garlanded people back. Rosalind-as-Jecintho literally gave devotees pearly, plastic rosary beads to place around their necks, distinguishing them—but not every devotee got one. Not everyone, apparently, was deemed worthy of such an honor (*mariyātai*). Those whom she did garland, however, received distinction, and those whom she did not had something to work toward. As Mātā gave each garland to *āṇṭavar*, she placed one, too, around the necks of those most devoted to her—just as garlands in the precolonial period were placed around the necks of kings.

WHAT HER SERMONS SAID

Despite the distinction within prayer house ranks that marked certain people as having higher status than others, prayer house members advertised the place as a home that welcomed everyone. The devotional book opens with an introduction, in Tamil: "Like the three oceans where the three persons of God flow together, our loving mother's pure-hearted Jecintho Prayer House is the place where the people of three religions (Christians, Hindus, and Muslims) come for rest and comfort. . . . God the creator, through the wisdom of our Jecintho Annai, releases us from the bondage (*piṭi*) of darkness. . . . She will bear in the pearl of her womb an amount that the universe cannot tolerate. Our mother will tell us in a simple way that which even common people can understand, through giving examples (*uvamaikaḷāka vaitta*, "giving comparisons by simile") of things found in our daily life and in the universe."

During prayer meetings, Francina, who was not only Rosalind's assistant but also her closest friend, would write furiously in a notebook while Rosalind-as-Jecintho gave messages.[41] Notably, the teachings did rely on similes and metaphors—almost like parables. Sometimes the teachings would flow linearly; sometimes they would move associatively and skip between subjects; but Rosalind-as-Jecintho would always sew them up by the end—like pearls strung together—some rougher, some polished. On living a Christian life, for example, she mixed metaphors: If we want to walk in the path of Jesus, we need to bear our crosses. We need to be like tailors who sow a brightly colored shirt with a thread of love (*aṉbu*) and a needle of faith (*vicuvācam*). "You can't be afraid of the point of the needle," Rosalind-as-Jecintho said. "When faith diminishes, our thread of love (*aṉbenkiṟa nūl*) will break, and the Christian life will become dull." Another teaching likened forgiveness to the sap of a rubber tree. Jesus himself was like a rubber tree; when he was wounded, the sap spilled out. "You, too, be like him," she invoked. "You pray for the person who does evil to you—that he will be filled by the Holy Spirit and that the prayer kicks out the evil spirit (*tīmaiyiṉ āvi*)." If you can't pray, she advised, just forget about it. "Forgetting is better than forgiving."

She repeated themes: hubris; the arrogance that leads to daily problems and world disasters; human inability to face change. She stressed surrender, entrusting ourselves to the "hand of the Holy Trinity" as if it were the hand of a mother feeding her child. One night she said that faith and belief were train tracks that kept us from getting derailed into problems as serious as suicide. I looked around. Lata and her family were sitting to my left.

Prayer was about selflessness, "intrinsic/inner love" (*uḷḷārnta aṉbu*), and developing a connection with God. "Prayer should not be 'give this; give that,'" Rosalind-as-Jecintho said. "Rather, it should make our relationship (*uṟavu*) strong with God the Trinity."

It was also about faith. "Prayer without faith is like a house without a roof. . . . God's blessings are like rain. To avoid getting wet in the rain we use an umbrella and a raincoat. If we hold an umbrella of faithlessness and wear a rain coat of disbelief, how can we get wet in the sweet showers of god's blessings (*aruḷ*)? How can we get his gifts of love's *prasādam*?"[42]

Aṉbu, *prasādam*, getting wet (even drowning) in the love of god—these were the distinct words of Hindu devotion. The home that Jecintho was building for devotees was familiar, and the actions performed in it shaped their bodies and hearts for proper happiness in the home of *this* world. People literally took this bliss home with them. Besides giving people substances to spread around their homes, Jecintho Mātā gave women saris that she had worn. The women who wore them likewise experienced her grace (*aruḷ*)—as well as her sartorial style.

Jecintho was literally a model for proper living. The inner disposition of praying for others, which had first begun in Rosalind's and Alex's own family and was cultivated through repeated practice, had become the heart of the discourse of the Jecintho prayer community. The dictum to pray for others and for the world distinguished its members' self-understanding: they were called to cultivate *aṉbu*, a specifically Tamil form of love and affection, transformed from Greek *agape*. This *aṉbu*-cum-*agape* suggested a new form of embodied knowledge, both specifically Christian and distinctly Tamil. Prayer house members repeatedly spoke about the changes in their lives wrought by this inner cultivation of an outward focus.

Robert elaborated on the cultivation of happiness (*santōsham*) that comes from praying the Rosary in this way, "Mary says, 'You offer forty to others; then, ten to yourself. So you don't worry about yourself; you worry about the others. Then I'll take care of you. I'll see [to] your needs.'" Humility was key to this happiness. "Faith should be only within us," Robert said. "We should not show it to other people." He illustrated with his own story:

One day some fellows, they built a church and they invited God for the opening ceremony. But God said, "No, sorry, I am busy. Another fellow has built a church. I want to go there." Then they asked that very fellow, "Where have you built your church? We have not seen it anywhere." That fellow said, "I built a church *here*. In my heart."

Key to this process of construction was effort (*muyaṟci*). "The Lord is not feeding the little birds in their nest," Rosalind-as-Jecintho said repeatedly. "A chick comes out from the eggshell by pecking the shell through its own effort. . . . A woodpecker makes a nest by pecking a hole. . . . So without being lazy, work without expecting benefits (*palaṉ*)."

Surrender, then, was not the only path to God's love, not even with Rosalind. Despite her assertions that she did nothing, that Mātā did everything, Jecintho herself modeled *muyaṟci*, the effort required to *create* a disposition of surrender—to build a home for Mātā in one's body and to build a church in the heart. The prayer house in Kodungaiyur was but one example.

WHAT THE INDIAN GOVERNMENT SAID

I wondered all the more about Dhanam and longed to leave the city. Our Lady Jecintho had been whispering into my ear during blessings, "You do not worry. You will be successful. I will take care of everything. You don't worry about anything at all."

But I was exceedingly worried. I had been there seven months, and still there was no word from the Central Government about my immigration status—no release from city arrest.

I had to get home. One of my sisters was getting married, and I was supposed to officiate. I also needed distance. I had started to feel like more of a participant than an observer at Our Lady Jecintho Prayer House, and this worried me. I already had my white, plastic Jecintho rosary and was expected to wear it. Now, after another night's prayer meeting, Jecintho had instructed Francina to give me some rose-infused oil, jasmine, and roses and tell me how to use them at home. I took the rosary off after leaving, but I followed her instructions, dabbing the oil in all four corners of my front hall, at each door lintel, and in each corner of my bedroom.

The next morning, I gathered my courage and phoned the director of the American Institute for Indian Studies in Delhi, the organization that had first schooled me with summer Tamil courses. I am not sure why I had not thought to call him earlier. He was kind—and connected. In two weeks, the Central Government of India ruled in my favor: I was free to move. "You are owed a huge apology from the government," the director said.

I headed home for a brief hiatus, with a return ticket. I was free to go and come.[43]

CHAPTER 3

Authenticity and Double Trouble

The Case of Nancy-as-Jecintho

When I returned to Chennai, in late September 2004, I took the bus straight to Rosalind's house. She pinched my cheek and scolded me for not being in closer touch while I was gone.

What had I missed? Nothing, she said with a wave of her hand: everything had been going as usual. Julie, her thick black braid hanging even longer past her waist, served me the chicken sambar that Celine, Rosalind's father's younger brother's wife (her *citti*), had spent hours preparing. I mixed the rice and spicy chicken with my right hand, rolling it between my thumb and fingertips. "Do you want curd?" Charles asked attentively, watching my every bite. "Get her some curd!" he called to the kitchen. I accepted the requisite second round.

"Actually, one thing has happened," Charles said. While I'd been gone, a local television station had produced a short series about the Jecintho Prayer House and about another Chennai woman who also claimed to be possessed by Jecintho.

Rosalind was dismissive. "Why would you want to know about such things?" she said with a twist of her hand. Charles also expressed chagrin.

"The poor girl has some psychological problem," he said under his breath. "Some family problem is there."

Problem or no problem, I wanted to see the show—and a few nights later, I eagerly slipped a pirated disc of *Kutram* (loosely translated as "crime") into my laptop.

WHAT VIJAY TV SAID

A deep-toned narrator's voice announced in Tamil that the other young woman claiming to be possessed by Jecintho was S. Nancy Browna[1] (Figure 3.1), an unmarried woman from a "Scheduled Caste"[2] who was twenty-one when she had first visited the Our Lady Jecintho Prayer House. About a month later, the narrator continued, in August 2004, Jecintho Mātā started to "come on"[3] Nancy while she was at home. *Kutram*'s series on Rosalind and Nancy ran for three nights in 2004, on Channel 15, and mimicked American investigative crime reports: a deep-voiced male narrated; opening frames cut quickly between scenes; a speeding bullet shot red through the title *Kutram*, promising to cut through crime in the streets of Tamil Nadu. Now off the air, the show had featured investigations into a variety of so-called holy practices, ranging from a child Hindu *bhabha*-priest to a "computer *cāmiyār*" who claimed to visit all seven worlds, and promised to cast a scientific light on these events. One of these events was Nancy's possession by Jecintho Mātā.

In its explicit comparison of Nancy's occupation to that of Rosalind, the show seemed to suggest that Mātā's possessions of Rosalind were authentic, and that Nancy's were not. Nancy's bodily actions during these occupations, *Kutram* noted, bore an uncanny resemblance to Rosalind's while she was possessed. Her carriage, her gaze, her manner of attending to visitors—all these seemed just like those of Rosalind-as-Jecintho. There was one crucial difference: Nancy claimed to receive stigmata.[4]

Soon after Mātā's first visit, Nancy's eyes, hands, and feet started to bleed, as did a poster of Jesus hanging on the bedroom wall, several witnesses stated in interviews. The TV series made fun of this purported miracle.

CUT TO SCENE: NANCY

Nancy lived with her mother, younger brother, and grandmother on a dense street in Kodambakkam. Nancy's father, Maatavan Shanthakumar, worked abroad in the United States as the manager of a donut shop. Her mother, Leela, was a housewife. On the show, a close-up of Nancy revealed a remarkably thin girl who appeared rather "dull," as Tamils will say of a lackluster face. Eyes downcast, she stood between her father, a strapping forty-seven-year-old with a dark handlebar moustache, and her mother, also in her forties, with a habit of licking her lips. Behind them stood Nancy's younger, taller brother, Antony, in jeans and a Western-style T-shirt, looking bored.

The next scene showed Nancy lying on her back on a cot, eyes closed. The camera zoomed in to her face to show what appeared to be a trail of blood falling from her eyes. On the wall above Nancy's feet hung a large poster of

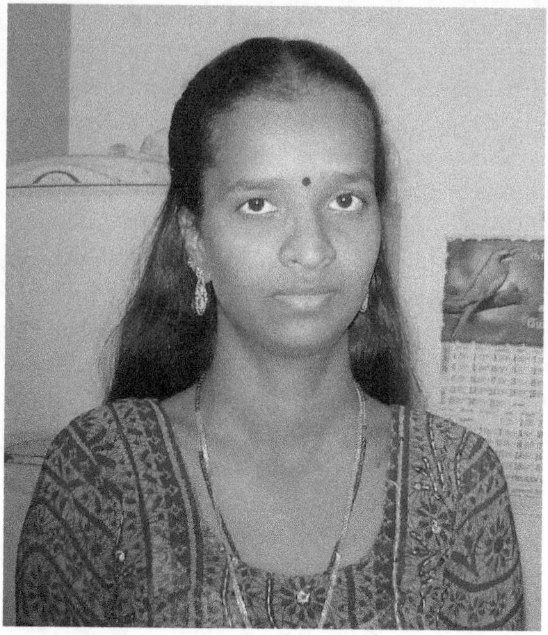

Figure 3.1: Nancy, 2005. Photo by S. Padma Balaji.

Jesus wearing a crown of thorns, from which a dark bloodstain also descended down the dirty wall. Neighborhood witnesses—all women, apparently culled from the outside crowd at night, clad in polyester saris and speaking colloquial Tamil, signs of lower-class standing—told the interviewer that when "*cāmi Mātā*" visits, Nancy makes strange noises and everyone comes running, afraid. This happens every few days, the neighbor said.

But when the camera crew asked Nancy to submit to a test and verify the neighbors' claims by touching something, Nancy refused. The narrator continued, "Noticing little by little that their true colors (*suya-rūpam*, lit. "self-form") were shining through [their deceit wasn't working], Santhakumar and Leela got shaken and agitated."

The documentary then took a crudely "scientific" tack. Returning to the stilled frame of Nancy lying with bloody tears running down her cheek, the narrator said: "Here is a demonstration of what a real blood flow looks like." The camera superimposed a computer-generated, "natural path" that a viscous liquid would take, due to gravity, from the corner of Nancy's eye down her cheek. The two paths, "real" and computer-generated, clearly diverged.

But what happened next, the narrator said, was even more interesting.

"A female deity (*peṇ tēvam*) descends (*iraṅki*) on her and bestows holy blessings (*aruḷ āci*), and during this, she appears like an old woman," he continued. The next scene showed Nancy during one such possession session, outside her house, surrounded by a crowd. Hunched over, blinking, she was led by her mother through the crowd as she strewed rose petals—the spitting image of Rosalind-as-Jecintho.

The scene then shifted to the Kodungaiyur prayer house, where a middle-class male witness described, in measured, educated Tamil, how Rosalind appeared when she became possessed by Mātā. His voice suggested he was a reliable, calm, educated witness, in stark contrast to the excited voices of poor and uneducated women of Nancy's neighborhood. The interview was followed by one with Rosalind. Speaking calmly and dressed in a pressed sari, Rosalind suggested that Nancy was possessed by evil spirits (*tēya shaktikaḷ*), or *pēy*, and was "using our name" (that is, the name "Jecintho") to make money.

"Use whatever name you want to use, and do whatever you want with it," she said, the speed and volume of her words rising. "But instead you've come here. What the heck?! 'Specific'-ally we use this name! A name such as this is given nowhere else!" She raised a finger and shook it. "Having used the name given here, you will spoil it."

If *Kutram* called into question both women's authenticity, it also suggested that, if there was a spectrum of authenticity, Rosalind was more authentic. But why? Rosalind came first, of course, but there also seemed to be other reasons: socioeconomic conditions, status, caste, reputation, local gender norms, and the like. As I ejected the CD and shut my laptop, I considered other possibilities for the portrayal of Rosalind's authenticity versus Nancy's. Was Nancy portrayed as inauthentic because she had introduced the element of stigmata, and had mixed that Christian metaphor with other Hindu, Tamil tropes? Was it because she had introduced an element of impurity into a religious terrain that had retained Brahmanical Hindu notions of blood as polluting? I had to talk to Nancy.

HOW I MET NANCY

My new female field assistant was Padma, a middle-class married Hindu woman with gorgeous brown eyes and two grown sons. She had been recommended to me by researchers at the Madras Institute of Development Studies, my institute of affiliation. Originally trained as an attorney, she had excellent shorthand skills, was fluent in both Tamil and English, and was a sensitive and incisive interviewer.

In mid-October, Padma and I set off to a Kodambakkam auto-rickshaw stand and told the drivers that we were looking for "the girl with the blood" (we pointed dramatically to the palms of our hands). The drivers knew exactly whom we meant, and zoomed off to a small area in Kodambakkam called Trustpuram. The street was so narrow that the auto rickshaw, wide enough for three to sit snugly hip-to-hip, could not easily pass through.

A middle-aged woman in the street pointed us to a staircase that led to a second-floor flat, which indeed looked just like the staircase in the crime show. At the top was a low, cast-iron gate; a long-toothed dog barked and leapt toward us, sending Padma and me nearly toppling back down the stairs. A woman, whom I recognized from the video as Leela, burst through the door, and a thin young woman I recognized as Nancy came out and took the dog's collar. She held it back while Leela opened the gate and hospitably invited us in.

Nancy and her mother took us to the inner bedroom and the cot on which Nancy allegedly had received stigmata and bloody tears. A dark stain still marked the wall from the poster of Jesus that, the video said, had wept blood.

Nancy told me that she regularly received stigmata, though she did not use the Tamil word *maraṇapāṭu*, or the "death-wounds" of Christ. "Blood comes to me," she said in Tamil (*eṉakku irattam varum*), from her palms and her eyes. Her Tamil grammar, like the expression of an emotion that "comes to a person," seemed to disavow agency. Then she told me about Mātā's shocking threat: Jecintho Mātā had spoken directly to her parents while she was possessed. She had told them that Nancy must not wed "because she is made for a life of service." But, Mātā had added, if Nancy did wed, she had to do so before August 9, 2006—otherwise, her hands and feet would split open permanently and she would turn forever into an old woman.

Nancy and her mother agreed to meet us the next afternoon for a longer interview. She recommended that we meet at Nancy's grandmother's house a few doors down—a cooler, more spacious place, better for receiving visitors.

WHAT HER GRANDMOTHER SAID

Nancy's grandmother's house—a relatively bright, pink-walled, marble-floored, single-level structure—boasted five minimally appointed small rooms and a shining white-tiled floor. Nancy and Leela welcomed us in and introduced us to Vadivambal. A thin, frail widow of seventy-two, Nancy's grandmother had shrunken, wrinkled cheeks and protruding, stained teeth.

The front room held a cot, a twenty-inch color TV with a big stuffed teddy bear on top, an old foot-pedaled sewing machine, and a bookshelf displaying mostly Hindu and Christian kitsch. A poster of an open-armed Jesus hung on a wall under a large electric clock. A Suzuki motorcycle stood in the hallway next to a fridge and a gas stove. Behind the kitchen, bathroom, and bedroom was a *puja* room—a prayer room—the size of a large pantry.

The *puja* room offered a visual example of the integration of the religions of Nancy's maternal (Catholic) and paternal (Hindu) grandparents. The top shelf featured Murugan, the patron god of Tamil Nadu and the son of Shiva and Parvati. Lakshmi, Krishna, Radha, Lord Venkateshwara, and elephant-headed Ganesh stood beside and below brass *puja* bells, camphor (*cūdam*) lamps, and a brass pot for water, another important element in Hindu worship. The lower shelves displayed Christian images, including several of Annai Velankanni and two others of Mary—as well as two plastic water bottles in the shape of Annai Velankanni, commonly sold at the Velankanni shrine in Nagapattinam to hold holy water. The lower shelves also displayed icons of saints, the Holy Family, Infant Jesus, and the Sacred Heart. The largest icon of all—a framed black-and-white photograph of Nancy's paternal grandfather, "M. Maatavan, d. May 19, 1999," stood propped on the floor, fully garlanded.[5]

After the house tour, Nancy and I sat cross-legged on the bed in the front hall. Leela produced a chair for Padma and sat on the floor with Vadivambal. I spoke with the old woman first, out of courtesy. We spoke in Tamil.

Unlike her daughter-in-law and granddaughter, Vadivambal was a Hindu. She gave birth to Maatavan Shanthakumar, her first son, on December 16, 1959, five years after her marriage to M. Maatavan, Sr., also a Hindu. When after four years of marriage, she still hadn't produced a son—an inauspicious lapse—she and her husband made a pilgrimage to Velankanni and prayed ardently to Mary;[6] Nancy's father was born a year later. Maatavan Shanthakumar converted to Christianity after his marriage to Leela, who was Roman Catholic. Theirs was a love marriage.[7]

Since her first trip to Velankanni in 1958, Vadivambal's faith in Mātā had grown, but until Nancy started getting possessed by Jecintho, she had never heard of Mātā possessing anyone. "But I have heard of Hindus being possessed by Mariamman," she said, referring to the fierce goddess associated with smallpox. It was time for her family to be making marriage arrangements for Nancy, and Vadivambal worried that anyone who found out about these possessions would either want nothing to do with her or would want an expensive dowry. The family was considering marrying Nancy off to her older maternal uncle (*māmaṉ*) Joseph,[8] a jail superintendent and a fervent Pentecostal Christian. Leela, in particular, favored him.

"What do you think?" I asked Vadivambal. "Is he a good person?"

"These days we cannot predict if a person is good," she said dismissively. "He prays a lot."

She was worried about Nancy, who was losing weight and fainting regularly.

But did Vadivambal believe that Mātā was truly possessing Nancy?

"I cannot believe, but I cannot totally not believe," she said. Whatever the case, the family had better hurry to arrange a marriage for Nancy "before some disaster occurs," she said. "What to do?" She waved a bony hand in the air.

WHAT HER FATHER SAID

Nancy and I had barely started talking when the landline rang. It was her father, calling from the United States. Though he came home only three or four times a year, Maatavan Shanthakumar seemed to keep a tight grip on his family from afar; he called the house three times during the interview, asking to speak to me. In heavily accented English, he explained that he and his wife married as Hindus August 19, 1983, in Velankanni, and they later remarried as Catholics at their local Our Lady of Fatima Church. He converted to Roman Catholicism in 1991. As a small boy, he said, he had prayed to Hindu gods. But his August 29 birthday coincided with the first day of the Marian Velankanni festival in Nagapattinam, and as a young man, he had pulled the chariot carrying the Mātā statue during the festival procession every year.

Maatavan said that he was in the house when blood first started coming from his daughter's hands and eyes.

"I believed," he said. "I believe in Mother Mary, but I worry. Fifty percent, I am worried. But 50 percent, I am happy also."

I asked him what he was worried about.

"I worry that my daughter is at marriage age," he said.

Had there been any marriage offers? I asked.

"No," he said. "She is twenty-one years old. At that, after twenty-one, is marriage." Then he added, "I leave it to Mother Mary whether she's doing well or not well. Mother Mary is either doing good or not-good. If something bad happens to my daughter, my wife and I will (commit) suicide."

I could feel my heart rate accelerate. "That's very serious," I said. "And what does it mean, 'to do something bad?'"

"My daughter is without marriage," he said. "If it is possible for her to live—then me and my wife, we will also live," he said. "But if something happens, we will suicide."[9]

"And how will you feel if no husband comes forward?"

"If no husband comes, then I will also be happy," he said. "If that is Mother Mary's decision, I will be happy. I believe in Mother Mary."

WHAT NANCY SAID

When it seemed polite enough to do so, I excused myself from the call and passed the phone back to Nancy's mother. Wanting to start the interview with Nancy on what I thought would be more abstract and theological ground, I asked Nancy to whom she prayed more: Mātā, Jesus, or God the Father? Her answer revealed her familiarity with Catholic doctrine, as she seemed to navigate deftly between Tamil and English.

"Father, Son and Holy Spirit, all are one," she said. "*Orē kaṭavuḷ* (only one God). Mātā Jecintho said there is only one God—Jesus. 'I am not a God,' she said. 'I am a blessed lady among women.' *Peṇkaḷukkuḷ pēru peṯravaḷ* (She has earned the name 'among women)."

Meeting Jecintho in Kodungaiyur had had a tremendous effect on her, Nancy said. She had gone only twice, and the first time, Rosalind-as-Jecintho had whispered into Nancy's ear. "She told me, 'You have been born for service,'" Nancy said. The second time Nancy went, she took her family, including her father, who at the time was home for the month. Again Jecintho whispered into Nancy's ear. "She said, 'Don't get married. You must do *bhakti*. . . . You must believe in Jecintho Mātā. Married life is not for you.' She poured the water over me, blessed me, and gave me a rose." Then, she continued, "on the twenty-second (August, 2004) Mātā came to me (*eṉaukku vantaṅkaḷ*)." Nancy was at home with her parents. She said she remembered nothing about what had happened. The last thing she remembered was that she and her mother and father had all been watching TV.

WHAT HER MOTHER SAID

At this point Leela took up the story—but in order to do so, she backtracked to the first time she had accompanied Nancy to Our Lady Jecintho Prayer House. She spoke in Tamil. She and Nancy had both gone home with rose petals. However, Leela said, she had done something extremely disrespectful in Tamil culture: she had thrown the roses—*prasādam*—into the dustbin. "The second time we went," Leela continued, "when Rosalind was possessed by Mātā, she gave roses to Nancy and told her, 'Boil the roses in oil. Any sick person to whom this oil is applied will be healed.' We put the petals near the image of Jesus (*cāmi*)."

Maatavan, having just returned from the United States, had accompanied them on that visit. He had been drinking, "as was his way," she said. Then they all came home.

"We were watching the TV news," she said. She and her husband were lying together on a cot. Nancy joined them. "Nancy's father and I were talking in a 'jolly' manner.[10] If the two of us ever sit together as one, Nancy will not be able to bear it. She will come and lie down between us. Her father will play with her. Both she and her father will play-wrestle (*mallukkaṭṭi*).[11] Just then, the eight o'clock news came on. Nancy's father said, 'Put on the news so we can watch it.' I said to Nancy, 'Turn on the TV and we will watch the news.'" The orders cast Nancy out of the cot.

Leela then scolded Nancy in front of Maatavan for not having been more careful with the petals (despite her own disrespectful act of dispensing with the first round), and ordered her to pour the newly made rose oil into a bottle. "She took the bottle, brought it over, and sat opposite the *cāmi* (image of Jesus)," Leela said. Nancy started pouring the oil into the bottle, following her mother's command. Again, Leela scolded her daughter. "Hey! People say, 'Don't just pour sacred oil with blind obedience; then anything can happen!'"

That's when Nancy seemed to fall into trance. "Sitting and praying with a lot of power/strength (*nalla valamaiyāha*)," Leela said, "she spoke all sorts of alien/unknown languages (*anniya pāshai ellām*)"—in other words, she was praying in tongues. "Then she just sat holding the Mātā oil she had put in the bottle," Leela said. "When she became calm, we (my husband and I) also became calm."

After the news program was over, Leela looked at Nancy. "She had gone completely bent over." (Leela demonstrated this in front of me as she sat cross-legged, her torso bent toward the floor, acting just as Rosalind had before getting possessed). "I thought, 'Why has my child gone like this?' Both of us (my husband and I) got off the cot. We called her. But she stayed like that—as if she were sunk (*putaincuṭṭāḷ*). I thought the child was fainting. At that point I didn't know that Mātā had come. I didn't know anything. I shook her; I tried to wake her. I said, 'Nancy! Get up, get up!' . . . Meanwhile, her father lifted her and held her against his chest, saying, 'Nancy-mā, Nancy-mā.' But she didn't gain consciousness. As soon as he lifted her, she started swaying/dancing (*āṭikkiṭṭu*)[12] like that, closing/clenching her hands, closing her eyes. That was the first time Mātā came down (*iraṅkināṅkaḷ*).[13] When I saw her aged appearance, I felt the life go out of me. Because I had seen her (Jecintho) at Kodungaiyur, no?[14] I started beating my chest, saying, 'Nancy-mā! We don't need all this.' "

Then, Leela said, Nancy motioned with her hands that she wanted water. "I brought water from the fridge and gave it to her. I thought she was asking for water to drink, but she refused. Then we gave her water in a glass. She motioned for us to pour it in a bowl. She did not speak. After, she was clenching her hands. 'What, Mā, what do you want?' I asked. 'What, Nancy?' She made some signs. Her eyes were closed. She did not speak. She was totally unable to speak through her mouth. She touched that water and wrote "*uppu*" (salt) on the floor. I ran and brought rock salt (*kaluppu*). She put the salt in the water, prayed, and sprinkled the water through the whole house. She also gave it (the bowl of water) to us. We drank." Then, she said, Nancy wrote these words with water on the floor: She is not your daughter. "Those were the first words. Then (she wrote), 'She is my daughter.' Then she looked at Nancy's father[15] and said, 'Don't drink! Save your life. You have only one heir. That is your son Antony. Your daughter is meant for a saint's life.' "

Then, Leela said, "We brought a close woman friend from next door. As soon as she entered the house, she said, 'I knew it would come like this on Nancy.' She encouraged us, saying, 'There is some power on Nancy.' Her two daughters also came. We prayed with them. Then slowly, slowly, she [Mātā] left, saying, 'I'll come after some days; think, and then tell me.' "

Then, Leela said, Nancy fainted.

About a week or ten days later, Leela said, Mātā again came on Nancy. That's when Mātā issued her threat.

"I am also a mother," Mātā reportedly said. "I lost my child when he was thirty-three. If you want to give your daughter in marriage, you should do so within two years. If not, on August 9, 2006, at three o'clock, her hands and feet will split (*veṭittu*) and become injured (*kāyamākiviṭum*); her skin will shrivel and she will become an old lady. After that she will walk like a hunchback. Her hair will become gray."

WHAT I SAW: SHIFTING POWER

Months after the interview with Vadivambal, Nancy, and Leela, Maatavan returned from the United States. I was sitting quietly in the front hall talking to Nancy and Leela one evening when he came home drunk. Behind his back, Leela motioned with her hand that he had been hitting the bottle, but Maatavan sensed what was going on. He stomped to the kitchen. Minutes later, he called Nancy loudly. She lurched out of her chair so fast that it toppled backward as she ran to attend to him.

In this intense family context, I realized, Jecintho had enabled Nancy to wrest power, at least briefly and at a key moment in her life, from both her parents. She had also removed Nancy somewhat from an intimate triangulation. Nancy's possession episodes did not keep her father from drinking, erase whatever trauma she may have experienced in her life, or save her from being in the middle of her parents' disagreements. But her signals of possession demanded a response, and respect. When Leela asked, "What, Mā? What do you want?" Nancy wrote *uppu* (salt). This demand echoed not only Rosalind-as-Jecintho's practice of putting salt in water, but also a centuries-old Tamil Catholic practice,[16] and a global one.[17] Nancy not only mixed salt with water; she mixed it with an act of literacy. Writing is a sign of power; it gave voice to Nancy's silence.

The content of this floor writing further differentiated Nancy from her parents: "She is not your daughter; she is my daughter." With newfound authority, Jecintho ordered Nancy's father not to drink and to take care of his health, especially as he had only one heir, Antony—a gendered reference to Nancy's lack of the power of inheritance. Mātā furthermore said that Nancy was not for married life, and thus would not give him progeny. Rather, she was "for a saint's life." That meant no sex. Who had the power over Nancy's body now?

The neighbor whom Leela called (a Pentecostal woman) confirmed there was indeed some "power" on Nancy. Repeatedly, in certain contexts, Leela and Nancy used the English word "power," as opposed to the Tamil words "*valamai*," or "*makimai*," which also mean "power," "force," or "strength," or *shakti*, "sacred power" or "feminine sacred energy."[18] Leela and her neighbor's use of the word "power" was perhaps appropriately ambiguous and all-encompassing, in that Nancy's "power" seemed to mix sacred energy (*shakti*) with social authority/power (*valamai*).

When Mātā returned on Nancy the next time, she issued the explicit threat over Nancy's sexual body. But first, she gave Leela some increased social power, manipulating and negotiating emotions and relations between family and community members (or at least between Leela and Nancy), by identifying Leela also with Mary and her suffering. It is often thought that the particular suffering of motherhood gives women *shakti*.[19] Mātā, then, gave not only Nancy but also Leela more power by enabling the drama of Leela's heightened suffering: now she could suffer not only because she might lose her dream of marrying her daughter off, but also because she might lose her daughter to premature old age and loss of sexuality, something akin to death.

As for the odd threat itself—Nancy's turning into an old crone with permanently split hands and feet—what lent *that* force or authenticity?

First, Nancy's bodily actions and manner of speech shared basic, structural attributes with Rosalind's practices while possessed. The two women not only acted alike while possessed; they also acted differently than they did on a daily basis "as Rosalind" or "as Nancy"—differences that included not just their bodily carriage, but also the manner in which they spoke: in more formal, high Tamil than daily speech, and in diminutives rather than in honorifics (in Tamil, *nī*, rather than *nīṅkaḷ*), for example.[20] The widespread South Indian belief in spirit possession, and the readiness to accept Mary as a possessing spirit or goddess, was another crucial factor. This resemblance-with-difference lent potential authority to Nancy-as-Jecintho's actions, at least to certain onlookers, depending on their social position and relation to her.[21]

In the end, it was the relation of the actors to one another and to their audiences, as well as the context of the performance, that gave the performance weight—or not. From the point of view of a middle-class audience, Nancy's social context made her performances ineffectual, compared to those of Rosalind. Like a person saying "I do" in the wrong place and without a proper justice of the peace, Nancy struck some people as the wrong person for the job, or as someone who was in the wrong place at the wrong time, thus making her speech and actions misfire.[22]

For those who were positioned to see Nancy-as-Jecintho as real, however, what lent weight to the threat's performative force—the possibility that it would "work"—was the strong taboo in Tamil society against women remaining unmarried into their mid-twenties. This taboo against "late marriage" has much to do, of course, with social control over a woman's sexuality, her most fertile childbearing years, and the importance of having children in order to confer auspiciousness on the family and, hopefully, produce a male heir. Nancy's age and position in relation to this expectation of marriage lent extra weight to Jecintho's threat to turn Nancy into an old woman.

WHAT "OLD WOMAN" AS TROPE SAID

When I had asked Rosalind why Jecintho was old, she had explained that Jecintho was *not* old; she was bent because she carried the weight of the world on her shoulders. Nancy may or may not have understood this bending the way Rosalind did, but her variation similarly capitalized on the visual of old age. This "old Mary" not only inverted the usual image of Mary but also offered a variant to a preexisting theme in both Tamil Hindu/Shaivite and Christian mythology. Old-women tropes such as Shiva as Mother, Avvaiyar, and Karaikkal Ammaiyar abound in both classical Tamil literature and in modern renditions of it.[23] They also exist in biblical literature in the forms of Elizabeth (mother of Jesus's cousin, John the Baptist, who first speaks the words "Hail Mary"); Anna the prophetess (who appears in Luke 2:36–38); and St. Anne, Mary's mother, who is also widely known throughout Tamil Nadu as a healer and has her own shrine. Rosalind and Nancy were both likely aware of all of these old female characters, as were their devotees.[24]

Also available to Rosalind and Nancy were tropes, meanings, and practices in the Pentecostal and Charismatic Catholic world in Tamil Nadu, including praying in tongues, exorcism, laying on of hands, healing, prophesying, and even—in recent incarnations as well as early and medieval Christian ones—stigmata. Nancy seemed as inspired by such practices as she was confused by the Protestant Pentecostal ones that eschewed outward devotions to Mary and paid more attention to possession by Satan and evil spirits. Nancy told me about such influences as she narrated the story of her early life.

WHAT NANCY SAID: EARLY INFLUENCES

Nancy was born on August 9, 1984, and attended Chennai primary and secondary schools that had various secular and religious leanings, ranging from Hindu to Roman Catholic, and English-medium (classes taught in English) to a Tamil-speaking Government School. Unlike her mother, she graduated from 10th Standard, the American equivalent of sophomore year in high school. At the time of our interview, she was enrolled in a lab technician course and later finished it.

Nancy often thought of her school days, when the lives of priests and nuns had inspired her. "I also thought of doing service to God," she told me. "Full-time service. I knew that if I had a family, apart from doing family work only a little time would be left to do service. So I thought of becoming a sister."

In addition to Roman Catholicism, she was exposed to evangelical Protestantism through a bevy of maternal aunts, uncles, and cousins, and she occasionally attended their Pentecostal church, as well other Church of South India (CSI) Pentecostal services through another wing of her mother's family in a town near Kodaikkanal.

CHARISMATIC CATHOLICISM AND THE BLOODY EUCHARIST

The Charismatic Catholicism to which Nancy was exposed has gone increasingly global, spreading from Spain to South America and the Midwestern United States in the 1960s, and to India in the early 1970s.[25] The beating heart of the movement in India is in Potta, Kerala. There, in 1987, a priest of the Vincentian Congregation named Mathew Naickomparambil had a vision to transform his small Charismatic prayer group into a large healing ministry. It became The Divine Retreat Center, which has "grown into a veritable moral metropole within the movement, even bragging its own train station."[26] Potta's website states that it is the "largest Catholic retreat centre in the world," with more than ten million pilgrims having attended retreats since 1990.[27]

Nancy was exposed to Charismatic Catholicism through priests, religious, and lay people who visited her parish from Potta. Nancy and her mother have visited the center many times, starting from when Nancy was in sixth standard. These visits to what Nancy calls "Chalakudy," where she stayed because of its proximity to Potta, planted in her a strong desire to be a nun. She began having intense experiences of *bhakti*, as she put it, yearning for Jesus from her early teens. Yet at Chalakudy, she also saw women and men "dancing," possessed by Satan and by *pēy*. The experience made her question the status of Mātā's coming onto her. She was battling now, not just with her parents' plans for her marriage and peoples' conflicting notions about the authenticity of her Marian possessions, but also with her own discernment of spirits. This divination process had a long tradition: early Jesuit missionaries to Tamil country drew clear boundaries between their own "true religion" and "pagan practices" such as deity and spirit possession.[28]

"Before Mātā 'came onto me' (*eṉ mēl varutu*) I went (to the Divine Retreat Center)," she said. "Before I went she didn't come. After she came, I thought, 'Is this a *pēy*? Is this Satan?' Because if we go to the Retreat Center, big, big priests (*periya* "fathers") all are there. When they pray, they drive out the spirits so the *pēy* won't come, won't dance (*āṭu*)."

Had Nancy danced?

"No," she said. "Only if it is the devil they will dance," she added. "People in the last row come to the front and dance. I prayed that if it is Satan it should go away from me. When I asked the Father (priest), he said this happens with the blessings/miracles (*ācīrvātatuḷ*) of God and told me not to forward propaganda (*pirapala paḷuttātīṅka*, lit. "don't be famous")."

In both Tamil Hindu and Christian healing and exorcism practices, this "dancing" (*āṭu*) can manifest when a person possessed by a *pēy* faces a priest or *pujari* who wants to exorcise that *pēy*, or when that person enters a sacred space thought to contain the presence of a deity. The divination of the entity possessing a person occurs through opposition of a fiercely healing or benign energy against a harmful or disruptive one: for example, of a god/goddess to a *pēy*, or of the Holy Spirit to Satan.

But there was yet another potentially authenticating sign of Nancy's having been chosen by a god—and one that was associated not just with Chalakudy, but with other Tamil and Christian tropes dating back centuries. One day, about a month before her first visit to the Our Lady Jecintho Prayer House, during a Mass at her own church, the Eucharist (*naṉmai*) turned to blood on her tongue. The Mass was being celebrated by one of the Charismatic priests connected to the Divine Retreat Center, she said. She received the Eucharist on her tongue, returned to her seat, and noticed that the wafer tasted like salt. The woman she was sitting beside told her that her mouth was red. When she touched her hand to her tongue, she saw what looked like blood, and quickly put her hand down. After the Mass, she asked the priest why the Eucharist would have turned to blood in her mouth.

"To that he said, 'It happens to so many people; God loves you so much,'" Nancy recounted. "'Therefore,' he said, 'hold onto God tightly or your life will change in another direction.'"

The priest who (by authority of his office) had consecrated the host and placed it on her tongue suggested that the agency for this bloody change came from God, who "loved her so much" that he had chosen her for the experience. But that same priest also exercised power over Nancy, not only as someone authorized to consecrate the host (as act reserved only for men), but also as someone authorized to interpret what had happened. While he told her that the Eucharist had turned to blood because of God's love for her, he also used it as a threat: she should "hold onto God tightly" or her life would "turn the wrong way." This relegated Nancy to the role of recipient—both of God's power and that of the priest—not an agent of her own life. And yet, as a recipient of such an unusual sign (*kuri*), she was marked as special.

Nancy's bloody Eucharist was not the first of its kind in India or in larger Asia. Three times in 1997 and 1998, a woman named Rani John, from Trissur, Kerala, had manifested what was said to be blood on her tongue after receiving the Eucharist. The first two of these events occurred in her home parish of Kanchikode, Kerala; the third occurred at Potta during a Bible convention. Prior to and following these "miracles," as they were dubbed by priests, religious, and lay witnesses, Rani John also received stigmata—a total of twenty-five times since 1996, according to the website dedicated to her. She also claimed to have witnessed a specific apparition of Mary, Our Lady of Kanchikode, who had given her special messages.[29]

One could say, then, that even Nancy's experience of the bloody Eucharist was an act of mimicry. Yet she could not claim any agency in relation to it, or she would certainly be considered a fake. She *had* to confer all power to the priest—and to God. In so doing, she not only performed authenticity;

she also maintained as ambivalent a relation to power and agency as she did to sex. This stance of ambivalence was perhaps necessary for her to claim any social power as a woman in her position in Tamil society, where modesty and female chastity (*kaṟpu*) must be maintained as proper female virtues.[30]

But what sort of real power, if any, did the experience give her? Under the tight, patriarchal constraints, of these gendered norms of the Church and of her own family, Nancy was left with few options for escape—both from such constraints and from the special calling she had received. It was no wonder her body emitted other signs of unruly blood.

WHAT THE RELIGIOUS BROTHERS ALLEGEDLY SAID

The month before Nancy visited Rosalind's Jecintho shrine in Kodungaiyur, the priest from Chalakudy—to whom Nancy had reported the bloody Eucharist on her tongue—visited her parish in Kodambakkam with two Charismatic lay "brothers." When this "Father" put his hand on a person's head, Nancy said, they would fall backward. Leela, Nancy's mother, herself fell back after he put his hand on her head: "I felt as if some 'power' was pushing me," she said. "Nancy caught me." The two Charismatic religious brothers who had escorted this priest to Chennai prophesied to Nancy and Leela that two miracles would come to the family. They told Nancy that if she waited, eventually lakhs of people would come,[31] and she would get the Holy Spirit and be very "powerful." (Again, Leela used the English word "powerful" in what was otherwise a Tamil lexicon.) They asked Nancy and her mother if they could visit Nancy at home "for counseling."

Leela explained to the brothers that her husband was a "full-time drunkard," that even though he was in the United States, the family was still very poor and had many debts. Someone, she thought, had worked black magic on the family. The brothers told Leela that there was no harm (*ceyviṉai*) or black magic (*āṉiyam*) in the house, that their sorrows would end and that they would prosper. Then they said they wanted to counsel Nancy. "Because I didn't want to leave my daughter alone with two men, I asked my neighbor Linda to be with her," Leela said.

When the neighbor emerged from the house, Leela learned something about what had happened inside. The two men asked Nancy "so many questions," Leela said. "They even asked the women questions about sex. They asked, 'Is your hand dirty? Have you committed some mistake with your hand? Have you loved anyone (*yāraiyāvatu* "love" *paṇṇukirāḷa*; lit., "Have you done love to anyone")? If you have loved like that, then how much?'"

On hearing this, Leela barged in and told them that she didn't want her daughter to become a nun. "She is my only daughter!" she told them. "She should get married; I want to see my daughter get married." But the brothers told Leela that one day thousands of people would come to pray. "This house will change to a big prayer hall," she recounted them saying. "There will be constant praying and singing. Nancy will be very 'powerful.'" They told her that anything Nancy prayed for would happen. "They said there would be miracles and wonders."

WHAT KODUNGAIYUR MĀTĀ SAID

Shortly after the Charismatic brothers' visit, Nancy asked to go to Kodungaiyur, to the Jecintho prayer house, for the first time. Against her mother's wishes but with her father's permission, she went. Then she wanted to go back and bring her parents. (Her father was home on a visit.) The family went with their neighbor Linda. They took two autos all the way to Kodungaiyur: an expensive ride. Nancy's father was very curious, Leela said. He also was not well. It wasn't clear whether he was sick from drinking or something else. "He had high fever," Leela said. "He was shivering and unable to sit inside the church." He lay in the auto while the others went inside.

In the prayer house, in front of the altar, Rosalind started her rocking and shaking. After "Mātā came on Rosalind," as Leela put it, the prayer house volunteers took Nancy aside. When Nancy returned, she told her mother that Jecintho Mātā had asked her to be a volunteer at the prayer house, and that she had accepted. Leela cried.

"I don't know what happened to me. I shook and wept, thinking of my fate. When Mātāmmā came praying on everyone, she came near me. She whispered in my ear, 'I saw your tears. Don't be afraid. I am always with you.'" By then, Leela's husband had come in. With little prompting, he also kneeled in the line. "That Amma put her hand on his head and washed his body, his legs," Leela said. "I will bear your fever," she reportedly told him. "Don't be afraid. I will be with you.'"

THE BLOOD: WHAT HER MOTHER SAID

Leela's narrative then turned to themes of suffering: her own and Nancy's. After Mātā had possessed Nancy, about a month after their visit, Leela saw blood on Nancy's hand and thigh. "I didn't think she was menstruating or anything," Leela said. "I thought she was completely clean (*cuttamāka tāṉē*). "How much we are dropping (blood) all over the house!" I thought. "No one was having their period; I thought that even Dripsy (the dog) was good. Even a dead rat wouldn't leave blood like that. While I was sweeping the house, I wiped the blood with my feet.

"The next day, when Mātā came (on Nancy), she asked me, "Have you seen drops of God's blood?" Leela was horrified. "'*Aiyaiyo*!' I said. I'd wiped it with my feet, thinking it was something else!" On another day, Leela recounted, at about two o'clock in the afternoon, Nancy was sleeping on the cot. Leela tried to wake her up to go to some event, but she would not wake up. Leela assumed this was God's work. She started to address Nancy's limp body.

"I said to her, "O God (*āṇṭavarē*), forgive me! Not knowing that you've come, I've been busy with housework!"

Leela didn't know what to do. She called various people. "But no one consoled me. No one dared to come to my house. They should either have said, 'It is Satan,' or 'It is Mātā,' but they didn't say anything! They just left me." This, too, was a fulfillment of prophecy: Mātā had also told Leela that she would be abandoned and inconsolable. Her anger swung to submission, and then despair. As she sat by Nancy's side, crying, looking up at the poster of Jesus, Nancy—her eyes still closed—limply pointed to the poster. "I looked at the picture; I looked back at her. I did it again. A third time she pointed to God's picture. She was unconscious (Nancy-*āy niṇaiviṉ illai;* lit. "she had no knowledge") while she was pointing. When she pointed again, I saw that picture pouring. The picture of God was dripping blood! I was shocked. I shouted and shouted, saying, 'Nancy! Nancy!' But Nancy was still under the spell (*mayakkumāka iruntāḷ*). I ran out; I ran in. I ran out again asking for Linda. I sent a boy to fetch her. The blood was slowly running down the wall. Linda came running in from the next street. 'Why are you crying?' she asked. 'What has happened to Nancy?' 'Blood is coming from the picture of God!' I said. She saw it and also started shouting."

Shortly following the bleeding Jesus poster incident, Leela was washing clothes outside when she saw two drops of blood on the door, as if a hand had left it. She wiped the drops with a white cloth so she could show it to others and held onto it. When Nancy's father, who was still back from the United States, came home for lunch, Leela told him about the blood. "He couldn't believe it. He was confused. 'Yes,' he said, 'it is fresh blood.' Just then, another drop of blood dripped down the wall from the poster. Then Linda's mother came. Her daughter had told her. I showed her the blood."

Soon, it seemed that everyone from the narrow street was coming. They started to want Nancy to touch things—a chain of rosary beads; a small Mary statue; a white bottle shaped like Velankanni Mātā, holding holy oil—so that they could see the trace of blood, and take it home with them. Suddenly, it seemed like everything the house had started to bleed. Once, Nancy went to morning Mass with a rosary that her father had given her, and came back partway through the service, holding a bloody rosary. Another time, Nancy was telling Leela about a song they had sung at church, when she suddenly said, "Mummy, my eyes are burning." Leela saw tears of blood running from her daughter's eyes.

ON GETTING MARRIED: WHAT NANCY SAID

Nancy sat quietly that afternoon while her mother recounted these stories, as Nancy had no memory of them. She also seemed a little down. Repeatedly during our interviews, Nancy's cell phone would ring and she would step outside to speak to her *māmaṉ* Joseph—her uncle on her mother's side, her potential husband-to-be. Nancy returned from the second call practically skipping.

These back-and-forth swings of mood in relation to Joseph were notable. Nancy seemed ambivalent: on the one hand, she would like to marry him; on the other hand, she said, she liked that Mātā possessed her. "But I get scared when I bleed and faint," she said. "I am becoming very weak." Her mother, meanwhile, had decided that she really wanted Nancy to marry her cousin Joseph. "He's a nice boy," she said, whose only defect was his dark complexion. "But Nancy's father does not like this. He says she doesn't need to get married now. On top of that, he wants Nancy to become a nun."

She licked her lips and put her hand to her head. "I don't know what to do."

WHAT MĀTĀ SAID

Nancy had said that she had no control over when Mātā came, but one day in mid-October, she agreed to call on Mātā. She seemed to want to do it with Padma and me, alone. She asked Leela and Vadivambal to leave the room, then lowered her head and closed her eyes. Her lips began to move as if in prayer. She leaned forward and, as if she was in some pain, squeezed her eyes tight. She spread her right hand on the floor in front of her so that it supported the weight of her body. She opened and shut that right hand, clawing the tile floor; if we had been sitting on grass, she would have been tearing it out in clumps. She lifted her wan face and clenched it. The corners of her mouth turned down; her nose crinkled; she appeared to be in pain. She started rocking back and forth, and did so for several minutes. Eventually, she opened her eyes, blinking as if looking into bright light. She squinted, blinked, and started to speak. The similarity of her facial movements to those of Rosalind-as-Jecintho was uncanny.

I tried at first to jot down what she said, but I felt my fingers stiffen. How do you interview the Mother of God? This dance between intimacy and estrangement in fieldwork was familiar to me, but now, for a moment, I lost my step. In my confusion, I vacillated between writing in English and in Tamil, missing whole phrases:

Jesu kristu . . . however much *tukkam* (sadness) there is, pray to . . . Sahāya Mātā. . . . each Mātā . . . Jecintho Mātā . . . You must pray. You must read the Bible. . . . *tēva* Mātā ('god/Mother'). . . . If you are Hindu . . .

Leela, who had stepped out when Nancy had asked her to, re-entered the room. She stood stock-still, in an attitude of attentive and humble service to Nancy-as-Jecintho, who motioned to Leela to help her stand. Her mother brought a chair; Nancy-as-Jecintho leaned on its arm as her mother helped her to sit. Padma and I remained seated on the floor.

I slid my notebook to Padma, who started writing Nancy-as-Jecintho's rolling Tamil.

"Prayer is decreasing," Padma wrote. "There are so many kinds of sin in the world. You must control them through prayer. I am not God (*kaṭavuḷ*). Jesus only is God (*kaṭavuḷ*). God (*āṇṭavar*) speaks in human form. He came to get rid of sins in the world. Pray. Sins will not leave. You must fight; you must pray. You don't know when Jesus will come. He will come like a thief. He will come very soon. . . . There is no intention here to earn money."

Then Nancy-as-Jecintho looked at me, squintily, and asked if I had any questions.

This was the invitation for a real interview. Padma was writing it for the record. "Do you feel pain when the blood comes?" I asked in Tamil.

"Nancy alone knows if her body hurts," she said. "This is Jecintho. They may say Nancy is acting. But can a regular woman stand for three or four hours?" These were practically the same words Rosalind had used as evidence of Jecintho's abilities. (During the height of her popularity, Nancy-as-Jecintho had apparently also stood and blessed people for hours.) "My heart always worships God (*āṇṭavar*)," she continued. "God's heart is a temple. You have come to do research. If God comes into this world, they won't believe it. I am in three places: Kodungaiyur, Perambalur, and Kodambakkam. I have already announced: an earthquake will come; an accident will come to Kumbakonam." Then she added, "My womb is a pot/vessel (*pāttiram*). God (*kaṭavuḷ*) is like milk. I am bearing God (*kaṭavuḷ*). I am a *pāttiram*."

I had never heard a reference to Mary like that in Christianity before. To me, it was distinctly South Indian, distinctly a reference to a goddess.[32]

"Do you have any more questions?" Nancy-as-Jecintho asked.

"Why did you come on Nancy?" I asked.

"Because Nancy prays so much," she said. "Because Nancy wants to become a *kaṉṉiyāstiri* (a nun, a female virgin/celibate). The blood that I get is not my blood. It is God's (*āṇṭavar*'s) blood. God sheds his blood in order to put an end to sin. If you see my blood, it is because we are committing many sins. We are committing many sins through our hands. We are committing many sins by way of our feet. We are committing many dirty/bad (*keṭṭu*) sins with our tongues. We are speaking many sins. If you worship Mātā, you can come out of this."

Her words echoed those of the Chalakudy brothers, as well as those of the Hebrew Bible and New Testament.[33] I wondered whether Nancy had been sexually abused by anyone—or at least, been made to feel guilty or ashamed about her own sexuality at this vulnerable time in her life. Such shame could certainly have added to her ambivalence about sex and marriage. But I couldn't ask her these questions, not while facing Mātā. I felt in my own body some boundary of propriety. Nancy-as-Mātā asked if I had any more questions. That was enough for the moment, I said.

She nodded. Her blinking slowed and her eyed closed. Her chin slowly dropped to her chest; she seemed to withdraw into herself. Her body relaxed and slumped forward. Then she was Nancy again. She slowly sat up.

"How do you feel?" I asked gently.

"Tired," she said. Then she held up her hands and opened her fingers.

In the center of each palm was a spot of red—what appeared, on closer inspection, to be fresh blood. I had never noticed Nancy prick herself or take hold of anything that might have ruptured her skin—and I had been watching carefully.[34] Nancy was sitting less than arm's distance away. I reached out toward her, gesturing with my eyes whether I might touch her hand. Nancy nodded yes, and held her right hand toward me. I cupped it in mine and lowered my face to peer more closely. I could see no wound; only a small dot of red, which was now seeping slightly, spider-like, into the fine lines and creases of her soft, light-brown palm (Figure 3.2). I looked up again at Nancy's face.

"Can I touch it?" I asked in Tamil. She nodded. Holding her right hand now in my left, I held my right index finger somewhat tentatively above her palm. I dabbed it gently into the small red pool, then put my bloodied finger to my tongue. It tasted slightly salty. Padma looked at me in utter horror.

"Hm-m-m," I said, looking back at Nancy. "Tastes like blood." Nancy and I burst into laughter, perhaps shocked at the intimacy and transgressiveness of the act. I asked what her parish priest said about it. "Does he say it is a gift? Does he ask you to consult a doctor?"

"Father told me not to see a psychiatrist," Nancy said. "They shouldn't take me to a doctor. This is not the work of a *pēy*. This indeed is God's gift. He told me not to spread propaganda (*pirapalappaṭuttattiṅka*) about this." I asked again whether it hurt when she bled. "Yes," Nancy said. "It hurts and my body (*uṭambu*) gets warm. The particular spot where the blood comes hurts a lot, and it gets hot."

"How does your body feel now?" I asked. "Are you in pain? Do you feel tired?"

"I had fever, so I am tired," Nancy said, closing her eyelids momentarily. I asked Nancy to recommend a priest who might be willing to talk to me about her stigmata.

"You can talk to our church father," she said. "But he told me not to talk to anyone who comes and asks about it. Already, Vijay TV misrepresented me. So he told me not to talk to anyone about it after that. I haven't even told him about your visit."

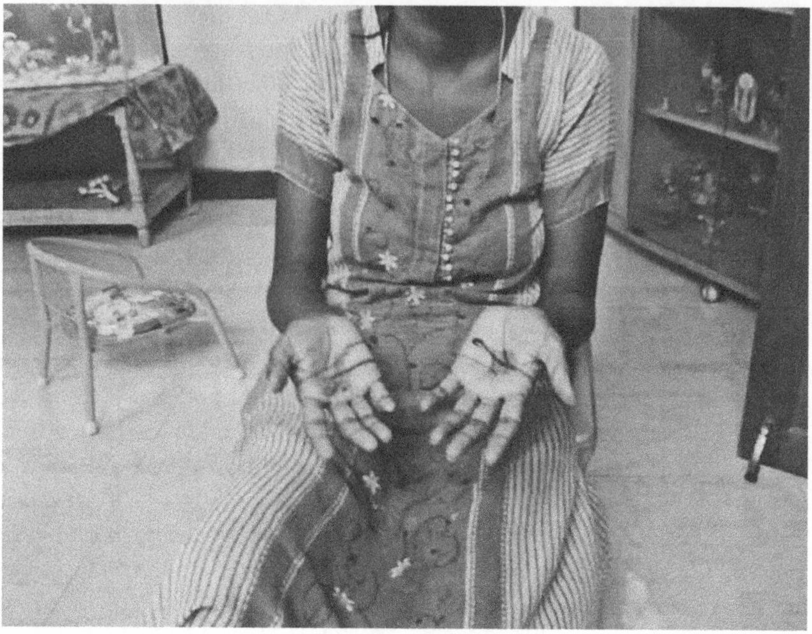

Figure 3.2: Nancy showing stigmata, 2005. Photo by author.

WHAT THE PRIEST SAID

Our Lady of Fatima Church in Kodambakkam originated in a garage. Now it was a church with a spire, surpassed in Chennai only perhaps by Santhome Cathedral. Its congregation comprised about ten thousand members. Padma and I walked past the grotto at the church's entrance, stopping briefly to look at the Our Lady of Fatima statue placed high in a fake rock-cave. The statue of a girl kneeling at her feet represented one of the two shepherd girls—Lucia or Jacintha—who had claimed to have seen the apparitions.

Rev. Fr. Ambrose, the pastor of Our Lady of Fatima Church was a mild-mannered, white-haired man who said that attitudes in the parish about Nancy's claims to Marian possession were split, reflecting a larger schism within the Church over such matters of popular devotion.

"People believe, and they go for the favors," Ambrose said, "but the Church doesn't approve. Church authorities in general teach us not to encourage such beliefs. The genuinity [*sic*] of Our Lady coming into a human person is a question. Even the Holy Spirit is not so easy."

He seemed reluctant to speak about Nancy's case in particular.

"I am close to that family," he said. "She actually started with a . . ." He paused. "She had a personal problem and started from there." He paused again; clergy privilege bound him not to discuss it. "Actually, there are two levels of response to that question. First, there was a personal problem: somebody disturbed her personal life. After those disturbances, she went to Chalakudy," where, he said, "she started to pick up behaviors." In any case, Ambrose suggested that the issue was becoming moot, since the frequency of the episodes was declining.

How many church members would he say believed that Nancy was possessed by Mātā?

"Before, maybe a hundred people," he said. "Now, nobody . . . The people feel some artificiality is there."

And his own opinion?

"Mary is so great, she can't be so cheap as to come onto a human woman," he said.

Many Catholic priests in Tamil Nadu spoke this way to me, but not to their parishioners.[35]

When I told Nancy what Rev. Fr. Ambrose had said to me, she seemed hurt. "Why would he say one thing to you and another to me?" she asked.

WHAT NANCY SAID, DECORATING MY HANDS

Later that day, Nancy held my hands in hers and reddened my palms with *mehendi*, otherwise known as henna—the temporary tattoos women wear on festive occasions, especially weddings.[36] Young women also enjoy decorating each other's hands just for fun. Nancy had made me promise to let her give me *mehendi* a few days earlier and had bought ready-made *mehendi* that came in a paper cone, like a pastry bag. Now, as she cradled my hand in hers and traced intricate leaf and paisley patterns from my wrist to my fingers, I asked her more about her *māmaṉ* Joseph. We spoke mostly in Tamil as my tape recorder rolled.

She told me her uncle (her mother's cousin) had a lot of belief in God. His siblings were all old and unmarried.

"They have sacrificed their lives to God," she said. "They are in the Pentecostal Church and praying a lot. But they will get married, because my uncle says a lot of prayers. It is said that he has a lot of power. So I shared my experience (of Mātā) with him. He gave some Bible songs to me. I did what he said according to the Bible. But I did not go to that church. I have not converted to Pentecostalism."

Why not?

"Because they don't accept Mary," Nancy said. "The Bible does not say one should have no belief in Mary. First is Jesus; then, only God. But for him, Mary sacrificed her life. She became pregnant without getting married. If I become pregnant without getting married I'll be driven out of my home. But Mary bore all the ill speech and sufferings, carried Jesus and gave birth to Jesus.

How much suffering she had! So I am giving her the respect she deserves. But I am not saying she is a god."

Another uncle and an aunt on Nancy's mother's side, meanwhile, are Roman Catholics. Her mother's sister, who is also Roman Catholic, lives in Chennai. That aunt married a Pentecostal man and attends his church. "But when she goes to church, she also worships Mary," Nancy said. Nancy herself had attended at least one Pentecostal church. A neighbor three doors down, a Pentecostal, had urged Nancy to accompany her to church, convinced that it was not Mātā who had possessed her, but a *pēy*. "Then they said that I was 'possessed' by Mary," she said, using the English word, and asked her to return the next week. "Then, I thought, 'They are calling me so that I will convert.' So I stopped going there."

Then, without my prompting, she became defensive. "We have not taken even one *paise* from anyone. If it (the possession) is due to Satan, it will scare us at night, or give us some problem. If it is Satan, we won't be able to read the Bible. But I go to church. I read the Bible. I do everything. I also have belief/ faith (*nambikkai*)."

I asked Nancy whether she thought she had been possessed by Mātā or by something else. She held my hand for a moment, yellow cone in her right hand, suspended. "The Bible does not say Mātāmmā comes," Nancy said. "It says that Jesus comes. No one can see saints, Mary, Jesus, or the Holy Spirit. The Father only sees them. As a thief comes, the Bible says—in that way Jesus comes. So the Bible tells us to be conscious and pray. It does not mention that Mātāmmā comes; I don't think so. It is said that when the world ends, or when God comes, a lot of miracles will happen. Sometimes just like that they come—they come somehow. Jesus said, 'In the last days I'll shower the Holy Spirit on everyone,' but it is not said that Mātāmmā comes."

"But maybe it is Mātāmmā," I said, still holding out the possibility.

"I think it is Mātāmmā," Nancy said. She traced the curved edge of a leaf up my index finger. "But I don't know if it can be confirmed that it is Mātāmmā."

Recently, she had gone with her parents to Velankanni and consulted a woman named Sister Mini. "She called me (from the waiting area) and asked where I was from. I told her that we were from Madras. When we said we had come for the festival, she asked us if we knew any good people for the convent. 'Maybe this is God's invitation,' I thought, and so I told her everything. I told her that these things have been happening since last year. She asked me to tell the head priest. But that father was busy counseling someone." So Nancy asked to go to another counselor. This counselor, whom she called a "psychiatrist," put his hand on her head and prayed, and said, "Mātāmmā allowed you to be born in order to serve her." "This was the first time I had heard anyone say this," Nancy said. Jesus has said that whatever you ask in my name you will get. With his help we can do anything. He has said, 'You will do more miracles even than I did.' I think that maybe it's been like that with me."

She had finished the design. A beautiful green vine now crept up my hand and forearm. I sat with it open in my lap, to dry.

"You have a lot of belief/faith (*nambikkai*) on Mātā," I said.

"If my belief in Mātā increases, I talk, forgetting myself," Nancy said. "I am not saying that I have the grace (*aruḷ*) of Jesus's presence. When I have *bhakti* on Jesus, when I keep his help (*tuṇai*; also "company" or "succor"), when I pray for others through him, saying, 'God, they are like this—they have this problem—you should do something for them'—when I speak like that, he will help them. That is in the Bible."

I thought of the reference to Mātā's body being like a vessel, a *pāttiram* full of milk. Did Nancy think that if she believed in Jesus, he would make a miracle inside her?

"Jesus will not possess us," Nancy said. "But he will be with us. He will not come inside us. But the Holy Spirit (*paricutta āvi*) comes inside us."

Who says that only the Holy Spirit comes inside a person? Does it say so in the Bible?

"No one has said that," Nancy responded. "Only I am telling. . . . The Holy Spirit came inside Mary and Jesus came. God sent the Holy Spirit and Mary became pregnant; only then was Jesus born. Jesus said, 'On the last day, I will pour (*ūṟṟuvēṉ*) the Holy Spirit on everyone. The old and young will see me. The Holy Spirit will come as fire and rain, and I'll pour on everyone.' Jesus has said so. Therefore I have seen the Holy Spirit possessing us. Therefore the Holy Spirit will come. Jesus won't come. God won't come. Mātāmmā won't come. I have read this in the Bible. . . . In the Bible it says, 'When you are not able to talk I'll put my words in your mouth.' Jesus said that but did not say, 'I'll come inside you.' Not in the Bible. But then, I have not read the Bible fully."

Did worry (*kavalai*) come to Nancy about Mātā's coming?

"Fear does not come to me," she said. "But I am affected."

To comfort herself, she would write letters and talk to Jesus—just as if she were speaking to a friend. "I have so much affection (*pācam*) for him. . . . Even in my dream, a man appears in front of me in a white gown. I think it is Jesus. Wearing this pure gown—and he comes to a place that looks like a garden. I have never seen his face. I have seen only his back. Seeing his hair, and a red-color shawl, he looks like an angel. He runs in that garden. It's as if we are playing hide and seek; I'll run to catch him. I cannot catch him—he runs. This dream came to me two or three days continuously." Her longing surpassed everything. "I don't want Mummy, Daddy, food, water, anything. I want to see God while living or after death. I want to see Jesus."

Hours later, as Nancy washed off the brown *mehendi* paste, leaving red flowers the shape small hearts on my hands, I asked directly: "Do you want to get married to your *māmaṉ*?"

She shrugged and laughed lightly. "*Pārppōm*," she said. We'll see.

WHO IS ELIGIBLE?

Who or whether Nancy would marry indeed remained to be seen. So did the answer to another big question: How would the Roman Catholic Church hierarchy react to women possessed by Mary, who threatened the authority of local priests? How did the local church decide who, if anyone, was eligible to practice Marian possession, and who seemed so authentic that they would have to step in? I would have to spend more time in Rosalind's neighborhood to find out.

But one thing was for sure: Nancy had come to dislike the place of her first inspiration, Our Lady Jecintho Prayer House. During one of our last interviews, Nancy complained that it had gone commercial; Rosalind's family, she said, had received lakhs of rupees. Rosalind's criticism of Nancy on TV, furthermore, had really stung.

"She said, 'She's acting,'" Nancy said, quoting Rosalind from the news series.

Leela piped up from her corner, "*She's* the one acting."

The question of who, if anyone, was acting in the theatrical sense of the word had yet to be determined. But the drama that was about to unfold between the Madras-Mylapore Archdiocese and the Jecintho Prayer House was about to make this fight look like child's play.

CHAPTER 4

Possession, Processions, and Authority

At least once a year throughout South India, people pull chariots of gods, goddesses, and saints out of shelters and garages for grand processions. In Kerala, Syrian Christians process Mary down the street to meet her Hindu "sister," Bhagavati, and in Manarkad, Hindus and Christians together honor processions of the "sisters" Mary and Kaṇṇaki.[1] During various Vishnu processions in South India, men swing the god's palanquin side-to-side in slow and graceful movement, signifying that the god is "dancing" and alive. In Madurai, men carry the *utsava murtis*, or "festival images," of the Goddess Meenakshi and her divine consort Shiva Sundareshwara through the streets—proving that she stirs yet in the hearts of her devotees—by reenacting the goddess's conquest of the world, her coronation as queen, and her marriage to Sundareshwara.

In South India, "car festivals," or sacred chariot processions, have long asserted social power and patronage.[2] In the medieval period, they became a way for petty kings to consolidate power in new territories and transform their kingdoms amid rapid commercial change. Kings and warriors could build their political power base through religious affiliations and ritual festivals—often Syrian Christian or Muslim.[3]

Jesuits, seeking to convert as many South Indians as possible, co-opted the wildly popular, nine-night, Hindu practice of *Navarāttiri* goddess festivals to win souls to Christianity. In the sixteenth century, they brought a statue of Mary as Our Lady of Snows from Manila to Tuticorin, on the coast, and installed it in an impressive new church that became known as *Mātākōvil*, the "mother temple." This place of a Catholic Mother Queen was a concept Paravas, people of a coastal fishing and pearl-diving caste, could relate to, familiar as they were with Hindu goddess temples. The *Navarāttiri* rites often contained a graphic ceremony of rebirth, the *Hiranyagarbha*, "golden womb," in which the patron of the rite (usually a ruler) was "reborn" from the womb of a life-size golden or gilded bronze cow.[4] The Jesuits asserted their authority over Parava converts with a ten-day procession, using Our Lady instead of a Hindu goddess. By the middle of the seventeenth century, the church of Our Lady of Snows in Tuticorin had become "a treasure trove of gold leaf and jewels"[5]—a Catholic golden cow.

In 1720, Parava leaders of Tuticorin arranged for the construction of a great ceremonial chariot known as the *poṇ tēr*, the Golden Car of Our Lady of Snows, and instigated a procession.[6] As with the Hindu chariot processions, the Tuticorin Golden Car festival began with a flag hoisting led by the Parava caste headman, and, as with the Hindus, the Catholic Paravas distributed *prasādam*, tossing consecrated flower and rose petals from the garlands adorning the Virgin and her chariot.[7] This and the Hindu processions became models for two of the most important Marian processions in South India each year: the nine-night celebration leading up to Mary's birthday, believed to be September 8, and the nine-night celebration in May, the "Month of Mātā's Devotion" (*Mātāvin Vaṇakka Mātam*). In May of 2005, this nine-night devotion became a flashpoint between Our Lady Jecintho Prayer House and Roman Catholic Church officials. In some ways, it was not unlike the caste clash around the Kandadevi and Aiyanar festivals near Dhanam's village. Like that conflict over ritual rights, this one too was about social power. Luckily, however, it did not result in violence.

CAR FESTIVALS IN KODUNGAIYUR

As in many Christian communities throughout India, the Marian May festival galvanized Kodungaiyur. It drew people from across religious lines for significant pre-festival preparation, as well as for the main day's pageantry. At Our Lady Jecintho Prayer House, planning the ten-day, nine-night event required tremendous effort, involving a theme for each day, a Mass and sermon on the theme each evening, and a grand procession on the last night.

As usual, members of Our Lady Jecintho Prayer House had invited priests from outside the parish to celebrate Mass each night. In addition to the consent of these priests, which they had no problem getting, the festival required patronage—an opportunity for monied members to display their loyalty and economic status. The final procession served as an act of generosity as well as a form of advertising: as the grand chariots moved down the streets, Hindus, Christians, and Muslims would come to their front doors and out on their balconies to watch, throw petals and confetti, or offer candlelit shrines in front of their homes to bless and be blessed by Mātā.

What not everyone knew was that all this hard work—the making of decorations, preparing the car procession, designing the floats, dressing Mary's statue—had been divinely ordered by Jecintho herself,[8] through the possessed body of Rosalind.

WHAT BORDERS SAID—OR DIDN'T SAY

In the prayer house's early days, the Madras-Mylapore archbishop had actually blessed the special Jecintho prayer—the one interjected before the third decade of the rosary[9]—with a formal letter of support, complete with insignia. In 2004, however, the local parish priest who had jurisdiction over the prayer house complained to an interim bishop, who, after a meeting with the Diocesan Senate, banned holding a Mass during festival days, albeit with little result. In 2005, the local priest complained again, this time to a newly seated archbishop, who released a letter ordering all diocesan priests to ban all Catholics from attending. Parish priests from around the Archdiocese stood at their pulpits and told their flocks to stay away from Our Lady Jecintho Prayer House.

Rather than being a deterrent, however, the ban attracted more visitors than ever.

The priest who had complained presided over yet another Annai Velankanni Church, located just a few kilometers away from the Jecintho shrine. The church was part of a new parish, Muthamizh Nagar, which the Archdiocese had bifurcated from the growing Madhavaram parish in 2001. After the bifurcation, the prayer house fell in the new parish, under the jurisdiction of Rev. Fr. A. Thomas. It was a poor parish:[10] most of the nine hundred parishioners lived in apartments built by the Housing Board, and Fr. Thomas held Masses only in Tamil.[11]

The oral history of the church's origins, however, revealed a communal and ecumenical sensibility common in South India. An energetic group of people had erected a shrine that was eventually absorbed into the hierarchical, orthodox religious structure—in this case—of a Christian church.[12] A decade before it became the center of its own parish, the Annai Velankanni Church had sprung up as a substation to the Madhavaram church, three kilometers away, when a group of five or six men simply built a hut in Mātā's name.[13] The local parish of St. Sebastian wouldn't support them, so the men purchased the land—about one hundred acres—from the Housing Board. In about 1991, they built a chapel, *Punita Ārōkkiya Aṉṉai* (Holy Lady of Good Health), and placed a statue of Our Lady outside the chapel under a thatched hut.[14] On the other side of the land, they erected a small Hindu temple. After they had raised 10 percent of the money to build the church, an archbishop offered the rest. Hindus, Christians, Muslims—the whole neighborhood—contributed sand, cement, seats, and even a bell tower.[15] Both Jecintho Prayer House and Annai Velankanni Church were the result of grass-roots efforts, yet the two communities were destined for conflict.

WHAT REV. FR. A. THOMAS SAID

A short man, in his early forties, with slightly graying hair and an angular profile, the Rev. Fr. A. Thomas was a convert from Hinduism to Catholicism. I had met him in 2004, when he had arrived at Our Lady Jecintho Prayer House to give annual house blessings. He'd invited me to come along on his rounds, where at each home he'd sprinkled holy water in every room and blessed each family member. In their eyes, he was warding off evil spirits or inviting blessings; whereas I saw his blessings as a sort of territorial marking, an establishment of authority. Now, in 2005, having discovered his opposition to the Jecintho Prayer House, I paid him a visit.

I found Fr. Thomas in his office in the bleak concrete rectory, wearing a white cassock and sitting placidly behind his desk, hands clasped, awaiting our appointment. He told me that maybe 5 percent of his parish membership attended the Jecintho prayer services regularly, but that he had been there only for two quick visits.

"I don't know what is happening there, really," he said, "other than what people report." It was the Mass that the prayer house established during Marian festival time that irked him. Its members had approached him in 2004 to ask permission to hold it, and he had refused. "When there is Mass in the (parish) church, you are not allowed to have any other Mass. . . . That was my stand." He had eventually relented on the Mass, he said, and shifted his opposition to their car procession.

"They were not listening," he said. "They had a *grand* car procession."[16] In addition, it had become clear to Fr. Thomas that the Jecintho community was offering Mass *daily* during the May festival. That's when he complained.

"They could pray, recite the rosary, and have any kind of prayer. But they weren't allowed to say Mass." Fr. Thomas told this to the Jecintho members, as well as his to own Annai Velankanni congregation, but the Jecintho devotees—even many from his own parish—had ignored him. Fr. Thomas's parish council had then gone directly to the Auxiliary Bishop, Rev. Fr. Lawrence Pius, to report the bucking of orders.

"The [Auxiliary] Bishop said he would take that issue up when the new archbishop arrived," Thomas said. The new archbishop, the Most Rev. Dr. A. M. Chinnappa, had decidedly banned the procession and Mass at Jecintho Prayer House.

"I sent my council members to convey the message [from the letter] to the . . . Prayer House," Fr. Thomas said. "But they were not ready to listen. They were not ready to stop."[17]

Furthermore, when Fr. Thomas heard that a Catholic Charismatic priest from Pondicherry—an outside diocese—was going to say Mass for the Jecintho devotees during the May festival despite the bishop's ban, he called the priest, as well as the priest's diocesan bishop in Pondicherry. The priest, who was also to hoist the flag on the festival's first day, argued that it was too late to cancel the Mass or his own participation. Fr. Thomas cited canon law and reported the priest to the Bishop's Commission. The priest was later relocated.

What was the canon law the priest had violated? Fr. Thomas looked worried and unsure. I told him he could give it to me later. But why had he not gone to any of the Jecintho prayer meetings, at least to observe?

Thomas shook his head and brushed something invisible off his desk. "I am not interested at all," he said. "I kept hearing that she [Rosalind] is telling something, or foretelling something, and that Mother Mary comes to her, and she becomes like an old lady. . . . I personally don't believe that Mother Mary can come in such a way, and take possession of a lady like this."

He held up his right pointer finger. "The first thing Mary gives is a message to the bishop, or a priest," he said, and listed the signs that Mary had given to the authorities at Marian shrines throughout the world: Lourdes, Guadalupe, Fatima, Velankanni. "I tell my people—we should not go after these miracles. Even the mere breath you get in the morning, after you sleep, that is the greatest miracle you can have in life. . . . You are able to see; you are able to breathe; you are able to enter the blessing of God. . . . So why seek another miracle?"

He grasped the sides of his desk. "The presence of Mary is *on this campus*. . . . This is a church, and Mother is present here. I strongly believe that we have her presence and guidance here. I too pray to her, even to make it clear to me what is happening there." He sat back. "It is my responsibility to tell people. For two years, I have been turning to Our Lady to guide me. Even just now, before you came, I was praying. And I think these steps [taken by the bishop] are one of the signs that I have received from Mary [about] whether it is true or false."

He held up his finger again. "Another thing. My strongest conviction is that Mother Mary will not go into the church against the priest or against the Bishop. . . . The mere fact that they are ready to disobey, they are ready to go against the church, in spite of instruction—it is not Mary's work.

"God will make use of any fool or any small thing to see that His will be done," Thomas added. "I may even see that it is demolished."

I thought I might have misheard him. Demolished? Did he mean the prayer house?

"I may see it demolished," Thomas repeated enigmatically.

BACK AT THE PRAYER HOUSE: WHAT THEY SAID

"We never got any letter," Rosalind said when I returned from my interview Fr. Thomas.

It was May 27, 2005, and the festival was well underway. Rosalind, Charles, and the entire Our Lady of Jecintho core crew had stopped their decorating for the seventh night's celebration and had gathered around to hear what Fr. Thomas had said.

"He may have announced in his church," Rosalind said of the ban on the Mass and procession, "but he didn't inform us of anything."

She had, indeed, gone to see the Auxiliary Bishop, Rev. Fr. Lawrence Pius, as Fr. Thomas had alleged, to request a donation. The prayer house wanted to sponsor an essay contest at Stella Maris College on the subject of poverty and disease. The Auxiliary Bishop had denied the donation and added that the prayer house must cease giving Mass.

Then came bomb threats, anonymous phone calls, and harassing visits. A group of Muthamizh Nagar parish council members had appeared and angrily threatened that if the prayer house held a car festival, it would be "destroyed" (language that echoed Fr. Thomas's).

But the show went on. The Rev. Fr. Pittchaimuutthu had indeed come from Pondicherry and hoisted the flag. The community had hosted at least one novena a night, drawing hundreds of people each time. Priests continued to come from outside the parish, as invited, to preside over each of the nine evening prayer meetings, and to give messages pertaining to Marian themes. When they arrived, however, Charles begged them not to say Mass, dutifully explaining the Archbishop's order. "Please don't say Mass," I heard him tell a young priest who had arrived quite happy to do so. "We don't want to get in trouble, and we don't want you to get in trouble."

The priest had seemed disappointed. An articulate man in his thirties, he had said he wanted to say the Mass because his own mother was an ardent devotee to Mary. To him, it was completely possible that Mary was possessing women in Tamil Nadu. Time would tell, he said, whether what was happening with Rosalind was ordained by God. Meanwhile, what mattered was that the healing practices were bringing people relief and strengthening their devotion to Mary.

Because the prepared sermons such as that delivered by this young priest had not been accompanied by a Eucharistic liturgy, they were, in Vatican-speak, simply "messages." (Notably, women, who cannot be priests, may give "messages" at the pulpit, but not "sermons.") The demotion in rhetorical status from "sermon" to "message" by removal of the Eucharist meant that the priests were able to follow the orders of their archbishop, but did not seem to weaken the priests' zeal.

WHAT SHE (JECINTHO) SAID

As the festival at Our Lady Jecintho Prayer House moved toward its zenith, the question of whether they would hold a final procession, let alone a Mass, hung over the group like a cloud. Yet opposition had also increased feelings of unity and purpose. As people organized flowers, strung garlands, and painted murals, the prayer house seemed enlivened by a sense of injustice.

On Day 8, after the young priest's "message" and the beginning of the group novena, the crowd chanted the rosary's third decade particularly loudly, and seven devotees, instead of the usual one,[18] prepared to take notes of Jecintho's message.

Rosalind started rocking. Mātā occupied her. Someone shut off the ceiling fans. Fr. Pitchaimuuthu, dressed in his saffron robes, sat motionless, facing Rosalind, on a chair in front of the altar of roses. Rosalind-as-Jecintho now placed rose petals on his head: he stooped to collect those that fell to his sides. Rosalind-as-Jecintho broke into tongues as the smell of roses permeated the room.

"*Illiha, niha niha nishallah, naha . . .*"

She switched between Tamil and English, speaking about the Trinity and about Mātā's showering people with love. "Many people are walking in the rain, but it is not showering on them because they are not feeling it. . . . You have to feel. . . . Unless you feel, my children, you will not realize."

Shifting gears, she then spoke about a human man, a *maṉitaṉ*. "He thinks he can do anything. But he cannot stop the tremor. He cannot stop the earthquake. Only God can do that. Only your prayers can do that."

She asked us to pray for specific people and places. She asked us all sincerely to pray for Fr. Pitchaimuutthu, that he be able follow his mission successfully. She turned and started praying over people, laying hands on them. Then, just when I thought the prayer meeting was over, she turned toward the crowd and announced that they would indeed hold a grand procession.

"I want everyone to take part," Rosalind-as-Jecintho said, glasses off, head shaking. "Each person is an actor . . . . I want you to celebrate with your family. You should not be sad. You should be happy, okay? . . . Pray. Anything can be changed through prayer."

Still possessed, Rosalind-as-Jecintho marched down the aisle toward the door. A few people followed her to the veranda and gathered around the flagpole. Narendiran, a member of the prayer house's core group, came outside and started reading loudly from his black Bible. "Do nothing from selfishness or conceit, but in humility count others better than yourselves," he read, continuing with the rest of Philippians 2. Meanwhile, inside, people prayed the Rosary: a young woman led the decades. The crowd sang one of the many devotional songs that Rosalind had written, inspired directly by Mātā, "*Kaṉṉi*

Mātā koṭutta varam" (The boon given by the young maiden Mātā).[19] Meanwhile, Narendiran was re-reading the same verse from the Bible, louder now so that he could be heard over the singing. Rosalind-as-Jecintho continued to touch and pray over people. Rosalind-as-Jecintho turned toward those of us who had gathered outside and spoke.

"Avoid distance from the Lord," she said in what seemed like a reference to the call, in Philippians, not to be frightened by opponents. "Everyone are [*sic*] called, but only a few are chosen."

Alex, held a bag of milk. The community was about to perform *abhishekam*, a ritual bath usually associated with consecrating Hindu gods, on the Mary statue. Rosalind-as-Jecintho continued to speak obliquely about the controversy with the diocese.

"You know very well," she continued. "Everyone who is speaking against you will read your writing."

"What can we do?" some in the crowd called out.

"Nothing is done by ourselves," Rosalind-as-Jecintho said in English. "The Lord is doing everything." Then she lapsed back into Tamil—"It is all though God's grace (*aruḷ*)"—and then into glossolalia, the sounds of Sanskrit, Arabic, and Tamil rolling together. "You don't worry when people are talking about you," she said in Tamil. Then, in English: "I am doing this only to glorify the Holy Trinity," aligning herself with the authorized male-gendered trinity and fourth-century Vatican doctrine.

Then she started giving orders about the celebration's tenth day: when the priests arrived, devotees should meet them on the street corner. "You bring the fathers," she said. "You ask them to stand there. We'll be having six ladies [greeting them]." She chose six women from the crowd. "That song also . . ." She turned to her attendant and best friend, Francina: "You'll be knowing that?" Francina nodded yes.

"I want a small one, a *kuḻuntai* (child)," Rosalind-as-Jecintho said, holding her hand waist high. A little girl of perhaps eight was pushed up to the front. "You can garland the father," Rosalind-as-Jecintho told her.

"Okay?" she said finally. "So there is no confusion? And you bless the flag."

Francina interjected, "Which day?"

Rosalind-as-Jecintho sighed with seeming impatience. "I'm talking about the *last day*," she said in the tone a middle-school teacher might use with a classroom of dull students. She returned to the subject of the priests. "So you'll be giving them garlands, and you'll be honoring them. You get the point, no? . . . So everyone will get their chances. I want everyone to dress up neatly. I want everyone to wear a tie."

"Everyone?" someone shouted out.

"*Everyone*," she said. "But not like that tie." She pointed to a man with bright, wide, diagonally striped necktie. People started giggling.

"Color?" someone shouted.

"It's up to you," she said. "You can wear any color. Except for the last day, that will be special. Last day, I want you to wear any color blue. You must dress well—*nalla* dress *paṇṇaiyiruvaṅko*," she said, using the Brahmanical formal second-person. She was speaking from the high ground here. Ladies, she continued, should wear bright-colored saris. "After that: The *tēr* (car/chariot). It is to be a very special *tēr*."

Yes, yes, several people said, their hands clasped like children, gazing up at her with wonder-filled eyes. An eleven-year-old boy, a small boy, would process toward the front, she said. "I want Alex to hold one side," she said, apparently speaking of the *tēr*. "Where is Alex?" Alex surfaced from the crowd. She whispered to him, and he nodded.

"How far should the procession go?" a man asked in Tamil.

She named a street. She reminded people to send invitations to "all the fathers" and "all the sisters" in the diocese, and to advertise the event in "all the papers. . . . You make it so that it reaches everyone." Then she ended with a sudden, dramatic reprimand: "I am very much offended by your words and your doings." The nature of the offense was not clear to me. She started to turn toward the prayer house, then turned back and added, "At the proper time, I want you all to pour milk, and all of you to wash your hands."

Lawrence approached her, unfolded the fabric he had been holding, and held it up: a blue-clad figure of Jecintho and child, hand-painted on white silky cloth, an exact replica of the other iconographic portrayals in the prayer house. Rosalind-as-Jecintho nodded in approval and prayed over the fabric in glossolalia. Everyone made the sign of the cross. She said, "You don't need to put it in the *garbha* (womb).[20] You just pour the milk, and I'll come."

Lawrence folded the cloth back up. A woman commented that it was wrinkled. He re-folded it. Everyone padded barefoot past the Jecintho statue, washing their hands in the green bowl filled with cool water. Then they turned to Alex, dipped their fingers in his tumbler of milk, and sprinkled the statue. Once we had all had had our turn, a few men from the core group rubbed and washed the statue with the remaining milk, performing the final rite of *abhishekam*[21] on Mātā.

WHAT *KUṬṬI* (LITTLE) CHURCHES SAID

As Annai Velankanni Church in Mutamizh Nagar and Our Lady Jecintho Prayer House were gearing up to celebrate their processions, so were other small neighborhoods in the area. Streets and neighborhoods all over the city typically raised money to host Mātā processions in late May. It was clear that the Archdiocese was singling out the Kodungaiyur Prayer House to discipline its members for reasons other than a supposed breach of canon law.

George Peter, an energetic prayer house member in his thirties, dressed in a striped cotton sports shirt, invited me to check out the neighborhood. We zoomed in an autorickshaw down dark, narrow side streets around sharp corners, and bursting out of dark alleys into bright, thickly populated areas of festivity. It reminded me of an American Fourth of July—fireworks, exploding lights, mirth, and risk—the sort of adrenaline-boosting excitement of a carnival. In one hour, we saw at least four boisterous Mary processions and parts of two Masses—one being said under a tree behind a makeshift altar, the other in a tiny corrugated-iron shed painted bright blue inside. On the shed, facing the street, was a huge mural of a Rubens-like, fair-skinned, light-brown-haired Mary and child, with the words *Punita Sahāya Aṇṇai Ālayam* (House of Our Holy Lady of Refuge) in Tamil script. Beside the shed was a cart bearing a bright-colored palanquin holding a statue of *Sahāya Aṇṇai*—a pink-skin-toned Mary, smothered in garlands of jasmine.

In all of Tamil Nadu, in all the processions I witnessed, whether Hindu or Catholic, only men pulled the cart.[22] If the palanquin stood on a truck's flat bed, a man would drive the truck and at least one other would accompany it on the flat bed. Women might process ahead of the cart, but men always carried, pulled, or walked beside it, in the honorary role of icon-bearers.

WHAT THE ARCHBISHOP SAID (IN THE PULPIT) AT MUTHAMIZH NAGAR

The procession for the groundbreaking ceremony for the new Annai Velankanni Church building in Muthamizh Nagar, Fr. Thomas' parish church, would feature not Mātā but another special guest: the Madras-Mylapore Archbishop Rev. Fr. Chinnappa. He and Fr. Thomas were to concelebrate Mass after the procession. It would be a double celebration of Annai Velankanni, the "White Virgin" (the Virgin of Good Health) and of the start of construction of the larger church that had long been Fr. Thomas's dream. The procession would involve a mix of traditions: high and low, Tamil and Keralan, Hindu and Christian.

A large crowd of several hundred people gathered outside the small church. Fr. Thomas and Archbishop Chinnappa, clad in long white cassocks—Chinnappa's belted with a wide pink silken sash—walked slowly down the street toward the church, trailed by another hundred people. Archbishop Chinnappa, by far the tallest man there, loomed over Fr. Thomas. A heavy gold cross the size of a large Olympic medal hung over his sash, and a pink garland of roses hung almost to his knees. As they strolled along, nine well-dressed laymen shaded them with silk Malayalam umbrellas. The umbrellas, fringed with small sparkling mirrors, glinted in the late-evening light. Dozens of prepubescent girls walked beside the umbrella men, sporting white, flouncy, taffeta dresses and white veils—like small brides-to-be—casting rose petals from wicker baskets. The procession passed a bus stand and a corrugated metal fence plastered with posters of Our Lady Jecintho Prayer House—advertisements for the nine-night May celebration.

Thomas's and Chinnappa's opposition to that celebration was based on some as-yet-unspecified canon law—but what was so strictly Catholic about the competing procession in Muthamizh Nagar? It seemed to cater to the Archbishop's Dalit roots: eight young men in white shirts danced a traditional stick dance (*tārai āṭṭam*) in front, their bamboo sticks clacking and clattering as they jigged in and out of two lines. Women did a flag dance—another borrowed "Hindu" rite. This hybridity was as common in Indian Roman Catholicism as Pizza Masala in Chennai. The crowd, which collected onlookers, moved slowly toward the church.

A canopy and stage had been erected in the front square. A middle-aged woman, jasmine bound into her hair, performed *ārati*[23] before Chinnappa, lifting and circling a stainless-steel bowl—filled with water, perhaps, instead of fire; I wasn't sure—clockwise in front of him. She offered him and Fr. Thomas sandalwood paste and *vibhuti* to dot their foreheads. The bell tower, purchased by a local Hindu, tolled.

People filed in under the canopy. Women and children sat on the ground facing the altar while men from the parish council and other core groups sat behind them in plastic chairs. They invited me to join them, which I did, the only woman in their ranks. Hundreds of other men stood outside the gate, spilling into the street, watching and listening. The crowd, by now, numbered maybe three hundred.

A pink styrofoam model of the new church, proudly displayed on a table, reminded me of a small Christian Taj Mahal. Chinnappa—who had donned a tall mitre hat—sat with Thomas on a stage behind the gold-lamé altar. They had changed into the red, gold, and white silken vestments of liturgy. Tall floor fans were blowing their hair up in back.

In his sermon, given mostly in English, Chinnappa spoke of obedience. "You listen to my words," he repeated. "You will be *my* property." He pointed his finger at the crowd when he said "you," and pointed it to his chest when he said "my." "The one who obeys will sing victory," he said. "Obedience is like traffic rules: you have to obey the rules and orders of a particular institution."

At the end of the sermon, three women approached the altar, each carrying a brick—the new cornerstones of the new church—and Chinnappa made the sign of the cross over each one. Men and women passed out "dum boxes" for donations. A man gingerly walked to the altar, carrying the styrofoam model of the new church, which the archbishop blessed as well.

WHAT THE ARCHBISHOP SAID (OUT OF THE PULPIT)

The next day, I stopped at the Bishop's House next door to Santhome Cathedral, located by the beach in south-central Chennai. A huge colonial structure, standing behind a tall iron gate on Santhome Main Road, it looked like a stone mansion plucked right out of Portugal. In addition to housing the Archbishop, the building held the Madras-Mylapore Archdiocese's central offices.

Rev. Fr. Bernard Lawrence, the parish priest of Annai Velankanni Church in Besant Nagar, where I was living, had introduced me to Fr. Chinnappa some weeks earlier. By chance, I had run into Lawrence there, and he had introduced me, along with a visiting Taizé priest from France. Chinnappa had welcomed both of us; I had told him briefly about my research, and had scheduled this second appointment.

Now he sat behind a large, dark wood desk. I told him that I had attended the Mass in Muthamizh Nagar the day before.

"I spoke about obedience," he said.

Yes.

"Obedience as in the reading yesterday," he continued.

Yes, I said again.

"Father James!" he called out for assistance. I thought he was calling him to offer an example of obedience. "Give us tea." He looked at me. "Tea or coffee?"

I said water would be fine. We settled on lime juice.

Chinnappa spoke more about the previous day's Bible reading, and about Mary. "She was ready to surrender herself to God," he said. " 'Let me surrender to your Word,' as a gesture of obedience to the Word." He enumerated many kinds of obedience: "Obedience to the parents. Obedience to the teacher. Obedience to the statutes of any institution. Obedience to the ministers of the head of the College of Ministers. Obedience in the religious community, to the superior, and the institutions of the congregation. So you cannot do away with obedience. When we obey God, He blesses us."

I took notes. I told him I was hoping to speak to him about the Kodungaiyur prayer house. He seemed slightly reluctant to talk about it, even disappointed in my interest.

"Those people have started some four years back, saying that that lady had a vision and Our Lady asked her to build the biggest parish in the world," the Archbishop said. He said that Mary has not asked for such a thing so far;[24] usually, he said, an apparition is meant for conversion, evangelization, prayer, or renewal of priests and the religious. "But she says Our Lady wanted her to build a church."

The matter was being studied, he said. "Here, in the Catholic Church, we have a method for checking, promoting, controlling. We have to. Otherwise, tomorrow, why not say, 'Our Lady appeared to *me*!'?"

What's more, he said, Rosalind had never come to meet him, as she should have when he first arrived. And furthermore, her family never attended church. I asked him how he knew this.

"I know," he said. "They tell me."

"Who is 'they?' " I asked.

"They don't go," he reasserted. It was clear Fr. Chinnappa felt offended by Rosalind's apparent failure of hospitality and submission.

I said I understood that they did, indeed, go to a local parish church, and his reply suggested that it was not the *proper* parish church. He responded indirectly, using sweeping examples, "If you are in Madras, you go to a Madras church. If you live in Delhi, you go to a Delhi church. They have to refer to their own community first. If you want to be a Catholic, follow the directions. If you want to be a Pentecostal, or an evangelical, you do what you like. . . . They should be receiving direction from me . . . . It's as simple as that." The followers of Jecintho, he said, lacked "religious maturity." It wasn't a question of "argument," he said. It wasn't a subject of "research." He paused.

"Are you talking to me?" I asked, confused.

"Everybody," he said.

Sensing that the interview was over, I closed the notebook into which I had been writing furiously, and began to thank him.

"This is not an interview," he said. "I ask that you not use anything I have said."

I reminded him that, when I made the appointment, I had asked for an interview.

"Well then, you need to conduct it properly," he said. "You have not presented me with any visiting card." I dug into my purse and handed him a letter from the U.S. Fulbright office in Chennai, and said that I had my police registration papers if he wanted to see them.

"No, no, that is not necessary." He glanced over the Fulbright letter. "You should take more care of this," he said, handing it back to me. "It's all creased. You should keep it in a file."

"If you would like, I can get you a proper copy without creases," I said.

He demurred. "Still, this was not a proper interview," he said. "In a proper interview, you ask me questions and I answer."

"But I did ask you questions, and you spoke," I said.

"But then in the end you will criticize," he said.

"No, Father. I will analyze." I began to stand. "Thank you, Father."

"And please come back at one o'clock for lunch."

The lunch table seated twenty priests. One insisted that I take a center chair. Fr. Chinnappa and Auxiliary Bishop Fr. Pius walked in, and we all stood.

Fr. Chinnappa sat to my right; Fr. Pius sat opposite. A visiting priest sat to his right. Over our first course of soup, the two bishops spoke to him about the prayer house and festival.

"It seems they disobeyed orders and went ahead with the Mass," Fr. Chinnappa said.

"Excuse me, fathers," I said, appalled that they'd gotten it wrong. "Could I jump in?"

"No," Chinnappa said, glancing my way. "You eat your lunch. It will get cold."

BIG DAY IN KODUNGAIYUR

Day 10 of the May festival at Our Lady Jecintho Prayer House: the culmination of nine nights of prayer. It would soon be time to break fast. The afternoon sun was high and the place bustling with activity.

"Everyone is doing something," Robert told me with a beaming smile. "No one is left out." In many ways, this festival promised to be even more syncretic than the one Fr. Thomas had hosted. On the patio, a five-man band, sitting cross-legged on a straw mat, was playing Karnatic music. Two men played a *tavil*, a two-headed drum tapped on one side with a stick and on the other with the hand and finger cymbals; two others played *nātasvaram* (horns); the fifth played a small organ.

Inside the prayer house, some three-dozen people sat in circles while, in a corner, women made flower garlands. Their fingers moved nimbly, stringing the tiny jasmine (*malli*) blossoms together with white thread—an art they had practiced since childhood. Along with the jasmine, they wove yellow chrysanthemums, white tubulars, bright orange cassandra, and *Bengalūr rōjā*, "Bangalore rose."[25] The bright pink petals lay scattered over large portions of the white floor, dotting it like a Seurat painting.

In another corner, Francina, Julie, Ruby Mary, and a mother and young daughter worked with roses, too, peeling petals off the buds and filling trays with them. The women on the hospitality committee, who had been chosen by Rosalind-as-Jecintho, would offer the petals to guests, along with *cantaṉum* (sandalwood paste), which they would use to dot each guest's forehead. From another tray, they would offer the guests sea salt and sprinkle each with holy water.

Along with preparing the roses, Francina was also making a *shakti karakam* in a *tavalai*, a wide-mouthed pot made of metal. A *shakti karakam* is an item also used in Hindu festivals to represent the power or *shakti* of the goddess.[26] This pot, too, represented *shakti*, Francina said. She placed margosa leaves and a coconut on its mouth, just as did Hindus in their goddess festivals, and dotted the pot and the coconut with red *kumkum* and orange sandalwood paste. The pot, in this case, represented Mātā, understood by the people of our Lady Jecintho Prayer House as a form of *shakti*.

Eight men, wearing lungis tied up around their waists, were sitting in a circle, legs folded easily in a half-lotus, working on the walls and roofs of the wooden chariots, the *capparams* (a small wooden chariot, often used interchangeably with *tēr*) in which St. Michael the archangel, the Sacred Heart of Jesus,[27] and Jecintho Mātā would be carried. The men's hands flew with wood, string, and flowers. Some of them tied flower buds to what looked like long popsicle sticks. The smallest chariot, the first, for St. Michael, was mostly finished and stood about the height and width of a man. The medium-sized chariot—for Jesus—would look like the spire of Velankanni; one of the men had drawn a sketch. The chariot roofs, strung with flowers, would cover litters made of heavier wood; solid poles extended from the beds, about eight feet high, to support them. The beds for St. Michael and Jesus were set on palanquins; Mātā's poled bed would be set on a tall cart with wheels.

When it was time to hoist the roof of Mātā's chariot onto the poled bed, the men grasped the edges and looked at one another. Someone yelled *heh*! and, with much yelling and grunting, they lifted the flowered roof over their heads. They worked fast, in ordered chaos; two men jumped on the bed of the chariot and held the roof its center. Arms over their heads, they adjusted it on the poles till it nestled perfectly.

The building of the chariots was a job for men only, and a moment of spectacle, like an Amish barn raising. Women stood by in fancy saris, watching in suspense, exclaiming "*Aiyaiyo*!" when the abundantly flowered skeleton stood firm. Eventually, the whole red-orange contraption would be set atop an ox cart. Men would pull the grand chariot for Jecintho Mātā and carry the other two "floats," the palanquins for Jesus and St. Michael—the lesser deities here—on their shoulders.

A woman in the back of the prayer house was already dressing the Jecintho statues. The small statue wore a new red and green silk sari. This statue would remain in the prayer house. The woman was making bridal veils of fine white netting for both statues. The large statue—the Jecintho-and-child that stood to my waist—would be decked in red and orange flowers for the ride. The grand chariot—the chariot for Mātā, the size of a small merry-go-round—stood finished, in all its splendor, on the street outside the prayer house, surrounded by little girls in white dresses and veils. One wore a bright orange-and-white flowered dress that matched the *kanakāmbaram* flowers and jasmine on the roof of the grand chariot.

Already, women were beginning to greet the guests, welcoming, decorating, and blessing people. Representing the hospitality of Lakshmi, they pressed sandalwood paste onto foreheads, offering rose petals and salt and sprinkling holy water. One middle-aged woman, Anna Francis, a core member of the community, wielded an aspergillum: the silver, scepter-shaped sprinkler with holes at its head. Several men clambered up scaffolding and, high over the heads of the female hospitality committee, erected the *pantal*, the festive gateway made of cloth and bamboo.

People started emerging in fancy dress: women in bright *saris* and *churi dars,* men in white button-down dress shirts and blue neckties—Western dress, the uniform of a high-rise office worker. On their chests, everyone wore badges—women's yellow, men's blue—the size and shape of first-prize ribbons at a country fair. The paper medallions were embossed with a blue heart sending out rays of light.

The marching band showed up in the late afternoon, playing two snare drums, a base drum, and a horn. The Karnatic musicians had stopped playing.

Muslims did the cooking. Next to the prayer house, Salim Bhai, in charge of five huge vats of rice and chicken sambar, oversaw a team of men who stirred the vats with long wooden sticks. Seven policemen had come from P6-Kodungaiyur to help with traffic control, at the request of Rosalind's brother Benjamin, the one with political connections.

WHAT THE PROCESSION SAID

Day 10, early evening Jecintho Mātā's coronation celebration (*muṭicāṭṭu viḻa*) was about to begin. Rev. Fr. Pitchaimuuthu, the priest who was later relocated, and Rev. Fr. Sauri Rajan, from another parish, had been greeted properly and garlanded as per Mātā's request. In the empty lot across from the prayer house, a large stage three times the size of Fr. Thomas's and a thousand folding chairs suggested that a Mass, a *tiruppali*, would indeed follow the car procession, both against Archdiocesan orders. But who was to say? Mātā could lead otherwise. The open-ended question lent the night an added air of expectancy. The sun was almost setting, and at least a thousand people had already arrived, most of them standing and milling around the prayer house.

This *tēr pavani*, or car procession, was to begin with the removal of the main icon, in this case, Jecintho-and-child, from its usual holding site inside the enclosed, sacred space and into public view in the grand chariot. The crowd pushed toward the prayer house doors, and Robert and a few other men shouted for it to part. Suddenly, the doors opened and the grand statue of Jecinctho Mātā emerged in the arms of four men, eyes wild and focused on the chariot. Time slowed down, atoms seemed to split, as they hurried out of the dark entrance amid a frenzy of shouting. "*Pārankaḷ, pārankaḷ!*" (Look, look!) "Take care!" people yelled. The men carried the blue-and-white statue, garlanded with jasmine and roses, down the steps of the veranda to the chariot parked just outside. Her blue eyes gazed out from beneath her lace veil. They lifted her, again with much fanfare, and she was inside the litter, with two men, then three. They seemed to take forever to install her. How many men would it take to arrange Mary's veil and garlands? (Figure 4.1).

Figure 4.1: Men arrange Jecintho and her chariot for the grand procession in Kodungaiyur, 2005. Photo by author.

Several other men dramatically held back bunches of jasmine garlands that hung from the roof, so the crowd could catch *darshan*.

Blue and white Jecintho flags, lining the street, swung in a light breeze. Hundreds of three-pointed leaves known as *tambaram* also hung from strings and danced like small birds.

Now, with Jecintho in her *vahana*, or vehicle,[28] the two priests stood at the shrine's entrance, hands pressed in prayer, while a line of women wearing yellow ribbons passed out the *cantaṉum*, the sandalwood paste, on stainless steel plates, that had emerged from the prayer house. People took some and dotted their foreheads.

Charles and Robert rounded up the "VIPs," about a dozen people including myself, into the prayer house. It was time to light the brass lamp, which stood shoulder high, holding several small receptacles for camphor and wicks—just like what one might find in a Hindu temple, except that this one bore a crucifix at its pinnacle. We each lit a wick. Rosalind appeared for the first time, standing beside us and wearing an impeccably tied, bright pink and gold silk sari with gold silk blouse, and a gold ribbon pinned to her chest. Francina stood beside her in a similar red-and-maroon sari with gold border, also wearing a gold ribbon. The only other woman was a nun in a light blue habit. Fr. Pitchaimuutthu and Fr. Sauri Rajan, and several other men, also lit the lamp.

As we walked back outside, the setting sun pierced my eyes. The crowd was immense. The chariots were lit with neon lights powered by loud, diesel generators on wheels. Fr. Sauri Rajan, facing Mātā's chariot with a wireless microphone, uttered an elegant prayer while Rosalind, standing beside him, held her right hand over her heart and prayed under her breath, lips moving silently. Fr. Pitchaimuutthu swung incense; Rev. Rajan shook the silver aspergillum over the chariot. Rex, one of the core prayer house members, took the microphone and recited Hail Marys. The crowd chanted along.

Sr. Dr. Annamma Philip, the principal of Stella Maris, also was here, and Sr. Florine Monis, the college administrator. Someone handed Sr. Philip a basket of rose petals, and she threw a few handfuls over Mātā, showering blessings. Young women took up large white flags bearing Jecintho's blue insignia and lined up under the *pantal* gateway in two columns; a crowd of women, many with their children, crowded behind them. Flags fluttering and sari *pallus* trailing, the women began to move forward, the white jasmine in their hair glowing in the lights behind them.

Alex led the chariots. His spindly figure stood in dark relief against the backlight—one thin arm raised in warning, beckoning or stopping the chariots with an open palm. Then came the men and the gods in their chariots, trailing their loud diesel engines behind them: two rows of men bore St. Michael, the field commander of the army of God, and behind him, the Sacred Heart of Jesus, dressed in red. Priests followed them, leading the chariot carrying Jecintho Mātā, also pulled by men. Important men of the prayer house community rode on the chariots, tending to the statues, fiddling with the flowers and lights; others escorted them, managing the crowd, asking people to stand back to the sides, or to move along. The job of some men was to yell directions—*Pō! Pō! Pō!* (Go! Go! Go!) *Nil! Nil! Nil!* (Stop! Stop! Stop!), while other men lifted electrical wires over the chariot pires with long, forked, wooden poles. One false move, and a live wire—one of the many that had been jerry-rigged between houses and the poles—could come down on the crowd. Men and boys lit firecrackers along the way, adding to the sense of contained danger.

Meanwhile, the roughly five hundred processioners chanted the rosary. "*Mariyē vāḻka!*" (Long live Mary!) punctuated the decades. People of various religious backgrounds stood in doorways along the route, some throwing flowers and others reaching out to touch the chariot. Some households had erected small shrines outside their entrances, where the chariots would often pause for blessings.

Rosalind and Francina walked with the women in front of St. Michael. Rosalind took my hand. Hers was warm. The event itself was a sort of miracle, she said, "The fact that the car procession goes around at all, and that nothing untoward happens—that itself is something, no?"

We processed through residential streets and turned at the border of the cemetery,[29] walking for some time along its edge.

"That's Mummy's grave," Rosalind said, turning toward the cemetery with a look of longing. This was a side of Rosalind I had not seen, a rare moment of transparent grief. She stopped and turned once more before moving on. We were heading back to the prayer house. Soon, a hum of whispers and suppressed exclamations shot through the crowd of women.

Rosalind pulled me to her. "Do you see it?" she said to me. "Did you see when Father was blessing the statue? And now, when you stand and look? See? She is moving."

It took me a moment to process what she was saying.

"See?" she said again. "She is looking all around. Her face is changing. Her eyes are moving. Her smile, her lips, her expressions. You can only experience it." Rosalind's own eyes were glassy. "Here, stand here," she said again to me. "From far away you can see the realness."

Anna Francis approached me, excited. "See, how beautiful?! How alive?! She is looking like a bride, all dressed up!"

The nun who had been in the prayer house for the lamp lighting called Jecintho a *kalyācci*, a bride. "Didn't you see?" she asked. "In the prayer house too, Mātā had a smiling face (*cirippa mūkam*)."

Another woman called Mātā's statue "*jōthi, prakāsam*," brightness itself. "Like when a woman gets married," she said. "She is *santōsham, illaiyā?* (she is happy, no?) *Atai mātitri cirippu* (It is that kind of smile)."

It is not just people who are possessed by deities in India. Aniconic items, such as a rock, a tree, a flame, a pot of water, a *linga* (an erect stone, the sign for Shiva; Sanskrit for "sign," or "phallus"),[30] as well as iconic ones, such as a *murti*, are all within the bounds of a god or goddess entering them. The renowned Indologist Diana Eck writes that a *murti* itself is defined in Sanskrit as "anything which has definite shape and limits . . . a form, body, figure, . . . an embodiment, incarnation, manifestation. . . . Thus, the *murti* is more than a likeness; it is the deity itself taken 'form.' "[31]

During processions in India, all kinds of people—Hindu, Muslim, and Catholic—think of icons of deities or saints as truly being alive.[32] This is both part of the power of *darshan*, that is, of viewing and being viewed by the deity, and part of the dangerous and ambivalent power of procession—which implies movement of various sorts. The deity moves in and out of the temple; people move in and out of sacred space and sacred time;[33] the deity and the people move together around the neighborhood, transforming one another and being reborn. As the goddess leaves her sacred sanctum—the temple, church, or prayer house "womb"—and is paraded around the streets, she transfers power onto the locale and its people. For the brief time that the goddess is processing, she is also possessing places and people who themselves become moving temples, enlivened by the *shakti* of that goddess. It is a time when the masses enact and proclaim their unity across religious lines, even—or sometimes because of—orthodox pronouncements of heterodoxy.

WHAT THE MASS SAID: ANOTHER SORT OF POSSESSION

The processioners reached the prayer house grounds to find a classic South Indian performance in full swing: loud Karnatic music boomed over more than two thousand people as a young woman danced *Bharatanatyam*—the Indian dance originating in the ancient *Natya Shastras*—on a well-lit side stage. The jingle of her bangles and *kalaṅki* (large anklets of metal bells) punctuated the music as she swung her hands into precise *mudras* (hand signs) and beat her henna-colored feet on the stage. Muslim men in white skull caps dotted the crowd, as did women with their sari *pallus* pulled over their heads, sometimes a sign of a Muslim identity. A Hindu woman holding a baby told me she had come to give thanks to Mātā for the gift of her child. At the front of the crowd, in the VIP seats, Fr. Pitchaimuuthu and Sr. Annamma Philip sipped orange Fanta from bottles. Both the *nātasvaram* band and the Western-style "marching" drum band played simultaneously at the edges of the crowd. A nun carried the *shakti karakam* up to the main stage and placed it in front of an altar.

Suddenly, a male voice came over the loudspeakers and announced "*Mariyē vāḻka*! *Mariyē vāḻka*!" Jecintho's chariot was entering the gate. A small group of prayer house devotees rolled out a red carpet from the entrance gate to a parking spot beside the stage. Men rolled the *Mātā tēr* forward and back to park it. The noise reached a fevered pitch. Women in particular flocked to the car, touching it, then their eyes, lips, and chests. They jostled to grab petals. Six altar boys dressed in red processed past the car to the altar.

Fathers Pitchaimuuthu and Sauri Rajan mounted the stage in blue-and-white vestments bearing symbols of the Eucharist and the Jecintho seal. Sisters Annamma Philips and Florine Monis, sitting in the front row, beckoned to me, so I sat with them. After Bible readings, we sang the Gospel Acclamation, "Alleluia." The Karnatic band played the scriptural verse, sung by Fr. Pitchaimuuthu, also in Karnatic style. A young woman sang "Ave Maria," and another led prayer intentions. We prayed for the world, for peace, and for the Church: specifically, for Archbishop Chinnappa and Auxiliary Bishop Lawrence Pius. Above the altar, a huge red-and-white banner in large Tamil letters read, "Having said 'So be it,' she surrendered herself to God, and therefore became queen of the world."

Fathers Pitchaimuuthu and Sauri Rajan consecrated the host and the wine. This was the moment of transubstantiation, when the substance of the bread and wine changed into the body and blood of Jesus Christ, according to Catholic doctrine. This, then, was *the* moment of possession—the moment in the liturgy when God-as-Jesus possesses the substance of the thing in itself, *becoming* it.[34]

Pitchaimuuthu led us in Tamil, "Lord, I am not worthy to receive you, but only say the word, and I shall be healed." People prepared themselves for the entrance of God.

Dozens of priests and nuns started moving through the crowd, offering communion. People swarmed around them. I faced Sister Florine, with her blackened, healing finger. She placed a wafer on my tongue. The crowd moved like lava for more than an hour while hundreds received communion. We sang a song, and Rosalind took the mic, center stage. She thanked Fr. Pitchaimuuthu, hung a huge rose-and-leaf *mālai* around his neck, and crowned him with a hat that looked like a bishop's mitre—red, white, and pointy, with a blue Jecintho seal in the center.

It was time for Jecintho's crowning. Nine-year-old Fredy walked up the red carpet, wearing the red-and-white cassock of an altar boy, carrying two glittering rhinestone crowns—one for Mātā and one for the baby Jesus—on a white silk pillow. He handed the crowns to Pitchaimuuthu, who placed them on the statues.

"*Maryiē vāḻka!*" the crowd shouted.

People swarmed around the Jecintho statue, throwing rose petals. Fireworks exploded into the night sky. The crowd stood facing the chariot, palms pressed at their chests, or over their heads. Some held their hands up, palms forward. Rosary beads hung down their forearms.

Lawrence, Rosalind's brother, approached me, beaming.

"How do you feel?!" he said to me. It was not so much a question as an exclamation. He gestured toward the crowd. "It's limitless, isn't it? Like the sea! You cannot count the stars, also. It is like the stars. And like the sea!"

Interlude

MĀTĀPURAM, OCTOBER—AIPPACI MĀTAM—2005

The house and almost everything in it descended deep beneath the long spiral that was sleep, submerged under a heavy blanket of moisture, silence, and heat. In the small mud-and-cement room and on its porch, under the thatch, the bodies of a man of thirty-five and his wife of thirty, their three small children, the man's mother and eighty-five-year-old grandmother, and two visitors lay gently breathing. The women and children slept on bamboo mats on the cement floor of the eight-by-twelve room; the man, on the porch beside his grandmother, who lay on a rope cot. All slept facing east, along with the statue of Mary in the nearby chapel that also faced east, in part because Hindus sleep facing south, in the direction of Yama,[1] the god of death. A calendar to Velankanni Mātā marking Gregorian time hung on one wall of the room; an iron folding chair hung on another; and three large cardboard boxes wilted slightly with moisture beside a small table fan—though there was no table—on the floor. It had been raining for weeks—after all, it was *Aippaci mātam* (month) of the Tamil solar calendar,[2] and, as the well-known Tamil saying goes, *Aippaci maḻai, aṭai maḻai* (*Aippaci* rains are persistent rains). But the monsoon flooding had cleared, allowing passage of the two visitors. Most human beings in the village were asleep, and most animals under its sheltering ring—the cow tied to the tree in the lot across the red earth path from the house, and the two chickens there, and the goats that belonged to the neighbors down the way—and many other beings beyond that ring, slept. The mynas and herons and peacocks that usually flew or strut around the fields surrounding the village had all tucked their heads into their breasts, and the dogs that roamed its red earth paths lay curled in small packs. Even the snakes, the *kattu viriyan*, the common krait, remained underground. The neighboring Hindu Dalit village of Chinna Unjanai lay deep under sleep: the *panchayat* (village council) president and vice president—both women—and their sons, who had been arrested and released that June after yet another embattled Sri Swarnamoorthi

Eswarar car festival in Kandadevi, were also asleep. To the north, the Kali Amman tank[3] lay full, its water still and mostly dark, reflecting the stars. In the wet earth surrounding the tank, the temples, the church, and both villages—Hindu and Catholic—the young paddy springing from the muddy soil lay still, free of human touch; its bright green shoots now lay under cover of dark. The snails in the paddy remained deep in their shells, and even the cockroaches pulled their legs in and slept behind dry stores of seed. The whole region of the earth on which we are all transient listed deeply, slowly rotating under the shadow side of the planet as the stars burned in their majesty. The rising and falling of bodies in this moment made no perceptible sound. All was unified in silence.

And then, a breath: The mother of the man of the house lay whispering, as if through pursed lips, verses from the Tamil translation of the Bible. She held the thick book in the dim yellow ring of a flashlight.

What do people gain from all their labors
at which they toil under the sun?
Generations come and generations go,
but the earth remains forever. . . .[4]

One of the visitors woke to hear the whispering, and drifted back to sleep. The old woman continued.

Is there anything of which one can say,
"Look! This is something new"?
It was here already, long ago;
it was here before our time. . . .[5]

A few houses down the lane, another woman, Dhanam, also kept vigil. She fingered her rosary beads, whispering 153 Hail Marys, rocking slightly, to and fro, while the bodies under her own small roof—those of her husband, daughter, and two granddaughters—also slept.

aruḷ niṟainta Mariyē vāḻka (Hail Mary, full of grace)
karttar ummuṭaṉē (The Lord is with you)
peṇkaḷukkuḷ ācīrvatikkappaṭṭavaḷ. Nīrē (She is blessed among women. You!).
ummuṭaiya tiruvayiṟṟiṉ kaniyākiya Iyēcuvum ācīrvatikkappaṭṭavarē (And blessed indeed is the fruit of your holy belly, Jesus) . . .[6]

Meanwhile, the sky held onto everyone with her strength. She held herself apart, as if to watch: wide, high, lit, her stars like milk above our heavy dark—or: her web heavy with dew, an arc in which we were all caught. Bigger than earth, certainly, this woman, this sky, held us, momentarily, in her celestial skirts.[7] Higher than the sky, she held us. Too near, we and all our dreams would cave, or find ourselves subsumed in waters. Too far, we would lose both her and ourselves. But here: perfectly distant and close, watched and held—finally, we could rest. We could settle into deep sleep, that state where there is neither dream nor desire, the place where there is no separation, where all, finally, is one.[8,9]

CHAPTER 5

Return to Mātāpuram

Rainy season, Sivagangai District, 2005. My work was reaching completion—or so I thought. My visa restrictions, lifted in time for the tsunami, had finally enabled my wider movement. I'd helped in the relief work, talked to survivors, and wandered, stunned, through the ruins.[1] It was time for me to return to the village, to Dhanam, the woman whose story first triggered my circuitous quest.

"I see you!" I heard on my cell phone, as I stood with Padma in the dusty, bustling market square. We had taken an overnight train to Madurai, and then a bus to Paramakudi. Fr. Arlappan came ambling toward us, cell phone pressed to an ear, wearing gray slacks and a white button-down shirt. A brilliant smile spread across his face. I liked him right away.

My return to Mātāpuram, like my entrance to Our Lady Jecintho Prayer House, would be marked by the accompaniment of a priest. But unlike the priests who had led me to Rosalind's arena of possession, Arlappan was a native of Mātāpuram. His visit would not be considered an occasion for pomp, but rather as a beloved son's homecoming. Arlappan's brother, Aarokkiyam, a tenant farmer and mill worker who served as village catechist (*kōyilpiḷḷai*),[2] had long been my main contact in Mātāpuram, in large part because of his phone: he had one. It was through Aarokkiyam that I got messages to Dhanam, who lived a few houses down the lane from him. Four years after our first meeting—because of Aarokkiyam's phone—she was expecting me. Aarokkiyam had arranged for Arlappan, his younger brother, to come meet us, and his help would be essential: I didn't remember the way across all the back-country roads to Mātāpuram, a village so marginal that even most auto rickshaw drivers in the closest big towns didn't know how to find it.

Fr. Arlappan, at twenty-nine, was a friendly, well-educated diocesan priest known for his social work among Dalit Christians. A Dalit himself, he was the first man from Mātāpuram ever to become a priest. He had been ordained on April 27, 2003, in time to celebrate the village festival, the Feast of Our Lady, the next day. That annual festival[3] was marked by a chariot procession in which villagers processed a statue of Adaikkala Mātā around the hamlet's boundaries, much in the style of Hindu chariot processions and the various Marian processions all over South India—including the one at the Jecintho Prayer House. But there was a significant difference between those earlier Hindu processions and the one in Mātāpuraam—and a significant similarity between it and the one at Jecintho Prayer House. Whereas the festivals to Shiva and Aiyanar in and around Kandadevi had spurred violence because higher-caste Hindus had banned lower and outcaste Hindus from participating, in Mātāpuram, reportedly any man was allowed to pull the chariots, and some neighboring Hindus also participated. (Women did not pull, but processed with the car.) Like the Jecintho procession, moreover, Mātāpuram's was not instigated by men or a male god such as Aiyanar, but by Mātā, who had possessed Dhanam.[4]

Like many Dalit priests of his generation, Arlappan had been assigned to small outstations in his first years of service. The first was the town of Illiyaankudi, twelve kilometers north of Mātāpuram, which had a majority of Muslim groups as well as Jains, Buddhists, Hindus, and Christians. In his third year, he was assigned to Paramakudi, the dusty, busy, market town where our bus had dropped us. Paramakudi, the political and revenue seat of Ramanathapuram District (also known as Ramnad), was a center for Dalit politics. The Paramakudi parish where Arlappan worked was also the seat of the Sivagangai Multipurpose Social Service Society (SMSSS), the local wing of the Tamilnadu Social Service Society (TASOSS), the Tamil Nadu Catholic Bishops' Council's main organization "for justice, peace and development."

I had never met Arlappan before, but as we chatted, it became clear that he was devoted to his work at SMSSS, committed to helping the people of the area, supportive of the movement for Dalit rights. He seemed not the least bit resentful, as low-caste priests sometimes were, of being stationed in "the backwaters" and held back from rising through the ranks of the Roman Catholic Church hierarchy.

Although the Paramakudi area had not been affected by the tsunami, villages only an hour to the east had been devastated, and many of them were low- or outcaste. TASOSS had been key in helping people rebuild their lives. Arlappan showed us his simple office beside the Alangara Mātā Church before we climbed into the small, white Maruti car he had hired with driver, and headed northeast toward Mātāpuram.

I was excited to see Dhanam again. As we pulled out of Paramakudi's main square, weaving through dense crowds and markets displaying piles of chili peppers and reams of bright cotton, Padma pulled her sari across her nose and mouth to keep out the dust, and I settled in to catch up on the people of Arlappan's hometown. I asked him especially about those who believed in Dhanam's possession by Mātā. Perhaps I expected the kind of dismissal that the Archbishop of Mylapore had shown.[5] But Arlappan wouldn't be drawn in.

"It is a simple faith," he said with a smile and a shrug. "I don't interfere in these matters, because it is such a small village." Many of the priests to whom I'd spoken about Marian possession seemed to share Arlappan's neutral stance, either claiming ignorance of the practices or turning a blind eye.

We crossed the Vaigai River, which flowed beneath us toward the Bay of Bengal. Washermen in the pink-and-yellow sandy shallows slapped their cloth over the stones. A straight two-lane highway took us through reddish clay fields dotted with patches of green grass and brush. The Ramnad district had long been a religious crossroads, and churches, dargahs, and temples of all stripes still marked the landscape. I noted many large goddess (*amman̲*) temples on our way into the town of Devakottai, "Fort of the Goddess." One of the oldest municipalities of Tamil Nadu, Devakottai had been one of the most active seats of the Independence Movement. Mahatma Gandhi had come here in 1934 to condole with the locals in the death of a Dalit named Poochi, an activist in the movement against untouchability. He had mediated discussions between the Dalits and the Nadars, who were opposed to the Dalits wearing shirts; going about bare-chested had been a sign of submission to higher castes.

The area was still largely ruled by Nadars, Kallars, and Chettiars, mainly agricultural-mercantile castes. We slowed through the narrow streets of Devakottai, under the shadows of great Chettinad mansions, the homes of former landlords—Padma leaning across me to crane her neck at the tall walls and see the times posted for tourist visits—and I imagined the tensions as a Hindu of Gandhi's stature asserted Dalit humanity and dignity, and as members of relatively higher castes like Nadars and Kallars struggled themselves for status and self-respect, recoiling in fear at the threat of the Dalit and Gandhian negotiations.

As we left Devakottai, the land opened up into bright, green rice paddies and coconut trees. Around small hamlets, goats grazed. The bright *rājagōpuram* (lit., "king-tower") of the infamous Kandadevi temple—the site of so many caste tensions—rose before us, a kaleidoscope of color against a light blue sky streaked with white cirrus clouds. Arlappan asked the driver to slow the car as we passed, so that we could regard the ornate towers looming over the flat landscape, the ten-acre *teppukuḷam* (tiled water tank) stretching from the temple like an immense, shimmering skirt.[6]

The Kandadevi festival, the annual chariot procession at the Sri Swarnamoorthi Eswarar (Shiva) temple, had been the center of controversy for decades, and tensions around it and the Aiyanar festival had led to the attack on Chinna Unjanai. The temple served about two hundred villages at the center of a vast fertile valley that had been owned for three centuries by a monarch and ruled by feudal landlords, mostly Thevars.[7] It loomed in the lives of most villagers as a symbol of wealth, prestige, and access to divine power. Brahmin priests presided over its rituals and guarded the monument's *murtis*, the stone embodiments of divinity. The annual procession was one of the rare occasions on which high- and low-caste people came together, with very clear rules signifying caste dominance. Pallar men, until recent years, had to go shirtless; and the women, blouse-less, when they were in the vicinity of the higher-caste chieftans, or *ambalakars*, of the four districts that made up the temple membership. These *ambalakars*, all of them Thevars, were honored in various ways during the festival. Villagers garlanded them with flowers; they wore the silk that had touched the *murtis*, and they led the processions. Kallars and other Thevars pulled the immense chariot around the nearby streets, marking their ritual territory. Pallars and Paraiyars participated, if at all, in servile ways. They went from village to village, shirtless, beating their *parai* drums, announcing the upcoming festivities. They spread mat after mat on the road in front of the chariot for the *ambalakars* to walk on, an ever-extending carpet. But they could never pull the divine chariot, touch its coir rope, or come near the chieftans—not even fall within their shadow. At least, that's the way the high-caste people saw it. Some Dalits claimed that before roads were paved, the higher castes had used them for sheer brawn to help move the chariot, and many resented their exclusion from the central ritual of the celebration.

Dalit politics gained momentum in the 1960s, and in 1979, a large group of Dalit men, mostly Pallars, contested the *ambalakars*' prohibition of their pulling the chariot. The Kallars pushed back, and this mounting tension eventually led to the controversy around the Aiyanar festival and to the attack on Chinna Unjanai.[8]

Padma and I wanted to see the magnificent temple more closely and connect with the disputed tradition of its procession, so we stopped to enter and to gaze at the black stone *murtis*. Shiva as Lord Swarnamoorti Eshwarar, guarded by the bull Nandi, stood in the deep recesses of the *garbha griha* (womb chamber) in the form of a *linga* marked with three horizontal lines of silver across the top, which glistened under camphor flames. To the side and less prominent, the domesticated goddess Sri Periyanayaki Amman (a local incarnation of Parvati) stood in her own chamber. Only the priests could go beyond the *margosa* leaves draped at the lintel of her vestibule.[9] One small camphor flame lit her room; by squinting, one could see the black stone figure of a goddess draped in a bright pink sari. Back outside, as our eyes adjusted to the blinding light, we gaped at the immense teak wood chariot, the height of six men, that was parked across the street. A tall, beefy man—a Kallar—emerged from a market stall and showed us the huge stone ball that was used as a brake against the chariot wheel. The stone was twice his weight and two feet in diameter. He crouched, hoisted it onto a shoulder, and stood. He could lift it fifteen times in a minute, he said, beaming: "*Cumma* (nothing)! It's like exercise!"

It was hard to picture devotees fighting to pull the wooden chariot (*tēr*) in the annual festival. Yet the newspaper *The Hindu* had reported that as recently as the previous year's festival, the state had issued Order #144, the Prevention of Detention Act. Police had fended off the Dalits who were trying to take the chariot's ropes, and they had made many arrests.[10] The Dalits, in response, had hoisted black flags over their houses. The tensions that had contributed to Dhanam's first experience of possession were alive and well.

The village around the temple was humble, picturesque, and sleepy in the midday heat. Traditional one-story Tamil homes lined up behind the temple, by order of caste, toward the fields and into the *kāṭu*, the uncultivated places. The Dalit hamlets lay just beyond the *nāṭu*, or "cultivated areas," in the wild lands, the *pālai* tracts. Beyond the hamlets, we wound through a patchwork of *pālai* and *marutam*[11] (agricultural fields), approaching Mātāpuram, Arlappan's village, and Dhanam's.

On the outskirts, small groups of people bent in the paddies. Most of the men and women of Mātāpuram worked as farmers: half of the population cultivated their own tiny land tracts; the rest worked as sharecroppers and tenant farmers. Given how hard it was to survive from such labor, many of the village men also worked in a cotton mill. We passed its gate and the big blue sign that hung from it announcing the Sree Kaderi Ambal Mills, Ltd. I craned my neck to look back as the paddy gave way to dry land. To untrained eyes, there was nothing in these rough fields but brush. Local eyes, I would soon learn, could see medicinal plants and spaces where ghosts wandered.

As we turned into a clearing and threaded our way down a narrow dirt lane, children came running from the scattered houses, barefoot, and surrounded us as we stepped out of the car. "Hello, auntie!" a few bold ones laughed, and ducked away. Others threw up their hands in mock salute, grinning. I greeted them in Tamil, eliciting a cacophany of wide-eyed giggles.

Our first line of business was to lunch at the home of our primary hosts, Arlappan's family, even though I was dying to see Dhanam. We found Arlappan's brother Aarokkiyam, who was thirty-five, dark, and compact with a thick moustache, busying himself with some work on the porch. The strong features that I remembered so well—protruding brow, buck teeth, eyes reddened by the sun—opened into a smile, and he hollered a greeting as we emerged from the car. Sahaya Mary, his wife, thirty, ducked out from under the thatch and beckoned us up the steps with an effusive "*Vaṅka, vaṅka*—come, come!" Her energy was as high as ever, but she looked gaunter than the last time I'd seen her: her eyes more piercing, her cheeks and collarbones more pronounced. We grabbed and held onto each other's hands. Sahaya Mary had had only one child when I first met her. Now there were three: Advin, two; Jency, three; and Olivia, five, all with short hair—Advin's shorn to his scalp—and clear, wide eyes. Sahaya Mary's thick hair, too, was just three or four inches long, short and wavy. She had offered it to the Hindu god Pandi Muni[12] some months ago, she explained, pulling on it with a laugh. Her quick, jerky, movements spoke of high spirits and excitability. Aarokkiyam and Arlappan's mother, Sebastiammal, a small, strong woman in her sixties, all smiles, emerged onto the porch, took my hands, and drew them to her face. Behind her came their grandmother, eighty-five, Ubakaram, hobbling over to wait her turn to take my hands, her cataract-eyes huge through thick glasses, her stretched earlobes dangling.

Their house was in the style of traditional, Tamil dwellings: a long mud-and-cement building stretched left and right, and a low thatch roof extended over the front porch. Aarokkiyam's widowed mother lived in a room off one end, and his grandmother and other extended relations lived in a room at the other. Each living space had its own open-air cooking area behind the house, separated from the other by a low mud wall. (They would later enclose the area as money allowed.) Across the lane was a small lot that the family owned, with a few chickens, a cow, an outhouse, and basic tools for plowing and leveling fields, made entirely of wood.

While Sahaya Mary bolted around preparing chicken and sambar, villagers came by to greet us: eighteen or twenty children and the few neighboring adults who were not in the fields. Many remembered me, though I did not remember them. Relieved that I could now talk to them in their native tongue, I still didn't understand every word of their rapid chatter. Arlappan went into the house and came out with a silky purple shawl, which he draped on my shoulders. Shawls were often given to honored guests in Tamil Nadu. I held lots of babies.

Suddenly Dhanam appeared. I hadn't seen her coming, shrouded as we were by the low roof of the porch. She ducked smoothly under it and sat on the stoop: it took me a split second to recognize her, it had been so long.

She was even more beautiful than I had remembered her (Figure 5.1). Dressed in a bright, periwinkle sari blouse and a rose-colored, flowered sari, she had wrapped its *pallu*, or long end, around her waist and tucked it into the left side, as was customary among fieldworkers. Her hair was tied in a tight, neat bun; her lips were full, her eyes bright and warm, her cheeks rosy, her skin glowing with health. She smelled of fresh soap. And what must she have thought of me, this once almost-mute *farangi*? We exchanged greetings and chatted briefly. She explained that she had work to do but that I would find her at her house; we would speak more later. She ducked back under the thatch and was gone, leaving a whirl of scents—sandalwood, musk, and rose.

Sahaya Mary served a big meal of chicken, sambar, and rice on banana leaves, and we ate mostly in silence, as was customary. Arlappan, Padma, and I—the guests—ate first. Sahaya Mary poured water from a tumbler over our right hands; there was no running water in the village. When we finished, she

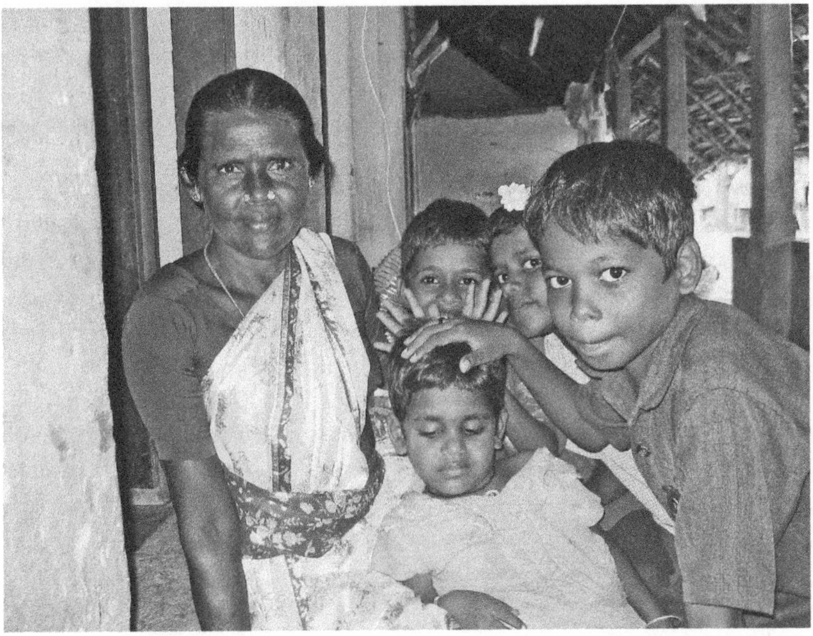

Figure 5.1: Dhanam with village children, 2005. Photo by author.

served the rest of the family in the inner room. Tamil tradition dictated that women eat last, after guests, men, and children, in that order; Sahaya Mary must have eaten eventually, but I wondered how much. She was, I knew, one of the people Dhanam had healed.

Like many social scientists and scholars of religion, I saw the phenomena of spirit possession as deeply imbedded in everyday practices. Relations with the spirits reflected and affected relations with other human beings and the norms that governed those relations in a given physical environment, and vice versa. In all my visits, I would approach the story of Mātāpuram with particular attention to people's work, relations of production, access to certain spaces, and the gendered relations that such work and access inscribed in bodies. I took "work" to mean not only paid work but also the labor of childbearing and child-rearing and the gendered meaning ascribed to such labor. I, meanwhile, would work at trying to understand what the villagers themselves said about their relations to the spirits of the place—the specific meanings people ascribed to their stories about Mātā, particular places, and the spirits that haunted them.

It was important to me, of course, to come equipped with as much understanding as possible of the forces—ancient and recent—that shaped villagers' sense of themselves and their places. The district in which Mātāpuram sat, Ramnad, had once been ruled by Hindu, Pandyan kings, and then, in the seventeenth and eighteenth centuries, by the Hindu Sethupathi kings of Ramanathapuram, a Maravar clan. These Hindu kings had successfully fought off the Muslims, who had been coming there to trade since as early as the sixth century. For a long time they also fought off Christian missionaries.

The key Christian player in the region was St. John de Britto, a Portuguese missionary. One of the Sethupathi kings had beheaded him, in 1693, and displayed his head impaled on a stake after de Britto made the mistake of telling the king that to convert to Christianity, he would have to send away four or five of his wives. Before running afoul of the king, de Britto had spearheaded a mass conversion movement in southeast Tamil Nadu.

In the end, though, the Sethupathi Hindus couldn't stop the British. The last king was deposed in 1795, and the British took over administration of the area. A revolt led to the imprisonment, and several hangings, of Indian rebels and leaders. For almost a century, from 1803, the British, with the help of the East India Company, used zamindars to manage the region.[13] Under "permanent settlement," these former rulers of kingdoms became gentlemen landlords of enormous estates who collected taxes from the peasants and gave a large portion to the British. The zamindari system ended as recently as 1892, when the British established their own tax collector. Meanwhile, however, the system had significantly reallocated power in the area as old and new orders competed for status and wealth, creating intense conflicts over temple honors.[14]

The Kallar caste, which was implicated in the festival violence at Kandadevi, as well as in the murders of the five Dalit men from Dhanam's nightmares, was officially categorized by the British, in 1918, as a "criminal tribe." Many individual Kallars, I knew, had struggled in the wake of this designation.[15] The word *kaḷḷar* in Tamil means, literally, "thief" or "deceitful person." Up until Independence in 1947, colonial officials habitually blamed Kallar men for cattle theft, blackmail, and highway robbery; they were fingerprinted, summoned for regular roll calls, and prohibited from leaving their villages without written permission whether or not they had been convicted of any crime.[16] Christian missionaries, meanwhile, stepped in during the early 1900s to develop agricultural reform settlements and a "modern" project of helping the Kallars refashion themselves. But the Kallars continued to internalize an identity as "savage" or "thieving," a self-concept that bore the deep imprint of colonial subjection. Now, from a rugged, outlaw existence on the arid southern plains of Tamil Nadu, they were trying to remake themselves as store owners and agriculturalists.

The British had oppressed the Kallars, and they, in turn, had oppressed, and—at the time of my writing—continued to oppress the Dalits. Yet I was climbing down the ladder of subjugation, into the world of Dalits, to inquire about a different kind of response to distress and persecution. How, if at all, might local idioms of spirit possession and healing—when taken on their own terms—express local knowledge about inherited hegemonies, social and bodily vulnerabilities, and specific women's responses to both? How might such knowledge expand our own materialist and psychological perspectives? What, if anything, might spirit possession practices and discourses in Mātāpuram reveal about the interrelatedness of bodies, memories, thoughts, feelings, and local landscapes—*tiṇai*—a type of home constituted by humans, natural phenomena, and ancestral and other spirits in that landscape? How might these possession practices and discourses shift relations between bodies—both at the microcosmic level of a family or of a small village, and at the macrocosmic level of the larger social, economic, natural, and nonmaterial world? Where, for that matter, does one body begin and end?

As I came to spend more time with the people of Mātāpuram, I came to realize their deep awareness of and heightened attunement to the incomplete and unjust nature of violent death and to the danger that women's bodies in particular faced at points of life transition in this world. I found myself inspired by the women's ability to persevere in the face of unthinkable odds and to live in intimate relation to one another with resourcefulness, resilience, self-worth, connectedness, and wholeness. Their possession practices expressed a kind of agency—a capacity, among other things, not only *to act* but also to be affected by injustice and violence and, in turn, to affect others. Their possession was a form of protest, against Brahmanical casteism, orthodox Roman Catholicism, and patriarchy, but it was also a way to empower, to provide hope, and to move energy that could otherwise be debilitating into vital pathways of self-care.

The bodily contagiousness of this movement of energy—this capacity to affect psychic, spiritual, and physical relations not only among healer and healed but also throughout wider communities of family and village—worked as a disruptive force in the face of violence that otherwise threatened to, and often did, overflow the brittle, fragile bounds of justice. This contagiousness and kinesthetic knowledge served to heal individual and communal memories of pain. In Chennai, at Our Lady Jecintho Prayer House, pain was related to fragmentation experienced in the tensive relationship between neo-capitalism and modernity, on the one hand, and the "old ways"—patrilocality, idealized gender norms, and notions about family, respectability, and home—on the other. Nancy's pain was likewise deep and related to convoluted family problems and expectations around marriage, status, and moving from adolescence to womanhood in modern Tamil society. Here in Mātāpuram, this embodied memory of pain was related to the history of the area—to the deaths of the five Dalits that Dhanam's community had witnessed—and to the pain of childbirth, the potential loss related to its dangers and to restrictions on women connected to this fear of loss and to the powers of fertility.

How did possession manage this healing? And who was this Mary, this Mātā, so central to the process of recovery, empowerment, and self-expression among Roman Catholic Dalits of Mātāpuram? How, if at all, was this Mātā different from the Mātā of Rosalind's Jecintho Prayer House or of Nancy's homegrown stigmatic protest?

WHAT THE VILLAGE SAID

In answering these questions, as with Rosalind's and Nancy's environs, the physical and social context of Dhanam's world mattered. So Padma and I went house to house, collecting formal surveys. We would eventually interview many of the patients whom Dhanam had treated in recent months, but we wanted a wider lens on the villagers, too: those who sought out Dhanam's help and those who didn't. We wanted a sense of the work they did, their standards of living, educational backgrounds, family histories, and religious affiliations and beliefs.

We conducted surveys in sixteen of the thirty-five households in Mātāpuram. The adults we interviewed were all either agricultural workers or mill workers, with the exception of one man who worked as a guard in the local health clinic. A number of men worked as migrant laborers, in places as far away as Malaysia and Singapore.

Most of the villagers, male and female, worked as farmers. Perhaps a dozen also worked in the cotton mill, where men were paid sixty rupees a day (about $1.50), and the married women, thirty rupees. Single women were paid fifteen rupees a day on a special scheme that promised thirty thousand rupees (about $680) at the end of three years if they didn't miss a day. Mill work had become less available owing to cheaper female labor from further away, so it was not uncommon for men from Mātāpuram to seek seasonal employment far from the village, even outside Tamil Nadu. Unlike the young women who came to the mill from afar, the women of Mātāpuram did not engage in migrant work. Like many of the men from the village, Dhanam's husband, Sebastian Samy, periodically went to Kerala for four to five months at a time. He worked at a small hotel with a staff of three. Excluding room and board, he was paid between eighty and ninety rupees a day, a good bit more than he would have earned at the mill. A few other men from Mātāpuram worked abroad.

The children of Mātāpuram were enrolled in local government schools and in Catholic schools, where some also boarded. (The system was similar to that of the British, ten-plus-two-plus-three pattern: ten years of primary and secondary education, followed by two years of higher secondary and three years of college education for a bachelor's degree.) Some of the teenagers we spoke to were studying for nursing or teaching. One young man said he wanted to join the army. (He later became an auto rickshaw driver.) Children tended to outdo their parents in educational status: most of the adults had never studied above eighth standard, if that, but many of their children had studied or were studying in the ninth, tenth, or twelfth standard.

Cross-generationally, people said that they didn't know how or when the village came to be. Generations before, many came, or were brought, to the area to work in agriculture for a rich landlord from the next district, who treated them very badly, some said, "like slaves." Their stories of the landlord's cruelty included beatings and starvation.

By all accounts, every person in the village was Roman Catholic or at least self-identified as Roman Catholic. I was never able to access baptismal records to confirm this. Part of the reason for the lacuna was that the village lay in a politically contested area in which there had long been tension and confusion between civil and religious jurisdiction. In 1987, Pope John Paul II created the Diocese of Sivagangai by Bull, severing it from the Madurai archdiocese to which it had belonged. The territory of the new Diocese of Sivagangai, with fifty-seven parishes, made up the two civil districts of Ramanathapuram and Sivagangai.[17] Also in the 1980s, civil district boundaries shifted, with accompanying disputes over whether civil or religious authorities should keep the records of various parishes. Local parish priests did not know where I would find baptismal records for residents of Mātāpuram (nor did the residents). To my knowledge, there was no written history of the village. This was itself a marker of the marginality of Mātāpuram. One priest, who was nationally famous for his social work among Dalits in the Hindu "sister" village to Mātāpuram, told me that he had not even known that there were Christians in Mātāpuram.

It was not at all clear how or when the people of Mātāpuram became Christian, but the older people of the village seemed to agree that they had been Christian for about five generations. This would be rather late in the history of Christianity in the region: Between 1640 and 1690, de Britto and another Jesuit, Antão de Proença (Paramandarswami) converted tens of thousands of people in the Ramnad area, often through mass baptism ceremonies.[18]

The people of Mātāpuram also didn't know how long there had been a church in the village, but they said that some sort of chapel had most likely been there as long as the settlement. The current building's stone marker noted that a Father Zacharias from Kerala built it in 1945. Men in a nearby village who had helped build the chapel said that Zacharias oversaw the transition of thatched-hut chapels in many Dalit villages to brick-and-mortar ones in 1945. The chapel in Mātāpuram originally had a bamboo thatch roof, they said, and that thatched hut had been built after a smaller one on the edge of the village, which had become a roadside shrine.

On Sundays, most villagers walked six kilometers to the diocesan parish church, Sahaya Annai Church (or Sahaya Mātā Church, as the people called it) in Devakottai.[19] The parish priest would make monthly visits to Mātāpuram to say Mass, and he would come for weddings or feast days. Otherwise, the prayers, the ringing of the bell, and other rituals were run by the catechist, a position that rotated among male villagers.

Almost all the people of Mātāpuram were either named after a particular form of Mary, had "Mary" in their name, or were named after a saint. All those we interviewed said they believed in Mātā. When we asked whether they believed in any particular *cāmi* (god) more than others, two answered "Mātā," and seven listed Mātā first over Jesus and the saints. Nine said they prayed to Mātā more than to any other god; two said they prayed to "Mary and Jesus"; three said they prayed to "Jesus"; and two said they prayed to "all the *cāmis*"—but "first we cross ourselves to Jesus."

We asked those who prayed to Mātā the most why they did so. "Because we pray to Mātā," came the circular answer. Or, "I don't know how to explain." Or simply, "I really like Mātā." Some prayed to Mātā to get results. "If I pray to Mātā, good things will happen." When asked whether they believed that Mātā ever "comes down on"—possesses—anybody, twelve answered yes, one answered no, and three said they didn't know. We asked those who said they believed that she "came down" why she did so, and they all said it had something to do with the body, with diagnosis or healing: "to heal others" they said, or, "if someone is sick and we ask what is wrong, Mātā will tell," or, "if a person's body isn't well, if a *pēy* has caught them, Mātā comes."

Toward the end of the interviews, we asked the villagers whether they believed that Mātā came down on Dhanam. Eleven answered "yes," two answered "no," and three answered, "I don't know." Ten said they had gone to Dhanam for healing at least once—two of those for childbirth. Eight said they believed in *pēy*, and four said they did not. Seven said that they or someone in their family had been caught by a *pēy*.

Everyone welcomed me kindly, and they often had their own questions. Was I "RC" (Roman Catholic)? Did I have family? Where were they? Did I believe in Mātā? I answered as honestly as I could, usually saying something like, "I believe that Mātā has a lot of *shakti,* and I am trying to learn more about her."

WHAT DHANAM SAID

After a few of these interviews, in the early evening of the day of our return in 2005, we found Dhanam at home, down the red dirt lane a few houses away from Aarokkiyam's house. She was by now forty-eight, and lived in a two-room house with her husband, Sebastian Samy, a mild-mannered man with compassionate eyes and a quiet demeanor who was ten years older than she. Their daughter, Sofia Mary, who was thirty, also lived with them, as did Sofia Mary's thirty-three-year-old husband, Peter Raj, and their two children, Chandana Mercia, eight, and Antony Daisy, five. Dhanam was watching the grandchildren when we arrived, and they played near her as we spoke. I was apologetic both about the long time that had passed since we'd seen her and about my Tamil. Last time, I'd hardly begun to learn the language and had spoken little, feeling "shy," I told her (lit. "shyness [*veṭkam*] came to me"). "This time I'll try to speak better," I said.

Dhanam was blunt. "Last time I understood everything you said in Tamil, but you did not speak well," she said. "This time I clearly understand you. Now, you are almost speaking well." We laughed, and Dhanam filled in a good bit of her story for me.

Her husband's mother had been born in this house, but her husband, Sebastian Samy, had been born in Pudukkottai, where his mother had married. His uncle, who had inherited the house, had no sons, and thus no inheritors, so he brought Sebastian Samy to Mātāpuram when he was six and raised him.

Dhanam was born not far from Mātāpuram, in the small village of Manapunjai, also mostly Catholic, near the better-known town of Puliyal. She had an older brother, a younger brother, and four younger sisters. Her parents were Roman Catholic and cultivated paddy. Her father, who had died many years ago, had been very religious and served as the village catechist. He had walked to Puliyal every day to see the statue of the Blessed Mother in a church dedicated to Mātā, and rang the bell at 6:30 in the evening.

The bell would start the prayers. He had trained all of his children to kneel and pray on the cement floor of the tiny chapel for an hour, or longer. He would keep adding to their prayers: petitions, petitions, petitions—there were so many needs! The children would be nodding to sleep, but he would keep pacing the chapel, saying the Rosary. When they finally went home, it was more prayer—family prayer for half an hour. Before bed, Dhanam's father would kneel and stretch out his hands, palms upward, for another ten or fifteen minutes. He showed great devotion to Mātā, and the villagers recognized it, showering him with honors at festival time. They would buy him a new set of clothes and have him walk in a place of distinction in the procession. He was poor himself, but he helped the poor through his catechism.

It was Dhanam's ill luck to be the eldest daughter of poor parents. Although her younger siblings went to school, Dhanam was sent away, at the age of seven, to live with her father's sister and brother-in-law in the Nilgiris, a rugged, hilly region of tea and coffee plantations. It was Dhanam's job to look after their son and do housework. Dhanam's older brother was also sent to live with relations. He worked in the fields and, like her, never finished school.

Meanwhile, Dhanam's younger brother and sisters attended a free government primary school and St. John de Britto Middle School, a Catholic school in Puliyal. Their father's brother, who worked in a mill, bought them books. Dhanam's younger brother would become a priest, studying in Rome and London before being assigned to Agra, in North India. Two of her sisters would marry, and the other two would become nuns, one working as a social worker, the other, the youngest, as a medical doctor, both far away.

At her aunt and uncle's house, Dhanam was neglected and did not have enough to eat. Dhanam's aunt sent her every morning to fetch milk from a distant estate. She had to climb two hills to get there. She would leave the house at six and return at about eight, traveling much of the way on a narrow path with tall coffee plants growing on each side. Sometimes a boar would jump out in front of her, but she had no fear. Rather than get scared, she would sing. "There was a Saint Anthony Church nearby, so I took courage," she said.

Yet the hardship of that daily journey over the Nilgiris hills—and the cruelty of her aunt and uncle—steeled Dhanam for the spiritual confrontations to come. "For me, *pēy* and *picācu* are like play toys," she told me. "I won't be afraid of anything."

Dhanam returned to the village of her birth, Manapunjai, when she was about fourteen because she was expected to reach puberty soon and marry. Within six months of getting her first menstrual period, at age sixteen, she was married to an older cousin by marriage, Sebastian Samy, whose mother's brother's daughter had married her own mother's brother's daughter. Like most of Dhanam's family, Sebastian Samy was an agricultural worker—a coolie (contract laborer) and a sharecropper.

In the early days of their marriage, both Dhanam and Sebastian Samy worked the fields. They owned an acre of land, but it was not cultivated, and so they worked on other people's land, clearing weeds for paddy. Sebastian Samy also occasionally found seasonal migrant work in Kerala.

At eighteen, Dhanam gave birth to her first child, a daughter. After the miscarriage that marked the onset of her possession by Mātā,[20] she bore three sons who lived. At the time of my 2005 visit with Padma, the eldest son was working in the cotton mill; the second was studying for the priesthood in Agra; and the youngest was studying in the eighth standard in a nearby convent school, also bound for the priesthood. The daughter, Sofia Mary, along with her family, was the only one of the four children still living with Dhanam and Sebastian Samy.

Dhanam didn't tell me the entire story of her possession by Mātā during that 2005 visit, at least not right away. I wanted to move gently, starting with simple questions such as whether her prayer and healing practices had continued as usual every Wednesday and Saturday over the past four years. (These were the same days that Rosalind held her prayer meetings.) The answer was "yes." "Talking to Mātā," Dhanam said, "healing sick people, seeing those who are *piṭi*—"plucked"—by *pēy*, those who are scared, chanting mantras—it is all still happening just as it did four years ago." But the practice had increased: during the past month alone, fifteen people had sought her care.

One woman of those who had come during the past month had been possessed by twenty-one *pēy*, Dhanam said. Unable to breastfeed her child and suffering from feelings of suffocation, she'd been in the hospital a full year, but had not found relief. I thought of Lata, from Rosalind's shrine, who had also felt like people were sitting on her chest. This woman, however, had started dancing (*āṭu*) in the church, and had sought out Dhanam. "She came here calling upon Mātā as her protection. Mātā saw that the *pēy* were on her. I drove them out. She stayed here for a month. Saturday, she left." Most of the people who came were women, Dhanam said, and most were newly married; had fertility or other problems related to childbirth; or were young, just past puberty, and marriageable. It surprised me to hear that most were Hindus, but Dhanam thought nothing of it. The majority religion of the population was Hindu, she pointed out with a smile and a shrug.

Men also came, suffering from *pēy* or black magic. "If they have black magic in their stomach, after suffering a lot and seeing lots of people for healing, finally they may come here." Through Mātā, Dhanam might diagnose, for example, three balls of black magic inside a patient. "These need to be taken care of by a Hindu practitioner," she said, a *mantravādi* (a mantra-sayer) or a *koṭuṅki* (a Hindu healer who works with small drums). She might tell them, specifically, to "blow and take medicine"—that is, to go to a healer who would say mantras and blow on patients' heads to rid them of black magic. The head and hair were often thought to be where *pēy* resided.[21]

One girl from Mātāpuram was still in the chapel that day, having stayed there the entire previous week. "She was affected by vomiting and loose motions, and it was uncontrollable," Dhanam said calmly, opening a palm upward on her knee. Before consulting Dhanam, the girl had gone to the hospital in Devakottai and received intravenous drips, but the problems had continued, the girl later confirmed. "She was behaving like a *paittiya* (a crazy person) running and talking," Dhanam said. "Then she was brought to the church. I knew that if she stayed here a week, she'd be all right. After I prayed for her, her diarrhea and vomiting stopped."

Usually, Dhanam said, she would chant mantras and tell the people seeking her help that they would be cured. "If it is not so, I will tell them that it will not work out and ask them to go to a doctor."

"They won't initially see a doctor?" I asked.

The first step for most families, Dhanam explained, was to take the patient to the doctor for an injection. "If they are not cured by that, they will be taken to the church. I'll chant mantras and, after that, immediately I will see Mātā and ask her whether it will be all right. She might say that it will be okay in three days." If the person is not cured in three days, Dhanam said, she will generally ask the family to take the patient right away to the hospital. But if there seems to be another problem—*piraccinai*—she can handle, "like a ghost problem (*āvi piraccinai*) or something like that," she will ask the patient to stay. "Mātā will cure them," she said. "Mātā will also come to heal some body problems. If they have a lot of belief (*romba nambikkai*), Mātā will come." This focus on belief—*nambikkai*—resonated with what Nancy and Rosalind had said. The internal world was dependent on the external, and vice versa.

Dhanam asked for nothing in return. People she cured might give something to the church—candles or paddy or money for upkeep—and they might offer something to Dhanam, she said, but "I'll not compel them to give. I'll take what they offer."

How did Mātā appear to her? What did she look like?

Dhanam paused. Her voice softened almost to a whisper. She came, Dhanam said, "carrying the child on her hip and wearing a crown. When she came like this, she usually did not come as *shakti* (feminine divine power)." What she meant, I later realized, was that Mātā appeared most often to her now as Velankanni Mātā, a more benign presence, as opposed to Adaikkala Mātā, who seemed to embody the fierce *shakti* required to exorcise spirits and to heal. This Adaikkala Mātā, the one whose statue was in the chapel, was the one who possessed Dhanam. "The Mātā here is Adaikkala Mātā. Most probably, Mātā comes to all as she is seen here."

I remained a bit confused about all these different Mātās until another visit, when I asked Dhanam about it in more detail.[22] But at present, one thing was abundantly clear: Dhanam worked hard, now, to summon Mātā. "I'll do one hundred and fifty *jeba mālai* (rosary prayers)," she said about her labors (referring to three rounds of the five decades of "Hail Marys" that usually comprise one Rosary). "With great dedication, after ten o'clock at night, I'll start saying the *jeba mālai*. I'll pray to God and ask about people's problems, saying that I don't know what they are. Then Mātā comes and says what to do." Mātā's lips will move, Dhanam said, as she gives instructions. Others will be present in the church when this happens, but Dhanam alone will see Mātā speaking and repeat what she has said.

Often, patients take a circuitous route to Dhanam, visiting not only doctors but also other healers first. "Those who do not have confidence [in Mātā] will not come," she said. "They will go first to a *koṭuṅki* or those who play *uṭukkai*," a small drum held in the palm of the hand and played with the fingers. It wasn't that Dhanam disapproved of the Hindu healers; after all, for specific problems, she sometimes sent patients to them herself. She just spoke matter-of-factly about how people searched for what worked for them, and suggested that many people waited too long to seek the help of Mātā. "After going everywhere they will finally come here. They'll have unbearable stomach pain."

Dhanam, then, was often a last resort. "Having been to so many places, they will ask me what Mātā says about their illness. I'll pray to Mātā and say [of the patient], 'She has suffered so many years,' and I'll ask her the reason. Mātā will say she has some specific problem."

Once Mātā specified the problem, the patient's pain often transferred to Dhanam. This, it seemed to me, was a form of kinesthetic knowledge,[23] an empathetic mimesis, or copy, within Dhanam's own body of the affected person's pain, used to discern and diagnose the problem. It was both the power of Dhanam's relationship to Mātā and her ability to empathize sensorily with her patient that allowed her to take on—and thus to expel—a patient's physical suffering. "However much I see Mātā, I will have their pain," is the way Dhanam put it. "After the pain comes to me, they will be all right." I would see the workings of this healing later that night.

Dhanam wouldn't provide patients with food or accommodations. Anyone who came from outside the village stayed in the church, accompanied by a friend or relative who cooked for them outside the church. It was not uncommon for patients to stay in the church for two weeks or more.

The patients were not passive recipients of Dhanam's care; like Rosalind, she assigned them rigorous spiritual tasks. "They won't stay idle," she said. "Every day they have to say 150 *jeba mālai*. I'll tell them, 'Ask Mātā. Tell everything to Mātā. You ask Mātā what you want; she will definitely give everything to you.'" Also like Rosalind, Dhanam encouraged the patients to develop their own strong relationship with Mātā. "I'll say, 'If you pray to her, just like she's telling me, she'll tell you too.'" Dhanam was generally disappointed in their capacity to summon Mātā, however. "After saying prayers, they will tell me that they were not able to see anything and ask me to see. I'll see for them because they were not able to see."

I'll see for them because they were not able to see. She was peering into a spirit world, it seemed, in a similar way that an ethnographer tries to peer into a distant culture. In Dhanam's case, she was entering into that world wholly; or rather, it was entering her. In my case, I was trying to enter, but could do so only partially, to expand the understanding of readers who could not travel to these places. In a more profound way, the healer was transforming a society, sending home oppressed, ailing, voiceless people—most often women, the lowest of the low—with a new experience of victory over malevolent forces, victory achieved through a feminine deity. Through Dhanam, Mary was being transformed from a Mary of colonizers to a Mary of formerly colonized subalterns—a Mary of suffering survivors.

History provides ample proof that early Christian missionaries colluded with colonialism and all of its violence—and that they also found creative ways to reach out to people across religious divides, creating new styles of Christianity in the attempt. The Italian Jesuit missionary Constantine Joseph Beschi, also known as Vīramāmunivar, or the "brave sage," introduced Adaikkala Mātā, or "Our Lady of Refuge," to India in the early eighteenth century.[24] At the Madura Mission, he adopted an Indian lifestyle, dressing in the saffron robes of the Hindu *sanyāsi* and writing poetry about Mary and Joseph in Tamil. He introduced this Adaikkala Mātā, a "localized" form of Mary, to the town of Elakurichi in Tamil Nadu during a devastating famine, when scores of Roman Catholics were converting to Danish Lutheranism in exchange for food. Soon after, rain came, the famine abated, and—according to Beschi's letters—many Catholics returned to the fold.

Today, though Adaikkala Mātā is sometimes represented with a child on her hip as Beschi had designed South India's first Mary statue (which he had brought to Konankuppam as Periyanayaki Amman, "The Great Princess"), she is generally depicted in her most famous form as she appears in Elakurichi: a young, light-skinned, dark-haired woman in native dress and dangling gold earrings, looking straight ahead, her arms outstretched, with no child.[25] Of the two Mary statues in the Mātāpuram chapel, the one of Our Lady of Fatima was an almost exact replica of the famous statue in Fatima, Portugal: light-skinned, swathed in blue and white robes, head bowed, hands lowered and slightly outstretched in blessing. The Adaikkalam statue, also without child, was less exact than to the "original" in Elakurichi: no earrings, hands pressed together under the chin in a gesture resembling either Christian prayer or the Indian greeting "namaste." However, like the reported original, she was swathed, each time I saw her, in a pink and gold silk sari (also like the Hindu goddess Periya Nayaki Ammaṉ in Kandadevi). Both of the statues in the chapel wore fresh floral garlands and crowns.[26]

Dhanam believed that all three of the hundreds of forms of Mātā found in Tamil Nadu—Velankanni, Fatima Mātā, and Adaikkalam—were only one (*orē*) Mātā, though she manifested in different ways at different times and places. This belief is quite like the commonly held idea among Hindus that the Goddess, Devi, though manifesting in innumerable ways throughout the world, is also always one: *shakti*.[27]

As the afternoon waned and we all relaxed into the conversation during that first visit to Dhanam's house in 2005, I grew bold enough to ask Dhanam where she understood the agency to lie when she "drove" the *pēy* out of her patients. It must have taken tremendous power to expel twenty-one *pēy* out of the woman who had recently come to her for healing. Had she driven out the *pēy* as Mātā, or as Dhanam?

While the woman danced, "I drove them out as Dhanam," she said. "Mātā tells me to do particular things and drive them out. I drive them out." She was only a conduit, she explained, to diagnosing the problem. She alone could not solve the mystery of the woman's ailments; she had to ask Mātā to "look into it." After she prayed to Mātā, she said, the *pēy* came to her and she drove them out. "Her chest pain and stomach pain were also cured."

But I was confused—and slightly disturbed. Here I had come all this way thinking that Dhanam was possessed by Mātā. Yet it was sounding increasingly as though Mātā simply appeared to her in a vision, spoke to her, and told her what to do. Had I distorted my findings by projecting my own exotic hopes onto Dhanam? If so, my whole thesis—the ideas powering my years of study and travel to India—would be busted. It didn't help that Rosalind and Nancy had held true to my idea that rural possession practices had migrated from places like Mātāpuram, far from the metropole, to places like Chennai. If not, who was to say that the possession practices I had witnessed in Chennai—the urban phenomenon—hadn't arrived through global networks of money, power, and trade to the village, rather than the other way around? At stake here was the question of full-on possession versus mere channeling, séance-style. Padma, to my luck—and to her credit—asked the next question.

"When Mātā comes to you, are you yourself, or are you another? Who speaks?"

"I know who I am, and I know what I speak," Dhanam said. "If I remember myself like that, Mātā won't come. Also, if I am unable to tell who you are, a *pēy* has come (to you). But when Mātā comes onto me, if others ask me to tell them what I said, I don't remember; I don't know."

When Mātā comes onto me. Here she was using the language of what we Euro-Americans (and English-speaking Indians, like Rosalind's father Charles) call "possession"; when Mātā comes, Dhanam is not conscious of herself and does not remember what she said. "If you then tell me what I said, only then I'll know. I'll think, 'Really? Mātā has spoken like that?'" She knew it was a *pēy* that was troubling a patient if it became hard for her to see—identify or differentiate—either the patient or the *pēy*. When she was in a state of what we call possession, however, she was unaware of herself. "Having seen Mātā, I won't know what I've said," she said.

Normally, of course, Dhanam would remember what people told her. Just as any modern, urban professional has to keep track of clients, supervisors, sources, or customers, Dhanam had to do business with her patients; despite the spiritual core of her practice, she had to be accountable, reliable. "If you tell me some problem you are having, and ask me to ask Mātā about it, and come the next day to find out what she said, I'll remember that. I have to speak to you, and ask Mātā, and remember that, and tell you the next day."

I was still somewhat confused. It seemed that Dhanam was talking about two different states: one in which she was possessed by Mātā and unaware of herself and one in which she was visited by Mātā and retained self-consciousness and memory. She seemed to use both states for purposes of healing. I made a note to listen to the taped interview again carefully, and to return to deeper questions in later meetings.

But for now, it was time to go to the chapel for evening prayers, and to see Dhanam's healing practices in action.

EVENING *MANTIRAM*—PRAYERS

Darkness fell quickly upon Mātāpuram. It was 7:30 p.m., and Sebastian Samy, Dhanam's husband, was leading Padma, Dhanam, Aarokkiyam's mother, and me from his house to the chapel. His flashlight slashed across a gravelly dirt path, picking out rocks and divots to avoid, illuminating bright bits of *noccilli* (a medicinal plant) and grass. The smell of wood- and dung-burning fires lingered in the air. We turned left on a path near Aarokkiyam's and entered a clearing. Sebastian Samy's light jumped ahead of us across the stubble grass to the chapel. Dim light flickered through its windows.

My eyes began to adjust as we crossed below the *margosa* leaves hanging over the lintel. The chapel had two rooms: a front room—a sort of sitting room, or front hall—and an inner room, which housed the altar. Entering the inner room, I could make out the silhouettes of a handful of people—women, by the drape of their saris—sitting on the floor and holding the candles whose light I'd seen through the windows. I couldn't make out the statues on the altar, but their shadows danced on the walls. I knew from earlier visits, though, that the two of Mary—Our Lady of Fatima and Adaikkala Mātā—held center stage, flanked by statues of other saints. The altar, many tiered in a common Tamil style, was unlike most others in that it held no icon of Jesus or of God-the-Father. Adaikkala Mātā, although the smaller and lower of the two Mary statues, was the more central figure, housed in a tall glass box adorned on top with three metal crosses. She and the smaller statues were draped in silk. A tall camphor lantern stood the height of the altar, on the floor to its left—part of the same ritual paraphernalia that Rosalind used and that was used in Brahmanical Hindu temples.

As my eyes adjusted, I could see by the candlelight and lantern that one of the women in the corner was young, maybe in her late teens or early twenties; one, a bit older, was pregnant; another was middle-aged; two were elderly. Dhanam walked quietly, barefoot, to the altar and knelt, placing the *pallu* of her sari over her head. We knelt behind her and to one side. Aarokkiyam's mother, behind me, whispered urgent Tamil prayers. The young woman approached Dhanam and knelt directly behind her, holding a lit candle. Dhanam's eyes closed, and her lips moved rapidly as she chanted a silent prayer. She held her palms up, close to her body, just below the shoulders. It seemed an intense, tightly controlled form of prayer. No drama.

It was very hot in the chapel, and there was no breeze. The women's candles and the oil lamp seemed to heat the room inordinately—or perhaps it was only the clay walls radiating the stored heat of the day. Shadows played on the wall. The young woman behind Dhanam looked thin and limp—her shoulders sagged—but she knelt stoically, waiting, holding her guttering candle. She seemed to know the routine.

After a few minutes, Dhanam turned, still kneeling, and faced the young woman, whispering something I couldn't hear. Then she told her to put her candle out with her tongue. The young woman extended her tongue, flat, as if a doctor was about to insert a tongue depressor, and touched it to the burning wick. The candle hissed and went out. I could smell the burnt wax as Dhanam tapped the top of the young woman's head lightly, with her fingertips, three times.

The young woman moved to the side, another woman knelt, and the process was repeated until all the women had extinguished their candles with their tongues and had received Dhanam's taps.

Within a half hour, Dhanam was on her way home to make a light supper. Nobody chatted or stood about; they retreated quietly into the shadows. There had been no dancing, no rending of clothing or loosening of hair, nothing but the quiet prayer and tongue-extinguished candles. Dhanam seemed to have calmed the chaos that had visited in her early reproductive years. The evening ritual of candle dousing was perhaps unusual among Roman Catholic practices—I had seen Hindu practitioners smack out camphor flames with the palms of their hands as ritual specialists exorcised them of *pēy*, or pierce their tongues with spikes during trance; colleagues had told me about Hindu, possessed women extending their tongues to have a lit piece of camphor placed on it, which they would then swallow. This act was part of a repertoire of practices that helped devotees and mediums identify a possessing spirit as benevolent (*cāmi*) or malevolent (*pēy*), and was sometimes, but not always, one element of an exorcism or removal (*kalippu*) of that spirit.[28] The candle-flame-eating scene in the chapel also reminded me of practices I had read about among devotees of Pomba Gira, an Afro-Brazilian spirit entity, in Brazil, in which a possessed woman "ate" lit cigarette after lit cigarette.[29] But neither I, nor anyone else I knew or whose work I had read, had ever seen candles used, at least not in India, in this way, by Hindus or Catholics. The women in the chapel seemed unfazed. The rite, in the end, seemed no wilder than the stateliest evening mass in Connecticut, Chicago, or Rome.

It was time for Dhanam to tuck her grandchildren into bed and pray her Rosary. As devoted a Roman Catholic as her father had been, she started prayers each night at eleven and ended two hours later. Nobody attended her night prayers; they were hers alone. "You cannot see that prayer," she told me, a cue for our exit. "No one can see." It was her time to cultivate her personal relationship with Mātā.

Outside the chapel, we bid Dhanam goodnight.

WHAT SHE SAID LATER ABOUT THE CANDLES

The next day, Dhanam described to Padma and me a few reasons behind the use of the candles. The first was simple: "Mātā likes them. That is most important."

Second: "It is punishment." Finally, the functional explanation: "The tongues of those who are possessed by evil will be burnt and the *pēy* will be driven out."

As candles go, these were nothing special: thin white tapers, bought from local shops, Dhanam explained. It was what they revealed that was key. "One should stand holding the candle," she said. "If we stand or kneel holding the candle, Mātā will see the *pēy* in that light." That is, Mātā will not only see the *pēy* but also recognize it, and reveal the *pēy*'s identity to Dhanam. This was all part of the process of divination, identification, and of driving out the now-recognized and, thus, now-disposable malevolent or mischievous spirit. Candles were lit regularly in the chapel, of course—at least two daily at the altar, Dhanam said. But if a person came to the chapel with very strong *pēy*, Dhanam would use one of those candles to light fifty or sixty more, one by one—which she would hand to the *pēy*-possessed person, who would put them out, one by one, with her tongue. (The women we had witnessed the night before, dousing one candle each, clearly did not have such strong *pēy*.) "For example, if a *pēy* is with me, that is the punishment given by Mātā," Dhanam said. "When the candle is burning, it has to be put out, using the tongue. Not all at once—but one by one they have to be put out. After putting them out, that *pēy*, afraid of getting burned, will leave. This is the punishment."

So Mātā is the disciplinarian. But *whom*, exactly, is being punished—the *pēy* or the woman? And for what? The *pēy* was being punished, Dhanam clarified. Still, it seemed to me I had stumbled onto slippery ground—for women who got *pēy* (and who got them more often than men, and for different reasons) became so afflicted only after transgressing some social norm specific to their gender, particularly during periods in their life when they were understood to be most vulnerable sexually. This had become clear in Dhanam's own story about transgressing a boundary while pregnant—stepping into Hindu territory and entering open water to fish—and it would become even more clear from Sahaya Mary's story, which I would hear shortly, as well as those of countless other young and newly married women whom we interviewed. I again recalled Lata from Rosalind's prayer house and Nancy's being interviewed by the Charismatic brothers.

Meanwhile, still focused on the candle-dousing rituals, Padma asked whether it was customary for clients coming to the chapel to hold lit candles. Dhanam answered that it was indeed customary—and immediately, without prompting, compared the practice to exorcisms among Hindus, who used wicks fueled by camphor. "Yes, Hindus, by doing a lot of things, drive out the *pēy*. But no, we can't do it like that. Candles are more liked by Mātā—that *pēy* gets controlled by that candle. It controls *pēy*. We will not use camphor."

This would be but one of a number of instances in which Dhanam would explicitly differentiate her own practices (and Mātā's preferences) from similar ones generally understood to be Hindu. This "similar-but-different" theme came up repeatedly in her narratives about spirits and deities that entered the village, and about the practices associated with them—and seemed key, even, to their efficacy. Perhaps she and her clients needed to feel that her healing practices—and Mātā's—differed from others in Hindu traditions so that hers could be considered more distinctly "another option," a different "brand." However, her practices could not be so different as to be unrecognizable from those more widespread practices of Hindu mediums, *cāmis*, *vaittiyars*, and *mantravādis* also popular in the area. Dhanam's practices had to be recognizable among Hindus as well as Catholics, in order to fit local understandings of efficacious healing and exorcism, and to translate as authentic. I would hear more of this "similar-but-different" discourse later, as Dhanam narrated to me, in precise detail, the specific experiences she had undergone in the early years of her possessions by Mātā, differentiating one sort of experience, and one sort of god, spirit, or goddess, from another. I would also begin to see more similarities and differences between her discourses and practices and those of Rosalind and Nancy, as well as similarities and differences between all three of these women and the ordained Catholic priests whose practices they were also mimicking and appopriating. In each of these cases—Catholic and Hindu, lay person and priest—healers and exorcists were using "similarity-with-difference" to their advantage.

But one significant difference between Dhanam and the other two women would soon emerge. While Mātā was absolutely, literally central to the villagers of Mātāpuram, another figure was just as important, though peripherally. His name was Aiyanar, the Hindu warrior god whose temple and statue, in the form of a terra-cotta horse, Dhanam had passed, during her second, doomed pregnancy, at the onset of her troubles. Aiyanar is a patroller of boundaries, and his temple, along with his many *muni* minions, stood at the edge of the next Hindu village. He and his *munis* were always ready to do battle with Mary. Where they stood, arguably, the Roman Catholicism of Mātāpuram ended. Or began.

In a subsequent visit, in 2012, Dhanam and I would delve deeply into the chaotic, tragic period of her early possession—and Aiyanar and his lesser minions, the *munis*, would figure as antagonists even more fundamental than the *pēy*. I had more digging to do in the fertile ground of the villagers' experience of Dhanam, of these *munis*, and of the Mātā who "came down on" Dhanam to battle with them. Aside from Dhanam, the villager who had experienced perhaps the most intimate and frightening contact with a *muni*, and who had been attended to by Dhanam, had been my own host, Sahaya Mary.

CHAPTER 6

Women's Work

Gendered Space and the Dangerous Labor of (Virgin) Birth

Padma and I both worried about Sahaya Mary. She was all angles—bony, nervy, high-spirited—and jumping up to care for everyone at the slightest need: her husband; her mother-in-law, who scolded her to move more quickly; her eighty-five-year-old grandmother-in-law; her three children; the goats; a cow (which gave little milk); a small patch of paddy field; and now, us—all on a shoe-string budget that allowed her little room to rest, let alone eat the proper food that she was supposed to cook for everyone. The monsoon rain was pouring down on the fields, and she was more housebound than usual—though she still bolted outside occasionally to tend to the cow and chickens. Still, she generously sat with Padma and me one afternoon for a long interview. The dark storm infiltrated the room with soggy air. Her children sat with us on the floor. Her youngest, two-year-old Advin, sat naked on her lap. The girls, Jency, who was three, and Olivia, who was five, pretended to be taking notes on their tiny outstretched palms just like Padma and me, who held notebooks. Rain pinged on the tin overhang of the veranda and plopped into the cooking pit adjacent to room where we sat. Pistachio paint peeled off the inner walls, on which hung a Marian calendar and a metal folding chair.

Sahaya Mary had been "plucked" (*piṭi*) by Pandi Muni, the bachelor god believed to impregnate virgins and newlyweds, when she was five years old—though she didn't know it at the time. Pandi is one of the seven *munis* ruled by the comparatively greater god Aiyanar; his title *munisvarar* can be translated as "he who is awakened, having realized Isvarar (another name for Shiva)."[1]

Much like Shiva, Pandi Muni—or *Pāṇṭicāmi*, as he is affectionately called—is a purveyor and administrator of souls, both living and dead. In this area around Madurai, where his main temple is located, he is also understood to be particularly hungry for virgins, to whom he gives children through intercourse.[2] It was his temple I had visited so many years before on the field trip organized by my Tamil language program, packed into bus 42, so it wasn't the first time I had heard about him. But some details were new. For example, I learned that he didn't necessarily manifest his occupation of a person right away: though he had "plucked" Sahaya Mary when she was five, he had lain "fallow" for twenty years, only manifesting his presence on the first night of her marriage. Suddenly, far from her natal family and alone with her husband, she had started "dancing" and exhibiting many symptoms of possession. Dhanam quickly diagnosed these, during exorcism sessions, as caused by Pandi.

Sahaya Mary explained to us that she had been out grazing goats, as was common on school holidays, when Pandi plucked her. Even at age five, she had been too beautiful for him to resist.

"Now I am like this," she said with a laugh, throwing a bony hand toward her face. "In my childhood, I was beautiful." She had been dark and wide-eyed, with delicate features. It had been a free and happy time; she had loved roaming the open areas, grazing the goats with the other children. Then she hit puberty.

By the age of twelve, like most of her female peers, she was no longer allowed to run freely through the *pālai* grazing lands. She was unaware of having been "plucked" so young—she had felt nothing, and had no memory of any strange sensations. Still, Dhanam's later diagnosis made sense. *Pēy* and other mischievous or volatile spirits, especially in this area around Madurai, where Pandi's main temple is located, are often thought to pluck beautiful young girls, newly pubescent girls, and new brides, the latter of whom give off a *maṇam* (fragrance) of sexual activity.[3]

Sahaya Mary was well known among villagers as a woman who had been troubled by spirits. Many had similar stories—as did women who came to Dhanam from outside seeking help. Her story, like theirs, revealed how gendered norms of purity and pollution, gendered notions of space, and the work connected to these norms and spaces, were linked to the experiences and local hermeneutics of possession. Key to these stories was the common experience of brides moving outside the safe, familiar confines of home and their natal families to the villages and families of their husbands after marriage. This move was often experienced as a source of great stress, even danger. These themes of fear, danger, and deliverance echoed not only in Sahaya Mary's story, but also in those of younger women facing new levels of education and work, older women who policed some of these younger ones, and Dhanam's own stories—including that of the "stone baby."

WHAT SHE SAID

Sahaya Mary came to Mātāpuram in 1999, right after her marriage to Aarokkiyam at the age of twenty-five.[4] She was one of two children born to a poor Paraiyar Roman Catholic farming couple from Kadiapatti, a village about an hour's drive north of Mātāpuram. She and her husband lived off his three-quarters of an acre of land that they farmed together, occasional manual labor, and the sixty rupees a day that Aarokkiyam made at the local cotton mill.

Aarokkiyam himself had had a tough life. He had left school after seventh standard, when his father died; as the eldest son, he needed to work to support the family. The face of his mother Sebastiammal, which seemed built around her smile, could just as easily collapse into despair when she recalled that time. Her children—Aarokkiyam, Arlappan, and her daughter, Arokkiya Mary—had been quite young. She continued to look after the farming while Aarokkiyam went to work in the local cotton mill, making twelve rupees a day. When a friend and coworker told him that there was construction work to be found in Hyderabad, he left for that northwestern city. Then the local mill wages rose by three rupees a day. Hearing the news, the friend returned—without Aarokkiyam. "He had no money for the return journey," his mother recounted. "We didn't know where he was staying. He was not even paid coolie wages for his work. After a year he was brought in a white Jeep like a dead body. He was unconscious. His brother (Fr. Arlappan) came home on his holidays and admitted him to the hospital. We borrowed money and got him treatment."

After Aarokkiyam had recuperated, the family looked for a bride. Sahaya Mary's family in Kadiapatti, like many local Catholics, put equal faith in Mary and many of the beliefs of their Hindu neighbors, such as black magic and astrology. Bad luck had been chasing them for years. For one thing, Sahaya Mary had been born under the planet *cevvai* (Mars). An astrologer the family consulted told them she had "*cevvai dōsham*"—the inauspicious ascendant on the position of Mars in the seventh house in her horoscope. It was generally believed that only when both a husband and bride have *cevvai dōsham* can they live together. As it happened, Aarokkiyam had also been born with *cevvai dōsham*, and his family was looking for a bride who likewise had it.

Aarokkiyam and Sahaya Mary were also found to be related through a distant aunt. Endogamous marriage is an ideal in Paraiyar families, as it is in many South Indian communities. Aarokkiyam and Arlappan traveled to Kadiapatti to view Sahaya Mary, and to propose marriage. It should have been good enough for Sahaya Mary that Aarokkiyam's brother was a priest, and that they were related with similar astrological charts. During the visit, Sahaya Mary kept her eyes averted as she was supposed to, but caught a glimpse—and did not like what she saw. "I don't want to get married," she told her parents after he left. "I don't like him. I don't like him at all." (She came to understand later that it was Pandi Muni that made her say this.) Her family scoffed at her pickiness and accepted the proposal. But the next day, when her brother went to his carpentry job he fell seriously ill. The family attributed this illness to Muni. Two days later, Sahaya Mary walked to Velankanni to ask for her brother's healing and to get Mātā's blessings on her marriage. She vowed that if Ārōkkiya Mātā (the form of Mary at Velankanni) healed her brother and blessed her marriage, she would remain a devotee forever. But her brother remained bedridden (as he would for seven years), and her sister-in-law also became mentally ill. Sahaya Mary's vow did not seem to be enough for Ārōkkiya Mātā to rid the family of this black magic.

After the wedding, Sahaya Mary accompanied Aarokkiyam to Mātāpuram, as per custom. They carried her dowry with them—a few jewels, a cot, and a bureau. At first, she wanted desperately to return to her mother's house for visits. Her mother was taking care of her brother; she felt guilty not being there to help, and she missed her family. Both families forbade her to return home.

Here Sahaya Mary's story turned to marital and conjugal problems. "During our first night, Pandi Muni slapped *(aṭi)* my husband," she said—meaning that *she,* Sahaya Mary, had slapped him physically—though it was Pandi who made her do it. She and her husband did not have sex. "During that first night Pandi Muni did not allow us to get united," she said. "I felt a burning sensation." Her whole body became hot, and her arms and legs felt like pillars. "I didn't want him. I pushed him."

Back in 2005, as the rain pattered on the roof during our first long interview, Sahaya Mary wanted to show me and Padma her scars. "My bangles broke and made me bleed," she said, holding out her forearms raked by thin dark lines. As her husband had tried to force himself on her that first night many years ago, she said, she had been talking excitably, "It was like I was talking to another man. My husband thought I had taken some lover. He got a doubt, and he beat me."[5] The "man" she had been talking to before her husband beat her, she said, was Pandi,[6] though she had been beside herself and unaware that it was him.

The next day, Aarokkiyam complained to Sahaya Mary's parents, who came to collect her. Back home in Kadiapatti, she "danced" for three days in the house, moving wildly, her hair loose. Her parents returned her straight to the Mātāpuram church, where she continued to dance. The villagers called Dhanam, who called upon Mātā, who made it clear: the problem was Pandi.

And the problems didn't stop. Outside the marriage bed, if Sahaya Mary even *saw* a man, she thought she would vomit. She would get very angry, very fast. She flew into rages unbecoming a new bride. Then, in October (her wedding had been in September), while she was distributing *maḻai cōru* (the "rain rice" that Roman Catholics bless and pray over for rain),[7] a dog bit her on the behind. This was a particularly inauspicious sign. Villagers told her to go straight to the village church. She did, intending to sleep there that night on the floor. Again, she started dancing wildly (*āṭam*). Again, Dhanam came—and Mātā came on Dhanam.

Mātā announced that the problem was twofold: Sahaya Mary was both possessed by Pandi Muni, who had grabbed her when she was five, and by the spirit (*āvi*) of her father-in-law, who had "come on" her when she moved into her husband's house. These two types of beings—*munis*, which are deities, and *pēy* or *āvi*, which are spirits of humans—operate quite differently, in village reasoning.

A *pēy* or an *āvi*, Dhanam later explained to me, may create trouble for a woman in her marriage or make her sick, but it will not literally separate a husband and wife physically by trying to have sex with the wife. Pandi Muni, on the other hand, will literally block the couple's conjugality—he will not allow them to join (*cēr*)—so that he can lay claims to the wife. (This understanding is true for both many Hindus[8] and Christians in the region.)

Diagnosed with this twofold source of trouble, Sahaya Mary stayed in the village church for two weeks. She chanted mantras. She had heard that some people called these *jebam*, or prayers, and that some people called them *jebam mālai*, "garland of prayers," or "rosary." She called them *mantiram*. It was all the same to her. These *mantiram*, like Hindu *mantiram*, were meant to undo the harm of another sort of *mantiram*—the kind said to inflict black magic. After much chanting, Sahaya Mary's father-in-law left her and allowed her to return home to sleep. But Pandi, it seemed, was still on her: she was still experiencing trouble with her husband; she was still getting angry in his presence—a sure sign. Again, she came to the church and danced. This time Mātā came on Dhanam and told Sahaya Mary to go to the Pandi Muni temple in Madurai and do offerings (*arccaṉai*) to him; only then might Pandi leave her. Furthermore, Mātā said, she would get pregnant only through Pandi. The warrior god had been safeguarding her; she would have been long dead without him.

In October the couple boarded the bus to Madurai. Halfway to the Pandi Muni temple, she could feel the god in her. "When the boundary stone of that temple came, automatically I started dancing," she told me and Padma. "It happens to everyone." Then, also along with most everyone as the bus came to a halt, she jumped off and started running—across the street, through the woods (*kāṭu*), and toward the temple, yelling "Hai Yuiiii!"

The family bought garlands and coconuts and worshipped Pandi. "We did everything as per Hindu custom," she said. Only if she came to this temple would she be given a child, Mātā had told her—and so it was believed about Pandi: he gave women children through "virgin birth." He would take a woman as his lover and have sex with her. Some women have talked explicitly about the orgasmic union that occurs being visited at night by Pandi.[9] Some of these women believe that Pandi is the true father of their child. Sahaya Mary and Aarokkiyam, however, both believed that Aarokkiyam was the father of their children, not Pandi, though Pandi had "seen to it." Despite the violence Sahaya

Mary had endured, Pandi had helped her to fight back—and he had blocked Aarokkiyam until Sahaya Mary was ready.

"After going to the Pandi temple, my daughter was born," Sahaya Mary continued—her first child. It was a very complicated birth, and Sahaya Mary was in severe pain. She had planned to have the child at home, as most Mātāpuram women do. Her sister-in-law was seeing to it. But during labor, all she could see was the child's head: it would not come out. It was too late to go to the hospital; choices were few. "When the baby would not be born at my house, I was brought to Dhanam's house and left there. Here," she said, looking around the small dingy room where we were sitting, "my father-in-law [his spirit] did not allow me to stay. I was scared. If I saw anyone I was scared. I was scared to stay in this house. So they brought and left me in Dhanam's house." There, she started to relax, she said—and Dhanam served as midwife. Dhanam found the umbilical cord wrapped around the baby's neck, but she maneuvered quickly, and Sahaya Mary delivered successfully. "If I had been taken to the hospital, I would have had a Caesarean." She or the child might have died. "But after a lot of suffering, I delivered. It was because of God."

It was also because of Dhanam, who delivered Sahaya Mary's next child as well. The third pregnancy, however, was even more complicated than the first. Dhanam recommended that Sahaya Mary go to the hospital, where she gave birth to a healthy boy.

Dhanam, it turned out, had delivered at least twenty babies in Mātāpuram. Among her clients were local women as well as women from outside the village. While midwifery was not her main practice—the number of visitors seeking other sorts of healing far outnumbered deliveries—birthing stories were among the many that she, Sahaya Mary, and other villagers told as signs of her reliable skill and abilities.

The stories offered yet more proof, albeit at times very troubling proof, that local beliefs and practices around women's fertility, Marian spirit possession, and gendered spaces—places restricted from women, especially at particular times in their life cycles—were all intimately connected. More than connected: they spoke to the ways in which women could act not only as caretakers, healers, and liberators to one another's pain, but also as carriers of continued oppression and policers of women's freedom. They did this, perhaps, in part, because of the very tenuous nature of their lives in the landscape of poverty and environmental conditions in which they lived, the conditions that both enabled and constrained their movements, the scarcity of choices available to them, the tight grip men held on them through patrilocal practices that separated women from their kin, and the physical violence those men could wield.

A DANCE OF (AT LEAST) TWO

Some scholars argue that exorcism and possession practices simply reinculcate women into the very structures of oppression that limit them—defusing stressful situations to achieve the larger goal of redomesticating women back into the world of normative female behavior.[10] In contrast, I am arguing that Mātā offered women ways, often in back-and-forth microsteps, to renegotiate their relationships to various forms of power. This didn't mean that they would escape their oppression; life is seldom so simple. Sahaya Mary was still beaten, and she eventually had sex with the husband who beat her. But Marian possession and exorcism practices did allow women to maneuver along a spectrum of possibilities that were always shifting. These strategies were rooted in the material and social body, and in the material and social body's interaction with the supernatural world, which was real for these women and which had real effects.

Because Sahaya Mary's husband believed that she was possessed by Pandi, for example, she was able to avoid having sex with him for a long period while the two negotiated their relations. Through the idiom of spirit possession, she was able to draw attention to herself and to her troubled marriage, to bring her problems out of the bedroom and into the more public sphere. She was able to get attention from her natal family, from Dhanam, and from fellow villagers. She was able to dance and sleep in the Mātāpuram chapel, ride a bus to the Pandi temple outside Madurai, and mix and talk with other women having similar difficulties. She was able to escape work for a time.

She was, in short, able to work more equilibrium and safety into her life, and she was able to establish intimate relations with Dhanam and with other women in ways that aided her at other life-and-death moments like illness and childbirth. She did all this with the help of Mātā and the spirits who roamed Tamil land—and they did it with her.

I call this a dance of "at least two" because, for Sahaya Mary and most of her fellow villagers, the deities and spirits were as real as the stones in the fields and the rain in the tanks from which they drew water. Meanwhile, the social body that interacted with this supernatural world—the body of Sahaya Mary, the bodies of her fellow village women, and the body of the village—did so within a symbolically constituted spatial and temporal environment, which in turn produced the body's practices and dispositions.[11]

WORK IN MĀTĀPURAM

The environment within which women and men moved in Mātāpuram was centered around work, and not just the work that produced what little economic capital they had, but also the work that produced social and cultural capital: the very real labor of childbirth, housework, caring for children and the elderly, and instilling moral teaching. This moral teaching involved creating dispositions in relation to spaces and times connected to the production and end of life—childbirth (including menstruation and marriage) and its opposite, death.

To understand Sahaya Mary's experience, then, it was necessary for me to understand the gendered divisions of labor, the spaces that demarcated that labor, and the rules governing behavior around purity and pollution in relation to both spaces and labor—especially since the villagers themselves spoke of these rules in relation to their experiences of possession. To be clear: the analytical frame of *akam* and *puṟam* is mine, gleaned from Tamil *Caṅkam* poetry,[12] a poetry that was generally written by and for, and that is still known by, educated elites. The words *akam* (inside) and *puṟam* (outside) did not come up in village conversation until I asked villagers about them. While the *Caṅkam* poems' relation to the contemporary social order, let alone any ancient one, is a matter of some guesswork, many scholars have argued that this literature continues to reflect and codify cultural attitudes that remain pervasive in Tamil society today.[13] Whatever words we use to frame our analysis, we can say with certainty that there is a long tradition in Tamil Nadu of comparing inside to outside, and of crossing critical boundaries between inner and outer selves.[14] My eventual task of raising the words *akam* and *puṟam* with villagers in discussion about men's and women's work resulted in some interesting discoveries.

Puṟam (Outside) Work

Agriculture

Compared to certain higher castes even in the same agricultural zone—and certainly to people in Chennai with whom I worked—most of the labor performed by residents of Mātāpuram was distributed comparatively evenly across gender. Unlike the higher-caste Chettiars, Nadars, and Kallars in the area, whose professions and class tended to involve more private ownership of property, the poor, agricultural-working Dalit women of Mātāpuram had fairly equal access to fieldwork and to the means of agricultural production as men. This also differentiated them from another low-caste Roman Catholic group just to the east, the coastal Mukkuvars, whose main work was fishing and whose women did not have access to the sea, boats, or nets.[15] Men in Mātāpuram usually cleared the paths to water sources and for harvests, and loaded the crops into trucks; otherwise, men and women in the village generally agreed that, as one villager put it, "We do the work equally." Dhanam clarified that what differences existed in paid agricultural labor were usually due to perceived differences in physical strength: "Women cannot do the difficult work. Men cut the trees and break them into two pieces. But such work cannot be done by women." During times when there was no harvesting or planting, women would go outside the village to cut wood and to water the fruit trees on their own small plots of land (if they had them). During dry seasons, they had to fetch and carry the water for the trees.

Thus, compared to women of higher castes, who were more exclusively restricted to the home and to the raising of children, Paraiyar women of Mātāpuram enjoyed relative spatial freedom. They walked many of the same paths into the fields as men, and shared much of the same space beyond their own domestic "inner" (*akam*) space. However, this relative equality of shared space was understood to make them more vulnerable to spiritual attack. That they had to walk the same paths as men and fetch water from outside the village, for example, meant that they could be "plucked" (*piṭi*) more easily by hungry deities and spirits.

Cultural control of women's bodies, meanwhile, was not only the province of the upper classes. Women in poor, nonpropertied classes also faced restrictions on movement and confining ideologies of femininity. The day-to-day disciplining of male and female bodies "marked" their bodies differently—not only shaping their inclinations and orientations, but also giving them access to different sorts of resources and cultural capital. These differences, and their effects on men and women's lives, played a significant role in possession practices.

Mill Work

As previously mentioned, many villagers also worked in the local cotton mill, which lay within walking distance of the village. The company offered three eight-hour shifts, and paid permanent workers six thousand rupees per month and casual laborers up to one hundred rupees for an eight-hour shift, according to the management.[16] This did not include money taken out of the wages for food expenses. The mill did not offer seasonal employment. Apprentices who qualified got permanent jobs after six months of training.

That was the official story. In reality, the mill had reduced its numbers of permanent workers significantly in recent years by hiring women from as far away as Uslimapatti and Aandipatti for lower wages. The women were paid thirty rupees a day, out of which fifteen rupees were taken to cover their food expenses. That left the women fifteen rupees (about twenty-eight cents) in daily take-home wages. According to the company scheme, if the women worked consistently for three years, they would be given thirty thousand rupees in hand, Aarokkiyam said. "But after three years they will be in trouble," he added. "They have to work the night shift. If there is power cut and they go to the rest house and sleep, again we'll go, wake them up and make them work. A lot of suffering comes to them."

In 2005 and 2006, Sree Kaderi Ambal Mills employed about two hundred women workers, according to managing director S.V. Pethaperumal. None were considered permanent, and all were unmarried. "After marriage they will not work; they will go to some other place," Pethaperumal said, referring to the common practice of women's moving to their husbands' villages. So most never got the thirty-thousand-rupee bonus.

Migrant Labor

Mātāpuram's men often sought seasonal employment far from the village. Women, on the other hand, did not engage in migrant work. Dhanam's husband, Sebastian Samy, would periodically go to Kerala for four to five months at a time to do hotel work. He worked at a very small hotel with a staff of three. Excluding room and board, he would be paid eighty to ninety rupees per day. "I'll send everything. If it comes to a thousand rupees, immediately I'll send it. I'll not even wait a month." He recalled one exception, "I was angry with her [Dhanam], so I left without telling. When I returned I brought the whole amount." There had been no quarrel between them, he clarified—only a small misunderstanding. Still, he said, "They did not search for me."

Dhanam, sitting beside him, responded calmly, with a smile, "Without knowing his whereabouts, how could we search for him? But I asked God, 'Where has he gone?' God told me that he had gone in so-and-so direction, and God told me that he would come back. Hearing this, I kept silent and did not search for him."

"There [in Kerala], I had one day leave," her husband continued. "I asked the owner if I could to go back to my *ūr* and return at once, but he refused. I came back anyway, telling him that I'd return immediately. When I got back, they were painting the house, so they needed me and I couldn't return." But he liked the migrant labor, especially in Kerala. "If I go there I'll be healthy, because I'll have food in good time, and that Kerala climate is good. Here it is very hot. There, the river is always full, and we will not get sick, even if we bathe in it. Wherever we go there, they will give work." Most of that work caters to the tourist industry.

Dhanam's son-in-law Peter Raj, who was thirty-three, had worked in Malaysia for two years before returning at the time of our visit. He was not always assured of a steady income, though he sent money home. He and his wife, Sofia Mary, who was thirty, farmed a half acre of land—not enough to live on. In a good year, paddy could yield six thousand rupees (about $125), once fertilizer and other expenses were accounted for.

So when Peter Raj was away, Sofia Mary and her children, Stella Mercia, eight, and Princy, five, stayed with Dhanam. When Peter Raj was home, he also stayed there. "We are looking after them," Dhanam said. "We are buying clothes for their children and looking after their expenses."

This was the way in Mātāpuram. While men worked far away, women were matriarchs.

Akam (Inner) Work

In addition to their agricultural work and any other labor in which they might be engaged, the women of Mātāpuram did most of the domestic work. During the years of my visits, Mātāpuram had no running water.[17] One water tank—the size of an oil drum—stood in the center of the village, in the clearing near the church, where the women brought their large, brightly colored plastic pots to fill from its faucet. Tankers occasionally rumbled in to fill the drum. But women also went outside the village to other water sources where they had rights, such as the large *uraṉi* (water tank, usually man-made, often lined with stone or cement) across the road from the village, which during summer often dried up to a mere puddle (Figure 6.1). On the other side of the *uraṉi* stood a Hindu temple to the god Pillaiyar, and beyond that, one to Muniswarar. This *uraṉi*, likely built centuries ago by a local king for irrigation and drinking, was considered public property. Now, women fetched water from it mostly for cooking—people claimed that rice tasted better when made with this water, lending it also a slightly yellow tint—and for drinking. They also carried water from this tank to wash dead bodies in preparation for burial, and to gather "holy water" for the Mātā chapel.[18] Hindu women also fetched water from the tank, though usually accessing it from their side. Further outside the

Figure 6.1: Dhanam fetching water from the tank, or *uraṉi*, just outside the village, 2005. Photo by M. Thavamani.

village, women from Mātāpuram would wash clothes and bathe in the river. They also grazed cows and goats in the fields outside the village. On any one day, one could see women coming and going from these tasks, alone or in small groups.

Times, though, were changing. Some of the younger, unmarried women of Mātāpuram were working as teachers in local schools or as social workers. It remained to be seen what sort of paid work, if any, they would do after marriage.

But the dangers young women faced in the "outside" world of professional work were arguably as onerous as those they faced in the rural work of laboring in "outside" areas of lonesome fields and *pālai*, or wastelands. Ghosts and *pēy* roamed these open spaces just as they roamed modern girls' hostels. Moments of stepping "outside"—whether into a field or to work in a factory or office—were often understood to be dangerous to women, particularly to young, newly married, or pregnant women. These were the moments when they were most vulnerable to be "grabbed" (*piṭi*) by a *pēy*.

WHAT THE GIRL SAID

Sitting in the cool chapel one day with a few women—one of whom was pregnant and there because she was not feeling well—and a thirteen-year-old girl, I heard stories about the girl's recent tussle with a *pēy*. She had been following me all day as I visited with and interviewed the villagers, and could not seem to stop touching my skin and hair. She had given me a pink plastic flower from the chapel altar and wanted me to keep it. She was stunningly beautiful, with long, thick hair she wore up in a bun in the morning, but later twisted down, loose, and gathered into an unfastened braid on her back. Her long green silk skirt (*pāvāṭai*), the traditional style of dress for prepubescent girls, brushed her ankles and tops of her bare feet, and a kameez, a long tunic, fell over it. At one point, as she stroked my left forearm and asked me about all the freckles on it, I asked her why she wasn't in school.

"I am not well," she said.

What was wrong?

"*Pēy piṭiccatu* (a *pēy* plucked me)," she said, matter-of-factly in a clear staccato.

She had been visiting her sister in the hostel at her sister's school. Night had fallen, and there was no light from a lantern or a candle, and no electricity. A cemetery stood nearby. "We heard a cat meowing," she said, her eyes opening wide. "We got scared. When we looked there was no cat. It was very dark."

The other women looked at her with some amusement. But they did not question her; rather, they seemed to elaborate on the details.

One of these women said that after coming back to the village, the girl had started acting like a *paittiyam* (a crazy person). She was running helter-skelter, in a frenzy—even beating people, the woman said—and when some of the villagers took her to the chapel, she started breaking things—doors and statues. She even tried to break the metal grille facing the altar. I imagined her swinging on it with her entire weight, which couldn't have been more than eighty pounds.

For three days, villagers tied her to the large tree next to the chapel, binding her hands to the trunk. For those three days, she didn't eat. She was given water to drink. Later, her family took her to the hospital to see if she had a mental problem. The doctors said it was nothing. Some villagers thought she had caught the *pēy* because of an old curse on the family that went back to an improper marriage from an earlier generation, which in their estimation had lacked close cross-cousin kinship ties. They felt she was bearing the weight of this curse just now, as she approached marriageable age.

Still, there was an air of playfulness to all of this discourse. The two women teased her, teeth flashing behind their hands, suggesting that she was highly dangerous, and warned me to keep my distance.

"Be careful!" one of the women said, in mock seriousness.

"Sit a little further from her!" the other laughed. She raised her hands as if to block the girl's energy, then fell over with her tongue sticking out.

The girl giggled and edged closer toward me, as if to prove them wrong, seemingly happy to be in this warm circle. The laughter was intimate, inclusive. The girl continued to stroke my hand. I was struck by the complexity of the situation, and the temptation for a Western-bred feminist like me to slip into simplistic conclusions. In one way, the women's chatter belied the seriousness of *pēy* possession. But it also normalized it, showing it to be not necessarily a horror but, rather, something playful about which one could chat and laugh. It also suggested a rite of passage—a moment in which this girl was now being included in "women's talk." While it pointed to the constraints placed on out-of-control girls—getting bound to a tree, for example—and the way in which women enforced normative behavior among themselves, it also revealed that the girl, and even these other women, may have enjoyed something about the rituals. Perhaps this young, blossoming woman appreciated the attention, and felt some relief at being tied to the tree in the center of the village.[19] People were, in a sense, "taking care" of her. And as a young woman coming into puberty, she was now eligible for possession.

WOMEN'S FREEDOM / RESTRICTION OF MOVEMENT

Many scholars have written about how purity and pollution restrictions tend to focus on moments in which women produce substances believed to be polluting. These moments range from birth and menstruation to sexual intercourse and death (including, and most notably, the death of a husband). Differences between Hindu and Christian practices on these matters abound, and yet they share similarities. There is a long history of attempts by Roman Catholic missionaries to incorporate certain indigenous customs, on the one hand (à la Beschi, and before him, another Italian Jesuit, Roberto de Nobili, who promoted practices—approved by Pope Gregory XV in a 1623 papal bull—that permitted rites such as wearing the sacred thread, applying sandalwood paste to the forehead, ablution before Mass, and various caste distinctions[20]), and, on the other hand, to differentiate Catholic practices from Hindu ones by banning many customs, including those that centered on notions of purity and pollution. Famous among these were the Malabar Rites, repeatedly condemned by several popes and finally banned by Pope Benedict XIV in 1744. These rites banned certain acts, such as puberty ceremonies and "pagan" practices during worship, and made room for others, such as allowing women to receive the Eucharist during their menses.

This last move countered local practices that banned women from entering temples and other sacred places when they were menstruating, practices still widely observed among Hindus.[21] And yet, at the time of my visit, many Christians practiced puberty rituals for a girl's first menstruation in only slight variation from Hindu practices. In accordance with many Hindu beliefs, Christian girls "in transition" were thought to be in a vulnerable state, likely to attract *pēy* or *picācu*, "evil eye" (*kaṇ tiruṣṭi*), pollution (*tīṭṭu*), or other agents of misfortune. Many Hindus secluded the girl (*vīṭukku dūram*, lit. "far from the house," a period of menstrual seclusion or separation), and practiced "rituals of removal" of harmful influences associated with their flow.[22] Often, these practices of seclusion went on for ten days.

Like many Hindus, the villagers of Mātāpuram would seclude the young woman on the onset of her first menses, but only for one day, as opposed to ten. Also like many Hindus, they poured water over the girl's head and gave her special foods believed to be cooling,[23] and often called relations to the house for this special event. However, some women told me that seclusion was no longer important—nor were the mud pots traditionally broken thirty days after childbirth, as they continued to be in many Hindu villages. Unlike many Hindu women, women in Mātāpuram cooked and fetched water, even during their first periods, and mingled freely—though there was some disagreement about such acts' propriety. Despite these differences in practice, the terminology that Mātāpuram villagers used to refer to women's menstrual periods—*vīṭukku tūram* (far from the house) or *māta vīṭai* (monthly cleansing)—remained the same as that of Hindus.[24] The differences that in Mātāpuram, the practices of seclusion, *vīṭukku tūram* was actually not far at all—just a little separate place in the house, maybe a corner.[25]

Despite some spectrum of opinion among Mātāpuram's women about the purity or pollution of different bodily states, one constant remained: they all spoke of certain places as dangerous or safe *in relation* a) to the state of a woman in her sexual/reproductive life cycle, and b) to Hindu spaces. In particular, they understood certain Hindu spaces to be especially dangerous to Christian women who were menstruating, pregnant, or newly sexually active. Many people in Mātāpuram, male and female, said that pregnant or menstruating women should not fetch water anywhere (or undertake any journey for that matter) that would require them to pass a *muni* temple. One young man in his twenties, whose mother died when he was very young, explained:

> On the way to fetching water there is a *muni* temple. When a woman is pregnant or when she is having her period, she should not go there to fetch water. Because my mother went to take water near the *muni* temple, she was slapped by Muni; during her delivery, she died unable to deliver the child. After she was possessed by Muni, she became ill. When I asked my father about why she died, he told me this.

Another notable distinction between Mātāpuram women and their Hindu neighbors was the belief that although they could go to church while menstruating, they should not go *inside* the church, and some women said they did not take Eucharist (*naṉmai*) during that time, either.[26] It was not that priests had warned them about this, they said. "This is our conscience—our *maṉacācci*," Aarokkiyam's mother said, "—that we are not clean, so we don't go inside." This custom, then, passed from woman to woman.

Another common Indian taboo pertains to the inauspiciousness of widowhood. This seemed not to be recognized in Mātāpuram, as I had seen in many Hindu communities. Aarokkiyam's widowed mother and grandmother both wore earrings and bright saris. They had full heads of hair. They were not secluded, rejected, or shunned but seemed an integral part of daily life—though they did complain, sometimes with a vengeance. If anything, the burden was on Sahaya Mary and most of the other, younger, female married in-laws of Mātāpuram to take care of these older women and, on occasion, bear their insults.

I also met more than one Hindu widow who came to stay in Mātāpuram. One such widow, Ignaci Ammal, was fed simple rice and vegetables by villagers for several weeks. She was related to no one in the village, and said she had been caught by Muni. She seemed to enjoy the care of the community, and would return periodically to be exorcised by Dhanam. Padma thought that she came just to be looked after, because she was perhaps not being taken care of at home.

Binding

Kenneth David, Kalpana Ram, Holly Baker-Reynolds, and Isabelle Nabokov have all analyzed binding as a recurring practice among Tamil women throughout their life cycles.[27] Not only are the breasts and loins bound—focal points of female *shakti* and sexuality—but also the hair. Such bindings correspond with ideas about proper women's chastity, and the degree of binding increases with the maturation of the woman.

In Mātāpuram as well, men of all ages could roam shirtless in the village—perhaps with a towel thrown over one shoulder—whereas women's upper bodies had to be covered and also their waists and legs down to their ankles. Phases of appropriate clothing corresponded to age and sexual maturity, increasingly restricting movement with age. Girls under the age of five might only wear underpants, or short Western-style dresses or skirts. After the age of about five, they might wear long skirts to their ankles and a top (*pāvāṭaiccokkai*)—though all schoolgirls wore uniforms (usually a short, pleated skirt, a button-up shirt, shoes, and socks). After a few years, in addition to the *pāvāṭai* and a top, a light cloth would perhaps be draped over the young woman's breasts. Before marriage, a woman would be expected to wear a sari—eight or nine yards of cloth—wrapped around her body. Girls were taught the importance of covering their breasts with the top of the sari, even during demanding physical labor. Beneath the sari, in addition to the blouse, women wore a long, heavy cotton underskirt into the waist of which they would tuck one end of the sari, further restricting their movement. One relatively new practice in the village was that young women, married or unmarried, could wear "nighties"—the loose gowns that were like long mumus—within village bounds when they were ill or for leisure, even outside the house.

The hair of young girls was cropped short and, at age five or six, oiled and plaited. After puberty, and certainly after marriage, adult women wore their hair coiled in tight buns at the back of the head. A grown woman should only have her hair loose when allowing it to dry after a bath. Unbound hair outside of the bathing context would connote either disorder or extreme emotion: grief, anger, sexual passion, or possession by a deity or spirit.[28]

Finally, other accoutrements and accessories in women's attire also suggested binding—bangles, ankle bracelets, and the wedding *tāli*. Mātāpuram Catholics, like most Roman Catholics in Tamil Nadu, had retained the Hindu practice of wearing the saffron thread or gold chain of marriage, as well as the central ritual in the Hindu wedding ceremony, in which the groom ties the *tāli* around the neck of his bride, binding her to himself.[29] The groom wears no such yoke.

WHAT SAHAYA MARY SAID: EMBODIED BOUNDARIES

Like many of the women of Mātāpuram, Sahaya Mary also abided by looser versions of the purity and pollution (*tīṭṭu*) rules that many Hindus in the area followed. These norms not only shaped women's daily movements and sense of self in relation to geographic space, but also their experiences of deity and spirit possession.

Sahaya Mary said she felt especially vulnerable to feeling the taint of pollution (*tīṭṭu*) after the birth of her first child. For her, rules around death and menstruation took somatic expression. If she went to the house of any person who had recently died, or the house of a girl who had recently attained puberty, she would feel as if ten people were sitting on her head. If she tried to eat, she would want to vomit. "If I go to any place where death occurred [recently], I'll stay at a distance, cry, and then come. If I go close, my eyes start burning. So most probably I'll not go near a dead body. If any close relative died, it's all right to go to their house. But if they are distant relatives, or third-persons, I'll have a lot of problems."

Many villagers practiced restrictions on movement around death and menstruation simply because, they said, it was proper to do so, and so as not to invite unruly spirits and the taint of pollution into their lives. Sahaya Mary's narrative reveals how these restrictions were *embodied*. She wasn't the only one to express this: the thirteen-year-old girl, for example, had talked about getting "chicken skin" when she heard the cat meow at the hostel, and many other women described bodily feelings indicating danger when they approached "outside" danger zones. The idea was that the spirits patrolled these purity rules—and, I came to think, the boundaries of gender. Sahaya Mary, for example, wouldn't go to the outside tank (*uraṉi*) to fetch water while she was menstruating.

"I won't go till it is over," she said. "No one goes to fetch water during their menses time. If anyone having their period goes to fetch water they will have problems."

On the other hand, there were differences between Catholics and Hindus in purity rules related to death. "If anyone from outside this village—if a Hindu—dies, they won't fetch water from the tank for thirty days. If anyone dies in this village, though, they go and take water. I don't know why." She did know one thing, though: "Mātā possessed Dhanam and said this. Because Mātā's church is within this boundary it is not a problem."

It is Mātā, then, in the minds of Sahaya Mary and other villagers who corroborated her story, who guarded them from the harm that could come from death and menstrual pollution—harm that might otherwise befall Hindus. Dhanam, as a conduit of Mātā, patrolled these boundaries as well. In both cases, it was Mātā who differentiated Catholic from Hindu behavior. Mātā, and by connection, Dhanam, was perceived by villagers as a protector, much like the fierce village gods and goddesses who patrolled Hindu boundaries. Like them, she protected in part by establishing or reinforcing boundaries around gendered space.

She was not the only one. Other gods and spirits also patrolled women's practices by creating "abject space"—taboo space into which entrance was prohibited. These gods and spirits were usually, but not always, Hindu (as we saw in the case of the ancestral spirit of Aarokkiyam's dead father, a Catholic). If women ventured into that space during an improper time in their reproductive life cycle, they might be "plucked" or troubled by these spirits. They would also reveal the attack through unruly behavior. The transgressive behavior would cause people, including unruly husbands, to take notice. Once recognized, these deities and spirits could then of course also be contained, exorcised or propitiated. The behavior, at times an SOS call, was the indicator.

In a somewhat convoluted way, the abnormal behaviors associated with these gods and spirits could rope men into relative submission as well, tempering their behavior. When Sahaya Mary and her husband went to the Pandi temple at Dhanam's suggestion, they felt a certain amount of "proper fear." Pandi Muni's anger, moreover, mirrored Sahaya Mary's own "righteous anger" at her husband.

"When we reached the temple, that god (Pandi) looked black and scary," she said. She described Pandi, "It will have a moustache; it will not allow anyone to go near it. It will protect. But it will get angry. It *should* get angry. When my husband was angry with me, I'll be angry. If he starts speaking, I'll be serious."

Dhanam told Sahaya Mary that Pandi was still "on" her now. Her husband should look out: if her husband gets angry, Sahaya Mary [Pandi] will get angry too. "I cannot control it," she said. "I'll get angry, like I'll beat him. We'll be like cat and rat." And the fighting would draw attention. Fr. Arlappan would call and speak to both of them. Neighbors would talk.

As she spoke, the children were sitting within arm's reach, playing quietly. Jency played with a plastic Snoopy; Olivia was again pretending to write on her hand as if it were a pad like mine. I felt a weight on my chest.

But why does Muni possess so many women and not men?

"It is a male god, so it possesses women," she said. "I don't know why. You have to ask the Hindus. We are Christians, what do we know?" She laughed. "I only know that it possesses me." She explained that many years may go by without one's knowing they have been "plucked."

"Only after the *maṅkal sutra* (marriage thread) is tied will it come out," she said. "Only then we will know." And only after giving offerings will it go.

"After we gave our offerings I stayed in the temple for a week. After that I did not have any problem." Unlike other deities who possess women and leave after they are propitiated, however, Pandi often remains.

"Villaiamma, Vellaicāmi are married gods; Pandi Muni is a bachelor god. So it will possess until death. This is a bachelor god so it will stay for protection. I asked Hindus, 'Why is Pandi Muni not leaving?' And this is what they told me." Bachelor gods are "hungry gods." Pandi Muni stays "until death" because, without a steady consort, he is thought to have insatiable sexual urges.

Dhanam explained further in a separate conversation. A *pēy*, she said, will stay inside someone "like a ghost (*āvi*)." While a man may be caught by a *pēy* or other spirits—and indeed, both Sahaya Mary's husband, Aarokkiyam, and Dhanam's husband had been caught by *pēy*, once each in their lives—most people caught by *pēy* are women.[30] For men, it is usually a question of astrological timing, Dhanam said, not behavior: "If the time is not good for men [if the time is inauspicious], maybe ten out of one hundred will be caught by *pēy*." When I asked why women were caught more than men, she answered, "We bathe by applying turmeric and wear flowers. *Pēy* like turmeric and flowers." The substances draw *pēy* because of their fragrance, which signals feminine beauty and sexuality.

But Dhanam was clear: cross-religious sartorial practices and vulnerabilities based on a person's sex did not mean that inner beliefs and feelings were the same across religious communities. "We cannot consider Hindu and Christian beliefs to be similar. Their god (*cāmi*) is very horrifying. The difference is that one should be scared of a Hindu goddess. We should be clean or it will harm us. But Mātā accepts whatever faults we have committed. She will not do any harm. We should also be decent (*kaṇṇiyamāka*) to Kali. Kali is there, in the land where we do agricultural work."[31]

Once, she said, she went to work in the fields without that decency (*atu illāma*)—when she was menstruating. After that she got very sick and her younger sister got a terrible headache that lasted a month. In such a state of uncleanliness, Dhanam was unable to see Mātā but chanted mantras to her. She and her sister also both went to the doctor, who thought they were sick from the rain. One night, when they were sleeping together in the same bed, Dhanam had a dream.

In my dream a black cobra (*karuppu nāgapāmbu*) came into my house. I shouted, "Snake!" But no one came. I went to beat it with a broomstick. But then that snake changed into a girl—a beautiful girl.[32] She was wearing gold bell-drop earrings, and everything. Seeing me, the girl asked why I was going to beat her. "Why did *you* come?" I asked. "I was going to beat that snake. Would I beat you if you were a girl?" I asked her why she came. She answered, "You all come like that [menstruating]—after coming like that, and doing that wrong, you come to beat me?"[33] I said, "Sorry, young girl. My sister came to your boundary (*ellaiyil*) unwittingly; we are farming. What can we do? Ok, I get it, so go." Suddenly she left. When my sister woke up in the morning, she was all right.

That is the difference between our god (*tēvam*) and their god (*tēvam*). Our god will not pluck (*piṭi*) anyone and give them problems. Even Hindus can come to our god. But to their god, only people who have a right (*urimai*) can go. Christians cannot touch the Hindu gods. But Hindus can come and touch Mātā.

The young girl in the dream was a form of Kali. "Would I beat a girl?" Dhanam had asked. Perhaps not unless Mātā told her to beat one possessed by Kali. But Dhanam didn't waste time to split hairs over that matter. Her point seemed to be that Christian women, especially menstruating or unclean Christian women, should not enter Hindu territory or approach Hindu gods. Hindus, on the other hand, need not worry about cleanliness in approaching Mātā. They, as well as Christians, could come to her at any time.

Mātā, then, like Kali, was a patroller of boundaries. But to Dhanam, Mātā's space was more inclusive and thus trumped that of other gods and goddesses.

WHAT OTHER PEOPLE SAID ABOUT DHANAM

While it seemed to me that the overall tone in the village seemed to be one of relative openness and equality, resources were tight, and people kept a keen eye out for people who seemed to have more than they. Everyone—male or female—was subject to scrutiny. And so, when Dhanam started treating patients who came to her for help, people started talking.

Some of the idle talk seemed to be about housework. We were sitting in the chapel.

"When I am at home doing my housework, my thoughts will be here only," Dhanam said softly. "Then just like that I will drop all my work and come here. I will come here, cover my head with my sari (*mukkāṭu pōṭṭukiṭṭu*) and stare, like this." She lifted her eyes toward the Adaikkala Mātā statue, and opened her palms on her knees. "When that happens, my husband will do all the housework and bring me food. At the very beginning, no one understood this. Initially, my husband felt very sad about this. But he did not quarrel with me. 'Her body is not well; that is why,' he would say. 'If Mātā comes on her, let her come.' Whatever people said about me, he would not listen."

It remained one of my regrets that I did not speak more with Dhanam's husband, Sebastian Samy, then—but then again, he was often away, and when he was home he was quiet. He seemed modest, gentle, and work-weary to me, while Dhanam was the stronger personality. As was appropriate to gender norms, he and I never sat alone for an extended conversation. But he insisted on walking Padma and me to the bus stop whenever we were taking the night bus to Karaikkudi and always waited with us until the bus came, which—even if we tried to time it close—could be as long as an hour. On one of these more private walks, he told us that he indeed believed that Mātā "came on" his wife.

"Even in my childhood days I had a lot of belief in Mary," he said, shining his flashlight ahead of us on the road. "My mother also had a lot of belief. I don't know whether my father had belief or not. He died when I was a small boy."

Mary had saved him from a bear once, when he was working in Kerala, he said. She appeared to him, glittering and carrying a child. "So nothing happened to me." She had also driven a *pēy* out of him once, through his wife, in the early years of her possession.

While Dhanam's husband seemed to have taken her possession mainly in stride, in the beginning she faced harsh judgments. In 2005, I had been speaking with Dhanam about how a village elder named Jebamalai, now deceased, had said *mantiram* over people in the name of Mātā for healing. Some villagers had referred to him as a sort of predecessor to Dhanam, but Dhanam had made it clear that he was no close parallel. First of all, she said, Mātā had not "come down on" Jebamalai (she had never seen or heard of anyone getting possessed by Mātā); second, he had had far fewer patients than she.

"I got so many problems because of this. People started asking, 'It hasn't happened anywhere: How could it happen to you? You have some power. A different *mantiram*. Some sort of *pēy*—you must have something like this," they started saying in this village. Now they realize it is true, that Mātā comes on me. Everyone has changed."

Or most people had, I thought, recalling the surveys.[34]

She said that the gossip had started some ten years back as increasing numbers of people had started coming to her for healing. " 'How does this happen?' the villagers started asking. 'In which world does it happen like this? Who becomes possessed like this? How does Mātā come on anyone? It can't be true. It's all because of *pēy*.' Like that they tortured me. They asked me to stop all these things. For one year, I stopped seeing anyone."

Or rather, she *tried*. But the people kept coming.

"I couldn't even stop . . . These people, they go to so many places. If they didn't get cured, they would come here. I would cure them if it was because of black *mantiram*. Then they would ask, "What should we do?" I would say, "We have to ask Mātā." Mātā would say, "To cast that away, the only weapon is a cross.[35] So you keep a cross in your house and come."

Dhanam tried to keep her practice contained and outside the chapel. And under the circumstances, what could she do but go to the person's house and put a cross there? In return, they might give her something: maybe a sari, maybe two hundred rupees—never more than that. "I wouldn't ask," she said. "They would give with pleasure. I would come away with that money or offerings. I wouldn't say no." India's was, after all, a gift culture. To refuse would be an insult.

However, "because of jealousy (*porāmai*)," a small group of people in the village—"maybe four or five men, or four or five women"—started to spread more gossip about her. They said that she was doing black magic and working for large sums of money.

"At that time, my husband was farming. My children were very small. When I got electricity, they all thought that I went out and got money, doing *maya jalam* (miracles, magic) in the name of God. 'What is the reason?' they said. 'Why are you possessed [by Mātā], and not others?' Even the small children talked about me: 'She is getting bribed.' My children scolded me, 'Why do you want this? Everyone is talking badly.' I didn't mind. So what? So somebody is talking rubbish—why should I worry? We have Mātā. Even if they close down the church, let them close it. We can see her in another place. But at that time, my husband and children!—when they scolded me, I felt very bad. I couldn't tolerate their speech."

Eventually, the village called a meeting. Dhanam, particularly broken by her own family's concerns, sat and listened while men and women alike spoke against her. Some also spoke in her favor, but it the end it was decided that the village did not want her to keep going to the church to see clients. She submitted. "Okay," she said, and went home.

But people kept getting sick, as people do—and some of them started coming to her house. Some of them brought babies or small children. Dhanam couldn't turn them away. That's when she started doing "family prayers" in her home. She followed the village ultimatum—she did not go to the church—but she kept a portrait of Adaikkala Mātā at home, and started doing *jebam* (prayer) there, regularly. "I asked my children to sit and do *jebam*," she said, repeating her own father's rigorous discipline. "In my house, Mātā came down and told me, '*Paravayillai.* Don't worry. Whatever you ask me, I will answer.'"

The crowds were not inconspicuous.

"They would all dance outside, whomever got *pēy*," Dhanam said. Family *jebam* in such circumstances seemed slightly inappropriate. What to do? "Okay," she thought. "I'll see them in my house. I'll cast away the *pēy* and then ask them to stay in the church."

For one year, she carried out this home exorcism and healing practice, praying to Mātā and directing people to stay a week or so in the church. After a year of this, she thought, "Why? Let them talk. I'm going to the church." She started seeing people there again. No one in the village said anything to her about it.

Over time, the numbers fell off somewhat. "It used to be I didn't even sleep," she recalled. "Saying prayers, saying mantras—that was my only job."

In 2005, with only a dozen or so people coming a month, she had gone back to working full-time in the fields, gathering wood and water, buying and cooking the food, washing the clothes, raising grandchildren—and praying and casting out *pēy*, as people needed it, in the chapel. If people came while she was in the fields or doing housework, well—they would just have to wait.

WHAT WATER SAID

There was one other, not-so-small problem: Water. *Taṇṇīr. Nīr*, for short. There was either not enough or too much. During rainy season, the rivers and fields would flood because the dry land could not absorb the rain fast enough. Inland Sivagangai was a place of extremes.

The one tank inside the village, in the clearing next to the church, was the closest and easiest place from which to draw water. This is where women would bring their brightly colored jugs and carry them home on their heads and hips, often two at a time. But the tank was not large enough—and not filled often enough by authorities via tanker trucks—to meet all their needs. So the women might have to cross the road outside the village, where there was another small pump, or to the *uraṉi*, the man-made pond outside the village across from which the Pillaiyar and, farther, the Muni temple stood.

To make matters worse, newcomers were starting to move in—just enough to stress already scant resources further. Over the past thirty years, ten new families had come to work in the mill or to build larger houses on land that was comparatively cheaper than that in Karaikkudi, Devakottai, or Chennai. These families were always related to *some*one in Mātāpuram—they were Catholic, and had rights to the land through purchase or inheritance. But they had hifalutin' ways: they needed water not only for drinking, bathing and cooking, but also for watering the trees and shrubbery around their houses.

One particularly vocal newcomer got along badly with Dhanam. A sturdy man with a large *mīcai* (moustache), this "outsider"—her sister's neighbor—had recently caused a decrease in her healing practice. He had called her a fake and spread rumors about her. And he got angry, fast. Dhanam felt particularly vulnerable to his ire when her husband was away doing migrant work.

This man wanted badly to speak to me, and of course I was curious to talk. I accepted tea and chatted on his veranda, but time was quickly slipping, and I desperately needed to exit so that I could speak to Dhanam before she went into the fields. I did not want to offend him, but he didn't seem to take signals. After some time, Dhanam came and stood quietly outside the fence abutting his property, silently mouthing some word I couldn't make out. I looked over his shoulder and watched her lips—was she saying "*pōr*" (war)? Right or wrong as I may have been, she was clearly afraid to speak and to enter his property. He did seem loud and aggressive compared to the other men in the village.

Dhanam told the story: The village had held several meetings about the question of whether or not to give the "outsiders" (*veḷiyakkaraṅkaḷ*) water access. Dhanam, for her part, told me that she *wanted* to allow the new people access, and simply explain to them that they should not water so many plants. But she felt pressure from the village majority, who wanted to contain their resources. Meanwhile, this man—who was also related to Aarokkiyam and Fr. Arlappan—seemed to have made Dhanam a scapegoat for his problems. Moreover, he had blocked the path to the fields behind his house, fields the villagers owned and worked. The barricade had forced many of them to walk a very long way around the village—into spaces that were not considered completely safe for women. It had taken a police order to get him to reopen it.

The path made a narrow dirt alley between this man's house and that of Dhanam's sister. Once, Aarokkiyam walked Thavamani and me out to the fields he cultivated. A small cross hung on an outer wall of the sister's house, at shoulder height (Figure 6.2). It was the last spot a walker might pass before leaving the enclosed village and entering the fields—another boundary marker. As I passed it, watching Aarokkiyam's hoe bob up and down on his shoulder ahead of me, I felt a shiver. I was simultaneously aware of the man in the house on the other side of the path, and of the spirits said to roam these parts. I also felt the thrill of going out into the fields for the first time, and entering what was, for me, entirely new territory.

PUṞAM: THE PLACE "BEYOND"

A shortage of clean drinking water and of water for crop irrigation not only exposed women to a greater likelihood of illness; it also made them spiritually more vulnerable to attack because they were forced to venture farther into unsafe territory. It was no wonder then, I thought as we passed the aggressive newcomer's house and crossed the road, that Dhanam and the other long-time villagers were fighting to restrict access to the scarce water. The road, a thin ribbon of asphalt, led one way to Devakottai and the other way to the graves of the five murdered Dalit men. It was a conduit for dangerous energies—to the unknown threats of the town, of upper-caste strangers down the road, and of death.

The narrow dirt path wound through bushes, low scrub, bramble, and palm trees. Thavamani pointed out to me many of the flora that I had read about in *Caṅkam* literature: the spiky *kaḷḷi* plant, in which a goddess resides; milky cacti; and the medicinal, yellow flowering bush *āravan ceṭi*. We crossed yet another road and passed through another wooded area, until finally, a shady grove opened up into bright, green paddy fields as far as the eye could see.

This is where women would come to weed crops and help with planting and harvesting. I could barely open my eyes for the sun's glare. It must have been well over a hundred degrees, and humid. The colors—green, yellow, blue—were

Figure 6.2: Walking a path in Mātāpuram, behind Thavamani and Aarokkiyam, beyond the last house and into the fields. Photo by author.

brilliant, and finally being outside the boundaries and scrutiny of the village felt expansive, exhilarating, even slightly transgressive. Aarokkiyam beamed with pride as I exclaimed at the beauty and noted the differences in color of the paddy and seeming precariousness of the fine shoots. We teetered like tight-rope walkers along the raised paths dividing the plots, waded ankle-deep through cool irrigation channels in our flip-flops, and pulled out a few large snails to consider. One barely moved its huge shell across my cupped wet palm. On the bank, in the shade, I offered my plastic water bottle to Aarokkiyam, who declined, and to Thavamani, who tilted his head back and poured water into his mouth without touching the bottle to his lips, as one does in India. I, too, poured the clear, cool water down my parched throat.

The trek increased my own, visceral knowledge about access to water and open spaces—and connections to spirit possession. Possession by *pēy* and release of such possession by Mātā was perhaps yet another form of expression of women's relation to scarcity, and of their protest. To have to walk a far distance for water—far from the *akam* space of the village and into the *puṟam* space of roads, crossings, fields, and dried-up water tanks—was indeed to open oneself up to being "snatched." *Pēy aṭṭam*, the dance of possession, was an event sometimes triggered by movements into dangerous spaces invited by such scarcity. It was no wonder that the aggressive neighbor, the newcomer who wanted to use this precious resource to water his imported trees and bushes, had wanted to close Dhanam's practice down—and that Dhanam and Mātā had resisted.

WHAT THEY SAID ABOUT *AKAM/PUṞAM*

From the beginning of my time in Mātāpuram, I was conscious that my interpretation of events was shaped in part by the categories of *akam* and *puṟam*, and of the categories of "public" and "private" that had long been used in feminist analyses of women's oppression.[36] But the people of Mātāpuram were not very familiar with the terms.

"I heard about this word," Dhanam said about *akam*, "but I do not know the meaning."

In 2012, Thavamani and I sat with her and her husband, and a few other men and women outside their house. No one else had heard these words before. We explained our sense of them: *akam* meant inside, *puṟam* meant outside. Applying them to men's and women's work, *akam* could mean, for example, "women stay home and do work," and *puṟam*, "their husbands go out to work."

The women started to talk at once. A paraphrase goes like this: "We do both! We work at home. We have the children, bathing and cooking and everything. At the same time, we go out to work. The men may not. My husband takes care of the bulls and livestock for a little while, but I always work. He digs; I carry the mud, or the soil. But then we come home; he just puts the towel on the floor and sleeps. I have to worry about his food and the children's food. I have to worry about the money also, which he brought in. If he gives me a hundred rupees, that's all I have to manage the house."

One woman offered a local parallel analogy to the classical binary frame of *akam-puṟam*. "Like *akam-puṟam,* there are two things," she said. "One is *vēlai* (work); another is *kavalai* (worry). *Vēlai/kavalai* is like *puṟam/akam*. As soon as we (women) come home, we cannot sit like them. When my husband is lying down, I will worry: when will I give him food? Then I will cook. When men go out they don't think about the wife; they buy a bun and maybe one other thing—enough for them. But we wives are not like that: we worry about our husbands and we worry about our children."

The men, to my surprise, agreed. Dhanam's husband added some wisdom. "*Akam* and *puṟam* should be equally distributed (between the couple)," he said. "If *puṟam* misunderstands *akam*, life will not be okay. For example, let's say I'm working in the field. She [Dhanam] brings food at ten in the morning. If I get angry with her, there will be a fight. If I ask, 'Why are you bringing the food so late?' then she will get angry with me. 'Oh,' she will say, 'I have to do work and clean and look after the children.' So the *akam* and *puṟam* should go together. *Akam* and *puṟam* should be mutual."

One old man was also sitting with us. "*Akam* is the same for women now as in the old days," he said. "They get up early and clean the house and cook the food. Then they go out to do work. For women in the villages, in those days they did only agricultural work: weeding, planting, collecting firewood. But nowadays the women are also working outside, equal to the men. Even digging. They want to make a new [water] tank; they have to work, partly because of the 100-days work scheme.[37] Everybody should work equally. The men say, 'Ladies, you carry the mud, we will dig.' "

The first man said, "*Puṟam* has given lots of opportunity for women to work: construction, bulldozers, leveling, drivers, coolies, conductors—more and more work is there nowadays if you know how to do it."

Another said, "In those days, when we went home, they came and met us. I would remove my shirt; she would bring the tumbler of water for me to drink. Now who is doing this?"

It was Dhanam who offered a class analysis. "There are two categories of *akam*: rich and poor," she said. "The rich, they don't go to work in the fields. The women stay at home. After doing the housework, they take rest. When the husband comes home, they are not tired. But women like us, poor people, we have plenty of work when we come home, so we cannot be inviting the men in, taking their shirts and all that."

On top of all this—above and beyond the labor of home, field, and now, everything from construction through teaching and social work—women had to give birth. Women were the source of life. This was another kind of power, labor, and danger.

THE STONE BABY

Perhaps nothing is more inside/outside than birth, and nothing more gendered than giving it. The twenty births that Dhanam had midwived reportedly had all been successful—all except one, depending on how you looked at it. The mother had survived. The "stone baby" had not.

Dhanam's account of the "stone baby" (*kal pāppā*) linked themes of women's fertility, gendered space, Mātā, and Muni. The incident had also tested Dhanam's authority as a healer and medium perhaps more than any other.

Thavamani and I were sitting on Dhanam's veranda with two others when she told the story:

A woman with five children who was from her sister-in-law's village had come to her for help with a very difficult and overdue delivery. Before the pregnancy, while menstruating, she had entered a water tank abutting an Aiyanar temple to catch fish. (This was a different lake than the one Dhanam had entered; a patroller of boundaries, Aiyanar abuts many lakes.) "When women have their menses and go [into his lake], he does not like that at all," Dhanam said. "That *cāmi* himself came into her womb. For ten months the *cāmi* was growing in her stomach."

The others sitting with us—an older female relation of Dhanam's and a young man, her distant nephew—must have seen the look of confusion on my face. "Like the *cāmi* statue," the older woman interrupted. "With a big neck and head."[38]

"Don't tell her the last part," Dhanam scolded the woman. "We should tell it from the beginning only—then she will understand." She turned back to me. "For ten months it was growing. She was almost ready to deliver the child. It was past its due date. The child had now been growing in her a year. She was having pain sometimes, and then no pain."

Had the woman gotten a medical scan?

"First they went to a *kuri* teller," Dhanam said.[39] "The man who told *kuri* had said that it was a boy, but that she would have a hard time giving birth. But she had unnatural feelings—not the regular feelings of pregnancy. *Then* they went to the local hospital and did a scan. They told her, 'There is a child, but it looks different.' They told her to go to Madurai. But that was expensive. Then they thought, 'Let us take her [to Mātāpuram] and ask Mātā; then if need be, we can go to Madurai.' So they came with fear, wondering what Mātā would say." People often recommended that women come to Dhanam for direction before pursuing other medical options.

The woman's family brought her in a hired car, along with a woman who had been with her to help with the delivery. The car dropped them in Mātāpuram, ten kilometers from the woman's village. Dhanam met them in the chapel. The woman was in a state of utter fear: "Aiyo! *Akka* (sister)," she cried to Dhanam. "I won't live even if I go to a hospital! I don't know what happened to me! Please ask Mātā to give me a safe delivery!" Everyone had told her she would not live through a Cesarean. Dhanam appealed to Mātā. "Amma," she said, "this girl is talking like this. Did something happen?" Mātā told Dhanam, "This girl is afraid, and she has a *pēy* in her stomach. Don't let her go to the hospital. We can cure her here itself. Keep her in your home." Dhanam told the girl, "Don't worry, Amma said you will deliver safely here."

Dhanam took the woman from the chapel to her house. The woman was in uncontrollable agony. It was about noon. The men in the group were becoming increasingly anxious. It would be hard to hire a taxi at that time of day, and they needed to know when to call one. "Wait until two o'clock," Dhanam told them. "After that you can take her wherever you want. Mātā had told Dhanam to wait an hour and a half—the woman would deliver by then. They waited. And waited.

"All the people were here," Dhanam said. "I was waiting and watching her. She felt like the child in her womb was coming up to her chest. She was crying, saying, "I am choking! I am going to die!" People were crying, saying, "You told us to stay here, but we could have gone somewhere to tear her open and take the baby. We are keeping her here only because of you."

Dhanam went back to the chapel.

"I asked Mātā: 'You said to keep her here, but she is in this condition.' Mātā said, 'Have courage; let the people talk.' I had courage in the church, but when I came out, they said, 'What, Mā? Because of you we kept her here and now she is going to die.' Which grief could I bear? I told them, "Be patient a little longer. Wait a half hour more. She [Mātā] said 'one-and-a-half hours.' Don't cry and talk. I have courage; don't lose yours." The woman was standing, holding onto a rope (hung from the ceiling).[40] She was standing like that, shouting, "I am going to die! The baby is coming up to my chest!" All the men stood, scared that she was going to die. "You said that in an hour and a half it would be alright, but the time has come, and nothing has happened!" I asked, "Amma, what is this?" Mātā said, "The time has come: beat her with a broom three times." The girl was breathing hard. The woman who came with her to help with the delivery was looking scared. I said [to Mātā], "I don't know anything; I am keeping her here only because you said so."

"She was there, her people were there, and the village people were there, all staring at the girl. They stood in horror thinking, 'We stupidly listened to this girl [Dhanam], and believed that Mātā had instructed us to keep her here.' Seeing them, I was losing courage. But Mātā *told* me, so I had courage. I told a man standing nearby, 'Take the broom and beat her.' Three times he beat her. We heard a *damar* (specific noise). She was standing. That *cāmi* had fallen there. From her stomach the *cāmi* fell out. With such a long tongue coming out of its mouth, blinking, showing its big eyes. The body was like stone. They poked it with a knife."

It had life?

"Yes, it had life. With popping eyes and a tongue hanging out. Like a *pēy* it was there. The whole crowd could see."

"The baby had the *rupam* (figure) of a *cāmi*," the old woman said.

Just like the *cāmi* at the temple?

"We were there from the beginning, so I know," the old woman said again.

Which *cāmi*?

Dhanam addressed the old woman from over her shoulder. "What: Kali or Muni?"

"Muni temple."

"Something," Dhanam said. "She does not know."

But it was not a stone? Did it have skin? Or like stone?

"Like stone," Dhanam said.

Like the *cāmi* statue.

"Like the statue," Dhanam said.

"But a baby only," the young man said, also now inquiring.

"A baby only," Dhanam said.

"It had skin?" the young man asked.

"No skin," Dhanam said. "Only stone. When we poked it, it was like poking a stone."

"It was that hard," he said.

"The tongue was out but there was no hair on the head," the old woman said.

"But it had life (*uyir*)," Dhanam said. "Ten minutes after the delivery, it died and it became stone."

A baby's cries came from next door—a relation's child. Thavamani and I sat speechless. Meanwhile, Dhanam and the old woman argued about how long ago this had happened. Was it fifteen years? No, longer: Maybe twenty. After the incident, Arusu was born—and he is twenty-five, twenty-seven years old now. Yes, it was around that time . . .

What was there to say?

"What an astonishment," Thavamani said, finally. "And wherever they went, nothing could be done?"

The old woman replied indirectly. "Like a child born from the womb, there was a *cāmi* there. When there is water in the [temple] tank, girls should not enter when they have menses. This girl entered the tank without listening."

That was the end of the story.

But not for me. I continued to dwell on it. Just like Dhanam, who had entered a lake in Hindu territory, next to the Aiyanar temple, where fights over who could carry the horses had triggered the death of the five Dalit men, this woman had entered waters patrolled by a Hindu god while menstruating. The Hindu "Other"—a *pēy*, a *cāmi*, or both (the real identity was unclear)—had entered the woman as retribution for her mistake. The story was told not as a sad event deserving of empathy, but as an I-told-you-so wonder story with moral weight: women, especially menstruating women, should stick to places deemed fit for their kind.

The other moral of the story, at least to some people, was that it proved Dhanam's authenticity as a midwife who could navigate dangerous births and save a mother's life because of her connection to Mātā.

Dhanam had mentioned the stone baby during an earlier visit, when I had come with Padma, but we had resisted asking more about it, I think because we were afraid. I, for one, did not want to come upon information suggesting that Dhanam would call a baby a stone and take a knife to it. Upon hearing the story again now, in 2010, I was angry: angry at a lack of medical care; angry at the lack of water; angry, even, at this belief in *cāmi*. I wanted a doctor in the house. Was the "stone baby" some sort of lithopedion—a dead fetus that that had calcified? Was this act euthanasia?

But illness and tragedy was part of the dark truth of life. Many rural villages in South India did not have hospitals or proper healthcare, and when they did, many people could not afford it. Fear of death was very real, and fear figured as an emotional character in almost all of Dhanam's stories. Fear was an opening to a dark, "other" world, an invitation to invasion from dangerous outside forces. Lack of fear—scoffing at the rules of elders, going into a water hole while pregnant or menstruating—did not show respect for death. Lack of fear could reveal itself as "unruly anger," as in the case of Sahaya Mary. Perhaps Mātā did help to reintegrate women into society at their own expense, women who had been relocated through marriage into "outer" zones, far from their nearest-of-kin. She helped them survive this sometimes violent separation.

While Dhanam did not seem to change the structures of oppression that kept women bound, she taught them, and their men too, to practice courage. She attended to them when, for lack of money or access or efficacy, no one else could. She did all this while engaging in battle with the gods and spirits who also roamed the landscape, and who were also as real as stones that cry.

This was indeed a world where a woman could give birth to a god, a *pēy*, or a *muni*. This "thing," this being growing inside of her, could be a dearly begotten son or daughter—or it could be an Other, a being who could suck a girl dry and open her up to the pain of other worlds. There was a terrible darkness to this world of bifurcation and permeability. This, too, was Mātāpuram.

CHAPTER 7

Memory, Mimesis, and Healing

When the five Hindu men from the neighboring village were killed in 1979, Dhanam remembered. She also possibly conflated the men's death, and her feelings of horror, the guilt of a mother who had lost her first son, a survivor's guilt, with another sort of survivor's guilt—that of not having been in the Hindu Dalit village that had been the target of the 1979 attack. She may have borne a vague sense of ancestral guilt, the guilt of a great-granddaughter of converts who had left behind their fellow Hindu untouchables upon converting to the religion of the white conquerors. She may have borne the guilt of an "Other."

What had she done to invite such horror? She had passed the graves of the five dead men—the five Hindu heroes, those handsome ones who had wanted only to live in peace and self-respect with their families. She had crossed the road to fetch water and firewood, the very road that opened toward town—down which the fire trucks had come and back up which the bodies had been carried before their return. She had waded into a lake in Hindu territory while pregnant.

Well, the gods would show her. They would take her son. And they did. They took his body, and Dhanam's too. They occupied her—just as the Mughal kings had occupied Tamil-land; as the Brahmin, Kshatriya, and other higher castes had removed rights of the lower- and outcastes; as the Portuguese, Dutch, and British had taken over the country from the sixteenth century to the twentieth; as wealthy landowners before and after independence had relegated outcastes to areas far from the high temple, away from water sources in a "wasteland" of *pālai*. Then Mātā came and showed *them*.

She showed everyone that Mary was benevolent, yes, but also fiercely protective, able to slay a demon, a *muni*, or a god with one blow. She knew the agony of a son's early death. And Mātā's deep knowledge of a woman's pain had left her with an ability to heal others' pain like no one. Her heart, her *maṉacu*, was bigger than that of so many other male gods. Her space in the chapel at the heart of the village may have been small, but her *kōyil* could make room for everyone. Mātā knew the meaning of ultimate sacrifice, and she would do anything to help save anyone who came to her with deep suffering. Mātā had saved Dhanam by entering her. Once entered, Dhanam's body became Mātā's body—an instrument for healing, redemption, mimesis, and memory.

WHAT I LEARNED TO ASK: QUESTIONS ABOUT AGENCY

The form of agency that manifested in Dhanam's possession did not involve Western notions such as conscious choice or the willful conquest of obstacles. Rather, it involved habits that cultivated intimate relationships with others (people, deities, and spirits) over time—what in Tamil we might call *paḻakkam*, or "habituation." This form of agency required a permeable, fluid self that could expand and adjust to the immediate social body to make room for the other.[1] In the case of a healer like Dhanam (or Rosalind or Nancy) who has turned her affliction by deities and spirits into an ability to heal, this habituation required not just *accommodation* of the deities, spirits, and clients who came to her, but also a virtuosic ability *to call* upon those deities, spirits, and clients—and to do so *over time.*

Dhanam had generously and repeatedly incorporated me into her life over the years, and I was increasingly finding her make her way into mine. I felt this inclusion most notably in 2012, when my visit coincided with the ordination of her second surviving son, Aananthan. He and his younger brother were both now seminarians, and both were home—as were many of Dhanam's siblings and other relations—in preparation for Aananthan's village-wide ordination. Hosting this event must have been one of the biggest labors of her life (other than giving birth). And yet, she incorporated me both as a guest and as an ethnographer, quite spontaneously, into it.

WHAT HER SON SAID: ON THE EVE OF ORDINATION

It was late November of 2012. Thavamani had taken precious time off from his farming and family to travel with me. We arrived in the town of Karaikkudi and hired a driver named Varun, a tall, lanky, twenty-five-year-old bachelor of engineering who had been hanging out at the Internet shop across from our hotel. As we rode in his white Tata Indigo, he told us about his own family—Hindu Shaivites—who practiced spirit possession almost daily, reminding me of just how prevalent these practices were locally.

The village, as we entered, was prepping full throttle for the ordination. It echoed with the sound of hammers and voices. Varun parked the car at the end of the main lane, and as we walked toward the chapel, women and children looked up from their tasks of drawing rice-flour *kolams* and of stringing brightly colored origami garlands between houses (Figure 7.1). The hammering grew louder as we reached the clearing behind the chapel. Men teetered above our heads on wooden scaffolding like tightrope walkers, building a makeshift stage. Two men walked past us shouldering long poles of cassurina wood for another *pandal* outside Dhanam's house.

We stopped first, as usual, at Aarokkiyam's house. He stepped outside to greet us, face beaming and glistening with sweat, dressed in shorts and a

Figure 7.1: Women in Mātāpuram draw *kolams* in front of their homes in preparation for Aananthan's ordination. Photo by author.

shirt with the sleeves rolled up, hands and arms grey, up to his elbows with cement. He explained that he was pouring a new floor for the house, which he and Sahaya Mary were readying for the celebrations. Sahaya Mary ducked out from under the new back roof of the once-open cooking area; smiling, all aflutter, she wore a thin towel wrapped around her head as a stabilizer for carrying buckets of cement. Her face was fuller than when I'd last seen her. She felt well, she said, and happy—and the children were also very well, boarding in a local hostel for school.

We walked down the dirt path to Dhanam's house and passed under the shade of the palm-leaf-roof *pandal* in front of it. She emerged in a dark-green sari. She had been expecting us. "*Vaṅkaḷ! Vaṅkaḷ! Nalla irukiṅkaḷā*? (Come! Come! Are you well?) I'm so happy to see you!" she said in Tamil. She looked older, her face a bit chalky compared to the dark, rosy complexion I recalled, but her hair still showed no trace of gray. She was now in her fifties.

In a South Indian village, an ordination is like a huge wedding, and the parents of the "groom" are the main organizers. We knew it would be hard to find time to sit and talk; when I had called weeks ago, we had planned to do so after the ceremonies. Still, she apologized for not being more available. "I am working in the fields, and then I'm doing housework, and then traveling about giving out invitations, so I am looking like this," she said, smoothing her hair and tucking it tighter into a knot. "My children are scolding me for working too hard." I begged her not to worry—we were happy and grateful to be there at all, and would wait for a time when it was convenient to talk. She was preparing to go to into Devakottai to shop for the event, she said, and invited us inside. Her young daughter-in-law, Jothi, pulled up two plastic chairs and offered us tea. Jothi's husband, Dhanam's eldest son, was well and working construction in Singapore. Dhanam introduced her youngest son, a tall, nineteen-year-old seminarian who had come from Agra with his brother Aananthan. He sported a high coiffure, Elvis-like, and a big comb in the back pocket of his jeans.

Then came Dhanam's husband, Sebastian Samy, looking distinguished as ever in a checkered lungi. His full head of wavy hair had greyed slightly, and the lines in his face had deepened. He sat with us briefly before excusing himself to change into a *veshti* and shirt for town. I presented Dhanam with the sari I had bought for her in Chennai—blue and purple cotton with *kambi* ("gold thread border"). Thavamani boldly forwarded that I brought it so she could wear it to the ordination (though that had not been my intention). She seemed thrilled, showing it from person to person in the house, asking what color blouse she should have made. Purple, her daughter-in-law suggested. Purple, her daughter Saara agreed.

Into the fracas stepped Aananthan, the son about to be ordained, in a white cassock. His dark eyes, accented by his thick black beard and complexion, would have converted me on the spot. We had never met; I immediately stood. He greeted us warmly. "I would have sent an invitation if I had known you were coming," he said in impeccable English, and speedily handed us two glossy twelve-by-fifteen-inch invitations: one in Tamil, one in English. The English version invited us to the event "[w]ith deep sentiments of love and profound gratitude to God and Mother Mary." The Tamil version went into further detail, inviting us "by the grace (*aruḷ*) of God (*iṟaivaṉ*) and by the help/succor (*tuṇai*) of *Aṭaikkala Aṉṉai*." The Tamil invitation distinctly thanked the village's local Mātā, Adaikkala Mātā. Her specificity, which went unnamed in the English invitation, mattered in Tamil.

I told Aananthan that I had been coming here since 2001, and that I had brought my doctoral thesis for the family's blessing.[2]

"My mother has a charism," he offered in English. He was referring to the charismatic gifts mentioned in the New Testament (1 Corinthians), which I knew well from my own family.[3] "She used to do much more healing, but it takes so much out of her. She becomes weak and tired more easily now that she is older. She has had to reduce her practice. She fasts a lot," especially on Friday, Saturday, and Sunday mornings, he said, and this also weakened her. His bold, supportive response had surprised me; other Devakottai priests, with the exception of Fr. Arlappan, Aarokkiyam's brother, had either denied knowing about Dhanam's practice or had spoken negatively about it.[4]

There was no time to question Aananthan about how he squared his mother's work theologically, if at all, with orthodox Roman Catholic teaching. He was headed to the parish rectory to spend the next day and a half in meditation and in prayer. The next time he returned to Mātāpuram it would be in a large, white car with the bishop, who would escort him back into the village in a ceremonial procession with his parents, visitors, and the entire village. A few days after being ordained, he would leave the village for North India. "So much faith is here in the South," he told me, sitting in his mother's house. "There is no faith there, so we are spreading it. There is a need." From that point on, he would be a member of the church hierarchy, his first loyalties to his bishop.

Meanwhile, Dhanam and her family were going into major debt for this ceremony. The whole event would cost about 1.5 lakhs, or 150,000 rupees, and the diocese would help only with the cost of the stage, or about 6,000 rupees. No one really knew how Dhanam's family would pay the loans back. Gifts would help. Later, I would watch male guests drape shawl after shawl of fine cloth over Aananthan's shoulders as part of the ceremony, and he would humbly remove them and put them in a pile; but they would not necessarily give cash. The nuns sitting behind me, meanwhile, sucked their teeth at the pile-up. "What waste," they said, and coyly showed me small envelopes of cash stashed under their pink sari blouses. I, myself, would quietly give 1,500 rupees to Dhanam after the ordination, and she would discreetly slip it under her own blouse.

REVISITING WHAT DHANAM HAD SAID

Later the next day, Dhanam and I sat in the shade of the *pandal* that had become her extended veranda. With us sat Thavamani, who helped to translate when needed; Dhanam's sister-in-law, a large, slightly sour-faced woman; and her twenty-something son. Now was my chance to ask Dhanam to re-narrate the onset of her possession, and to move the interview toward questions about *exactly* when she understood herself to be *possessed*—that is, when Mātā actually occupied her body, if at all—and when Mātā simply *appeared* before her at Dhanam's invitation, to help her discern the cause of a person's ailment.

She began by recounting the fishing incident that had marked the onset of her possession when she was seven months pregnant, before the stillbirth. "I went fishing with my husband," she began—

"You told her all that before," her sister-in-law butted in.

"No I didn't," Dhanam said. "She asked, but I didn't tell her."

Indeed, in earlier years, Dhanam had told me the rough outlines of the story: The *pēy* of the five Dalit men had long been haunting her; she had entered the lake in Hindu territory while pregnant. What she had *not* told me was that to get to the lake, she had had to pass not only the gravesites of the five murdered Dalit men; she also had to pass a temple that housed the god Aiyanar—a patroller of boundaries—and, as is common at such temples, seven *munis* and the god Karuppar. This was the same Aiyanar for which the five Dalit men had wanted to carry the terra-cotta horses, before they were attacked.

The boundary marked not just Hindu territory but Mātāpuram's as well; it was part of its larger imagined landscape, its geophysical space in relation to Hindu caste, and its cosmological relation to local deities and spirits. Both Mātāpuram and Chinna Unjanai (Little Unjanai) fell within the larger territory of Unjanai, the *nadu* (or "kingdom," once feudal, now a regional administrative unit).[5] For all the residents of Unjanai—high caste and low caste, Hindu and Christian, Brahmin and non-Brahmin—Aiyanar held tremendous cosmological and social meaning. The Brahmanical temple at Kandadevi drew seventy-five villages from four different *nadus* for its annual car festival for Shiva. But unlike Shiva, a king, Aiyanar was a warrior, a patroller of the king's boundaries. He lived on the outskirts of Unjanai, close to the low-caste and Dalit dwellings, and was considered a slightly lower god than Shiva—but extremely powerful. Aiyanar, lying as he did on the edges of the *nadu*, often near bodies of water and out beyond the high-caste dwellings, was often connected to non-Brahmanical practices, though upper castes tried to appropriate him. He was a village god—a village, or "petty" raja. One might consider him a *kshatriya*, a "warrior," who protected the outer boundaries of the kingdom. Meanwhile, as the "high" goddess Parvati protected Unjanai from its spiritual center at Kandadevi, the "low" goddess, the village Amman, protected each village from the center, as a mother protects her child.[6] Likewise, in Mātāpuram, Aiyanar marked boundaries—*fluid* ones—between Catholic and Hindu, high caste and Dalit. Mātā, its local Amman, stood in the center.

After returning from the fishing excursion just beyond the Aiyanar temple to her own hut near the Mātā *kōyil* in Mātāpuram, Dhanam began to miscarry the child that would have been her first son. From a medical point of view, the miscarriage may have resulted from severe food poisoning (though no one else in her family got sick) or falling on her belly on the bank of the *kammai*, or severe dehydration caused by her acute vomiting and diarrhea—but this was not her understanding. Whatever the cause, the trauma of her illness and loss was central to her narrative. Mātā possessed people *through* affliction, just as she came to *oppose* it. The *pēy* and other spirits who could cause affliction served as the very reason for Mātā's presence. No affliction, no need for Mātā.

But why Mātā, *munis*, and *pēy* and not, say, Satan? So far, Satan had only arisen in my discourse with Nancy, who had been exposed to so much Pentecostal fervor through relatives and neighbors. Neither Catholics nor the many Hindus who came to Dhanam seemed to speak of Satan. This local Roman Catholic way of thinking seemed much more compatible with South Asian myths and traditions that did not treat good and evil as necessarily opposing states or realms than with forms of European Catholicism or Protestantism.[7] This local Catholicism seemed, rather, to treat spirits and deities as ambivalent, even fickle. In Mātāpuram, Mātā was the goddess who could both afflict and heal, and Hindu gods, goddesses, and *pēy* were the deities and spirits who could also afflict, *but not heal*. Although Hindu gods and goddesses healed in some Hindu villages, they did not do so here. In this sense, Dhanam had to some degree demonized certain Hindu gods and goddesses; she had created, absorbed, and/or adopted (perhaps from Roman Catholic teaching) a split between good and evil—not toward Mātā, who could cause affliction as well as heal it, but toward Hindu deities. This perspective differed from those of many Hindus who came to her. For them, the cause of affliction could be a karmic inheritance, an astrological fate, or a violation of a prohibition as easily as it could be a malevolent spirit or fickle deity. Transgression (one's own or that of someone else who had cast a spell of black magic) and illness were often linked. It could even be that a seemingly positive event such as marriage (envied by another, including another man who desired you) could open one up to negative possession by spirits who would show themselves eventually through "abnormal" (non-gender-normative) behavior. In terms local to Mātāpuram, these malevolent or mischievous *pēy* or *munis*—beings whose existence in this arid landscape had been documented at least as far back as the *Caṅkam* poets—had become the foils for the opposing characters who could also heal, such as Mātā. These oppositions were necessary to Mātā's very existence.

Aiyanar not only patrolled the boundaries of Hindu/Catholic territory; he patrolled the boundaries of the Hindu-related, gendered purity rules that Dhanam had transgressed, and he patrolled the boundaries of local forms of Roman Catholicism. In retribution of her gendered transgressions, it made sense to Dhanam—because of the sacred geographies and cosmologies surrounding her—that Aiyanar and his minions, along with the *pēy* (all of whom were Hindu), had possessed her.

It was Mātā who had named the culprits. In her re-narration, Dhanam told me that fellow villagers had reported her initial Marian possessions back to her. She added that in her own doubt and confusion, she had prayed to Mātā and had asked for direct explanation:

When I asked (Mātā) why this *cāmi* (Aiyanar) got me, I came to know that when Hindu people go there (to the lake), they say "*Aiyanā*, or *Aiyā* (Lord)," and then get into the water. I didn't say that. I said, "*Iyēcu, Appa*" ("Jesus, Father"). But the seven *cāmis* (the *munis* in that temple) didn't like hearing that. So they got me. I said "*Iyēcu, Appa*," thinking, "I am like this [pregnant]." Then I made a sign of the cross and got into the water. Then the god might have thought, "Why did this girl do this, and not follow me?" The same night, I got vomiting and diarrhea . . . and I could not bear the stomach pain. There had been a Hindu girl who was pregnant and had died there [in that Hindu village]; she also got me [as a *pēy*]. Then my family took me to hospital. In the night I had fits. Then they brought me back to the *kōyil* (the Mātā chapel in Mātāpuram)."

Even after returning from the hospital to the *kōyil*, Dhanam had tried to work at home and in the fields, but the *pēy* of the five Hindu men kept disturbing her. Unable to stand the pain and anguish, she went back to the Adaikkala Mātā *kōyil*.

"I was like this—arms out, eyes rolled up—for three days. If I were Hindu, they would have taken me to see someone to call the *cāmi* or *pēy* [to discern the problem], and tie and expel the spirit. They (Hindus) will do so many things. We don't have that habit (*paḻakkam*). Since we don't have all these resources, I just surrendered. All that time, Mātā never spoke to me.

You just prayed to Mary and Jesus?

"I didn't do or know *anything*. All the *pēy* just started to dance."

Who was dancing?

"I myself was dancing."

So you were possessed and dancing.

"Yes. Without my knowing, they (the *pēy*) danced. My hair loosened and [no subject] danced, twirling."

I noted here that now "they" danced, and that the subject of the verbs "to dance" and "to twirl" was missing. Who was the agent here? I asked Dhanam whether this was the first time this had happened to her.

"Yes," she said. "Looking at the statue (of Adaikkala Mātā), the *pēy* itself said [through Dhanam's own mouth], 'Mother (Amma), without knowing you would be here we came.' The *pēy* sees very well Amma's greatness (*makimai*), but we do not know."

How does she know that? Did anyone tell her, or did she herself come to know?

"I did not know. Others told me. Only then I came to know. *They* told me, 'You danced like that. You said, "Amma." You called.' "

How did she know all this?

"I did not know anything. Only the *pēy* knew about Amma. I didn't know. Only the *pēy* said, 'Amma. I am afraid. If I see you, I am afraid. I will go.' Then people realized Mātā's greatness. Through seeing the *pēy* they could see Mātā. After the *pēy* left, I just lay down. I did not know what happened. Then they [the villagers] asked me, 'Ma, what happened to you?' I said [in an upbeat voice], 'I'm feeling well. What happened to me?' They said, 'You came from somewhere and you danced. You danced so much, and said "Mātā," and then, "I am going." . . . They told me, 'You yourself danced and rolled.' I told them, 'You people alone are telling me this, but I do not know anything.' I was there [in the chapel] for three months. . . . For three months I never came home. It [the *pēy*] danced and it spoke. But then, suddenly, it was Mātā who spoke. How did she speak? She said, 'I am here. From where have I come? I came from Poondi.' "

Poondi is the place where the missionary Constantine Joseph Beschi[8] built a now-famous church to Mary, probably the first in the area. People know this Mary as a particular, local incarnation: Poondi Mātā. Beschi later placed a slightly different form of the Poondi Mātā statue in the Adaikkala Mātā church in Elakurichi. One Mātā spawned another, which spawned another, and so on. The mimetic iterations of Mary seemed endless.

QUESTIONS OF AGENCY: MĀTĀ CALLS ON DHANAM

Imbedded in Dhanam's narrative were details that spoke to my own, long-held questions about agency, permeability, and Hindu-Christian oppositions versus (or in tension with) conceptions of a shared identity. Only *through Dhanam's body* was Mātā able to reveal herself in opposition to the *pēy*, the *muni*, and Aiyanar. Moreover, only through the witness (*cāṭci*) of the community—the social body of the village, of which she was a part—was Dhanam able to know that she was possessed. While Dhanam began the story in the shadow of the Hindu Dalit men's deaths—an incident narrated as an invasion—she likewise narrated her move to go fishing as an act taken as a member of a social body that stood in relation to an opposing one. What mattered to me at this point in the story was that, when Dhanam walked to the lake, she didn't stop to think; rather, she got caught up in the excitement and kinetic movement of the village, and in the needs of her own body to eat and to feed her family. Catholics joined Hindus in this shared act of need. Once she was in the *kammai*, she did suddenly think, "Oh, I am like this (pregnant)," said "*Iyēcu, Appa,*" and made the sign of the cross for protection. But *Iyēcu* and *Appa* did not protect her.

Again after the fishing excursion and the miscarriage, Dhanam lost control over her body. The discourses of her community also fell outside her control: during that first, three-month period of illness and possession, it was her community that told her what she had said and how she had acted. She had not only been "caught" by six *pēy*[9] and a *muni*, according to fellow villagers, who had heard her speak as Mātā; she was also caught in a communal and historically situated web of meaning and motion. She was behaving in ways that fit her community's expectations of the somatic signs of suffering connected to the spirit world. Some might want to call her a victim of social pressure. But such a claim, I felt in my own body, revealed an outsider definition of agency. Rather than losing her agency, Dhanam was becoming a very important sort of agent: she was being "called," interpellated, brought into a particular way of being,[10] as an agent to be used as instrument for the spirit world and as one who had a limited range of somatic options (one might say "somatic semantics") at her disposal. These semantics both enabled and constrained certain possibilities for ways of acting—including calling on the deity. But first, Dhanam was a body out of her mind with pain, an instrument for the work of spirits and deities.[11]

If we understand that concepts of agency are historically and culturally constructed—if we think of a precondition of having "the ability to act" as having a body, a vessel, that can be filled with particular, local ways of acting, or of being "one who acts"—we take the first step toward the possibility of thinking outside a specifically Euro-American conceptual toolbox. We can also acknowledge that different forms of agency fall across a spectrum.

Dhanam may have been at death's door when Mātā came to her. But she was instrumental to Mātā's healing. She was, one could say, being "played" as an instrument might: by the *pēy* of the dead men; by the death of her son; by the history of subjugation that her people had undergone for centuries; by her own village's spiritual and gendered hermeneutics; by the exigencies of her life—and by Mātā. This process was also mimetic. Dhanam's instrumental form of agency, located in her own culturally constituted and habituated body—one that carried a history both of Dravidian spirit worlds and of colonial conquest, of "Hindu" as well as "Christian" practices—*repeated* somatic semantics familiar to her community. This community at times required, and even honored, an *ability* to be played.

Notably, moreover, this particular form of instrumental agency did not last. In the later microworkings of possession that Dhanam described, she clearly oriented her body, over time, in reaction to a possession that had begun as a trauma, an occupation of her body put into motion by agents largely outside her control. She then moved across a spectrum of agency closer to that of an agent who increasingly controlled her instrumentality through habits of exchange.

At first, Dhanam lay on the floor in total submission while Mātā waged a battle over the spirits and deities that had invaded her. Eventually, however, she began to make small gestures that played a role in the ensuing drama, inviting Mātā into the experience of occupation by these troubling "others." During the first three months of her ongoing episodes of possession, Dhanam said, she started putting the end of her sari over her head as a *mukkāṭu*, or veil—a gesture of submission and respect that women in South India commonly perform when in church.[12] This gesture served as an exterior sign of an interior state; whenever Dhanam put this *mukkāṭu* over her head, Mātā would come. As soon as Mātā left, she would remove it, and Aiyanar would come. This play between Mātā and Aiyanar went on for three years, she explained. Exactly who was exercising (or exorcising) what sort of agency here, who was doing the placing and removing of the *mukkāṭu*—Mary or Dhanam—was at first slightly unclear to me. Indeed, this ambiguity is perhaps key to the trope of spirit possession. But whether triggered by Mātā's presence already—a response to it—or an invitation to Mātā to come, Dhanam's language suggested that *she* was the one moving the veil, and not Mātā. She used the pronoun "I" before the verb "put." The gesture of putting the end of her sari over her head signaled Mātā's presence, and lay within the realm of Dhanam's direct agency.

On the other hand, the play of opposition between Mātā and Aiyanar, whose boundaries she had transgressed when fishing, did not. As Dhanam told the story, it was Mātā, not Dhanam, who ordered Aiyanar to stay *for three years*—the two pummeling Dhanam's body with their presence. The reason? To reveal Mātā's *makimai,* which in the end trumped Aiyanar's.

It took some time for me to tease out the details of this confusing drama. Dhanam first explained the moving and removing of the veil in this way: "As soon as Amma went away, I removed the *mukkāṭu*. As soon as I removed the veil, the *pēy* came. The same one (the *pēy*) who went away from me (when Amma came), as soon Amma went away, came back to me. . . . The *cāmi* Aiyanar stayed. . . . With Aiyanar, the other *pēy* who died also were with me."

I was admittedly getting confused with all these *pēy* and Aiyanar, and the *mukkāṭu*, back and forth. So I asked Dhanam to clarify. She seemed slightly frustrated, but continued.

"With Aiyanar, the other *pēy* (of the men and the woman) who died were with me. Then they all ran away. But when Aiyanar wanted to go, Amma caught hold of him, and held him. When Aiyanar asked, 'Why, Mā, are you holding me? Leave me. I want to go. Without knowing, I came.' 'No,' [Mātā said]. 'By keeping you, I want to introduce myself to the people. If I only *tell* this girl [Dhanam] about you, who will know? People will think she is just making things up. They won't believe. But by keeping you, I want to introduce myself to these people; *then* you go. . . . You will stay for three years. After spreading my *makimai*, you (*nī*) can leave.'. . . Amma spoke like this. But as soon as Amma goes and this *mukkāṭu* is removed, [the *pēy*] comes, dances, goes here and there. . . . That *cāmi* ("god," Aiyanar) joins the *pēy*, no?—he chases and beats all of them and stays."

The young man, who had been listening intently, caught the look of confusion on my face. "The big *picācu* (ghost) chases the small *picācu*," he offered.

"Yes, the big *picācu* chases the small *picācu*," Dhanam said.

Thavamani asked, "What about the people who came there?"

"The people who came to see the show (*vēdikai*), she calls," Dhanam said. "'Come here, you have a sickness in your body. Go immediately to the hospital.' Some people kneel down and ask for a child. She will say, 'You have a chance to have a child. After a certain year, you will get a child.' Exactly as she said, it would happen. She spoke like this. Then it was over. . . . That was indeed the first scene (*kāṭci*)."[13]

During the three years following that first scene, in the course of this drama of opposition, Mātā looked over all the people, healing them, diagnosing their problems, making her *makimai* known. "For those three years, if anyone came with *pēy* or sick, Amma would call Aiyanar," Dhanam said. "*That* Amma." She gestured to the Adaikkala Mātā in the chapel.

All this time, you would be in the *kōyil*? I asked.

"I would be in the *kōyil*," she said. "That's where she (Amma) comes." Then Dhanam made two further statements, both of which revealed to me a very complicated sense of agency. For full effect, I will give them first in Tamil, and then in English translation. To some readers, this part of my story may seem like a very nit-picky analysis of language. But bear with me. It is key.

"*Nāṉ Shivaṉē eṉṟu Mātāvē eṉṟu jebam ceytu irukkirēṉ*," Dhanam said. *Nāṉ* is the first-person pronoun, "I." "*Shivaṉē eṉṟu*" ("thinking only of Shiva") is a very popular colloquial expression throughout Tamil Nadu, across religious boundaries. It has roots in local Shakta sectarianism dating to the medieval period.[14] Dhanam follows it with "*Mātāvē eṉṟu*" (thinking only of Mātā), and then "*jebam ceytu irukkirēṉ*" (I am praying). Altogether, the statement can loosely be translated as, "Doing nothing, thinking only of Shiva and thinking only of Mātā, I am praying." (Recall that Tamil often employs the present tense when referring to past events.)

The expression *Shivaṉē eṉṟu* bears echoes of the Shakta cult from which it came. It was the Shaktas, devotees of the goddess who emerged in popular devotion in the Tamil middle ages, who brought both Vishnu and Shiva under the control of Devi, the great goddess. Shakta sectarianism sought to lessen the importance of Shiva and Vishnu in favor of Devi. From Shakta *bhakti* (devotion) came the popular Tamil expression: "Shiva without Shakti is *cava*, or corpse"—lifeless, without power.[15]

I didn't ask Dhanam whether she was only using the expression colloquially, meaning, "I was just thinking 'Mātā,' and praying," or whether she was referring explicitly to Shiva as an analogy to her state of "doing nothing." One way or the other, she was at the very least saying something akin to "Doing nothing, thinking only of Mātā, I was praying."

What form of agency was this? It was at once "giving up" action ("doing nothing"), which is an action in itself, and "doing" an action ("praying"). This was an action, then, of both submission and appellation—a call to the deity, embodied in an attitude of focused, single-minded devotion. Dhanam was calling upon Mātā to animate her. As with Shakti and Shiva, so with Mātā and Dhanam: no power exists without the feminine divine principle animating existence.

This process expressed a progressive dynamic: first, Dhanam's body was "animated" (or afflicted) by divinity due to little no direct agency on Dhanam's part—though causally connected to her act of walking past the graves, into the water, and so forth. Then, Dhanam cultivated receptivity to this original experience of intrusion, and—over time—an ability to call upon it. This interpellating process, along with its continued social authentication as onlookers and participants responded to it as familiar and true, seemed core to the process of spirit possession—not only with Dhanam, but with Rosalind and Nancy as well. All this was consistent with many other experiences of possession among Tamil Hindus.

On the matter of active cultivation of her own inner disposition, Dhanam said something else very important: "I was saying prayers (*jebam*) to Mātā with my innermost heart/mind (*eṅkaḷukku uḷḷam*). As soon as I pray with a melting heart (*maṉacu urukkuttōṭu*), Aiyanar cannot be there. *This* Aiyanar."

The statements were telling on many levels. Dhanam employed the Tamil *bhakti* language of "melting" (*urukkam*) to imply that she was completely immersed, her subjectivity completely melded into Mātā as she prayed. As soon as she intensified the modality of her prayer like this, Aiyanar became uncomfortable. He could no longer be in that space, as the space of her body had melted into Mātā. That mode of her being destabilized him. Also important was the particularity of her statement: "*This* Aiyanar"—echoing and reflecting the particularity of her earlier statement, "*that* Mātā," Adaikkala Mātā. At such a level of particularity—of *this*-ness, of proximity, deep interconnectedness and personal relation—there was not only a particular Mātā; there was a particular Aiyanar who could be singled out from all the other manifestations of Aiyanar. Both *this* Mātā and *this* Aiyanar were present to Dhanam—so present that they took turns inhabiting her body. But of the two, Mātā was bigger. She made the other, Aiyanar, feel uncomfortable. In the end, Mātā destabilized his existence.

Historically, this deterritorializing that Mātā enacted could be understood on many levels, both metaphorically and literally. The Indian subcontinent had long been equated with a woman's body—first, in early conquests by outsiders; later, by Orientalist scholars, administrators, adventurers, and missionaries who viewed India as an erotic, exotic Orient; and later, by Indian nationalists themselves, as "Mother India." So when had the foreign territorialization of Dhanam's body begun? With the invasion of Mughals into southern Tamil land? With the invasion of Portuguese colonists and their missionaries? With corporeal traumas enacted upon her ancestors, involving slavery and sex? With inter-caste violence that could lead to death—such as the deaths of the five Hindus of Chinna Unjanai who had merely wanted equal rights to worship their gods?

Like her land and those who lived in it for generations before her, Dhanam had been possessed—her own body compromised, her own child killed. This rupture was at once intensely personal and also linked to wider social (and sexual) trauma. I saw her possession both as a mimetic reenactment of invasion and as a sympathetic response, a ripple of an "original" crime—a crime against all sons and mothers. This was the poetic of *puṟam*, of war (*pōr*). This was the trope of the mother who goes to the battlefield seeking her son's dead body; this was the mother who also becomes, through the loss of her son, a brave warrior. Mātā's son had also been taken. And Mātā was adamant: her ability to protect the *kōyil* of this Dalit village would not be compromised. She would demand justice.

As for Dhanam's own conscious understanding of what was happening here, she herself spoke of a lack of clarity and a search for meaning. During those first three months in which she was in the chapel, praying and acting as a moving vessel for Mātā and for Aiyanar, she had started to have all sorts of doubts. How could she know that it truly was Mātā inhabiting her? How could she discern her authenticity? How could she know that this wasn't just another *pēy* messing with her, masquerading as Mātā? She had no memory of the experience. She only knew about what had happened to her through her neighbors.

Here, Dhanam's story resembled that of Rosalind, who had difficulty believing that her cousin Alex had indeed seen Mātā—that it was Mātā who had left the rose petals outside the bedroom window. It also resembled that of Nancy, who didn't know whether Mātā, Satan, or some psychological problem had inhabited her. Both of these women had asked for proof, and both got it—one through rose petals, and another through blood. Dhanam, in the midst of her own doubt, did the bravest of things: she dared Mātā to show herself, face-to-face.

"When I came home after three months in the church I told her, 'Amma, you are saying that you are with me, but unless I see you I won't believe you. Unless I see you face to face I won't believe that you are in me. Others are telling me Mātā is on me. But I don't believe (*nambikkai kiṭaiyātu*) whether you or the *pēy* is on me. Unless you stand in front of me and tell me that you are in me, I won't believe.' I slept in the church. . . . I had a doubt: 'Is it Mātā?' People were saying all the *pēy* ran away. They say I said (as Mātā) that they ran away. But how can I believe this Amma? The villagers are saying this, but how can I believe? To believe, I should see Mātā face to face. People can say it's Mātā, but I should definitely believe. I should definitely have that knowledge. I should realize that Mātā is like this only. Only then I can say that she is with me. Then what I did was this: I bathed[16] and lay down. I said, 'Mā, if you are really on me, Mā, if you are here with power (*makimai*), chasing that *pēy*, you must descend and come now. I must see your body ("form," *uruvam*).'" Dhanam paused, and her voice softened. "I saw (*pārttēṉ*)."

In the church?

"In the church. After some time, after about an hour, she came and descended (*vantu iraṅkinārkaḷ*). I saw (*pārttēṉ*)."

That—

"That Amma with life like that came and descended. I was all alone; no one else was with me."

This, it seemed to me, was an ultimate moment of reciprocal exchange. It demanded risk and intimacy. Mātā, then, not only tamed Dhanam; Dhanam tamed Mātā. Their relation was becoming one not only of occupation and withdrawal, transgression and abjection,[17] but also of reintegration, mutual love, and equivalence. It was a relationship of reciprocal desire.

RECIPROCAL AGENCY: DHANAM CALLS ON MĀTĀ

The question of whether possessed people are self-aware while possessed, and the problems that their claims of lack of self-awareness bring to scholarly study is not just one that Western academics and skeptics bring to their analysis of spirit possession. It is one with which possessed women themselves grapple. In the end, the question boiled down to the importance of materiality—the evidence of seeing, of *darshan*. Whether through the appearance of flower petals, of bloody stigmata, or of Mātā herself descending in a vision *in front* of the perceiver, this "seeing" relied on the ability to make demands on Mātā, which in turn was part of a *process*, a long-term cultivation of reciprocity.

Dhanam's narrative continued. For three years from Mātā's self-revelation in the form of a face-to-face presence, a fierce drama ensued: Dhanam continued to get possessed bodily, alternately by Mātā *and* by Aiyanar et al., and continued to drive out afflicting spirits and deities from Hindus and Catholics who came to her for healing. As opposed to the first three months in which Dhanam was relegated to the chapel, Mātā now released Dhanam to come and go as she pleased. "She (Mātā) said I could go to work and go anywhere." Aiyanar would be with her as she moved about that whole time, Mātā expressed, but he would not hurt her. "You go with courage," Mātā told Dhanam.

That's when Dhanam increasingly regularized—one could say, further ritualized—her practices. She would come to the chapel on Wednesdays and Saturdays,[18] and other days as people needed her. People might just show up, unannounced, having traveled for miles by foot or bus. When Aiyanar came on her, she would dance, but when Mātā came on her, she would sit quietly and look up at the Adaikkala Mātā statue, pulling the *mukkāṭu* over her head. When she danced, onlookers would light and give her candles, as if to drive the *cāmi* away, and she would put out the flames with her tongue. (This preceded the ritualization of later years, when *she* would give afflicted women the candles.) Sometimes the god would demand the candles. "With anger, it [Aiyanar] would ask, 'Why are you doing that?'" Dhanam said, recounting the words people had told her he had uttered. Then it [Aiyanar] would announce: "'Fine. Bring the candles!'" It would "eat" the flames one by one—and her tongue never burned, she said.

Dhanam referred to Aiyanar as "it," both distancing herself from the god-being and using the Tamil pronoun for animals, babies, and beings understood to lack any fully human consciousness. As such beings can, he behaved in all sorts of transgressive ways. "At that time, I was carrying my son who is now married," she said. "I would dance with that son in my stomach and crouch, jump, growl—I would do all sorts of things." Onlookers—women especially—would gasp at how she must be suffering to act in such physically challenging ways while pregnant.[19]

"Oh, soon after the first miscarriage you conceived a second son," I said.

"I conceived."

And the gap?

"One year," Dhanam said. "After the *pēy* came and went, Amma came on me and I conceived. She (Mātā) said, "I only gave you this child. 'He' (Aiyanar) ate the first child. Let us see what he can do to this child."[20]

It was the ultimate dare. Moreover, it was yet another, dramatic show of Mātā's strength that she enabled Dhanam to become pregnant ("I only gave you this child") while Aiyanar was also "with her," periodically inhabiting her body. And though Sebastian Samy was the human father of this second child, the slippery discourse suggested that he had little to do with it. It was Mātā who gave Dhanam the child—Mātā, the protector, whose threatening language ("let us see what he can do to this child") suggested a standoff. Now it was Mātā against Aiyanar, her body against his, with nothing less at stake than an unborn child.

Here was a radical subversion of orthodox Roman Catholic theology. In a gender-bending moment of assisted reproductive technology,

Dhanam's discourse turned the patriarchal myth of incest upside-down: that of a male god, God-the-Father, impregnating Mary, his virginal daughter. When talking about Mary (not only with Dhanam, but also with Rosalind and Nancy), the word "virgin"—*kaṉṉi* (also "unmarried woman" or "maiden")—never entered the discourse. Rather, Mary was a mother (*amma*) who was both an active agent for impregnation and a fierce protector. Dhanam's story furthermore acted as a mirror—a mimetic counter-narrative—to popular stories and local discourse about Pandi Muni, the giver of virgin births, who by association was connected to Aiyanar.[21] In Dhanam's story, *this* Mātā—this *Adaikkala* Mātā—trumped both patriarchal impregnators, Hindu and Christian, Pandi Muni and God the Father, as well as, perhaps, her husband. This mimesis—imitation that is not the same, but that *approaches* sameness (verisimilitude)[22]—also evoked authenticity par excellence.

Dhanam gave birth to that second son (her first living son), and called him Adaikkala Raj. And in the third year of her ongoing possession by Aiyanar and Mātā, she became pregnant again, with a third (and second surviving) son, Aananthan—the one who would soon be ordained. Finally, after Aananthan's birth, as if in defeat, Aiyanar went away—and Mātā also stopped possessing Dhanam's body. The need to oppose Aiyanar had disappeared. Dhanam became pregnant again, with a fourth, or third surviving son (the son who would also attend seminary in Agra with his brother) without trouble from Aiyanar, though she continued to pray to and work with Mātā in order to heal others.

After Aiyanar left, Dhanam's healing practice subtly changed. From that point on, she explained to me, she would no longer become bodily possessed by Mātā; rather, she would call upon Mātā, and Mātā would descend *in front of her* and speak, divining people's problems, and acting through Dhanam to heal them. This practice of calling upon Mātā, of seeing her, and of diagnosing the problems of patients was what I had seen in 2005, when the women kneeled in front of Dhanam and put out candles with their tongues.

This was yet another form of mimesis. Dhanam continued to engage bodily with and sometimes even get possessed by the *pēy*, *muni*, or other spirits who possessed her patients. She would feel them in her own body as she prayed in the chapel to Mātā. It was this empathetic feeling and bodily sensation—of the patient's particular pain in her own body—that would help her discern the afflicting spirit. This exhausting process caused her to suffer and required enormous endurance and energy (often after a full day working out in the fields). Now, as she was getting older, she had to be careful not to exhaust herself; her children begged her not to overdo it. Her possession practices were waning.[23]

THE STORYTELLER, THE ETHNOGRAPHER, AND THE PROBLEM OF LANGUAGE

It is no wonder I had been confused. The process was complicated, and the terms permeable. English is inadequate to portray the subtleties of Dhanam's lived reality accurately—more inadequate, even, than discursive Tamil itself might be, to the extent that it too cannot describe what any one body, even one raised speaking Tamil, exactly feels. To make matters more complex, Dhanam was talking to a white foreigner, someone she knew might not understand. Thus, she later explained to me in 2012, she had sometimes "dumbed down" her language to make it more accessible to me. This ended up sometimes making things more confusing. For example, rather than "stillbirth" in explaining the loss of her first son, she had used the term "abortion." Later, when it was clear to me that she had surely meant "stillbirth" in relation to her first son, I returned to ask why she had used the English word "abortion." She said she had done so because she didn't think I would understand "*iruntapiruntāta*"—meaning "(one that is) dead and born."[24]

Likewise, perhaps, she used interchangeably the terms "*cāmi*," "Aiyanar," and "*pēy*." She only stopped doing so when I asked her, with Thavamani's help, to be very specific with what she meant: to say "*cāmi*" when she meant "god," and "*pēy*" when she meant "*pēy*." I also had to prod her to be careful when she used *piṭi, iraṅki*, or *vā* to talk about different forms of possession. It seemed at certain points she got sloppy about it, and Thavamani pressed her to be specific. I couldn't help but think how ironic this all was, that we were perhaps creating an illusion of certainty about these concepts, when actually they were indeed very fluid and given to change, partly based on the person being addressed.

Padma, with whom I worked in 2005 and 2006, was a Hindu, and had been offended at the way Dhanam would occasionally use the term *pēy* to talk about Hindu gods (*cāmi*) like Aiyanar and Muni. To a small degree, Dhanam's treatment of these Hindu gods and spirits reflected the discourse of nineteenth-century Christian missionaries, who had branded as "demons" all of the gods and spirits of these "Hindoo pagans." While I did my best to pin Dhanam down on the terms *pēy, muni,* and *cāmi*, to think about what she meant and to be clear about it with me so that I would not make mistakes in my text, I knew that in doing so I might be creating new discursive truth. I knew that in my anthropological quest for certainty—ironically, in my quest for "truth"—I could be shifting language meant to describe real, lived experiences from permeable or metaphorical meanings to rigid categories. This permeability of terms, however, could not only cause misunderstanding; it could cause better understanding. "The big *picācu* chases the little *picācu*," Dhanam's nephew had tried to clarify for me when he saw I was getting confused, using a category that he thought I would be able to understand. His explanation had suddenly made things click. I knew he didn't mean "ghost"—but I got a cartoon image of a big guy punching a little guy, that helped me understand a hierarchy of power among *pēy*, *picācu*, and *cāmis*. The more I sought to chase down meanings, however, the more mirrors and labyrinths I faced. I realized that we were all creating a sort of fiction—one that an audience could take or leave, but should not take as forever or everywhere true.

In some ways, the fluidity of these terms mirrored the subjective character of the reality of which we were speaking. We were speaking about crossings: of humans into nonhuman worlds, and vice versa; of virgins giving birth to gods, and of gods giving birth to humans; of women becoming male gods, and of female gods trumping male ones. This form of speaking was, in many ways, poetic. Discursive language (let alone science) would never capture the land of gods and the spirits; certainly, English would never replicate Tamil speakers' attempts to signify their experience of reality. I, in particular perhaps, felt terribly isolated by this rupture. At other moments, when I felt myself coming closer to understanding, I relished the sense of intimacy.

STORYTELLING, HEALING, AND MIMESIS

Narrative plays an important role in the ongoing process of discernment—both for the ethnographer and for the possessed person she or he is trying to understand. Because of the nature of language and of memory, the possessed healer's life story never actually captures the "exact truth" (whatever that might mean). And yet, the very exchange of words and the experiences they engender themselves matter—literally. They *materialize,* or *call into being,* mutual subjectivity. They invoke spirit/s. They *materialize them*—in speech acts, as well as in bodily acts of mimesis. Through imitation, not in the sense of pretending, but in the sense of performative social iteration and reiteration, bodies create a new "real." Speech is only one part of this communication, of this calling new, altered states into being.

Meanwhile, Dhanam's telling of her story—of her affliction and relief from it; of her harnessing trauma (as an outside force "done" *to her*) and turning it into healing was perhaps healing in itself. It could only be so, however, with the participation of the community. The community had both *to tell* Dhanam her own story, and *to hear* it (and see it), repeatedly. The story required reiteration, and the story building required an exchange. Changing here and there, both the story and its context enabled possessed women's claims to authenticity. In every case, the story required witnesses to exist.

What matters most in this long process of discernment of what is true or false, real or unreal, authentic or inauthentic, however, is the healer's efficacy—which also requires witnesses. Those can be split into at least three kinds: believers, skeptics, and those who move between. My presence as a friendly researcher, a potential skeptic who held on and kept coming back—perhaps at times *wanting* to believe, perhaps at times not—must have also, at least somewhat, authenticated Dhanam's position as an able healer, as it had Rosalind's and Nancy's. Meanwhile, most people in the village witnessed this tall, unmarried *farangi* repeatedly return from halfway across the world to talk to Dhanam and to them, and to record and write it all down. They were kind enough to authenticate my enterprise—that of a field researcher and scholar of religion wanting to make a coherent and cohesive story.

Further complicating these stories and my interpretation of them was that people's mere talking with me about their experiences was likely to have changed them.[25] The relationship at times became clinical, though it wasn't always clear who was interrogating whom. Like so many other villagers, Dhanam had asked me whether I was Roman Catholic (yes). She asked whether I was married (no), whether I ever had been married (no) and why not. She asked whether I had children (no), and why not; whether my mother and father were still living (yes); whether I lived with or near them (no), and why not (this was normal in my culture); whether I had siblings (yes, two younger sisters); were they married (one was), and—again—were there no brothers (no)—"*pāvam.*" *Pāvam* means "pity," as my lack of brother, husband, and child made me rather pathetic according to local norms. In my early visits, Dhanam repeatedly told me I would marry. By 2012, she told me that if I was meant to marry, it would happen; if I didn't, it was God's will.

Dhanam and I had to cultivate a relationship of reciprocity for this project to succeed. Having entered the relationship in good faith, we worked to maintain it. A delicate balance extended over many years, and I believe that Dhanam gave much more to me than I ever did to her. In fact, I was careful not to give much at all, for a plethora of reasons. Whatever she gave, I tried to copy with my recorder and pen. For her part, she tried to understand me, not only linguistically, but imaginatively: to imagine what I might know and not know, what I might need to see or not see. She was, perhaps, trying to see into my *maṉacu* (heart/mind) to discern whether it was "pure," as I was trying to see into hers. She was in a sense discerning my spirit.

What struck me increasingly about Dhanam as I got to know her was that her capacity to make room for Mātā included her capacity not only to make room for others, but also to make room for "other," non-Catholic, so-called Hindu deities and spirits. She did so not only in the healing space of the chapel, but also *in her own body*.

This making room for the radical Other, I came to understand, was not only evidence of how religion is fluid and unbounded in the ways we generally do not acknowledge in the study of religion or in common Euro-American discourses and practices. It was also evidence of a long process of social healing and memory. This process required a kind of *paḻakkam*, or embodied familiarity, with a violent colonial past, with the Otherness of European Christianity as introduced by a foreign conquering force, and with the Otherness of caste Hinduism as an ongoing threat in the daily lives of Dalit South Indians. It also required a *paḻakkam* with the abject body. This abject body could be male or female—but most commonly and specifically in the case of Dhanam and most of the people whom she healed, the subject was that of the abject female body: the body that did not fit into the meta-narrative of "proper femininity."

Moreover, the mutually constituting relationship between these deities/spirits and women—especially regarding the spirits' ability to help or to hinder women's fertility (marking such lack as abject)—made room on the stage (*kaḷam*) of possession both for the "ideal" woman (married, child-bearing), and for the abject woman (non-married, non-childbearing). This abject woman, yet another radical Other, could seek healing, get attention, and find shelter from a patriarchal world that threatened to snuff her out, contain or violate her, or mark her as invisible.[26] This stage made room not only for the familiar Mātā of the orthodox, Roman Catholic Church, but also for a fierce Mātā—one who incorporated more volatile and combative characteristics of local village goddesses and other local deities and spirits into her body. The stage also made room for humans understood to be volatile—possessed women in particular, women who were "Other." The entire lineup of dramatis personae—all these spirits and deities, all these humans on the stage and off—needed each other for their ongoing survival. Each required the other in order to exist.

My own deepening understanding of this process of healing was enabled by my own *paḻakkam*, my own growing familiarity, with Dhanam, with her village, and with my field of study. Perhaps I wanted to make space for the home that had shaped me, the home of the domesticated Mary and the undomesticated chaos of Charismatic spirit possession and exorcism, as well as for a more expansive home of the world. I was being challenged to incorporate this Other as part of myself. In many ways, I was the one seeking healing.

Certainly, I had power in this relationship of exchange. Try as I might to level the field—to represent myself as non-threatening, to admit my lack of knowledge, to present myself as a friend, and so on—I could not fully do so. It was I, in the end, who would write this story, no matter how much I tried to acknowledge its co-creation. It was I who had access to forms of capital beyond which anyone in the village could ever dream of having.

On the other hand, they had access to other sorts of powers—varieties of cultural and, one might say, spiritual capital, different forms of bodily knowledge—that I would never have. They had power to access ancestors and spirits, power that came from intimate knowledge of the land and their own resilience to particular forms of oppression. By studying the object of their desire, I could at times feel a ripple of it in my own flesh too. The longing could be lonely and painful at times, or—in flashes of insight—thrilling and deeply satisfying.

So who, exactly, had the power here? Power is constituted in many directions through relationships of exchange.[27] This is not only a Foucaultian concept; it is a particularly Tamil one, perhaps a particularly South Asian one, if we look to Diana Eck's work on *darshan*[28] or Christopher Fuller's on popular Hinduism,[29] among many others. Here in this Mātā *kōyil*, as in many so-called Hindu spaces, it was the reciprocity of the relation between goddess and *bhakta* ("devotee") that enabled the flow of power. In this case of Mātāpuram, power flowed in the exchange between Mātā and Dhanam, between Mātā and Aiyanar, between Mātā and villagers, between Mātā and *pēy*, between Mātā and me—indeed between *all* of us as a social body—and, by extension, between the villagers of Mātāpuram and their Roman Catholic priests, and between those villagers and their Hindu neighbors who worshipped Aiyanar. Shiva was animated by Shakti. The village was animated by Mātā, as well as by Aiyanar and the lesser gods and *pēys* of the so-called Hindu pantheon (which was not only Hindu). Mātā animated and was animated *only in relation* to these gods and goddesses of the Tamil region, to the *pēy*, the spirits of the dead that wandered its earth, and to the people dwelling on it. The priesthood was enabled by the goodwill of the villagers—as I would see in the days ahead—and challenged by lack of it. Likewise, the village was animated not only by the spirits of the dead—Hindu and Christian—but also by the spirits yet to come, children-to-be, whose well-being was dependent on the well-being of the bodies and spirits of the villagers, particularly of the women who would carry and bear them into this world of the living.

To do this work of bringing forth life, Dhanam and others had to preserve the memory of the men, women, and children who had passed on to the world of the spirits, and do so in a region marked by violence that attempted to snuff out their experience: caste violence, colonial violence, physical and symbolic violence of various orders. Forced to relegate their own, indigenous ways of knowing and remembering into a hegemonic order that sought to control them, the women of Mātāpuram had to do so in the face of a double rupture: one constituted by nature of being Dalit, and another, by nature of being female. However, it was this violence—of the body, of language, of original rupture (from the mother, from our pre-conscious "selves")—that enabled communication and perhaps existence itself. It was violence, suffering, and loss that enabled the very conditions for healing. It was pain—the desire to heal it and its memory, the desire to mimic the original rupture and be made whole again—that enabled spirit possession.

CHAPTER 8

Conclusion

Departures and Homecomings

WHAT THE ORDINATION SAID

A different sort of ritualized memory of death, sacrifice, and new life was about to occur: the ordination Mass for Dhanam's son, a reenactment of Jesus's Last Supper. The ordination would begin at five o'clock and go into the evening, culminating in a feast.

By 4:45 p.m. the village was quickening, and Dhanam was hustling barefooted through the dusty light along the dirt lane that led from her house to the road crossing. Everyone was moving in that direction: in minutes, the bishop of Meerut would arrive in his big, fancy car with Aananthan. Dhanam was dressed in the blue-and-purple sari I had given her—complete with newly stitched purple blouse—walking as fast as she could without unseemly haste. Her hair, drawn into a bun at the nape of her neck, was adorned with fresh, white jasmine and orange blossoms. Still, I noted from behind her, she walked elegantly, with an ever-so-slight waver to her hips in the sari that constrained her movement. I caught up.

"Truly, happiness has come to me," Dhanam said. "This is the luckiest day, for me to see this. To me there is no *kavalai* (worry). God has chosen me to see this."

The sun was beginning to set, leaving a dusky-rose glow. A small crowd stood at the crossing. In the center, the seven-piece "New Star Band" (so read the English words on the marching bass drum) played what sounded to me like Romanian music; the musicians, dressed in white shirts and red vests, together played four drums, a clarinet, a saxophone, and two silver shakers. The Devakottai parish priest, Rev. Fr. Aasir Vatham, swept in dramatically on a red Honda Hero motorcycle, white cassock billowing, and removed his leather aviator hat and reflective goggles. A single firework went off in the field behind me, so close that I jumped. Soon a white SUV pulled up, out of which stepped more white-cassocked men: the Bishop of Meerut—the tall, light-skinned, graceful, white-bearded Right Reverend Francis Kalist, wearing Gandhi-like spectacles and a raspberry skull cap; Dhanam's younger brother, Rev. Fr. Michael Antony, also tall and sporting a short-cropped gray beard (I could imagine him sipping espresso in Rome, where he had studied); and behind him, Aananthan, shorter, darker, looking stunned. The crowd broke into applause, and dozens of villagers pressed toward him. Several men, led by Aananthan's father, Sebastian Samy, crouched to touch the bishop's feet, and Dhanam and a few other women did the same. The bishop touched each of their heads as more of the crowd swarmed in to be touched. Dhanam's brother Rev. Fr. Antony waved the throng forward and the band led us back to the village. Enveloped by villagers, Rt. Rev. Kalist, Rev. Fr. Antony, Fr. Vatham of the Honda motorcycle, Aananthan, Sebastian Samy, and Dhanam walked together, with Aananthan's young seminarian friends from Agra following. More fireworks were shot off from the edges of fields, sending up dark plumes of smoke.

The crowd paused briefly at the small, roadside Mātā chapel—once a small hut—that predated the one in the village center. Some people stopped in front of it to cross themselves and receive *darshan* before we turned down the narrow main lane to Mātāpuram. I had usually approached the village from the back, western side; now we entered from the east, into the heart of the village, toward the chapel. (With very few exceptions, all *kōyils* in South India, including Hindu ones, face east, toward the rising sun.) We walked slowly down the lane lined with houses, and the crowd bottlenecked.

Firework smoke blocked my view to the chapel, save for the blue steeple cross and flagpole hovering above, and so—wanting to see what was going on in front—I hurried forward around the edges of the crowd.

The bishop, two priests, and Aananthan stood facing the chapel entrance while two women performed *ārati*[1] facing them under the lintel—one held a *karakam*[2] and one, a plate of burning white candles just like the ones I'd seen ailing women put out with their tongues.

The chapel was decorated as if for a party. Tinsel garlands glittered from the rafters. Each statue was adorned with new silk and fresh flower garlands—especially Adaikkala Mātā, strung with more garlands than any. Fluorescent electric lights illuminated the statues and altar. Gazing up at them now in a row were the four men of honor—the bishop, Fr. Antony, Fr. Vatham, and Anandam. Dhanam stood behind them, arms spread at shoulder-level, palms up, like a risen Christ on the cross. She was holding all this up to Mātā, I thought. Then the literal truth struck me: she was the one behind all this, her son's ordination, the village's faith, the presence of so many. Innumerable times, she had faced this altar with no priest between her and Mātā. Now she stood behind four men, unseen by them but in full view of the crowd.

By the time we had moved outside, about two hundred people were seated in the rows of beige plastic chairs in the clearing, facing the stage. Behind them, a small pack of two dozen priests were "vesting up," taking their gold-and white cassocks and red stoles from a table. I'd watched one village woman carefully fold and lay them all there beforehand. The men lined up jovially in pairs at the far end of the roped-off aisle facing the stage; I was surprised at how jolly they seemed after the seriousness in the chapel. The bishop donned the most elaborate vestment: a tall red-and-white mitre, a red pectoral cross over his white cassock, and an enormous gold staff, a "crosier." At the far end of the clearing toward the stage, twenty nuns sat together on the plastic chairs. Front rows were reserved for the dozen or so priests and seminarians, and for Dhanam and Sebastian Samy. Across the aisle, about eighty women and children sat in front on blankets; another hundred, mostly men, sat behind them on chairs. Police, mostly if not all Hindus, stood on the crowd's borders, looking a bit less like patrollers than participants caught up in the ceremony.

The crowd stood as the liturgy began. Aananthan walked slowly between his parents down the aisle; Dhanam, her eyes glassy and fixed on the altar, looked like she was about to go into trance. Four young girls danced classical *Bharatanatyam* below the stage while three of Aananthan's adult female relations stood on it, again waving *karakam*s—one filled with candles—in vertical circles. The women stole nervous side glances and stalled, seemingly unsure about which direction to wave the pots. They decided on clockwise (correct by Hindu standards), and bowed to the men. The bishop took the lit *karakam* and also performed *ārati* to the crowd—until it started to catch fire and someone took it away. Half the priests ascended to chairs up on the stage and half remained down below, in front. The crowd settled.

After the usual Introductory Rites of the Mass,[3] all of which were in Tamil, Dhanam climbed the stage and approached the lectern. "The first reading," she said in Tamil into the microphone, "is from the first book of Jeremiah, verses 4–10." I held my breath: she had told me she was illiterate. The top of her head barely cleared the top of the stand. She spoke slowly, deliberately, her warm velvet voice spreading over the village. (When I later asked how she had managed this reading with so little schooling, she looked up to the sky, smiled, and said, "*āṇṭavarē*"—"God only"! Also, she said, she had practiced.) She spoke the verses clearly and carefully, stumbling only a few times, and a woman stage right would call out the proper word.

> The word of the Lord came to me, saying,
> "Before I formed you in the womb I knew you,
> before you were born I set you apart;
> I appointed you as a prophet to the nations." . . .

> Then the Lord reached out his hand and touched my mouth and said to me, "I have put my words in your mouth. See, today I appoint you over nations and kingdoms to uproot and tear down, to destroy and overthrow, to build and to plant."

I have put my words in your mouth. These verses were not about Dhanam—they were about God putting words into the mouth of Jeremiah, a Jewish prophet who began his mission in about 627 BCE. The possible choices of scripture for this occasion, like all scriptural readings for Sunday Mass and special Ritual Masses (such as ordinations), had been set by the Vatican: this reading was one of the four possible choices for the first reading at an ordination. But this context—of a Dalit woman's performing the reading, a woman who claimed to be possessed by Mary and whose practices went ignored by most priests—lent the message poignant irony. Had the Lord made Dhanam a prophet? Had he put words into her mouth? Did this include the words spoken by Adaikkala Mātā? Was God authorizing Dhanam's possession and healing practices? There was a sort of metaphorical poetry being enacted here, relations of power being negotiated and renegotiated.

Dhanam's daughter Sofia Mary read the second scripture, and then Aananthan himself read the Gospel of Luke 4:16–21.[4] The reading included two important verses quoting Jesus, Luke 4:18–19, which fit clearly in the stream of liberation theology:

> The Spirit of the Lord is on me,
> because he has anointed me
> to proclaim good news to the poor.
> He has sent me to proclaim freedom for the prisoners
> and recovery of sight for the blind,
> to set the oppressed free,
> to proclaim the year of the Lord's favor.

It was moving to hear Dhanam's Dalit son read this Gospel on people's liberation. I thought it telling that the reading stopped at verse 21. Either he or someone else had chosen to stop it here, or this was a mistake, as the established reading for this occasion continued through verse 22. Directly following verse 22 is another well-known passage, in which Jesus is tested in the wilderness by Satan, drives out an impure spirit from a man, and heals many "with authority and power." The story might as well have referred to Dhanam. But it was omitted.

Next, the bishop rose to give the sermon. His topic was priesthood; his main message, in Tamil: that a priest (or "*guru*") becomes Jesus. "The priesthood is the love at the heart of Jesus," he said. "The priest ("*guru*") *is* Jesus." This seemed a bit theologically off to me. The priest *is* Jesus? I had been taught in my Wednesday night CCD (Confraternity of Christian Doctrine) classes as a kid that the priest *stood in* for Jesus, and that only the bread and wine became Jesus's body and blood. But it turns out that as recently as 2010, Pope Benedict XVI taught otherwise. In a General Audience in Saint Peter's Square, Benedict announced that "the priest, who acts *in persona Christi Capitis* and representing the Lord, never acts in the name of someone who is absent but, rather, *in the very Person of the Risen Christ*, who makes himself present with his truly effective action."[5] Benedict's words suggest that the priest and Christ are one during Mass. How is this different than the priest being possessed by Jesus? One difference, to my South Indian-inflected thinking, is that the priest's identity is not believed to leave his body; a second is that he remembers the event. I am sure the Vatican would have some other explanation.

In any case, despite the stress in the Tamil invitation that this celebration was being offered in gratitude to Adaikkala Mātā, the bishop's homily included no mention of mothers, or of Mary—except for one. After stressing the importance of the priest's role in the sacrament of confession, the bishop focused on the ending of the rite, when the priest says, "I forgive your sins." Then he paused and raised a finger.

"When he says that, do you think that Mother Mary is forgiving your sins?" the bishop said, wagging his finger. "No. The priest is saying, '*I* will forgive your sins.'"

I was struck. Why would he feel the need to say this, if not to scold the faithful for excessive Marian devotion, and to attack the popular idea that devotion to Mātā leads to forgiveness? The question would have to remain unanswered for now, as Aananthan was taking his vows. "Do you vow to renounce sin?" the bishop asked him, beginning a long list of questions that included vows of chastity, poverty, and obedience. Having assented, Aananthan lay prostrate at the bishop's feet, face down, arms extended as if he were on a cross. Dhanam watched all this from below, stage left.

From where I stood, the ordination offered a bottom-up view of the interdependent power relations within hegemonic orders such as the Roman Catholic Church in village India, and the Church's relation to Brahmanical and non-Brahmanical Hinduism through appropriating some of its practices. On the one hand, the Church hierarchy depended on women like Dhanam—women who cultivated popular Marian devotions (including, in the Tamil context, exorcism and healing) and who raised "proper" sons, often in poverty, sending them to Catholic schools and eventually to seminary to bolster the ranks of the Catholic priesthood. An unschooled village teacher-healer with virtuosic local knowledge, Dhanam had helped fill Sahaya Mātā Church in nearby Devakottai with people whose faith she had invigorated, and whom Catholic priests needed in order to keep their jobs.

On the other hand, women like Dhanam also depended on the Church hierarchy. In her work among poor Hindus and Christians, Dhanam needed the symbolic tools and rituals of Roman Catholicism and Hinduism to be helpful—indeed, to mean anything at all to her patient-clients. While many Catholic priests would accept the "mixing" of some such tools in the name of enculturation, others they often found unacceptable, such as possession practices, Marian exorcism of *pēy*, and propitiating Hindu gods. To some degree, both dominant Church fathers and subaltern lay people had to code switch between cultures. Each had to negotiate with the other, through various symbolic worlds, to communicate at all.

Some clergy felt the need to turn a blind eye to women like Dhanam, while others recognized and even supported their semicovert actions. But in the public sphere at least, Church hierarchy had to limit certain discourses and practices in order to retain dominance, whether that meant setting the rubrics for Mass or investigating claims of Marian apparitions and miracles. Ultimately, the Pope was "the decider" about who had access to salvation and forgiveness—and who would do the forgiving. To this bishop, at least, it was the priest who did that, not Mary.

In the face of such patriarchy among the religion of the colonizers, I came to see Dhanam, then, as more than a covert operator. She was a survivor, healer, and keeper of local cultural and social memory. She was needed for the church's survival, for the survival of local beliefs and practices in the face of such domination, and for the survival of real men and women, Hindu and non-Hindu, Dalit and non-Dalit. She was not effecting any obvious structural change. But to the local priests who either bemoaned or ignored her, she posed a tiny, but potentially insidious threat: to the status quo, to patriarchy, to orthodoxy, to Marian doctrine, and—perhaps most importantly—to their own personal, local power. But their silence also spoke of negotiation. They knew that work like hers not only helped to fill churches; it also helped fill the ranks of the priesthood.

At the same time, Dhanam and Adaikkala Mātā together were helping women negotiate locally normative gender roles among few options. It had never been a serious option for Sahaya Mary to leave her husband, for example; doing so would likely have had dire ramifications.[6] Rather than see Sahaya Mary face such consequences, Mātā and Dhanam helped her negotiate her position within extremely narrow constraints, allowing her to establish a slightly more balanced relationship with her husband, and to birth her three children safely. But as Dhanam helped women like Sahaya Mary move fluidly through their fractured universe without losing their cultural and religious identity, she also helped them back "into the fold" of gendered norms, returning them to a space of respectability and relative physical wholeness. She did so, moreover, by manipulating her own and others' bodily practices that were both inside and outside local, patriarchal norms of proper female behavior.

These "inside" and "outside" behaviors themselves were reinforced by postcolonial Christianity, Brahmanical caste Hinduism, and patriarchal, patrilocal marriage practices, and vice versa. By making specific, ritualized space in the village for non-normative, "improper" female behavior—for wild-haired women, sick women, women having reproductive troubles, married women far from close kin, women who spoke "out of order," women who crossed into taboo territories—she both reinforced and refashioned norms of "proper behavior." She opened space both for disturbing the status quo and for repairing it, thus leaving it changed and ever changing. She worked with tools of the Master and with tools that did not belong to the Master. There was indeed more than one Master here—and if we consider each "tool" an instrument, then Dhanam was a jazz virtuoso. She worked within margins, on the margins, outside margins. She played all sides. This was not a space that Catholic or Brahmin priests could get into; this was not a stage on which they could properly play.

As I sat below the stage several rows behind Dhanam, I imagined that she must have felt pride and perhaps relief, as well as some pain, to see her son initiated with such pomp into a faraway, comparatively privileged, male world. This separation, this ritual of initiation, would not likely involve Aananthan's reintegration into the village.[7] Rather, her son was being initiated into a new home: a masculine world, a world transcendent to the immanence of the village, a world ordered by a different sort of hierarchy and submission.[8]

Despite the pomp and extravagance of the affair, however, there was no guarantee he would rise very far. Once Aananthan returned to Agra, he might become just one more village Dalit among the ranks. As long as he remained a priest, he too would have to negotiate the structures of hierarchy and oppression within the Church to which he had consented to submit. Perhaps he would never become the sort of priest to oppose or look down on a woman like his own mother.

Perhaps, in the unlikely possibility that he became a bishop, he would have a little more empathy, a little more respect for outlying forms of popular devotion on the margins. Perhaps the substance of his *ūr* would always remain in him and, like Fr. Arlappan, he would help Dalits and low-caste people empower themselves through grass-roots social change. Or, rising through the higher ranks of priests, he would become a different sort of conduit for change, one who would accept Marian possession practice as a "charism." There was no guarantee of such open-mindedness by nature of his being Dalit, of course: the Archbishop of Madras-Mylapore, Rev. Fr. Chinnappa, after all, was a Dalit—and he had opposed Rosalind's operation. But structurally, regarding any possibilities for institutional change, the only hope I could find was Aananthan. It would take many strong mothers like Dhanam to raise sons like him—and these sons, in turn, would have to negotiate directly with the power of Vatican empire.

The ordination had helped me clarify the peripheral[9] and yet powerful nature—the under-the-radar micromovements and negotiations—of Marian spirit possession in South India in relation to various hierarchies: patriarchal family structures and practices (such as patrilocality), orthodox Roman Catholicism, Brahmanical Hinduism, and caste. It also helped me to reconsider Rosalind and Nancy. What sorts of transubstantiations had they negotiated through their possession practices? What sort of boundaries, if any, had they shifted in relation to the hegemonic orders within which they lived?

WHAT NANCY SAID

On December 13, 2007, Nancy had stepped outside Our Lady of Fatima Church into the pouring rain of a winter monsoon, the saffron thread of the wedding *tāli* newly tied around her thin neck. Her husband, a strapping, distant cousin of the Pillai clan, like her mother, tried to shield her head and silk sari from the rain. A Roman Catholic priest had just celebrated the wedding Mass, complete with the Eucharist. I was in Chicago at the time, but Nancy and her family had invited Padma, who we later discovered was very distantly related to Nancy's father as a member of the Gounder clan. Nancy's paternal grandmother, Vadivambal, had stomped out early due to some irritation, Padma told me—but no matter, at least not then, not to Nancy. Her wedding had been a long awaited, much debated moment—and her own body the site of contestation.

After three years of prenuptial drama, numerous hospital visits due to Nancy's fainting and bleeding spells associated with her claims to Marian possession, and several visions of Our Lady in the form of Jecintho Mātā, Nancy was now—both ritually and legally, in the Roman Catholic Church and in the state of Tamil Nadu—a wife, a *maṉaivi*. As such, more importantly, she now possessed the potential to be a proper "good wife," or *cumaṅkali*,[10] thus fulfilling her proper role as a mature Tamil woman.

It had been an auspicious occasion for more than one reason. Not only was Nancy then twenty-three, almost past marrying age and therefore saved in the nick of time from possible spinsterdom (or from convent life, as her father had once wished for her); the marriage had also fulfilled a divine directive from a perfect, divine mother—Jecintho Mātā: *cumaṅkali, tāy* ("mother"), *amma* extraordinaire.

It had only been three years since Mātā had pronounced that Nancy must not wed "because she [was] made for a life of service." On the other hand, Mātā had also threatened that if Nancy *did* wed, she would have to do so before August 9, 2006—or her hands and feet would split open permanently and she would turn into an old woman.

The date had come and gone. Mātā, who continued to possess Nancy, had apparently allowed an extension. Nancy did not turn into an old woman, though she continued to bleed occasionally from the palms, even just before her wedding.

In 2010, I returned with Thavamani to Nancy's family home in Kodambakkam. I immediately saw one small, structural difference from my earlier visits: the small apartment on the roof had been renovated. Nancy greeted us at the door: "Akka!" she exclaimed. I was happy to see that she had gained a slight bit of weight. A little girl with curly black hair peeked out from behind her legs, holding onto her *churi dar*: Nancy's three-year-old daughter, "Z." Nancy introduced us to her husband—a tall, likeable-looking man with warm, gentle eyes. Z danced about, trying on my wedge sandals, clopping around the tiled floor in her tiny feet. Nancy's husband worked as a baker and a tailor. The Pentecostal uncle and jail superintendent, it turned out, had been disregarded; the family had slowly pulled out of the nuptial agreements mainly over concerns that he did not have enough money.

Nancy was still occasionally possessed by Jecintho Mātā—and still, though less often, exhibiting stigmata. Her husband did not oppose the practice, but said that he simply did not like to be around to witness it; he found it disturbing. The two showed me their wedding album: large glossy, photo-shopped pages of them against a backdrop of the minor basilica of Velankanni. One photo showed a close-up of Nancy's wedding *mehendi*, the red-dyed designs with which she had once painted my own hands. She presented me with a small gift: holy oil and a small, olive-wood cross that she had brought back from Jerusalem. Late in 2005, she had traveled there with Vadivambal. Her father had sent money from the United States for the church-sponsored trip. Two years later, Vadivambal converted to Catholicism.

The family had set up a special table to feed us. We were eating spicy mutton and rice when Nancy's father, Maatavan Shanthakumar, emerged through the front door dressed in the saffron *lungi* and *veshti* of a pilgrim: he was about to set out walking for Velankanni.[11] He was now working for an airline catering company; his boss, he said, was an avid devotee of Mary. Maatavan called the boss and handed me the cell phone, perhaps to enjoy some status from the international connection. When we hung up, Maatavan asked if I could get him a visa to come to the United States. I said I was sorry but didn't have any contacts.

Nancy swung her daughter around by her hands, both of them laughing. Z was vivacious. Maatavan raised a hand to her more than once, moving between cuddles and raised-voice threats. She squirmed away.

In 2012, I came again with Thavamani.

"Akka!" Nancy looked just the same, and greeted me with a huge smile. Nancy's mother, Leela, was also home; Nancy's husband was at work, and her father was out. Vadivambal was in the hospital with a heart ailment. I had brought a sporty new outfit for Z, now five. The little girl danced around in it saying, "Alleluia."

Suddenly, Nancy's father walked in the door. "*Mātāvē*!" he roared. He stank of alcohol. Nancy and her mother tensed up, and Leela looked at me stiffly. He picked up his granddaughter, who resisted.

He said something to Nancy in Tamil, too fast for me to understand, to which she responded with some firmness. He shot back a louder retort. She yelled back—a primal, bark-like, territorial yell. I had never seen Nancy stand up to her father like this. The veins on her neck stood out, and she glared at him, seething. He left the room for the kitchen. Then, suddenly, the blood seemed to go completely out of Nancy's face. She looked ashen.

I asked her if she was all right. She nodded. Everyone in the room exchanged tense glances. Nancy started to regain color.

Her father returned to the room.

"I don't believe in ANYTHING," he said loudly, now shouting at me. "Not God, not Jesus. I believe only in Mātā. ONLY MĀTĀ. No Jesus." I nodded, holding my breath. I glanced at Nancy. Again, the color was seeping out of her face.

"And I drink!" he yelled, almost with pride. "You can write that down. I drink! But I work. And . . . ask anyone here in the neighborhood if they believe. No one believes!"

He left the room; my eyes followed him until I heard Nancy gasp. I turned back and she lifted her palms toward me. It appeared that her palms were bleeding again. "*Aiyo!*" I said. Thavamani sucked his teeth. Leela went to get a towel. It didn't hurt, Nancy said, but her hands were both shaking. I cupped one and felt the tremor. Her hand was hot. This sometimes happened when she got upset, Nancy said. Her mother wiped her hands with the towel. We remained silent for a bit.

We asked how she was feeling—"only afraid."

Thavamani asked, "Don't you feel some sort of power on you?"

"No," she laughed softly. "I feel only fear."

Later, I quietly asked Nancy how things were with her father.

"The year before I met you," she said, "I was very much attached to my father. But I didn't know his character. When I learned, *verappu* (hate) came to me."

He had never done anything physically to hurt her, she said; but he had *spoken* to her very badly, very inappropriately. She didn't say what he had said—and I didn't ask. I felt I had already asked so much—but it was something very bad, Thavamani told me later, given the way she had expressed it in Tamil.

Maatavan wanted to walk us to the auto stand, but Nancy insisted that she do it, alone. And she was firm: she would take Z with her. He shrugged, disgruntled.

Nancy and her daughter walked with us to the main road, where we hailed an auto. We exchanged updated phone numbers. As Thavamani and I climbed in, Nancy hoisted her daughter onto her hip, and held her little hand up in a wave. "Bye, Akka!" she yelled. We waved through the back window as the auto pulled away. I watched them get smaller and smaller until they melted into the crowd.

In 2015, Nancy was eager to meet, but did not want to do so at home because her father was there. I waited for her at Mannah Chat Center in Kodambakkam—a neon-lit, easy-to-spot shop with chrome-edged tables, waiters, a tremendous display of fresh fruit, and about a hundred ice-cream flavors to choose from. Nancy arrived with both her husband and her mother. We embraced.

Nancy looked better than I'd ever seen her in a well-tailored, modern *churi dar* and high-heeled, strappy sandals; a small rhinestone thunderbolt pendant hung around her neck on a delicate gold chain. Her husband wore a "Finest Tommy Hilfiger Denim" tee shirt with jeans. Her mother, dressed in a modern sari with geometric designs was notably missing her big red *pottu* in the middle of her forehead. She had become "more Pentecostal," she said, referring to the plainer style of adornment. Z was in Kodaikkanal with relations for a brief school holiday. Just as we pulled our chrome chairs out to sit, a group of women at a table in the corner called out and hailed Nancy over—they turned out to be neighbors with whom she met twice a month for "Bible study and praising" at their local Fatima Church. The meetings were " 'Pentecostal'-*māttiri*" ("Pentecostal-like"), she said—a form of Charismatic Catholicism. Clearly, she had community and social life.

We settled down with our juices. "The blood still comes," she said in Tamil when I finally asked about the stigmata. "But it comes less often." This was partly because she calls on Mātā less, due to concern for her daughter. About six months ago, Nancy said, Mātā came on her, and her daughter got scared. Then, "at [Z]'s school, one lady asked, 'Are you the girl with the bleeding?' " Nancy and her husband decided that they didn't want to expose their daughter to such comments.

Still, sometimes, the blood will come on its own accord, she said. And occasionally, when Z is not around, Nancy will call Mātā—especially if someone comes to her for help with a problem. "But if Mātā wants to say something, she'll just come."

Nancy's husband nodded. Nancy used to bleed more often, he said, and he had worried: "Because she was weak. Now, she is okay and I am not worried," he said with a head bob. The two seemed in harmony. It was sweet.

I was finishing the last of my delicious pink pomegranate juice when Nancy said something that made me stop sucking halfway through the straw: Her blood type had changed since the marriage. "It used to be

O-positive," she said. "Now it is 'O, light-positive.'" I asked what this meant, and she repeated "light-positive," shrugging her shoulders. Did this mean her "O-positive" blood had moved . . . closer to "O-negative"—if this was even possible?[12] Nancy didn't know anything except what she had been told: her blood had changed. "This is a very rare blood group," she said. "I went and told people at the church, and they said, 'Your blood has changed because it is Jesus's blood.'"

So the blood was not Mātā's, but Jesus's?

"They are two separate things," she said, consistent with what she had told me in 2004.

We talked a bit more about Z, and about her husband's work, which he said was going well. We stepped out to the street, and took photos outside the neon-lit fruit stand. Nancy reached behind her neck, unclasped her necklace, and handed it to me. I tried to decline, but Nancy insisted on my turning around and holding up my hair so she could clasp it around my neck. The small lightening bolt hung against my clavicle. Again, we went our separate ways, waving: she, squeezed between her husband and her mother on his motorcycle; me, in a hired car and driver.

Several things were clear to me now, having seen Nancy off and on all these years, and I could draw some clearer comparisons. Of the three women, Nancy seemed to have benefited most from Mātā at the microlevel of family dynamics. Nancy married by Mātā's choice, not her father or mother's—and challenged their authority, especially that of her father. On the macrolevel of larger-scale social practices, however, the comparative *lack* of change seemed more pronounced: she did not retain much of a following, and her possession practice had powered down. But the community of believers to which she belonged was tight and intimate, and this circle of seemingly jovial women seemed to add to her self-esteem.

Despite remaining within locally normative patriarchal structures—she and her husband still lived in the same household as her father, for example (though now on the renovated roof)—she had moved further from dominant patriarchal dynamics in her intimate life. She had escaped both the jail superintendent and her father's wish that she become a nun. She had a husband and daughter whom she loved—and she had "moved up in the world" as a properly married woman and a mother. And in relation to her father, she had reclaimed a strong voice: one that was not just Mātā's but also her own.

WHAT ROSALIND SAID

By the time of my visit to Rosalind in 2010, the family home had been painted bright orange and yellow and the front hall had been reappointed with a bright-orange, faux-leather couch and matching chairs. Plopping down on the couch next to me, Rosalind moved in close and pinched my cheek. "Hello, how are you, how do you do?" she joked in English. I had come early before the prayer service that night. We had been in touch a bit over the phone, asking about health and simply making contact. Charles and Robert sat with us. Celina was making lunch. What had I missed in the past few years?

"Where is the photo?" Rosalind asked and flicked her hand in the air. Julie disappeared into the bedroom—her beautiful long braid trailing down her back—and returned with a glossy 3x5.

Rosalind handed it to me. "What do you see?"

It was a close-up of something. A large orange and white blob.

She covered part of the photo with her hand.

"Now what do you see?" she asked.

I still saw a blob. "Ummm . . . ," I said.

"It is a bun. A close-up of a bun," she said. "But look." She pointed again to something in the center of the photo. "See?"

Robert looked at me expectantly. "Don't you see it?" he asked. "The nose? The eyes?"

Rosalind turned it slightly in my hands. "Now?" she asked, somewhat impatiently.

Charles spoke in a serious, low tone. "It is the face of Christ."

Rosalind turned the photo sideways again. "If you look at it this way"—she covered another part with her thumb—"some people see a lamb."

The lamb I couldn't immediately see, but—yes, if I looked long enough, I could start to make out the face, a beard, and even what could be interpreted as a crown of thorns. This was a new sort of Rorschach test. I was no longer being asked to see Mary. I was being asked to see Christ. In a bun. I thought of the ten-year-old piece of toast with Mary's image imprinted on it, which had been auctioned on eBay for $28,000.

But this was no joke. Rosalind told the story as it had been reported to her. During a prayer meeting one night, Jecintho had suddenly asked for a "bun." Not a *dosa*, not a *roti*, not *nān*, but a "bun," a British concoction. And she was duly presented with one: a common, palm-sized roll available in many roadside bakeries like the one up the street. Jecintho said some prayers over it, broke it into pieces and distributed it among the crowd. Like the parable of the loaves and fishes, the pieces had seemed to multiply endlessly. The last of these pieces—a fairly large chunk—was saved and placed in a monstrance on the altar, like a consecrated host. Days passed. Then weeks. Miraculously, Rosalind told me, the bun did not grow any mold. It did change shape, however—and the face of Christ had appeared.

Everyone had seen it.

But was this bun of the same sacramental quality as a wafer consecrated by a priest? Had it actually become the real body of Jesus, a "host" transubstantiated by Christ's real presence?

"Of course!" Rosalind exclaimed. "She [Jecintho] is Christ's mother, is she not? Who else, if not she, could bring his body and blood into the world? There are so many bad priests these days." Certainly, Mary's consecrated Eucharist was at least as valid, if not more so, than theirs.

That night, the overall structure of the prayer meeting proceeded as it had six years ago, in 2004—but now the monstrance displaying the remains of the bun stood next to the Jecintho statue. It had become part of Jecintho's repertoire. A large, blow-up photo of the bun—the same one I had seen—stood nearby on a poster board. As usual, the crowd began to recite the third decade of the rosary, and Rosalind started rocking. Francina helped her stand. Bent, shaking, Rosalind-as-Jecintho blessed the crowd with lavish amounts of rose petals and salt water. The overhead fans slowed to a halt, and she sounded less like an old woman, and more like a newscaster. She reeled off a litany of names and world events that needed prayer: President Obama, the Pope, something about Bin Laden. She said the world was in a more precarious state than ever—even since the 2004 tsunami. Her message had become increasingly apocalyptic.

"There is no one to protect us, no one to save us," she said. "So who can give you the protection—complete protection? Only the Father, the Son, and the Holy Spirit can give you that. We want you to know it. We are with you *always*."

Here again was the Trinity: in Tamil, *mūvoru iṟaivaṉ*, or literally, the "three-people God,"[13] it was the language of orthodox Catholic theology in Tamil translation. Rosalind had been schooled at Stella Maris; she knew the Trinity well. But the discourse got slippery: Jecintho referred to herself and to the Holy Trinity as "*we*." "We are with you always," she said again. "We are with you . . ."—she paused expectantly—and the crowd shouted, "Always!" This was not only political rally discourse: this was call-and-response, Pentecostal-style preaching. "If you want to receive the Lord, what do you have to do?"

"Pray!" someone shouted.

"Have faith!" someone else said.

"You have to receive the Holy Spirit," Jecintho corrected. This was full-blown, homegrown Charismatic Catholicism, with Mary at the helm.

As in my previous visits, Rosalind-as-Jecintho asked the crowd to pray not only for the Pope, but also for cardinals, bishops, priests, and nuns. She broke into glossolalia. Then she broke out a new move. She took a few steps back, lowered her vocal register, and stretched her arms out straight from her sides as if she were Christ on the cross. Her eyes rolled back in her head as she looked upward. Then she lowered her arms, looked down at the altar, took the monstrance in both hands, and raised it high above her shoulders. She stepped forward quickly, presenting it to the crowd while raising the level and register of her glossolalia. Then she moved back, just as quickly, lowering her register along with the monstrance, and then forward again, raising both object and voice. She moved back and forth like a pendulum.

The crowd reacted, and it had also developed new gestures. When Jecintho stepped forward, Francina, seated directly in front, raised her rosary beads in front of her face and shook them violently, her face in an almost seizure-like expression. To the left and the right of me, a few people sitting cross-legged started beating their knees up and down, pumping their fists on their knees, and breathing loudly as if hyperventilating.

Rosalind-as-Jecintho continued her swinging back and forth motion. When she retreated with the monstrance-and-bun and lowered her voice, the crowd calmed. When she came forward, the tempo and pitch of her glossolalia riled people up. Francina shook the prayer beads more, as if in a fit. "Amma, Amma!" people cried, as if in pain. "*Jecintovē, Jecintovē*!"

Then Rosalind-as-Jecintho started chanting something new—in the pitch and cadence of a priest's Eucharistic doxology.[14] She also held a rosary. As she waved the monstrance back and forth, chanting, the hanging beads clicked against the metal like the chain on a censor.

"This is his body . . ." Rosalind-as-Jecintho said in Tamil, raising the monstrance one final time.

This was perhaps the pinnacle of ritual success: Jecintho, in her consecration of a simple bun, through the body of Rosalind, was fully enacting the role of a priest, bucking all Church authority. She had, in fact, worked a double transubstantiation and—from the point of view of the Vatican—probably a double heresy. Not only had Jecintho "transubstantiated" Rosalind's body into that of Mary; she had transubstantiated bread into the body of Christ. Mary, standing in Rosalind's body as Jecintho, was now standing as priest, who stood in for Christ, who held up—and gave up—his own body for others' salvation.

The Vatican is very clear about women's inability to consecrate the Eucharist. It had codified the doctrine of transubstantiation by 1563 at the Council of Trent, relegating the sacrament only to male priests—and has since then banned women from becoming priests solely because of their female bodies.[15] According to the Vatican, only ordained men may stand in for Christ during the Liturgy of the Eucharist, because only male bodies may symbolize Christ's. In Roman Catholic liturgical doctrine, the species of bread and wine *becomes* Christ *in substance*, and Christ becomes incarnate in the bread. The bread, one could say, is possessed by Jesus: like a Tamil *murti*—an image that does not simply represent the deity but *is* the deity—the bread *is* Jesus. The Catholic priest is not himself possessed by Jesus—on this the Church is clear. Nonetheless, he becomes *in persona Christi capitis,* Latin for "in the person of Christ the head."

The priest, then, takes on a *persona* of Christ—in Latin, *persona* means "mask," or "character played by an actor"—and the person behind this *persona,* or mask, is a man. Tamil understandings of possession, one could say, reverse this understanding. The human being is the mask, and the agent behind (or within) it—within the skin, the body of the possessed person—is the deity or spirit. Jecintho, then, in the body of Rosalind, was taking on the persona of priest, who takes on the persona of Christ. Like Dhanam at the ordination—in the chapel, back to the crowd, offering her son up as priest—Jecintho was now offering up the body of her son, reenacting her own original sacrifice at the foot of the cross.

Over the years, as a result of her possession, Rosalind had accrued immense status from that of a single mother running a tutorial business, a woman whose husband had left her. Members of her community also enjoyed newfound social position. An alternative family of the prayer house community had been established, and countless lives transformed. While certain members of the church hierarchy had come to scorn Rosalind—even the Stella Maris nuns had stopped coming after the Archbishop's ban[16]—a community of lay people had gathered around her, supporting her and one another, benefiting from this new family. Together, they were making meaning—creating a sense of wholeness and success—in a rapidly changing and increasingly alienating city.

Our Lady Jecintho Trust, over which Rosalind had served as president, had been dissolved ("It was a big headache," Charles said), but a new "Jecintho grotto" had been built on the roof of the prayer house along with a large air-conditioned prayer hall. Along its long back wall, a professionally painted mural depicting the life of Jesus figured Mary in two scenes: the birth of Jesus and the wedding at Cana. Before the mural stood an altar shaped like a huge gold chalice, on which stood a golden monstrance—a larger model, it seemed, of the one that Rosalind had held—displaying a piece of the consecrated bun.

As for microstructures, Rosalind's extended family was growing. Her brothers Lawrence and Robert, who had married and each had two children, now had separate but adjoining apartments in a neat, middle-class complex about fifteen minutes from the family house. Their children—fraternal cousins—could literally step over a short wall separating one rooftop patio from another.

Only two of Rosalind's cousins remained single. Julie of the beautiful long hair had barely survived encephalitis, after the prayer house community had chipped in for her hospital bills. With her long hair shorn and her face pinched with some paralysis, I had barely recognized her when she had come to welcome me at the gate. Alex, meanwhile, had enrolled in a training program for social organizing and uplift. He had also just launched a local Christian newspaper, *Investigation Today*, with a mission to expose and eradicate social injustice. Family members teased him about its potential success, but he took it all in stride. Out of the limelight, with no expectation that he get possessed at any particular time—or perhaps even marry—he was free to move in and out of the public sphere quietly, as he wished, through social work and writing. He did so with the support of a large family, an enlarged circle of friends, and faith in Jecintho.

WHAT MANY MARYS SAID

I saw no problem with Mary occupying three women at once. It made sense, given the patterns of human social behavior—including performativity, mimicry, and the contagious nature of bodily acts—that if Mary possessed one woman, she could possess more than one. And if Mary possessed two women, then why not three, thirty, or three-hundred-and-thirty thousand? And why not all at once? She had, after all, appeared around the world in different guises; who was to say she didn't appear in at least two places simultaneously?

Certainly, people around the world had long been *experiencing* her simultaneously—and in India, in more than one woman's body—and it was this experience, the phenomenological part, that mattered most to me. People can only recognize Mary through their own language, their time and place in history, their culture, their environment, their relation to the order of things,[17] their culturally specific notions of divinity in all its forms. Particular locales *enable the very possibility* of the perception of particularly different forms of divinity.

Meanwhile, theologically, what was time to Mary? Like her son who burst into historical time as if through a ripped curtain separating heaven from earth, Mary also seemed able to do so, bodily, multiple times.

Whether one takes a phenomenological or theological view, it is the *particularity of the time and the place* that matters most in *how* Mary reveals herself. Similarly, in Hinduism, vis-á-vis goddesses: though any pan-Indian, "high" Brahmanical goddess—such as Parvati, Lakshmi, Durga, or Devi/Shakti—can be as present in a Brahmin temple as on a home puja shelf, "local" goddesses proliferate with countless names specific to each village, neighborhood, or clan—and their names remain somewhat unique.[18] Each local goddess is often associated with a Brahmanical one, but the local avatar—her name, her associated stories—will vary from place to place, house to house, grandmother to grandmother (and to granddaughters).[19] Key to understanding goddesses and divinities in India is their *multiplicity*. Divinity, in India, is both one and many. It is particularly *immanent*, with an ability to possess people.

In the global Christian context, however, at least one question remains: why does Mary appear in so many names and guises around the world, depending on time and place, while the three persons of the Holy Trinity—God the Father, Jesus, and the Holy Spirit—remain comparatively stable?[20] The answer: she is a woman.

She is not a male god—no sky god like Zeus, Indra, or God the Father—ruling transcendent, unaffected by change. True, she is often depicted as queen: as early as the sixth century, the Roman Empire had already appropriated her as *Maria Regina*.[21] In the modern era, this royal status reached its apex when Pope Pius XII defined Mary's assumption in 1950 and, in 1954, proclaimed her queen.[22] Even as queen, however, she simultaneously represented immanence and unparalleled carnality:[23] a woman with a womb—through which god became man.

For deeper insight about the immanence of female deities, we can particularly thank Hinduism. As far back as we can know, its goddesses have been associated with nature and fertility.[24] Historically, repeatedly, men have both worshipped them for these powers and also, because of these very powers, harbored fear of the female body. The source of this fear may not only be women's power to birth life—and the "lack of control" that this female sexuality can represent—but also men's loss of control over their own genetic reproduction. If a woman can give birth after intercourse with any man, then any man can fear the possibility that a woman's offspring may not be his. One way to ensure knowledge about paternity is to contain women's sexuality.

THE VATICAN MARY VERSUS MANY MARYS

Of the Many Marys out there in the world, the Mary of the Vatican has been the most systematically dehumanized and desexed by Church Fathers, from the first century CE.[25] This "hole" left by Mary's lack of sexuality—indeed, her lack of a *body*—is exactly what has enabled the popular imagination to fill it, like a phantom limb that stoutly continues to assert its existence. Many Roman Catholics have embraced this "Vatican Mary"; others have rejected her entirely.[26] In between the two poles are scores of believers who have tried to reclaim her prophetic nature: a Mary who seeks to redeem the church from sexism,[27] a Mary who announces a preferential option for the poor, a Mary who perceives scandals, who shows "*com*passion" (suffering *with*).[28] This is the Mary of the Magnificat, the pregnant Mary who—in a visit with her also-pregnant cousin, Elizabeth (the one who calls "Hail, Mary!")—proclaims the canticle from the Gospel of Luke (1:46–55), "My soul magnifies the Lord! For . . . he has brought down the mighty from their thrones, and exalted those of humble estate." This is a revolutionary Mary who, like her son, lifts up those who are socially and economically among the lowliest of the low, a Mary who can upset the social order by turning things upside down. Mary has always contained this possibility, and the Church has always tried to harness it.

Although people all over the world "flesh out" this potentially volatile Mary in all sorts of ways, they do so particularly on the margins, and most particularly in colonial and postcolonial places—especially those with long-standing, widespread, and still-active practices of deity and spirit possession.[29] In the face of domination, one way that people hold onto cultural memory is to continue to "dance" their own, precolonial traditions into life. To do so is to retain dignity, identity, and a relationship to a world that will not be completely blotted out by colonial powers.[30] It is one means of refusing alienation and retaining wholeness. This "fleshing out," this "dancing," need not be conscious (at least, not in the way Westerners generally understand consciousness, that is, as "self-awareness" or awareness by the mind of itself) to be strategic, and it need not—indeed, I would argue, *cannot*—originate from the dancer. It must involve both repetition (that which has preceded the bodily act) and invention (that which proceeds from the new act, which may attempt to imitate that which preceded it, but which will never quite match it). It comes from somewhere else, though it moves through the body.

As we have seen with Rosalind, Nancy, and Dhanam, this "dancing" or "fleshing out" can create tension with the Vatican, as well as with its local subordinates. For centuries, priests and missionaries in India and across the missionized world have had to negotiate with the unruly popular imaginations of their flocks in order to retain their sphere of influence (including over what they have feared to be unruly in themselves), while negotiating with other clergy, dominant bishops and archbishops, and the Pope. The line from village to Vatican can be quite direct: the Diocese of Meerut's website, for example, features the Rt. Rev. Kalist who ordained Dhanam's son, shaking Pope Francis's hand in a well-appointed hall that appears to be in the Vatican.[31] Manipulations of all sorts abound, including those affecting salvation: on that same Diocesan website, the Rt. Rev. Kalist reminds priests to inform people that they can gain plenary indulgences by assisting with his local, pastoral visitations. Priests like Rev. Fr. A. Thomas, meanwhile, pressure church leaders like Archbishop Chinnappa to punish people whom they perceive as threatening or heterodox, and they can win points by smoking out such "heretics." Church members obey orders, ignore them, or push back. Wrestling with and within this vast sea of unruly, volatile bodies, local clergy and the religious across the world are constantly negotiating and renegotiating people's many imaginings of Mary, both among the masses and in more elite theological circles.[32]

As for the Vatican, however, there is a threshold beyond which it seems it will not negotiate. This threshold, this site beyond which it will not step, is Mary's body. The Church refuses to cross over in at least two ways: it will neither allow Mary a real body, nor will it allow her to possess the bodies of real women. Meanwhile, the Second Vatican Council conceded that the Holy Spirit may move in and through lay bodies: in the 1960s, Charismatic Catholicism was gaining such popularity that the Vatican realized it had better embrace it—and also police it.[33] Notably, the Pentecostal Movement is growing exponentially in places like Africa, China, Latin America, South Korea, and South India in part through this "movement of the spirit."[34] In Europe and the United

States, meanwhile, in a desire to reclaim a perceived loss of the feminine divine in Western contexts, theologians have pointed out that in the original Hebrew and Syrian, the Holy Spirit is gendered as feminine.[35] The Church seems less threatened by practices that invoke this feminine, "in-filling" spirit than by practices that invoke a possessing Mary. On life-threatening issues affecting women's bodies, moreover, such as abortion and contraception, the Church will not budge.[36] Likewise, Mary's body is territory the Church will not concede.[37]

WHAT WE CAN SAY ABOUT "CHRISTIANITY" AND "HINDUISM"

The stories of these women reveal the constantly contested nature of the boundaries that define any one "religion" as people necessarily borrow from and negotiate local idioms, discourses, and practices. They also reveal how seemingly "solid" boundaries come to be: when people in positions of relative dominance find that dominance threatened. These stories of contestation reveal the constant policing of what counts as "authentic"—as "real" Christianity or "real" Hinduism, "real" deities or "real" Marys, "real" women or "abject" women—by social bodies, and by bodies of people in dominant positions of power.

That such people borrow local idioms, practices, and discourses from one another does not make their "religion" (or their "real") any less authentic. Authenticity depends significantly upon context and judge. The Vatican understandably resists gestures toward relativism—as do many believers, regardless of creed or denomination. While its Second Council supported "contextual theology," including some variation of liturgical details (such as the use of local vernaculars, types of music, etc.), the church constructs authenticity on the "tradition" of apostolic succession, notions of papal infallibility, and that which has *already been deemed* authentic. What most orthodox standpoints fail to acknowledge, however, is that religion is *always* deeply contextual. South Indian Marian possession practices are no less Christian than the practices of many Roman Catholics—whether South Indian, American, or Native American. They are no less Christian than the non-canonical gospels Church fathers eliminated from the New Testament, partly out of concern to distinguish themselves from others—people who seemed too Jewish, too Hellenistic, too "pagan," too Zoroastrian, and so on. They also share much with and owe much to these "others" in their own self-construction, including Hindus.

Certainly, people have been wondering and worrying over what counts as Christian and Hindu for centuries, including in the modern period.[38] Certainly, to call something "Christian," specific basic idioms, discourses, and practices may need to exist—for example, belief in Jesus Christ, and the importance of the Bible. But the expression of Christianity is always context-dependent, always worldly and immanent, incarnational, embodied, somatic. The idea that a certain *sort of Christianity* is pure and whole, that it exists "out there," transcendent—or that something called "tradition" (whether it be Hindu or Christian) never changes—is not only a fiction; it contributes to unspeakable violence and suffering. It is only through constant negotiations, and through moments of schism and violence, that something we might call "Christianity," "Hinduism," or "religion" happens at all.[39]

WHAT THESE WOMEN CAN SAY TO US ABOUT AGENCY

What had always vexed me most amid this pro-Vatican discourse about Mary, was the insistence that Mary *chose* to say yes. While the notion is appealing to many women devotees, it had long seemed to me a like a grand theological hoax—even a cover-up for rape. What sort of choice is it when a male angel from God shows up in a young woman's bedroom, announcing, "*You have been chosen*"?

This discourse about "choice" carries a specifically Euro-American history, and the women with whom I worked in Tamil Nadu quite conspicuously never spoke of it. Their sense of personhood was not shaped by Enlightenment ideas of agency. Nor, in all my years of working in South India, did Mary's virginity ever enter the discourse. The disparity may be a matter of cultural difference and translation: sex is not discussed publicly in South India as it is in Europe and the United States, and the Tamil translation of "virgin"—*kaṉṉi*—does not carry the bio-medical connotation of "unbroken hymen," but rather one of life status: "maiden" or "young, unmarried woman." This goes for Velan*kaṉṉi* Mātā as well as for the Hindu goddess *Kaṉṉi*yakumari, the adolescent avatar of Shri Bhagavati.[40] Notably, both *kaṉṉis*—Velankanni and Kanniyakumari—also represent place names: Velankanni is a significant port town in the district of Nagapattinam, and Kanniyakumari lies at the southern tip of India, at the confluence of the Indian Ocean, the Arabian Sea, and the Bay of Bengal. Both *kaṉṉis* (the females and the places) are related to specific bodies of land and of water—the earth's body.

Key, then, to the South Indian devotees with whom I spoke was not Mary's virginity but her *body*—her mothering of Jesus, her carrying him in her own womb (translated in the Tamil "Hail Mary" prayer as *tiru vayiṟu,* literally "holy stomach/belly"), her feeding and caring for him, her suffering and grief upon his death. Also key was her faith, her *nambikkai*, strong and fierce, like Durga or Kali, and—also like that of these goddesses—her desire to rout out injustice. People wanting contact with such a strong goddess would cultivate habits of devotion through prayer, vows, and acts of pilgrimage. They would submit their bodies to her—perhaps daily, even to a point of total occupation.

Submission, motherhood, faith, strength, the body—these themes were all much more salient in Tamil Catholic discourse than any talk about conscious choice. To the contrary, behind practices of possession and intense devotion was the strong notion of a *lack* of consciousness as we know it. What mattered was full submission to a higher power to the point of self-evacuation, or even annihilation. This was true of patients as well as healers. In the cases of Rosalind, Nancy, Dhanam, and their followers, *Mary* was the redemptive agent—not the women themselves. Each stressed this repeatedly. It was *Mary's* embodiment of people on this earth, her intense love for them, and people's reciprocal and radical acceptance of this embodiment and love that healed, not human agency.

Throughout my many years of fieldwork, people back home would ask me, "So are these women rebels? Are their Marys real?" I asked myself these questions too, of course, and usually frustrated or disappointed my questioners with, "Yes and no." I also came to realize that these were not quite the right questions to be asking. If we allow Rosalind, Nancy, and Dhanam truly to speak to us, we may find that such inquiries tell us more about ourselves than about Dhanam, Rosalind, or Nancy. We might be smarter to ask what assumptions lie beneath our queries.

As many authors of the past decade or so have reminded us, our analytical tools often contain historically constituted categories and presumptions. Modern liberal ideas of agency forwarded by Western Enlightenment philosophers, for example, presume the existence of a fully autonomous agent—an individual who is the author of change.[41] These philosophers, in their development of the political project of liberalism, paved the way for feminism, which, in its first and second waves, focused on the equal citizenship of women and freedom from patriarchy.[42] The anthropologist Saba Mahmood, in particular, reminds us that the normative political subject of feminism "often remains a liberatory one, whose agency is conceptualized on the binary model of subordination and subversion."[43]

Agency need not presume such a binary. Agency can take many forms: it can be understood as a spectrum; it can spread across vast webs of relationships; it can exert its force over, under, or *with* other agents; it can ripple over generations, like *karma*. But always, it manifests in particular, singular moments, within the constraints of space, place, and time. An act is always situated in context. Speech acts—declarations about free agency, for example, and the politics and ideals they enable—are no exceptions.

If we doggedly insist on talking about resistance,[44] then yes, to some degree all three women were rebels: Rosalind consecrated the Eucharist as

Jecintho; Nancy spoke back to her parents and manifested signs of blood; Dhanam wrestled with *pēy* on a dirt floor, resisted death, and pulled others from death's door. Certainly, Rosalind, Nancy, and Dhanam's various forms of devotional work effected change and moments of resistance. But they were not *only* or *always* resistors—they did not seem to see themselves as such, and they certainly did not act autonomously.

Of the many things I learned in the course of writing this book was that agency never consists in being a "sole author"; nor is agency necessarily unidirectional. There is no such thing as a fully autonomous agent transcendent of historical circumstance. Even gods and goddesses, or any sense of divinity or "something bigger," must pass through the web of history.

Likewise, these three human women did not author change out of thin air. To some degree, they also brokered in the language of hegemony. They did not have the tools or conditions—or even, it seems, the intent—for revolution. Rather, they cultivated a virtuosic ability to improvise with their circumstances and tools at hand to be used as *conduits* for change, as they themselves stated repeatedly. What passed through them as conduits—and through the bodies of the people they sought to heal—were practices, discourses, and spirits that had long preceded them: deities, ancestors, people who had died untimely deaths, "abject" and "ideal" beings, languages, poetics, saints, tropes, mantras, prayers.

Such virtuosity in handling and being handled by spirits does not abide happily with Western notions of autonomy, nor with many strains of liberal feminism. Neither "agency" nor "hegemony" exists in a vacuum. The categories themselves are the historical results of discursive practices. They are, moreover, constitutive; that is, they constitute subjects in particular times and places. They have in part constituted me and my ability—and inability—to see. They have affected my choices about what and what not to include in this story, and how. As a person historically situated in this body and this moment, I recognize that while various categories of agency, resistance, rebellion, and self-consciousness have been liberating for many, they have also been deployed for colonizing and dehumanizing projects. They have served the logic of empire.[45]

Perhaps it is best that I turn my interpretive gaze in other directions, including—barring narcissism—back toward myself. Perhaps I was the one in need of redemption. Perhaps I needed spirits, having rejected them.

IN THE *ŪR*: WHAT SHE SAID

Two days after the ordination, the family traveled to Dhanam's natal village (*piranta ūr)*, to the very chapel where Dhanam had miscarried. Her second surviving son, Aananthan, was about to celebrate Mass. This event in the *ūr* had not been on the glossy invitation. It was known only by word of mouth, and was meant to be intimate.

In Mātāpuram, we piled into a little white Maruti outside Dhanam's house, trying to see how many people we could fit into it. While we negotiated, Dhanam's third son, the younger seminarian from Agra, leaned in to a rearview mirror, slicking his hair back with a comb. I sat in the back seat between Dhanam and a young woman having husband troubles, who held her three-month-old baby on her lap. Dusk was settling over the fields. We drove down a narrow street through higher caste settlements of Thevars: Kallars and Nadars. People looked out from the verandas of their *pakka*, two-story homes with curiosity. Once we were outside the higher caste colonies, the country stretched as far as the eye could see, and we wound our way through more *pālai* and scrub areas. Finally, a small village came into view. We drove up a dirt road till we could drive no more and unfolded ourselves from the car to walk the remaining short distance to the main village lane. Dhanam and I took a path that cut across a dry field.

At the end of the path stood the small Mary chapel, smaller than the one in Mātāpuram but of the same style. It, too, faced east, toward small houses lining a narrow dirt lane. Halfway down the lane, we came to Dhanam's family home—a small thatched house with a columned veranda. A group of women stirred rice and sambar in huge pots on bricks outside, and thick smoke from the wood fires bellowed out, thick and pungent. I squinted as we walked through it. A small, vibrant woman with white hair emerged out of the dusk and smoke, taking my hands in hers. "My mother," Dhanam said in Tamil—"*eṉ amma*." This beautiful, wrinkled woman beckoned us to the veranda and served us tea. A black-and-white framed photo of Dhanam's deceased father hung above the door, his portrait garlanded with orange and white blossoms.

It was getting dark. About sixty people were congregating in the lane. I could barely see going out there, off the lit veranda, but Dhanam led me across the street to a man she introduced as her older brother. Save for his graying hair, he closely resembled Dhanam. Like her, I recalled, he had been sent to work instead of school. He was a farmer.

Their younger brother, the priest from Agra, was also there, distinguishable from the crowd by his height and white cassock. Aananthan, broader and shorter, stood beside him, and as they turned together to face the lit chapel, we gathered around. Uncle and nephew held hands and started to walk very slowly down the lane, toward the chapel.

The crowd processed in almost total darkness. Ambient light from the small houses and the brighter glow of the chapel ahead lit the way. Every few feet, young men set off sparklers just ahead of Aananthan and his uncle, who stopped, aglow in the fizzling white light.

Slowly, people filtered into the chapel and sat on the floor. Aananthan and his uncle stood behind the altar. Bodies packed the tiny church. People leaned in doorways and through windows. Aananthan opened the Liturgy by chanting a prayer, hands uplifted.

This was where Dhanam had rolled in agony so many years ago, a few years before Aananthan's birth, feeling abandoned and out of her mind with pain. I couldn't imagine how she felt now in this place full of people, her own kin, chanting Catholic Tamil prayers in unison, and her son behind the altar.

I stayed halfway through the service, as long as I could. Finally, I motioned to Dhanam, who was sitting beside me, that I had to catch my flight home. She whispered to me in her calm, velvet voice to come back soon, "*Vaṅkaḷ, vaṅkaḷ.*"

"Okay, Mā, *nān pōyittu varēṉ* (having gone I will come)." In Tamil, there is no expression for good-bye.

As I walked across the fields outside the chapel to the car waiting on the dirt road, stars burned clearly in the night sky. Lights beamed through the chapel windows and open side doors, sending a yellow glow into the otherwise dark landscape. The *pālai* tract was full of spirits. The clear, high-pitched singing of Tamil hymns echoed across arid fields.

Epilogue

On the night of Saturday, October 31, 2015, Jecintho Mātā and her prayer house community—about two hundred and fifty members—presented Fredy with a birthday cake. It was the eve of his eighteenth birthday (as well as the eve of All Saints' Day), and everyone had gathered around him in the chapel.

"Fredy-boy," as his friends and family called him, was almost six feet tall and model-handsome, with a thick head of dark hair and a 100-watt smile. He'd been a participant at the prayer house since a young age—at nine he had taken the microphone and given an insightful message about the rosary. Now, on his eighteenth birthday, he blew out the candles, and his family cut the cake. Jecintho blessed him, asked the community to pray for him, and sent him home because he had a fever. Suresh, his cousin Ruby's husband, drove him, gave him a tablet for the fever, and told him not to go out that night to a party his friends had planned for him.

Fredy had been sleeping at home when his friends came and roused him. "I am taking the car," he told Charles, who had come home early from the prayer meeting. "I'll return immediately."

The year before, Fredy's family had presented him with this car: a brand new, dark red Maruti Suzuki Ertiga. He had passed his exams and needed a way to get to engineering college, so they had bought the car on a big loan and hired a driver. "FREDY" was plastered across it in red stickers.

Now, on the night before his birthday, the driver took him and three friends toward Mahabalipuram—a beachside town with a Western vibe—while two other friends hired a separate car to meet them. Rosalind came home to find both her son and his car gone. By midnight, he still wasn't home. The two had remained very close as he grew into his teens: after studying late into the night, he had always slept with her in the same bed. This night, she was in touch with him by text.

"I luv you my son, come home safe," Rosalind typed.

"C u soon," he texted back. "Tomorrow I will be a new Fredy."

Soon after, Rosalind called him—and got a cheerful, automated, Indian woman's voice: "The Airtel subscriber you are calling is not answering. Please call again later." (The message rang in Rosalind's head for more than a year: "Please call again later.")

When her call was finally returned, it was the parents of one of the other boys. There had been an accident, they said. They were at the hospital.

Rosalind left immediately with Alex, Robert, and Suresh. It wasn't until after they left that Charles saw the local television news: four boys had been killed in an automobile crash on the East Coast Road in Poonanthalum, about 60 kilometers south of Chennai, north of Pondicherry. At 4:30 a.m., according to the reports, the car was heading north on the East Coast Road when it veered off a flood canal bridge, brushed its side, flipped, and plunged into the canal. Four of the boys died on the spot. The other two were rescued by local villagers and rushed to Chengalpattu Medical Hospital. Charles and the others were not able to confirm whether one of the four was Fredy. Nor were they able to reach Rosalind, who was still en route.

The six boys had piled into Fredy's car after the hired driver had long since fallen asleep, family members later said. The boy in the driver's seat was underage. Fredy had climbed into the back seat with his head on a friend's lap. Airbags had saved the two in front.

At the hospital, Rosalind identified her son's body.

On November 2 they buried him. Rosalind was inconsolable. Robert also was particularly shattered. Charles forced himself to remain steady. "Someone has to stand," he thought. But he, too, was changed forever.

A friend of the family named Robin, who was in his early thirties and who had coached Fredy in swimming and weight lifting, washed and dressed the body in yellow clothes. Three priests came to the house to bless the body, which lay in an open coffin, and followed the pallbearers in a procession first to the prayer house, then to the local church. An estimated two thousand people came to the funeral. Three priests, including Rev. Fr. Pushparaj, a longtime friend and supporter of the prayer house, officiated Mass. Visitors poured out onto the street. The other boys had been Hindus. The death of the four was a communal catastrophe.

The grave could be seen from the main entrance of St. Sebastian's Cemetery, though it was far inside. "FREDY," spelled in delicate stainless steel letters, rose several feet over all the other black marble headstones and markers. Beneath the letters, a billboard-sized poster of Fredy hung behind glass. His friends had liked him to pose for pictures. He looked like a Tamil movie star.

Hair coiffed high, wearing red-tinted aviator glasses, he leaned nonchalantly on the handlebars of a black motorcycle. On the board's other side, in a photo also taken earlier that year, he leaned out the driver's seat of the red car, one sneakered foot propped up on door.

His plot lay near that of Stella Rani, Charles's wife. Family members placed flowers and rosaries in Fredy's open coffin, and—after it was closed and lowered—dropped handfuls of earth over it. Visitors lit camphor lamps, burned incense, and garlanded the grave regularly.

Rosalind remained plunged into grief. She neither ate nor slept. Celina tried feeding her with her own hands, like a mother feeds a baby, but she denied food. For days Rosalind did not speak; she only cried. Doctors prescribed sedatives.

After the funeral, on the night of November 2, a young woman named Jaya, a prayer house member with an MBA who works for Scope International, had a vision. She saw a cemetery, a beam of light coming down from the sky, and Fredy's body being lifted to heaven. Fredy was wearing yellow, just as Robin had dressed him. She also heard a gentle male voice: "Go tell Rosalind and her family."

On November 3, the vision came again to Jaya.

On November 4, it came again, but this time, Fredy was dressed in white and wore fine white shoes. He held a candle as tall as the prayer house. Jaya also heard a voice, "I'll be here only." She told Charles about her vision and asked him to go to the cemetery to see. Charles went with a few others, but saw nothing; Jaya cried. Later, however, the group was able to find what they took to be a sign: a photo of Fredy taken earlier in the prayer house. He was positioned in front of a statue of Christ the King and the crucifix, such that the crown and cross seemed to sit atop his head.

On November 6, in the middle of the night in the United States, my phone lit up with the news of Fredy's death. Charles's voice shook. "She is in complete shock," he said of Rosalind. "We are all in shock." He also told me about the visions.

Many people called to console Rosalind, but she wouldn't talk—not even with Rev. Fr. Vincent Chinnadurai, who had been such a support over the years.

After two months, she started returning to the prayer house—first, only on Saturdays, and then every Wednesday and Saturday, as before. Jecintho occupied her and dispensed blessings, often for three to four hours straight. Most attendees—about three hundred regulars—knew what Rosalind had been through. Many wondered, why would Jecintho have let such a terrible thing happen? They could barely imagine Rosalind's pain. They also noticed that when

Jecintho occupied Rosalind after Fredy's death, her whole "tone"—her face and her voice—became very bright—and that when Jecintho left, Rosalind became weak and deflated again. Rosalind left home only to go to the prayer house.

In May, six months after Fredy's death, two priests came to the prayer house to celebrate Mass for the unveiling of his portrait—his *tiru uruvappaṭam*—framed and garlanded according to South Indian tradition.[1] The family had placed the large portrait next to the altar in the prayer house, opposite the Jecintho statue. In August, the family hosted a 300th-day death memorial—a big Mass conducted in the prayer house—after which they fed guests and visited Fredy's grave.[2] Rosalind, who had been counting every day, had specifically asked for this memorial, though she did not attend.

I called periodically through the year, speaking always to Charles but never to Rosalind. "She won't come to the phone for anyone," Charles said. "It will take some time." Maybe after the one-year anniversary, he said.[3]

Aside from the Wednesday and Saturday sessions, Rosalind refused to attend any of the special events at the prayer house—including those that Jecintho had ordered, such as a flag hoisting and a procession with a banner in Fredy's honor, on October 1, 2016. Rosalind saw the pictures and heard what people told her—among other things, that the new flag and banner featured an image not just of Jecintho Mātā, but also of God the Father, the Son, the Holy Spirit, the Eucharist, and Fredy.

In mid-October of 2016, Charles sent me the invitation to the one-year death anniversary via WhatsApp. A four-page document filled with Bible verses and messages from Jecintho, it announced a three-day memorial, October 30, 31, and November 1—a feast for a "New Revelation Era." The feast would end with the "Revealing of the New Name of Our Lord Jesus Christ":

> No one can definitely deny anyone's spiritual experiences or can be a critic of other's [*sic*] apparitions or visions as they are beyond the understanding of human reason (Daniel 4:35). . . . I'll also give each of them a new stone on which is written a NEW NAME (Rev. 2:17). . . . I'll write on him the name of my God and the name of the city of my God, the new Jerusalem, which will come down out of heaven from my God. I will also write on him my NEW NAME" (Rev. 3:12).

The invitation listed several testimonials: "I was tortured by evil spirit [*sic*] for one-and-a-half years . . . [and was] relieved immediately when I called out the New Name of our Lord Jesus Christ," signed Jecintho Jayshree.[4] "Our house was about to get submerged in water due to . . . the Chennai flood December 2015," stated Jecintho Sirumalar. "At that moment I prayed in the New Name of Our Lord Jesus Christ. Not even one drop of water entered the house and immediately the rain began to stop." And so on.

November 1, 2016, exactly one year after Fredy's death, the new name of the Lord was revealed. It was "Fredy."

I arrived a few weeks after the one-year anniversary.[5] I ducked out of the auto-rickshaw in front of Rosalind's house with my suitcase; it was the first time I would stay with the family. Charles met me at the gate, crisply dressed as always, with a firm handshake. Rosalind emerged slowly from the shaded patio in a maroon housedress. She looked smaller than I remembered. She buried her head in my shoulder. "I lost my son . . ." she said through quiet tears. "He was my life. He was everything." Her voice broke. She clutched a small photo album of Fredy—and she continued to clutch it throughout my three-day visit.[6]

Inside her bedroom, on the side of the mattress where Fredy used to sleep, she had set up a display of about fifty photos—some framed, others just propped against the wall. She slept next to the photos every night, handling them, praying with them, putting them back in their place. A smaller copy of the formal portrait—Fredy's *tiru uruvappaṭam*—hung on the wall over a glass shelf flanked by two silver camphor lamps and two ceramic angels. Outside the room, it hung in three more places. A framed headshot of Fredy as a young boy in sunglasses stood on a corner table next to a garlanded statue of Jecintho and child, amid many other smaller Marys and plastic roses. A smaller photo in a circular frame read, "FREDY REIGNS."

"We sent [the news] to the Pope via Twitter," Charles said, referring to the New Name of Our Lord, as I sat beside him on the sofa. They had also sent a letter to the Vatican with the photo of the bread that Jecintho had consecrated in 2010. "So far we have not heard anything."

He handed me a small book—about the same size as the first one published about Jecintho in 2004. The cover featured a young teenage Fredy in dark sunglasses, holding a long-stemmed rose. "Rosalind has nothing to do with this," Charles offered. "She is not behind it."

The 136-page book featured many glossy photographs of Fredy, and was compiled by Robert, according to its front matter. The entire prayer house community had played a role in its authorship, as it contained page after page of members' witnesses to the signs and wonders they had experienced in the name of Fredy. The first to witness such wonders was three-year-old Yuvan, who, on the night after Fredy's death, had seen him standing on a mountain atop the prayer house. He called the prayer house "Mount Zion." Four-year-old Lolita had seen him on Christmas night, flanked by two angels. Irene Daphne, a grown woman with a B.E. and M.B.A., saw Fredy's face in Mother Mary's statue during a service in her local church and "in the side pose from the lower stomach of our Mother Mary till her ankle." On

February 8, 2016, during the hundred-day ceremony for Fredy, Mrs. Manju Kannan was offering prayers to him with her family when her cell phone went dead; the family asked Fredy to witness his presence, and the phone switched back on. Mrs. Deivanai, Fredy's former teacher, wrote that he was the best student she had ever had, and classmates wrote of his kindness, charisma, and selflessness. George and Dhanya of Perambur made difficult job transfers from Chennai to Kerala, all due to the intercession of "Saint Fredy."

Francina, who still visited Rosalind regularly after a two-hour, one-way commute from her job as a schoolteacher, took me aside into Rosalind's room to discuss a key essay in the book that she had written. The essay details clear patterns between Fredy and Jesus. On the third day, Jesus rose again. On the third day after his death, Francina said, Fredy also rose and was taken to heaven. As Jesus had appeared to Mary Magdalene on the third day, Fredy gave a vision to Jaya. Both Jesus and Fredy went out of the city to meet their deaths. Each had transformed what would usually be understood as a "bad death" into a "good death."

"In the olden days it was said that the crucifixion was only for thieves, liars and all that," Francina said, leaning toward me on the bed. "Jesus took that crucifixion and made it a victory. So it is with Fredy. Usually they say that [sort of accident] is usually for the cursed people, so they won't get a good death. Only the blessed people will have good deaths. . . . In the first resurrection, God took away the death, and he gave life. So in the second resurrection (of Fredy), he took the death that is usually given for the cursed. And," she paused, "He made it into a blessing."

There was more.

On December 11, 2015, Francina said, forty days after Fredy's death, she and Robert were sitting with Rosalind in her bedroom when Mātāmma came onto Rosalind. Robert had been eating a sandwich. Jecintho took a piece of bread from his plate, showed it to them, and said, "This bread is made of ordinary wheat," Francina recounted. "This bread has become the body and blood. This body and blood came down from heaven and stayed with you all for eighteen years and went back again to heaven. He came from the Eucharist and again he went back to that same Eucharist." Francina and Robert went immediately to the upstairs room in the prayer house devoted to the Eucharist. "We were praying to the Trinity," she said. "At that time I saw the face of Jesus in the host. I also saw Fredy's full body. The Holy Spirit possessed me very powerfully." Others also now saw the face of Fredy in the piece of wheat bun that Jecintho had consecrated, and the name "Fredy" written across the forehead of Jesus.

"We are going to present to the whole world that which the world cannot accept," Francina said. "God has given us evidence to show that Fredy is the new name of Jesus."

The next night, I slept on the floor in Rosalind's room. I had not slept at all the first night; I'd been offered a bed in a room with Julie and Charles, who snored quite loudly, and the room was stuffy. Rosalind's room was cool and quiet. I was grateful for the soft pallet on the floor beside her queen bed, which was half covered with Fredy's photos, and was desperate for sleep. I settled in. Rosalind came down from the bed and sat next to me; leaning on one hand by my shoulder, she draped the other lightly across my waist. "He was all I had," she repeated softly. "He was my life." I propped myself up on one elbow, and she reached for her cell phone on the bed. It was full of pictures of Fredy. Both of us knelt against the bed while she scrolled through. One, taken a few years earlier when he had a leg injury, showed him lying on a couch. "Look at his face," she said, spreading the screen with her fingers to zoom in. "He looked exactly this at the hospital . . . his eyes, his mouth." Her voice broke. Indeed, his face, magnified like this, down to the last pixel, was haunting; his mouth was slightly open and he appeared to be in agony. I wanted to ask her to put it away. But she was now holding it beside the enlarged picture of the consecrated bun. "Look at this," she said, holding the picture next to the magnified face of Fredy. "Can you see his face here?" She pointed to the right side of the enlarged photo of the Eucharist, and I could definitely see Fredy's face, in the same look of agony, open mouth, prominent cheekbones—and I said so.

She fingered the phone. "He was everything to me, Kristin," she repeated. "How I suffered—you have no idea." I had my hand on her shoulder now; her pain was physically palpable. She showed me the final texts she had shared with her son, and read them aloud.

But the pain had begun long ago, long before these texts, she said.

It had started with a dream.

"It was February 27, 1997, Lenten season," Rosalind said. In the dream, she was at her local church, taking communion, and the priest gave her only half of the Eucharist host. She awoke very upset, and told everyone about it. "I was saying to all my teachers [at the tutorial center], why did he give me half the host? *Why*?" The next day, Friday 28, she went to evening Mass at the same church. She felt tremendous anticipation. "The whole day I was very excited. I was feeling so much anxiety standing in the queue [for the Eucharist]." Then it all happened exactly as in her dream: "It was the same priest—the *same*. When he was about to give me communion—he usually says, 'Body of Christ'—he just looked at me, and he gave it to me. Immediately my body was trembling. Then I came to the place where I had been sitting, in the pew—I could *feel* the traveling—I knelt down and I was filled with the Holy Spirit. I held my abdomen. As soon as it reached the womb, I was conceived."

It took me a minute to realize what she was telling me: that she had conceived Fredy through taking the Eucharist.

"February 16, my last menses came," she said. "February 28th—the 13th day, isn't it? We went to the doctor and tested on March 15. The doctor gave us the [birth] date of November 23. But he was born November 1."

So Fredy came early. But her story had changed. "Rosalind," I said. "In 2004, when I asked about Fredy's father, you told me that you were married, and that he had left you when you were pregnant." I took a deep breath. "Was he there at the time that you conceived?"

"He was not there," she said. "He left."

"What—I'm trying to understand," I said. "Were you married when you conceived?"

"I'm—I'm not sure . . ." her voice trailed off.

She wasn't *sure*?

My face, despite my fatigue, must have communicated my confused shock. She started to cry. "You see, Kristin, this is very difficult. I don't talk to people about these things." Her voice got shaky again. "That time, it was full of tears. You have no idea. Four o'clock in the morning, I used to pray. You don't know how I suffered. My parents, how they suffered. You have no idea . . ."

Despite all the emotional intensity, my body was weak and my head, starting to bob.

"I think you are getting very sleepy," Rosalind said. Her voice started to fade.

Back in the living room the next morning, I sat across from Rosalind. Celina handed me tea. It was a school holiday, and the house vibrated with the flurry of Fredy's cousins. Rosalind watched their antics with amusement, occasionally shifting her attention to the television. I was reminded of Fredy when he was that age. The children tried to teach me the names of different bugs in Tamil, and laughed hysterically when I mispronounced the word for "butterfly" (*paṭṭāmpūcci*). I recalled to Rosalind an interview we had when Fredy was about seven: I had kept the tape rolling while he tested me on the names of animals. She smiled.

I told her I was concerned about her. Why didn't she appear in public at festivals or on feast days, or at least those in memory of Fredy? "I myself do not want to promote it," she said. "I want to be behind the screen. I don't want to get in the way of this plan."

I urged her to get out more. Go shopping with a few trusted friends. Try a short walk. Her brow furrowed. "I don't want to," she said. "I don't know why . . ." Her voice trailed off as if she were seeking the right words. She stroked Fredy's album.

By eight o'clock that evening, people were flowing in from work. The extended joint family and some guests were gathering for a meal: Lawrence, Robert, and their wives and children; Paul, Julie, Alex, Charles, and others. Sirumalar and her husband had brought their two children, and a young man named Joshua, a convert from Hinduism who had moved in with the family, also sat in the large circle. Julie couldn't make it but phoned to say hello.

Celina brought out heaping dishes of "special noodles" (spaghetti with chicken and Indian spices) that she had prepared in my honor. While people passed the plates around, Rosalind placed one on the table in front of Fredy's portrait.[7] The plate remained there by his image while we ate. Toward the end of the meal and before we finished, Rosalind took the plate, ate a few spoonfuls, and passed it to Lawrence's wife, Auxilia. She fed her children from it, then herself—and the plate circled the room amid the chatter, with everyone eating from it, including me.[8]

Six o'clock p.m., Wednesday, November 30, 2016. The exterior of the prayer house had changed significantly since my last visit; a baroque white façade now spanned its height. Compared to the humble chapel I had seen in 2004, this was a castle. On the façade, a fresco of a large hand held in its palm the Holy Family, who stood on the blue globe of the earth, encircled by a tremendous rosary. Above the hand hovered a dove, and above and below it, in Tamil and English, "Our Lady Jecintho Prayer House." Instead of the lit Jecintho sign on the roof, however, a billboard featured the now-iconic picture of Fredy holding a rose, rays of light shooting around his head like fireworks. The new entrance, a gate-like structure that lit up at night, beckoned devotees to walk between two life-sized images of Fredy, along with images of Jesus as King, a white-bearded Father, and the dove-like Holy Spirit: "Step in to Receive the Choicest Blessings of Heaven and Earth." The upstairs Eucharistic Hall now featured a brightly lit portrait of Fredy (Figure 9.1).

On the ground level, the community sitting on the floor of the packed main room was largely the same: there was Lata in the corner with her family; and Rex, the lay preacher; and Anna Francis, who smiled and mouthed a silent "hello" as she moved to make room for me. People sang the same songs and still held rosary beads and Bibles—along with identical palm-sized brown crosses I had not seen earlier. Fredy's portrait to the left of the altar was flanked by small statues of angels, just like the small altar in Rosalind's bedroom, and on the portrait sat a crown. Beside it was the huge, enlarged photo of the Eucharist bun. The altar, still covered in plastic roses, now featured not only a medium-sized statue of Our Lady Velankanni and child, draped in a bright blue sari, but also a taller Christ the King, draped in a red velvet cloak embossed with silver sequins spelling "FREDY, FREDY, FREDY" down the cape. To the left, Christ the King stood beside an equally large statue of Jecintho, crowned and draped in white gauze, holding a crowned infant Jesus. Out of

Figure 9.1: Upstairs Eucharistic Hall, Our Lady Jecintho Prayer House, November 2016. Fredy's portrait is on the left. Photo by author.

her right hand spilled rose petals and the message, "Lord's Mercy is Showered on the Mankind." Below the message lay an infant Jesus wrapped in a red cloak. The sequins on the red velvet also spelled "FREDY." Over all of this hung a crucifix, with a monstrance like a backdrop encircling Christ's face where the host would be.

Rosalind, sitting cross-legged in front of the altar of statues and roses, chanted the rosary with the crowd. She started to yawn. Her head fell forward, and she began to bob gently from the waist. People started singing "*Vāḻka Mariyē*!" and hands shot up. Jecintho, still seated, drew her fingers through a tray of salt, mixing the crystals for some time before sprinkling some in the bottles of water lined up in front of her. Then she stood and spread her arms out as if in crucifixion, and a wave of energy seemed to move through the crowd as bodied shifted and straightened. She took the silver censor and swung it in the sign of the cross, first toward the altar, then toward the enlarged picture of the Eucharist, then toward the portrait of Fredy, and then to the statue of Jesus. She reached down to the altar, took the infant Jesus wearing the "Fredy" dress in her arms, and, turning, held it up to the crowd. Another wave of energy went through it. After placing the statue back in the crèche, she picked up the smaller picture of the Eucharist and cleaned the glass with a hand towel, her head shaking. She turned again to face us, held the picture up high, and made the sign of the cross with it in the air. Then she turned it clockwise to us, and made the sign of the cross again. She repeatedly turned it, making a cross with each angle until it was right side up again. People were bowing, saying, "Father, Son, Holy Spirit" in Tamil, and speaking in tongues.

The fans stilled and Jecintho spoke for some time, mostly in Tamil. "Let the old tradition go, and let the new tradition come," she said, still holding the photo. She raised it over her head. "You will speak and the world will listen."

"*Āmmā* (yes)," the crowd responded.

"The whole world will cry," Jecintho continued. "It will mourn. Is there anyone to help us? Yes. He will know how the people are suffering. . . . Every second he is forgiving you. He says that he is not going to punish you. He is always seeing and always watching. He knows what to give and when to give it. What to give—only the mother can say. But even the mother has limitations, whereas he does not have any limitations. He can create everything out of nothing. . . . He has planned everything. No one knows the reasons. But he has brought you; he is using you. You must give total surrender; you must give total concentration in the hands of the Lord. He has brought you to understand the mysteries—the hidden things. He has said, 'I am the God of Abraham. I am the God of Isaiah. He has said, 'If people ask you who you are, you say, "I am—"

"Who I am!" the crowd replied.

"*Nān irukka irukkirēn* (I am who I am)," Jecintho corrected. "Remember the convenant I have given you. *I am the same Lord. I haven't changed at all.* . . . The coming year is the year of proclamation. So you will be proclaiming the words of the Lord. The world may be aware of the Second Coming, but they won't be aware of the Second Resurrection."

She instructed people to read from the book of Revelation. She asked everyone to pray for their own families, for people at the prayer house, and for all the world.

"So you just lift your crosses," she said . . . and people did, and she turned back to the altar, and held the picture of the Eucharist up again toward the crucifix. She moved the portrait up and down, singing in tongues in cadence to the movement.

She turned again and blessed the crowd with her right hand. People made the signs of the cross on their bodies. Jecintho walked the aisle, showering us generously with the salt water. Large droplets fell on me; black ink bled through the pages of my notebook. Rose petals fell into its open spine. We ate the petals thrown on us. Someone handed out sheet lyrics for a new song written by Jecintho—Tamil on one side, English on the other. The Tamil script, I eventually realized, spelled out the English phonemes so that the sounds, read in Tamil or in English, came out more or less the same:

Retreat! Retreat! Retreat!
Let us go back (2)

Let us go back to the Lord and Shine in his light (2)
Retrieve! Retrieve! Retrieve!
Let us set things right (2)
As we have set our foot in Mount Zion
Let us set things right (2)
Join together, *we will achieve*
Join together, *we will succeed*
Join together, *we will redeem*
Join together, *we will glorify*, we will *glorify* . . .
Hosanna! Hosanna! Hosanna in the highest (2)
Lord we will lift up your name (2)
With our hearts filled with praise (2) . . .
Holy! Holy! Holy is the Lamb of God (2)
Lord we lift up your name (2)
With our hearts filled with praise (2) . . .
Jesus! Jesus! Jesus is the King of Kings (2)
Lord we lift up your name (2)
With our hearts filled with praise (2) . . .
Fredy! Fredy! came and went back to the Eucharist (2)
Lord we lift up your name (2)
With our hearts filled with praise (2)
Be exalted O Lord our God
Fredy is the Lamb of God (2)
Hosanna in the Highest (2)

NOTES

INTRODUCTION

1. Eleanor Zelliot, *From Untouchable to Dalit: Essays on the Ambedkar Movement* (New Delhi: Manohar, 1996). Etymologically, the first meaning of "Dalit," derived from Sanskrit and first used in Marathi, is "ground," emphasizing Dalit people's closeness to the earth. Nirmal Selvamony, "Serving *Flesh and Fish Blood* as Neopostcolonial Poetics," *Journal of Contemporary Thought* 37 (2013): 105. Politically, "Dalit" is a relatively recent, and contested, term for a category of people formerly called "Untouchable"—that is, people deemed not merely to be of low caste, but to be so low that they stand outside the caste system altogether. Historically, they have been treated literally as "outcasts" (thus the origin of the English word), unworthy even to touch the shadow of higher people. The term "Dalit" is not preferred by everyone, but has been taken up by people across India as part of a transnational political movement. I use the term "Dalit" because Dhanam herself and her neighbors used it to describe themselves.

   Dalits are a mixed population, consisting of social groups from all over India. They speak a variety of languages and ascribe to a number of religions. According to the Indian Government's 2011 census, Dalits (or as the Government would call most of them, members of the Scheduled Caste) were almost 17 percent of the total Indian population, and in Tamil Nadu, about 20 percent—but these figures only included Hindus, Sikhs, and Buddhists, and would have been substantially higher if the census-takers had included Christians and Muslims. Many of those people, usually listed by the government as "Backward Classes" (BC) or "Other Backward Classes" (OBC), were thus left out of welfare schemes allotted to Scheduled Castes. The numbers of specifically Christian Dalits remain hard to ascertain. In 2003, *The Hindu* newspaper stated that at least one-fifth of India's population was Dalit. See S. Viswanathan, "The States: A Temple Car and Caste Tensions," *Frontline*. August 2-15, 2003.
2. "Caste" has often been confused with *jāti* (lit. "birth" in Sanskrit). *Jāti* denotes the hereditary clan or subgroup—usually endogamous—into which one is born. "Caste" denotes a larger system of categorization than *jāti*. Upon arriving in India, the Portuguese applied their word *casta* (which in Latin means "pure," and from which the English word "chaste" derives) to the various *jātis*, roughly according to the fourfold Sanskrit *varna* system (*varna* means "color" or "category" in Sanskrit). The system became known as the *varnashrama-dharma* (the duty of the stages and *varnas*), and in practice, categorized people largely according to occupation. The categorization was given metaphysical justification in the *Rig Veda*, which lists four *varnas* of society: Brahmins (priests), Kshatriyas (warriors), Vaishyas (agriculturalists and traders), and Shudras (servants and artisans). The three upper

varnas, which have always been a small percentage of the total population, were allowed an initiation ritual that made them the "twice-born"; the fourth was not. The members of the fifth category—considered even lower than the fourth—were left out of this system altogether because of their association with ritually impure occupations. It was the British, who eventually took over from the Portuguese as colonial administrators, who formally categorized all the *jātis* as "castes," in their Colonial Census of 1901. Upon independence, the Indian Constitution listed more than a thousand groups understood to lie outside the four *varnas*, and called them "Scheduled Castes," eligible for affirmative action. They also created the categories of "Scheduled Tribes," "BC," and "OBCs" to apply to non-Hindus. According to the Mandal Commission Report of 1980, OBCs accounted for more than half of India's total population. The Sachar Committee, commissioned in 2005 by Prime Minister Manmohan Singh, found that only 9 percent of all Christians were included in the category of Scheduled Caste.

3. Pallar (or "Pallan") is derived from the Tamil word *pallam* ("lowness," as of a ditch or furrow) for the artificially lowered rice paddy fields in which Pallars toiled. David Ludden, *Peasant History in South India* (Delhi: Oxford University Press, 1989), 86. The Kallar, or Kallan caste group, is a predominant caste in the southern Tamil country, commonly identified as having a warrior or thieving heritage. The British categorized the Kallars, who had tended to be economically disadvantaged and some of whom thieved for a living, as a "Criminal Tribe." On this and how they worked to raise themselves to an agricultural community with respectable status, see Anand Pandian, *Crooked Stalks: Cultivating Virtue in South India* (Durham, NC: Duke University Press, 2009). Also see Edgar Thurston, *Castes and Tribes of Southern India*, vol. 3 (Madras: Government Press, 1909), 72; Susan Bayly, *Caste, Society and Politics in India from the Eighteenth Century to the Modern Age* (Cambridge: Cambridge University Press, 2001), 39, 385. On clashes between Kallars and the Dalit Pallars and Paraiyars, see T. S. V. Hari, "Special Report: Ramnad Thevars Go Harijan Hunting," *Onlooker*, July 8–22, 1983, 40–44. On the caste tensions around the Shiva temple in Kandadevi, see several articles from 2005 by S. Viswanathan in *The Hindu* (sent to me on November 4, 2005, courtesy of S. Viswanathan).
4. Shiva, at this temple in Kandadevi, is worshipped as Sri Swarnamoorthi Eswarar. Shiva is one of the three "high" gods of Hinduism (the other two being Vishnu and Brahma) and the supreme god of Shaivism, the sect that worships Shiva. By "high" god, I mean a Brahmanical god, one associated with the Vedas, the earliest sacred Sanskrit texts, whose rituals fell under the control of the Brahmins and other high castes. By "lower" gods and goddesses, I mean deities that are not necessarily ritually controlled by Brahmins: local village gods and goddesses, often known to be fierce. Aiyanar (or Ayyanar) is one such village deity. Often represented as a warrior, on foot or riding an elephant or a horse, he is believed to protect village boundaries and to guard the people and the fields from evil spirits. He is often depicted with two female consorts and other deities like *Vīran* and *Cūran*. Some devotees claim him to have Brahmanical status, because when animals are sacrificed to *Vīran* or *Cūran*, priests or *pujaris* hold a screen-like cloth before Aiyanar so that he cannot see the sacrifice. If he is a Brahmanical deity, he could be a later addition to the village sacred pantheon (Nirmal Selvamony, personal communication, August 21, 2015). It is significant that the bloodiest intercaste conflict of the Kandadevi area, which occurred in Unjanai (the mother village of these smaller hamlets, such as Chinna Unjanai and Mātāpuram), erupted over this fierce god of boundaries, whose Brahmanical/non-Brahmanical status is ambivalent.

5. In the main part of this festival, men carry small terra-cotta horses on their heads in procession, and women sometimes carry clay figures meant to symbolize babies.
6. Hari, "Special Report," 40–44. Also see legal documents filed by Kallar/Nadars (the Nadars of this area are a higher caste in alliance with the Kallars) of Unjanai and the Dalits of Chinna Unjanai, public documents, 1979. The Unjanai Kallar/Nadars filed an injunction against the Unjanai Dalits for performing the festival of *Puravi Yedduppu* (the putting of horses). In their injunction against the Pallars, the Kallars/Nadars claimed that they owned exclusive rights to carry the horses. For details about the conflict and the arguments of the Kallar/Nadar plaintiffs and Dalit defendants, see Certified Copy of Counter Affidavit, Court of the Subordinate Judge of Devakottai, I.A No. 363 of 1979 on O.S. No. 86 of 1979. The document argued that "the atrocities committed by the plaintiffs is [*sic.*] unparalleled in the history of Tamil Nadu" (p. 7). The Dalits tried to claim their rights through an ownership petition but lost the case and appeal. After 1966, no one celebrated the horse festival in Unjanai, though the higher-caste Kallars performed folk dramas on a stage. No one, that is, until 1979, when the Kallars made preparations to hold the horse procession again. For weeks, beginning in May 1979, a fight ensued in the courts between Kallars and Dalits over who could participate. On June 29, the battle moved to the fields outside Chinna Unjanai.
7. Police records and a lawsuit filed by representatives of the Dalits of Chinna Unjanai, public documents, 1979. Eighty-six of these reported fifteen hundred (most of whom had been "rounded up" and shown on record as "arrested suspects") were charged for murder, arson, looting, possessing dangerous arms, and the like, and tried in the Ramnad District Court. The trial went on for four years. On May 18, 1983, District Judge Krishnamurthy acquitted all the accused; residents of Chinna alleged that the trial was "fixed." Hari, "Special Report," 40; personal interviews with residents of Chinna Unjanai, October 2005.
8. According to residents of both Dhanam's village and Chinna Unjanai, the court had ordered that the bodies be buried rather than cremated, in case of a later postmortem.
9. Paraiyars were considered outcaste largely because of their occupation of making and beating drums; handling the leather made from dead animals rendered them polluted.
10. Untimely deaths are "premature"—they occur through accident, suicide, murder, and the like.
11. Girl children are often less welcome than boys in South India, as they carry burden of dowry, even among many Christians. Furthermore, because Tamil Nadu is mostly patrilocal, married couples settle in the husband's home or community, and adult sons often reside with their parents into old age: thus, a boy is insurance for long-term care. Among many Hindus, moreover, it is sons who oversee their father's funeral rites. Dhanam and her husband both dearly loved girls—"they are more obedient," her husband told me—but a boy would better help look after them in old age.
12. *Vibhuti* has many meanings and uses in Hinduism, but it usually refers to a white sacred ash, ritually made of burnt dried wood. Devotees often wear it on their foreheads, after receiving it as *prasādam*, a consecrated substance from a temple first offered to the deity and then returned to bless the devotee.
13. Tamil-speaking South Indians seem to use the word *ūci*, "injection," to describe what happens during any number of doctors' visits. It remained unclear to me why people seemed to be getting so many "injections," for seemingly any and every malady.

14. Tamil women traditionally return home to their natal place to be cared for by their mothers in the last months of their pregnancies. In illness, in particular, this would not be unusual.
15. A sign of possession by *pēy*.
16. Villagers later told her all of this.
17. *Muni*—also known as Muneeswaran or Muniyaandi—is a local deity, famous in Tamil Nadu—a fierce, meat-eating, warrior god, sometimes known for smoking cheroot and drinking arrack. He has many forms; some are understood to be servants of Aiyanar.
18. Alf Hiltebeitel and Kathleen Erndl offer answers on both sides of the issue in their edited volume *Is the Goddess a Feminist? The Politics of South Asian Goddesses* (Sheffield, UK: Sheffield Academic, 2000). My own answer to this question is, "it depends."
19. Many scholars claim that the term "Hinduism" is a relatively recent construct—a term that came up in English usage, at least in Britain, no earlier than the late eighteenth century and was deeply implicated in the process of colonialism and nationalism that followed. The British had taken a geographical term that had been used by Persian speakers to refer to the lands and people beyond and around the Indus River, *al-Hind*, and loaded it with new religious meaning. They used the word "Hindooism" as a blanket term for the plethora of beliefs and practices found on the Indian subcontinent, from the Brahmanical (priestly) Shaivite, Vaishnavite, and Shakta traditions (that is, the people who worship Shiva, Vishnu, and Shakti), to the multitude of non-Brahmanical popular beliefs and practices that did not involve Sanskrit or brahmin priests. I use the term "Hinduism"—with the knowledge that it is problematic—both to make reading for the non-specialist easier, and because it is the term that many Hindus, themselves, have taken as an identity marker. I would rather eschew it altogether and simply say something like "the variety of religious practices of the subcontinent called India," but doing so is wordy. So I will drop the quotation marks from here. See Romila Thapar, "Syndicated Hinduism," in *Hinduism Reconsidered*, ed. Hermann Kulke and Gunther-Dietz Sontheimer (New Delhi: Manohar Publishers, 2001), 54–81; Brian Pennington, *Was Hinduism Invented? Britons, Indians, and the Colonial Construction of Religion* (New York: Oxford University Press, 2005); William Sweetman, *Mapping Hinduism: "Hinduism" and the Study of Indian Religions* (Halle, GE: Neue Hallesche Berichte, 2003); and Julius Lipner, "The Rise of 'Hinduism:' Or, How to Invent a World Religion with Only Moderate Success," *International Journal of Hindu Studies* 10, no. 1 (2006): 94. Cf. David Lorenzen, "Who Invented Hinduism?" *Comparative Studies in Society and History* 41, no. 4 (1999): 630–659.
20. A. K. Ramanujan, *The Interior Landscape* (Delhi: Oxford University Press, 1994), 103–115; and Nirmal Selvamony, "*tiNai* in Primal and Stratified Societies," *Indian Journal of Ecocriticism* I.1 (2008): 38–48.
21. Evidence for this oppression is extensive, ranging at least from the colonial period to present-day India. Examples include Bama, *Karukku*, trans. Lakshmi Holstrom (Chennai: Macmillan India, 2000); Anant Kakba Priolkar, *The Goan Inquisition: Being a Quatercentenary Commemoration Study of the Inquisition in India* (Bombay: Bombay University Press, 1961); and Ebe Sundar Raj, Sam Thambusamy, and Ezra Samuel, *Divide to Rule*. Rev. ed. (Chennai: Bharat Jyoti, 2000).
22. Hindus make up 80 percent of the population, and Muslims, 14 percent, according to the 2011 Census of India. Statistics on the number of Christians in India are controversial and vary widely, from the official 2.3 percent (about 28 million)

recorded in the 2011 Census of India to the 6 percent (72.6 million) recorded in the World Christian Database. Official statistics are often distorted by people self-identifying as Christian or Hindu depending on the situation, as the government bars certain categories of converts from state welfare as Scheduled Castes.

23. David Mosse, *The Saint in the Banyan Tree: Christianity and Caste Society in India* (Berkeley: University of California Press, 2012), ix.
24. Compared to South Indian communities on the southwestern Malabar Coast, where St. Thomas the Apostle is said to have arrived in 52 CE, however, the numbers are small: far below Goa, for example, which boasts a Christian population of 25 percent (though its total population is only 1.45 million), or Kerala, where Christians—mostly St. Thomas and Syrian Christians—are 18 percent of the total population of 33.4 million (2011 Census of India).
25. Norman Cutler, *Songs of Experience: The Poetics of Tamil Devotion* (Bloomington: Indiana University Press, 1987), 1.
26. Margaret Trawick, *Notes on Love in a Tamil Family* (Berkeley: University of California Press, 1990), 6.
27. Ibid. Also see Karin Kapadia, *Siva and Her Sisters: Gender, Caste, and Class in Rural South India* (Boulder, CO: Westview, 1995).
28. Men and women often sit on opposite sides of the bus in South India, though at the time of my writing, this practice was slowly changing, especially in large cities.
29. For a similar description of this trip, see Gillian Goslinga, "Embodiment and the Metaphysics of Virgin Birth in South India: A Case Study," in *Summoning the Spirits: Possession and Invocation in Contemporary Religion*, ed. Andrew Dawson (London: I. B. Tauris, 2011), 110.
30. Marcel Mauss, "A Category of the Human Mind: The Notion of Person, the Notion of Self," in *The Category of the Person: Anthropology, Philosophy, History*, ed. Michael Carrithers, Steven Collins, and Steven Lukes (Cambridge: Cambridge University Press, 1985), 1–25.
31. For similar reasons that I stick with the word "Hinduism" in this book, I often stick with the term "possession" when discussing a myriad variety of experiences, discourses, and practices that seem to fall under this category. This is partly a problem of translation—writing for an English-speaking audience—as well as the fact that English-speaking Tamils themselves use the term. Where possible, I break down the types of what we might call "possession" along Tamil categories.
32. Frederick M. Smith, *The Self Possessed: Deity and Spirit Possession in South Asian Literature and Civilization* (New York: Columbia University Press, 2006); Eliza Kent, *Converting Women: Gender and Protestant Christianity in Colonial South India* (New York: Oxford University Press, 2004), 58–60; Isabelle Nabokov, *Religion against the Self: An Ethnography of Tamil Rituals* (New York: Oxford University Press, 2000); and Karin Kapadia, "Pierced by Love: Tamil Possession, Gender, and Caste," in *Invented Identities: The Interplay of Gender, Religion, and Politics in India*, ed. Julia Leslie and Mary McGee (New Delhi: Oxford University Press, 2000), 181–202.
33. Nancy's father was of the Gounder community.
34. Kalpana Ram, *Mukkuvar Women: Gender, Hegemony, and Capitalist Transformation in a South Indian Fishing Community* (New Delhi: Kali for Women, 1991).
35. Richard D. MacPhail, "Finding a Path in Others' Worlds: The Challenge of Exorcism," in *Popular Christianity in India: Riting between the Lines*, ed. Selva J. Raj and Corinne G. Dempsey (Albany: State University of New York Press, 2002), 141–162.
36. See David Mosse, "Catholic Saints and the Hindu Village Pantheon in Rural Tamil Nadu, India," *Man* n.s. 29, no. 2 (1994): 301–332. He cites R. Deliège, *Les Paraiyars*

du Tamil Nadu: l'organisation sociale d'un village d'intouchables de l'Inde de sud (version abrégée) (master's thesis, Katholieke Universiteit te Leuven, 1986) and his own work in Alapuram, Ramnad, as sources for the "rare occurrence" of exorcism at Marian sites. However, I found it to be quite prevalent, and respectfully disagree with Mosse, who states that, with few exceptions, "Mātā has an entirely benevolent power, strongly associated with health and childbirth, and marked by the absence of punishment of demonic exorcism" (331).

37. Matthia Frenz, personal communication. Frenz attended one of these services in 2000. According to an article from March 3, 2004 in *Thina Thandi*, a local Tamil-language newspaper, Alphonsa Mary, age 50, was arrested for collecting 500,000 rupees from the public. I do not know what happened to her case.
38. Folklore Resource and Research Center, St. Xavier's College, Palayamkottai, Tamil Nadu, 2001.
39. Ironically, this woman had reportedly left the country to come to the United States for several months while I was in Chennai, and I was unable to track her down.
40. Thanks to Kaori Hatsumi, who introduced me to this.
41. Maurice Bloch, "The Slaves, the King, and Mary in the Slums of Antananarivo," in *Shamanism, History and the State*, ed. Nicholas Thomas and Caroline Humphrey (Ann Arbor: University of Michigan Press, 1994), 133–145.
42. Karen McCarthy Brown, *Mama Lola: A Vodou Priestess in Brooklyn* (Berkeley: University of California Press, 1991); Terry Rey, *Our Lady of Class Struggle: The Cult of the Virgin Mary in Haiti* (Trenton, NJ: Africa World Press, 1999).
43. Katharina Wilkins, "Mary and the Demons: Marian Devotion and Ritual Healing in Tanzania," *Journal of Religion in Africa* 39, Fasc. 3 (2009): 295–318.
44. Pope Benedict XVI approved the declaration, issued by the Congregation of the Declaration of Faith, that excommunicated the Community of the Lady of All Nations, better known as the Army of Mary, on July 11, 2007. See "Army of Mary Excommunicated by the Vatican," Catholic News Agency, September 14, 2007. http://www.catholicnewsagency.com/news/army_of_mary_excommunicated_by_the_vatican/ (accessed September 29, 2013).
45. Carla Bellamy, *The Powerful Ephemeral: Everyday Healing in an Ambiguously Islamic Place* (Berkeley: University of California Press, 2011); Joyce Flueckiger, *In Amma's Healing Room: Gender and Vernacular Islam in South India* (Bloomington: Indiana University Press, 2006); Eliza Kent and Tazim R. Kassam, eds., *Lines in Water: Religious Boundaries in South Asia* (Syracuse, NY: Syracuse University Press, 2013); Afsar Muhammad, *The Festival of Pirs: Popular Islam and Shared Devotion in South India* (New York: Oxford University Press, 2013).
46. Scholars notoriously disagree over dating the *RigVeda*, in part because it is difficult to trace such ancient origins. See Gavin Flood, *An Introduction to Hinduism* (Cambridge: Cambridge University Press, 1996), 37–39; and Wendy Doniger, *The Hindus: An Alternative History* (New York: Penguin Press, 2009), 85–102. Doniger, on page 86, says it was composed "in around 1500 BCE," and Flood, on page 37, dates it to "probably around 1200 BCE." Max Müller said it was probably composed somewhere between 1500 and 1200 BCE. See Max Müller, *The Six Systems of Indian Philosophy* (London: Longmans, Green and Co., 1899), 44–47.
47. Smith, *Self Possessed*, 245. In the Mahabharata as well as in Tamil *bhakti* literature, we see that people can be possessed by extreme emotional states, as well as by demons; by places and their entrance into them (which can cause risky emotional states); and by substantial forms that may cause them to shape-shift by their entrance into the body.

48. Susan Bayly, *Saints, Goddesses and Kings: Muslims and Christians in South Indian Society, 1700–1900* (Cambridge: Cambridge University Press, 1989), 40.
49. While there is no set number of deities in Hinduism, the popular perception that there are thirty crores (330 million) may be traced to verses from the *Rig Veda* and the *Brihadaranyaka Upanishad*. Lynn Foulston and Stuart Abbott, *Hindu Goddesses: Beliefs and Practices* (Brighton: Sussex Academic Press, 2009), 1–2.
50. David Mosse, "Catholic Saints and the Hindu Village Pantheon," as found in Parish Diary entry, Fr. Gnanaprakasam, 4.8.1896.
51. Ines Županov, *Missionary Tropics: The Catholic Frontier in India, 16th–17th Centuries* (Ann Arbor: University of Michigan, 2005), 24.
52. Ibid.
53. Historians have more or less agreed that Thomas likely did actually make the journey, though some, like Susan Bayly, caution that the Indian stories about him are adaptations of preexisting West Asian myths about heroes and martyrs. See Bayly, *Saints, Goddesses and Kings*, 245–246.
54. Mathias A. Mundadan, *History of Christianity: From the Beginning up to the Middle of the Sixteenth Century (up to 1542)* (Bangalore: Theological Publications in India, 1984), vol. 1, 9–66. Another possibility is that St. Thomas himself did not bring Christianity to Kerala; rather, West Asian merchants and navigators brought the sect of St. Thomas Christianity to South India via the Keralan spice market, which saw busy exchange since Roman times. See Bayly, *Saints, Goddesses and Kings*, 244.
55. Corinne Dempsey, *Kerala Christian Sainthood: Collisions of Culture and World View in South India* (New York: Oxford University Press, 2001), 5.
56. Ibid., 5–6.
57. This state served as the governing body of a host of Portuguese fortresses and colonies overseas. It was enabled by and enabled the *Padroado Real*, or "royal patronage," by which the Vatican had delegated to the kings of Portugal the administration of local churches. Through this arrangement, Portuguese kings were able to order the construction of churches, nominate pastors and bishops, and spread their empire in collusion with the Church based in Rome.
58. Dempsey, *Kerala Christian Sainthood*, 6.
59. The Portuguese had built their first Catholic *feitoria*, or port trading station, on the Malabar Coast in 1498, in Calicut, near Goa. They built the second in Mylapore, which would, under British colonial rule, be known as Madras (now called Chennai), and officially occupied it in 1543. See Bayly, *Saints, Goddesses, and Kings*, 258–262.
60. Ram, *Mukkuvar Women*, 39.
61. Margaret Meibohm, "Past Selves and Present Others: The Ritual Construction of Identity at a Catholic Festival in India," in Raj and Dempsey, *Popular Christianity in India*, 62.
62. F. R. Hemmingway, "Tanjore," *Imperial Gazetteer*, vol. 1 (Madras: Government Press, 1908), 250.
63. In 1961, the estimate of people attending the annual festival alone was one million, according to the Indian census of that year, and numbers have grown significantly since then, the Vicar General told me.
64. August 15 is both the Feast of the Assumption and India's Day of Independence.
65. The cult of Mary that first emerged in Palestine developed from the goddess cults already predominant in that region. See Marina Warner, *Alone of All Her Sex: The Myth and the Cult of the Virgin Mary* (New York: Vintage, 1976). Greco-Roman goddesses morphed well with her, as did Celtic goddesses later in Ireland, Aztec goddesses in Mexico and Central and America, and so on.

66. Innumerable studies note the preponderance of spirit possession practices among women compared to men. See Erika Bourguignon, "World Distribution and Patterns of Possession States," in *Trance and Possession States*, ed. Raymond Prince (Montreal: R. M. Bucke Memorial Society, 1968); Janice Boddy, *Wombs and Alien Spirits: Women, Men, and the Zār Cult in Northern Sudan* (Madison: University of Wisconsin Press, 1989); Emma Cohen, *The Mind Possessed: The Cognition of Spirit Possession in an Afro-Brazilian Religious Tradition* (New York: Oxford University Press, 2007); Bruce Kapferer, *A Celebration of Demons: Exorcism and the Aesthetics of Healing in Sri Lanka*, 2nd ed., Explorations in Anthropology Series (Providence, RI: Berg, 1991); Michael Lambek, "From Disease to Discourse: Remarks on the Conceptualization of Trance and Spirit Possession," in *Altered States of Consciousness and Mental Health*, ed. Colleen A. Ward (Newbury Park, CA: Sage, 1981); Michael Lambek, *Knowledge and Practice in Mayotte: Local Discourses of Islam, Sorcery, and Sprit Possession*, Anthropological Horizons (Toronto: University of Toronto Press, 1993); and Aihwa Ong, *Spirits of Resistance and Capitalist Discipline: Factory Women in Malaysia*, 2nd ed. (Albany: State University of New York Press, 2010)—to name a few. For a study on gender orientations as a possible source of this comparative difference between men and women, rather than sex, also see Simon Baron-Cohen, *Mindblindness: An Essay on Autism and Theory of Mind* (Cambridge, MA: MIT Press, 1995); and Simon Baron-Cohen, *The Essential Difference: Male and Female Brains and the Truth about Autism* (New York: Basic, 2004).
67. In the New Testament, she appears first in Paul's letter to the Galatians, in which Paul states, simply, that Jesus was "made of a woman" (Gal. 4:4). He never refers to her again. In the Gospel of Mark, she appears twice: once in an unflattering light (Mark 3:31) and once as the mother of Jesus (Mark 6:3). It is only in Matthew and Luke that we get a little bit more. Matthew, particularly concerned about his Jewish audience, links Jesus's birth five times to fulfillments of the Hebrew Bible, translating into Greek what first appeared in the Hebrew. For example, Matthew writes, "Behold a virgin [in Greek, *parthenos*] shall be with child and shall bring forth a son, and they shall call him Emmanuel" (1:23)—a translation of Isaiah 7:14: "Therefore the Lord himself will give you a sign; the young woman [or "maiden," in Hebrew, *alma*] will conceive and give birth to a son, and will call him Immanuel." Mary doesn't speak at all in the Gospel of Matthew. In Luke, she speaks for the first time—four times, briefly. John stresses her cooperation with Jesus in the marriage at Cana and her presence at the foot of the cross but contains no conception or infancy stories.
68. Jaroslav Pelikan, *Mary through the Centuries: Her Place in the History of Culture* (New Haven, CT: Yale University Press, 1996); Miri Rubin, *Mother of God: A History of the Virgin Mary* (New Haven, CT: Yale University Press, 2009); Warner, *Alone of All Her Sex*.
69. This image, attributed to the Coptic artist Isaac, is found in a manuscript from Fayum, Egypt. See Warner, *Alone of All Her Sex*, figure 33.
70. Rosemary Radford Ruether, "Mariology as Symbolic Ecclesiology: Repression or Liberation?," in *Sexism and God-Talk: Toward Feminist Theology* (Boston: Beacon, 1993).
71. Warner, *Alone of All Her Sex*; Mary Daly, *Beyond God the Father: Toward a Philosophy of Women's Liberation* (Boston: Beacon), esp. 69–97; Ruether, *Sexism and God-Talk: Toward a Feminist Theology* (Boston: Beacon, 1993); Karen Jo Torjesen, *When Women Were Priests: Women's Leadership in the Early Church and the Scandal of Their Subordination in the Rise of Christianity* (San Francisco, CA: HarperSanFrancisco, 1993).

72. James C. Scott, *Weapons of the Weak: Everyday Forms of Peasant Resistance* (New Haven, CT: Yale University Press, 1987).
73. Hegemony, in accordance with Antonio Gramsci, refers to a process whereby a fundamental class exercises control through its moral and intellectual leadership over allied, dominated classes. This hegemonic process legitimizes the authority of the dominating class. According to many Gramsci scholars, including Roger Simon, "hegemony [to Gramsci] is a *relation*, not of dominance by means of force, but of *consent* by means of political and ideological leadership. It is *the organization of consent*." Simon, *Gramsci's Political Thought: An Introduction* (London: Lawrence and Wishart, 1982), 21 (italics mine).

    Scholars' approaches to the term "subaltern" are complex, and the term's meaning has a long history, from signifying vassals and peasants in late medieval England to lower ranks in the military (by the 1700s) to historians and novelists writing from a "subaltern perspective" (by the 1800s)—that is, empathetic to and interested in the lives of "natives." David Ludden, "A Brief History of Subalternity," introduction to *Reading Subaltern Studies: Critical History, Contested Meaning and the Globalization of South Asia*, ed. David Ludden (New York: Anthem, 2002). The meaning of "subaltern," however, took a significant political swing in the 1960s, when the Italian Marxist Antonio Gramsci used it to address the non-capitalist, non-bourgeoisie subordinate classes or groups—the proletariat, the peasants, the lumpen masses, and the like—that were "non-hegemonic" (in short, "non-dominant") during the stage prior to the emergence of a critical consciousness. By 1982, this Gramscian use of "subaltern" was championed by the Subaltern Studies Group, a collection of South Asian historians who published a series of journals, edited by Ranajit Guha, to investigate history "from below." Instead of studying the political and historical roles of social and economic elites, these scholars explored the political-actor role of men and women who constituted the masses on the subcontinent. Although scholarly approaches to and uses of the term "subaltern" have run the gamut, a common theme is an interest in subaltern consciousness as a critical feature of subalternity. See Ajit K. Chaudhury, "In Search of a Subaltern Lenin," *Subaltern Studies*, vol. 4, ed. Ranajit Guha (Oxford: Oxford University Press, 1999), 237; Gayatri Chakravorty Spivak, "Introduction: Deconstructing Subaltern Studies," *Selected Subaltern Studies*, ed. Ranajit Guha and Gayatri Chakravorty Spivak (Oxford: Oxford University Press, 1988), 4; Dipesh Chakrabarty, "Invitation to a Dialogue," in Guha, *Subaltern Studies* 4:364, 376. It is this matter of consciousness, as well as a study "from below," that I am particularly interested in here. For a critical perspective of the term "subaltern" as essentializing, see the introduction to *Public Health in the British Empire: Intermediaries, Subordinates, and the Practice of Public Health, 1850-1960* ed. Amna Khalid and Ryan Johnson (New York: Routledge, 2012), 4–6.
74. Audre Lorde, "The Master's Tools Will Never Dismantle the Master's House" (1984), in *Sister Outsider: Essays and Speeches* (Berkeley, CA: Crossing Press, 2007), 110–114.
75. For a particularly interesting analysis of this stance, see Jason Springs, "'Dismantling the Master's House': Freedom and Ethical Practice in Brandom and Foucault," *Journal of Religious Ethics* 37 (2009): 419–448.
76. For a criticism of studies that treat possession as a lack of consciousness or a "multiple personality disorder," see Mary Keller, *The Hammer and the Flute: Women, Power, and Spirit Possession* (Baltimore, MD: Johns Hopkins University Press, 2002). Cf. I. M. Lewis, *Ecstatic Religion: A Study of Shamanism and Spirit Possession*, 3rd ed. (New York: Routledge, 2003), ix–xxiv.

77. Who are these dominant classes in this book? Who are the subalterns? Ranajit Guha used the term "subaltern" to mean the people who were in a subordinated position as against the *dominant foreign* (colonial officials, industrialists, merchants, financiers, planters, landlords, and missionaries), as well as against the *dominant indigenous* (big feudal magnates, industrial and mercantile bourgeoisie, and those in uppermost levels of bureaucracy). See "On Some Aspects of the Historiography of Colonial India," in *Subaltern Studies I: Writings on South Asian History and Society*, ed. Ranajit Guha (Oxford: Oxford University Press, 1982), 8. I would expand the term "subaltern" also to include the people (women and men) who are in a subordinated position to the *dominant patriarchs*—male heads of households, priests, male administrators, and the like, who may be foreign or indigenous.
78. Brahmanism, the practices and discourses of orthodox Hindus, is a category applied to the type of Hinduism whose followers stake claims to the authority of their beliefs on the Sanskrit Vedas. It gets its name from its followers' reverence for *bráhman*—sacred speech formulation, hymn, poetic formula, *mantra*—and from the class of priests (*brahmans/brahmins*) who hold custodial power over this sacred word formula. In later Upanishadic texts, *brahman* came to mean something closer to the divine substance of the universe, absolute reality. Non-Brahmanical Hinduism, an umbrella term that includes many discourses and practices that preexisted the Vedas on the subcontinent and, depending on time and location, informed them, is a category that some scholars use to refer to the plethora of discourses and practices that had roots on the subcontinent long before European colonization. Many scholars, such as Wendy Doniger, have warned against such false binaries as Brahmanical and non-Brahmanical, Vedic and non-Vedic, especially for what the latter term of the binary leaves out: in short, "[t]he non-Veda is not one thing but so many things." See Doniger, *The Hindus*, 101. I am using the terms in this book, however, as shorthand (as with "Hinduism"). I will not pursue the complex history of these categories here; rather, I will gesture toward the discursive practices that could roughly be categorized within them because I think they are useful. For excellent scholarly works that use the terms "Brahmanical" and "Non-Brahmanical" for analytical purposes, see Ram, *Mukkuvar Women*, 66–75; Sandra Robinson, "Hindu Paradigms of Women: Images and Values," in *Women, Religion, and Social Change*, ed. Yvonne Yazbeck Haddad and Ellison B. Findly (Albany: State University of New York Press, 1985), 181–215; and Diane P. Mines, "Gods of Yanaimangalam," in *Fierce Gods: Inequality, Ritual, and the Politics of Dignity in a South Indian Village* (Bloomington: Indiana University Press, 2005), 125–146. For a basic description of the Vedas, see Klaus K. Klostermaier, *Hinduism: A Short Introduction* (Oxford: OneWorld Press, 2002). For the meaning of *bráhman* in the Vedic ritual period, see Louis Renou, "Sur la notion de *bráhman*" in *L'Inde fondamentale*, ed. Charles Malamoud (Paris: Hermann, Collection Savoir, 1978), 83–116; Jan Gonda, *Notes on "bráhman"* (Utrecht, Netherlands: J. L. Beyers, 1950); Paul Thieme, *Zeitschrift der Deutschen Morgenländischen Gesellschaft*, Vol. 102 (n.F. 27), no. 1 (1952): 91–129; and A. Sandness, "On *Ritá* and *Bráhman:* Visions of Existence in the Rig Veda," *Annals of the Bhandarkar Oriental Research Institute* 88 (2007): 61–80.
79. Many Keralan Christian communities believe that Kuravilangad, Kerala, where St. Mary's Forane Church was built in 105 CE, was the first place Mary appeared in the world after her assumption into heaven. According to legend, she revealed herself to a few children who were tending their flock there, and asked them to build

a church from which a miraculous spring would sprout. Official church website, www.kuravilangadpally.com (accessed April 10, 2013).

80. David Mosse, "Possession and Confession: Affliction and Sacred Power in Colonial and Contemporary Catholic South India," in *The Anthropology of Christianity*, ed. Fanella Cannell (Durham, NC: Duke University Press, 2006), 99–133.
81. Ines G. Županov, personal communication, June 8, 2013. An exception to this would be the Goan Inquisition, when it was the job of priests to root out transgressions and write home about it.
82. Arjun Appadurai, "The Capacity to Aspire: Culture and the Terms of Recognition," in *Culture and Public Action*, ed. Vijayendra Rao and Michael Walton (Stanford, CA: Stanford University Press, 2004), 59–84.
83. I also interviewed Roman Catholic priests who believed that Mary spoke through them. However, these priests differentiated themselves from these three women in that they clearly stated, when asked, that they were not *possessed* as such but rather had experienced a form of *inner locution*: Mary spoke to them internally, and they simply repeated what she said.
84. Ramanujan, *Interior Landscape*, 104.
85. Ibid.
86. Of these five landscapes/states, the one mentioned setting the context for the poem above is *kuṟiñci* (pronounced *kurinji*), a mountain flower that only blooms only once every twelve years (somewhat in line with the onset of puberty). It stands for the mountain landscape, which is overseen by Murugan, the god of war, youth, and beauty, the god of Tamil land. It also corresponds to the lovers' experience of union. Its emotional opposite is expressed by the landscape called *pālai*, meaning desert, or wasteland. *Pālai* corresponds to the affective state of separation—not only of the lover from the beloved, but also of the couple's elopement, their hardships on the way and their separation from their parents. The third landscape, *mullai*, corresponds to the forest, and to the state of patient waiting/domesticity; the fourth, *neytal*, the seashore, corresponds to anxiety in love and in separation from the beloved. The fifth, *marutam*, or agricultural lands, corresponds to a lover's unfaithfulness, and to the sulking and resentful state that it brings. We will see all five emotional landscapes in this book.
87. This question of using pseudonyms points to another, related theme: the extent to which any narration is fictional. For more on the fictional quality of ethnographies, see James Clifford, *The Predicament of Culture* (Cambridge, MA: Harvard University Press, 1988); James Clifford and George E. Marcus, *Writing Culture: The Poetics and Politics of Ethnography* (Berkeley: University of California Press, 1986); Kamala Visweswaran, *Fictions of Feminist Ethnography* (Minneapolis: University of Minnesota Press, 1994); and Isabelle Clark-Decès, *The Encounter Never Ends: A Return to the Field of Tamil Rituals* (Albany: State University of New York Press, 2007), 4.
88. Barbara Schuler, *Of Death and Birth: Icakkiyamman, a Tamil Goddess in Ritual and Story* (Wiesbaden: Harrassowitz, 2009), 228.
89. *Kōyil* in modern Tamil usage literally means Hindu "temple" (*kō* means "king," and *-il* is locative). However, many Christians and Hindus use the word *kōyil* for both Hindu temple and Christian church. A stone marker in the chapel states that Fr. Zacharias from Kerala inaugurated its renovation. According to villagers who helped build it, and others, Zacharias oversaw the transition of thatched-hut chapels in many Dalit villages to brick-and-mortar ones in 1945. The chapel in Mātāpuram originally had a bamboo thatch roof, they said. By the time of Dhanam's crisis, the roof was made of dark wood.

90. Rev. L. Besse, S.J., *Fr. Beschi of the Society of Jesus: His Life and His Writings* (Trichinopoly, India: St. Joseph's Industrial School Press, 1918), 37. *Aṭaikkala Mātā* is also commonly transliterated in roman as Adaikkala Mātā, Adaikkala Matha, or Adaikala Madha. It will appear as the most common Adaikkala Mātā from here out.
91. "Idaiyar" (sometimes called "Konar" or "Ayar") is a pastoral group, associated in *Caṅkam* literature with the *mullai*, or forest tract.
92. Fear (*pāyam*) is an emotion that is locally thought to open the person to instability and disequilibrium, which in turn opens him or her up to possession by *pēy* or *picācu*.
93. One priest, a Dalit from another Tamil village, told me in 2005 that he didn't really want to use the broom, but that a family had come to his village begging him to use it, and he felt compelled to satisfy their expectations. So he tapped it on the person's head lightly.
94. My sole object, upon getting this notice, was to not leave India. If I did, embassy officials and the Indian scholars I knew advised, I could be blacklisted and never regain entry. They recommended that I ask the Ministry of Home Affairs to issue a "stay" to the notice and do everything in my power to remain in India until the Central Government had made a decision.
95. In Chennai, the waves mostly wiped away people on or near the beach itself.
96. Kristin Bloomer, "Notes from the Field: Retrieving the Dead," Martin Marty Center for Religion and Culture, Web Forum (Chicago: University of Chicago, February 2005). http://divinity.uchicago.edu/sites/default/files/imce/pdfs/webforum/022005/commentary.shtml.

CHAPTER 1

1. Tamil Nadu society is for the most part patrilineal (lineage and inheritance move from father to son) and patrilocal (women, as brides, move in with their husband's family). In a joint family a woman may live, then, with her husband's parents, his brothers, and his brothers' wives and children.
2. Such claims were part of a larger public discourse about illegal organ sale in India and revealed anxieties about the fragile lines between rich and poor, between those who could afford access to healthcare and those who could not. These claims connect to facts: the rapid rise of highly advanced medical technology in India—and in Chennai in particular—combined with high levels of poverty, has generated good business for organ transplantation, both legal and illegal. Villivakkam, a crowded area of northern Chennai where illegal kidney trade had been especially rampant—less than nine kilometers from Alex's house—was known as "Kidneyvakkam." See Lawrence Cohen, "Where It Hurts: Indian Material for an Ethics of Organ Transplantation," *Daedalus* 128, no. 4 (Fall 1999): 135–165.
3. I have, for the most part, retained speakers' use of Tamil verb tenses in translation. Because the past is more readily "present" in Tamil than in it is English. Some scholars have suggested that to the extent that language reflects consciousness, and vice versa, time is more fluid to a native Tamil speaker, and that the past informs the present more significantly than it does for people raised speaking English.
4. *Mātāmma* is the term used by many Tamils when referring to Mary. *Mātā* is a Sanskrit loan word for "mother," used in Tamil for various goddesses. *Amma*, another term for "mother," may also serve as an honorific, a term of respect,

usually used to refer to a married woman; it is sometimes added as a suffix to a proper name, for example, "Anjamma," or to professional titles to indicate that the person is a woman ("Doctor-amma"). Alone, it may be used as a term of address by elders or superiors to a younger woman. Male elders, for example, sometimes called me *Amma*, which I understood as a term of both respect and endearment.

5. Notably, Alex reports Mātā as using the diminutive form of "you" here: *nī*. She does not use *nīṅkaḷ*, the respectful plural form. *Nī* connotes intimacy; *nīṅkaḷ* connotes distance. In colloquial speech, speakers may use *nī* toward a person who is younger than they or in moments of intimacy—for example, between lovers.
6. The following events, sketched broadly here, have become part of the lore of the history of the Our Lady of Jecintho shrine.
7. The practice of praying the "family rosary," as it is called, is quite common among Roman Catholics in South India. Families most often say the ten-decade prayer in the evening.
8. I was not able to contact the nuns, or the parish priest, to confirm this part of the story. By the time I arrived, the priest had been reassigned to another parish.
9. This icon is ubiquitous throughout Tamil Nadu—not as thickly ubiquitous as the Hindu gods and goddesses whose images grace temples, commercial signs, and billboards, but notably common nonetheless. The Virgin Mary depicted in the form of the statue of Our Lady of Health at Velankanni is the most common popular image of Mary in Tamil Nadu. Velankanni Mātā's image can be found painted on walls and encased in glass in street shrines along the roads in and around Kodungaiyur. Benjamin's photo of the rose petals in the outline of Velankanni Mātā was later mass-produced on the back of pamphlets advertising the Jecintho shrine.
10. Rosalind, personal interview, spring 2004.
11. Rosalind used these exact words when describing her feelings at the time to me.
12. In a spring 2004 interview, Rosalind specified these "correct words" (quote) for what happens to her. P. R. Subramanian's modern Tamil Cre-A dictionary lists the following translations for the verb *ākkirami* (which the suffix *-ttal* nominalizes), in this order: "to steal; kidnap; take possession; occupy (a place, country, illegally, by force; annex)." Subramanian, *Kriyāviṉ taḷkālat tamiḻ akarāti* [Dictionary of contemporary Tamil], (Adyar, Chennai: Cre-A, 1992), 65. The verb *koḷ* means "to take hold" or "to keep" and is often used as an auxiliary verb for the preceding adverbial participle. This use of *koḷ* extends the notion of "take hold" to the meaning of the preceding verb.
13. I use "shrine" and "prayer house" interchangeably in reference to the Jecintho house. Devotees sometimes used *kōvil/kōyil* (temple), in addition to the English "church" or Tamil *jebavīṭu* (prayer house). The word *kō-vil* originates from forms of South Indian worship that precede the encounter with Christianity, and it has been used to describe Hindu temples for centuries. I occasionally use "shrine," however, because people approached the Jecintho meeting house as a place where miraculous healings might take place, a pilgrimage destination, and a local (and, in comparison to a mainstream church, temple, or mosque, usually small) place of worship dedicated to a saint, holy person, or deity—all of which are referred to variously in local vernaculars by South Asian Hindus, Christians, and Muslims.
14. In Tamil religious traditions, many people believe that human spirit-force is concentrated in the eye and radiates from it. Children are thought to be especially

vulnerable to the forces that glances may cast their way, particularly envious glances (from childless women, for example). To deflect the current of the gaze, then, parents often paint large black dots on their children's faces.

15. The word *farangi*, used in Urdu and Hindi, as well as Tamil and other South Indian languages, is derived from the Persian word *farang*, which means Frankish. It is also used in places such as Thailand—*farang*—and in Ethiopia. In the eighteenth century, Indians often used the term derogatively to refer to foreigners; meanwhile foreigners, not aware of the potentially negative connotations, used it refer to themselves. Vincent Cronin, *A Pearl to India: The Life of Roberto de Nobili* (London: R. Hart Davis, 1959).
16. The direction in which Hindus circumambulate a temple, and the way that Charles directed me to walk.
17. *Karpu* means something akin to sexual self-discipline: abstinence for unmarried women and, for married women, sexual relations within the bounds of marriage.
18. In classical Tamil poetry, kings, saints, and honored guests are garlanded with flowers and leaves. This practice continues today throughout Asia and the Pacific. *Mālais* are also notably used in Tamil marriage rituals: the verb *mālaiyiṭu*, for example, means "to marry by garlanding." P. V. Jagadisa Ayyar, *South Indian Customs* (New Delhi: Asian Educational Services, 1992), 55–57. In Tamil Nadu, one common type of garland often used in public or political ceremonies, comprising three or four golden medallions made of cardboard strung together with beads that look like sandalwood, adorn statues of political figures as well as of Hindu deities. They also could be said to resemble rosary beads.
19. *Bhārat* is a Hindi word meaning "India." On the connection between Tamil, the goddess, nationalism, devotion, motherhood, womanhood, and types of love that have informed all of these, see two works by Sumathi Ramaswamy: *Passions of the Tongue: Language Devotion in Tamil India, 1981-1970* (Berkeley: University of California Press, 1997) and *The Goddess and the Nation: Mapping Mother India* (Durham, NC: Duke University Press, 2009).
20. "O My Jesus" is also known as the Fatima Prayer. Although it is from the fifteenth century, the rosary was recognizable and its various elements amalgamated, the standardization of the vocal prayers, including the addition of the "Glory Be to the Father" and the second half of the Hail Mary ("Holy Mary, Mother of God, . . ." etc.), occurred in the latter part of the century. The "O My Jesus" was added to each decade after the apparitions of Our Lady of Fatima, in 1917, in which it is believed that Mary taught the following prayer to the children (one of whose name was Jecintha): "O my Jesus, forgive us our sins, save us from the fires of hell, lead all souls to heaven, especially those in greatest need." W. A. Hinnebusch, ed., "Rosary," in *The New Catholic Encyclopedia*, 2nd ed., vol. 12 (Washington, DC: Catholic University of America, 2003), 373–376.
21. This is the English version of the prayer offered to me by the family, and printed in the Jecintho prayer book sold outside the shrine. (The sale of such items is common outside temples and churches in South India.)
22. On the custom of salutation and prostration before deities, elders, and superiors, see Ayyar, *South Indian Customs*, 7–11. Also, on the practice of always being seated below one's guru when in his presence, see Wendy Doniger, trans., *The Laws of Manu*, with Brian K. Smith (London: Penguin, 1991), 2:198, 37.
23. The word *vāḻka* is the optative form of the verb *vāḻ*, to live. The expression "*vāḻka*!" means "(long) live!" It is the closest translation to the English exclamation, "Hail!"

24. Personal interview, David Shulman, 2011. In one of my last visits to the prayer house, Rosalind and her community had allowed me to tape, surreptitiously (so as not to signal to others that it was generally allowed), Jecintho Mātā's message. Shulman told me that the speech on the recording was unrecognizable.
25. Pentecostalism was on a steep rise in Tamil Nadu at the time of my visit.
26. At the Pandi Muni temple outside Madurai, for example, I saw women possessed by Muni or by *pēy* dance this way (see the introduction). I also saw disheveled, *pēy*-possessed women at Mel Malaiyanur, 32 kilometers from Gingee, southwest of Chennai, at the temple of Ankaḷaparameswari—a local, fierce form of the more benign and "high" Brahmanical goddess Parvati, the consort of Shiva. See also Ram, *Mukkuvar Women*; and Nabokov, *Religion against the Self*.
27. Frédérique Marglin, *Wives of the God-King: The Rituals of the Devadasis of Puri* (Delhi: Oxford University Press, 1985), 185–191; Nancy Auer Falk, *Living Hinduisms: An Explorer's Guide* (Belmont, CA: Thomson Higher Education, 2006), 141–142.
28. In Tamil Nadu, the body's becoming hot or cold is often associated with metaphysical states. In Siddha Vaidya, a South Indian branch of Ayurveda, ideal health is understood to be the balance of humors associated with either heat or coolness. Bodily balance, furthermore, is more than a matter of merely maintaining physical health; it is also a way of maintaining a balance between humanity and divinity. Many scholars of Tamil Nadu have noted the relation between the hot or heat-producing humors and female energy, sexuality, and desire—all considered to be dangerous openings to the world of supernatural beings. See Ram, *Mukkuvar Women*, 54–57; and E. Valentine Daniel, *Fluid Signs: Being a Person the Tamil Way* (Berkeley: University of California Press, 1984), 125–129. By these readings, Rosalind's becoming "hot" when possessed might indicate that she is open to the supernatural world of dangerous, non-Brahmanical female goddesses—as opposed to the cooling effects of a Sanskrit goddess.
29. *Tiruvācakam* is perhaps one of the best-known works of the Tamil Shaiva corpus. Considered by many to also be an example of *bhakti* poetry, it documents the development of the poet's passionate relationship to Shiva. The poems swing from experiences of suffering to elation, as Manikkavacakar expresses himself feeling "now hopelessly estranged from Shiva and now miraculously close to the god, even possessed by him." Cutler, *Songs of Experience*, 29.
30. For a classic moment of such reversal, see Laura Bohannon, "Shakespeare in the Bush," *Natural History*, August-September 1966.
31. David Shulman, *Tamil Temple Myths, Sacrifice and Divine Marriage in the South Indian Śaiva Tradition* (Princeton, NJ: Princeton University Press, 1980), 4, and throughout.
32. The hoisting of the flag outside a temple or shrine marks the beginning of most Hindu festivals. It is also an important ritual at Velankanni during the Feast of Our Lady and at many other Indian Catholic churches and shrines. Susan Bayly notes that flag hoistings at the start of Christian festivals "corresponded to the flag-raisings [Tam. *kotiyētram*] enacted at the start of the Tamil Hindu *utsavam*: the hoisting of the temple flag was a 'kingly' right which was once held by south Indian chiefs and rajas." Bayly, *Saints, Goddesses and Kings*, 344.
33. One *Oxford English Dictionary* definition of "witness" is "the inward testimony of the conscience," a legacy of 2 Corinthians 1:12.
34. For an analysis of the history of ethnography as a colonial, misogynist enterprise, see Ruth Behar and Deborah A. Gordon, eds., *Women Writing Culture*

(Berkeley: University of California Press, 1995). For the summary of an analysis of ethnography as objective fallacy informed by Cartesian dualism, see Paul Stoller, "The Scholar's Body," in *Sensuous Scholarship* (Philadelphia: University of Pennsylvania Press, 1987), xi–xv.

35. Michel Foucault, *The History of Sexuality*, vol. 1 (New York: Vintage, 1978).

CHAPTER 2

1. There is really no word for "religion" in Tamil, and some scholars argue that religion a concept was introduced rather late. The modern Tamil word for "religion," *matam*, is derived from the Sanskrit root *man*, "to think." *Matam*'s second meaning—"exhilaration," "joy," "madness," "drunkenness," "musk," or "rut (of an elephant)"—is from the Sanskrit root *mad*, "to be drunk". In Tamil, the two roots are homonyms—that is, they have same spelling or pronunciation but different origins. Margaret Trawick argues for some conflation of the two meanings in Tamil: that religion is not a "restricted, sacred domain cordoned off from the everyday, the profane. It [i]s *matam*, 'madness,' a connection with invisible, chaotic powers, present in all places, at all times." See Trawick, *Notes on Love*, 7. On "religion" as a particularly modern, Western category and on its conceptual failures, see Talal Asad, *Disciplines: Genealogies of Religion and Reasons of Power in Christianity and Islam* (Baltimore: Johns Hopkins University Press, 1993), 27–31.
2. Linguists are doubtful about this etymology, despite the number of speakers who understand *kaṭa* of *kaṭavuḷ* to mean "to cross." It is much more probable that the ancient root of this word is is *kaṭaṉ*, "loan," "debt," or "obligation." God is someone to whom we are indebted, to whom we wish to repay our gifts. David Shulman, personal communication, August 7, 2016. I prefer the local interpretation, though I also appreciate linguists' insights about etymological history. For another reference to the "cross over" meaning, see Trawick, *Notes on Love*, 37. For a folk creation myth about *kaṭavuḷ* being both transcendent and immanent, equilibrium itself, before (and, to some degree, after) all the elements within him were scattered as the result of *kama* (desire), see E. Valentine Daniel, *Fluid Signs: Being a Person the Tamil Way* (Berkeley: University of California Press, 1984), 3–5. Other Tamil words for god are *āṇṭavar* and *iṟaivaṉ*.
3. Pierre Bourdieu called this *habitus*, "a *way of being*, a *habitual state* (especially of the body) and, in particular, a *predisposition, tendency, propensity*, or *inclination*." The *habitus* is produced by "the structures constitutive of a particular type of environment (e.g. the material conditions of existence characteristic of a class condition)." See Bourdieu, *Outline of a Theory of Practice*, trans. Richard Nice (Cambridge: Cambridge University Press, 1977), 72. *Habitus* is neither a result of free will nor determined by structures but is created by a kind of interplay between the two over time. See Bourdieu, *Distinction: A Social Critique of the Judgment of Taste* (Cambridge, MA: Harvard University Press, 1984), 170.
4. According to Bourdieu, competition for different sorts of goods, or capital, operate in a "field": a social arena in which struggles and negotiations over resources take place. Each field requires, by nature of what is at stake, a different logic and structure that is both the product and the producer of the *habitus* appropriate to the field. Each field, furthermore, is structured by power relations, which stand in relationships of domination, subordination, or equivalence based on the access they afford to goods. These goods, or capital, can be divided into four categories: economic, social (valued relations with specific others), cultural (various kinds of knowledge), and symbolic (prestige and social honor). See Pierre Bourdieu, "Forms

of Capital," in *Handbook of Theory and Research for the Sociology of Education*, ed. John G. Richardson (New York: Greenwood, 1986), 243–246. Bourdieu may have considered Rosalind's family, for example, despite their relative lack of money, to be relatively dominant in cultural capital. Rosalind's power in one field, furthermore, may not have been so great in another.

5. Kent, *Converting Women*; Kenneth Ballhatchet, *Caste, Class and Catholicism in India 1789–1914* (Surrey, UK: Curzon Press, 1998); M. S. S. Pandian, *Brahmin and Non-Brahmin* (Delhi: Permanent Black, 2007).
6. On notions of *mariyātai* as a generalized Tamil idiom of rank and distinction, see Diane P. Mines, *Fierce Gods: Inequality, Ritual, and the Politics of Dignity in a South Indian Village* (Bloomington: Indiana University Press, 2005), 81–100.
7. For a full treatment of such works in anthropology and religion, see Janice Boddy, "Spirit Possession Revisited: Beyond Instrumentality," *Annual Review of Anthropology* 23 (1994): 407–434. On the study of gender, see Judith Butler, *Bodies That Matter: On the Discursive Limits of "Sex"* (New York: Routledge, 1992); Saba Mahmood, *Politics of Piety: The Islamic Revival and the Feminist Subject* (Princeton, NJ: Princeton University Press, 2005); and Sherry B. Ortner, *Making Gender: The Politics and Erotics of Culture* (Boston: Beacon, 1996), to name just a few.
8. Pierre Hadot, *Philosophy as a Way of Life*, ed. Arnold Davidson (Malden, MA: Blackwell, 1995).
9. Elizabeth Grosz, *Volatile Bodies: Towards a Corporeal Feminism* (Bloomington: Indiana University Press, 1994). Lacan first used this model of the Möbius strip, though for different purposes.
10. The Sanskrit-derived word *cittam*, which has found its way into Tamil usage as something akin to "reasoning mind," is of the Indo-European language family, not the Dravidian.
11. Charles Hirschkind, *The Ethical Soundscape: Cassette Sermons and Islamic Counterpublics* (New York: Columbia University Press, 2006).
12. A. Pandian, *Crooked Stalks*, 15–22.
13. These neighborhoods are called suburbs, though they are now technically part of the city corporation. The 2001 Census of India splits it into two: East Kodungaiyur (pop. 27,506) and West Kodungaiyur (pop. 24,857).
14. C. Chandramouli, "Quality of Living Index in Chennai: An Approach Paper," in *Proceedings of the Third International Conference on Environment and Health, Chennai*, India, ed. Martin J. Bunch, V. Madha Suresh, and T. Vasantha Kumaran (Chennai: Department of Geography, University of Madras and Faculty of Environmental Studies, York University, 2003), 75–81.
15. C. Chandramouli, "Provisional Population Totals: Paper 2 of 2001" (Chennai: Census Operations, Tamil Nadu, 2001). The urban agglomeration of Chennai had a population of 6.4 million, a number estimated to have risen to almost 7 million since 2001.
16. U. Kalpagam, "Secularism, Religiosity and Popular Culture: Chennai's Roadside Temples," in *Economic and Political Weekly* 41, no. 43/44 (Nov. 4–10, 2006): 4595–4600. Kalpagam argues that the proliferation of roadside Hindu shrines serves as evidence of "multiple modernities," a notion that allows for the flourishing of contemporary religiosity along with the modernization process, rather than a single trajectory of modernization that implies secularization. The concept of "multiple modernities," he argues, combines both aspects of tradition and modernization, "although the process of modernization may entail the transformation and pragmatic adjustment of tradition" (4596).

17. For an analysis of a nostalgic longing for a rural home and its relation to Marian devotion, see Meibohm, "Past Selves and Present Others," 61–83.
18. MGR served as chief minister of Tamil Nadu from 1977 until his death in 1987. He rose to stardom—and, eventually, political stature—playing roles that portrayed him as a hero to the poor.
19. The *tiruṣṭi bommai* (also *veruḷi*) is a mask, usually made of plaster of Paris, that is often hung at construction sites and sometimes at domestic entrances.
20. This is taken as a common sign of *pēy*.
21. This is another common trope in possession stories, particularly those involving a goddess. See Eveline Meyer, *Aṅkāḷaparamēcuvari: A Goddess of Tamilnadu, Her Myths and Cult* (Weisbaden, GE: Franz Steiner Verlag, 1986), 59. *Nāga*, Hindu deities who take the form of a snake, are also thought to bring rain and fertility. See Dhanam's story in chapter 6.
22. Mary is often depicted iconographically as crushing the serpent with her foot. The connection comes, at least in part, from Genesis 3:15, in which God speaks to the serpent: "I will put enmity between you and the woman, and between your seed and her seed; he shall bruise your head, and you shall bruise his heel." When St. Jerome translated Genesis to the Latin, however, he wrote, "*she* will crush your head" (italics mine). The *Old Catholic Encyclopedia* defends the Vulgate, as does Pope Pius IX's Apostolic Constitution of 1958, *Ineffabilis Deus*, "[T]he most holy Virgin . . . was . . . eternally at enmity with the evil serpent, and most completely triumphed over him, and thus crushed his head with her immaculate foot."
23. On the "snake dance" as a manner of expressing possession, see Nabokov, *Religion against the Self*, 107, 112, 147–149.
24. On people's longing for the authenticity of a healing guru in a contemporary, globalized world, see Amanda Lucia, *Reflections of Amma: Devotees in a Global Embrace* (Berkeley: University of California Press, 2014), 68–73.
25. See Bourdieu, "Forms of Capital."
26. I use the term *strategic* here as Catherine Bell does, focusing on "the more common 'strategies of ritualization,' initially defined as a way of acting that differentiates some acts from others." Like Bell, I view ritual as a framework of practical activity and as action that inculcates the embodied nature of ritual mastery. Catherine Bell, *Ritual Theory, Ritual Practice* (New York: Oxford University Press, 1992), 107–108.
27. For a complex analysis of submission as a form of agency, see Mahmood, *Politics of Piety*.
28. Bell, *Ritual Theory, Ritual Practice*, 93.
29. By discipline, I mean both the noun (the specific form of prayer, the structure of the prayer itself, to whom it is addressed, the posture assumed while making the address, the meditative practice involved, visualization, etc.) as well as the act of disciplining the body. On the history of spiritual exercises from Socrates to Foucault, see Hadot, *Philosophy as a Way of Life*. On the connection between Catholic meditation, embodied processes, and the global Catholic missionizing movement, see J. Michelle Molina, *To Overcome Oneself: The Jesuit Ethic and Spirit of Global Expansion* (Berkeley: University of California Press, 2013). On the disciplining of South Indian bodies through colonial missions, see Mosse, *Saint in the Banyan Tree*; and Županov, *Missionary Tropics*.
30. I never saw Rosalind eat, take a drink, or go to the restroom during all her hours of standing.
31. The cost of this book was partly covered by sixteen pages of advertisements from many families and businesses, including Stella Maris.

32. Robert, interview.
33. See Holly Baker Reynolds, "The Auspicious Married Woman," in *The Powers of Tamil Women*, ed. Susan Snow Wadley, Foreign and Comparative Studies / South Asian Series 6 (Syracuse, NY: Maxwell School of Citizenship and Public Affairs, 1980), 36.
34. To my knowledge, Rosalind-as-Jecintho does not put her hands on men's lower abdominal areas, though she will touch men's stomachs, backs, hands, arms, legs, shoulders, necks, and heads.
35. For more examples of such "inversion" in spirit possession, see Brown, *Mama Lola: A Vodou Priestess in Brooklyn* (Berkeley: University of California Press, 1991); Boddy, *Wombs and Alien Spirits*; Kelly Hayes, *Holy Harlots: Femininity, Sexuality, and Black Magic in Brazil* (Berkeley: University of California Press, 2011); Nabokov, *Religion against the Self*; and Elaine Craddock, *Shiva's Demon Devotee: Karaikkal Ammaiyar* (Albany: State University of New York, 2010).
36. Rosalind said that she behaved this way when possessed because Mary was carrying the weight of the world on her shoulders. Also, Robert added, she had explained that he had to bow before God the Father. "I don't want to stand before my Father," he reported her saying. "So, I am bowing my head. See how humble I am to my Father. Like that, you have to be humble for others."
37. A lakh is a South Asian numbering system in which one lakh equals 100,000. One hundred thousand rupees, then, is one lakh of rupees. At the time of my visit, one American dollar equaled about 48 rupees. One lakh of rupees at the time of that exchange rate equaled about $2,083.
38. While *mālai* beads have been around in India for centuries, the Catholic rosary was standardized in Europe by the 16th century, at around the same time the Portuguese made significant inroads in Tamil Nadu.
39. Michel Foucault, *Techniques of the Self: A Seminar with Michel Foucault*, ed. Luther H. Martin, Huck Gutman, Patrick H. Hutton. (Amherst: University of Massachusetts Press, 1988).
40. Homi Bhabha, *The Location of Culture* (London and New York: Routledge, 1994), 159.
41. My thanks to Francina for allowing me to copy these notebooks.
42. *Prasādam* (*piricātam* in Tamil) means "gift" in Sanskrit. In Hindu temples, it is usually a material substance such as food, blessed by a deity and distributed back to devotees.
43. "Having gone, I come" (*nāṉ pōyittuvarēṉ*) is the common phrase for goodbye in Tamil.

CHAPTER 3

1. A woman's name in Tamil Nadu is often preceded by her father's surname. Nancy's father's surname is "Shanthakumar," so his daughter's full name appears as S. Nancy.
2. Because Nancy's father was born a Hindu from the Gounder community, she considered herself a member of a Scheduled Caste (she used the term "SC").
3. Both the narrator and Nancy used the verb phrase *varu mēl* (come onto), the same language used for expressing Hindu deity possession in Tamil. Nancy also used the verb *irangi* (to descend), another common reference to Hindu deity possession (see the introduction).
4. Stigmata, bodily wounds or bleeding that seem to correspond to Jesus's crucifixion wounds, are not considered a Hindu sign (*kuri*). Blood and bleeding has its own

place within Hindu devotional traditions. Stigmata, however, is a word that originates from Saint Paul's Letter to the Galatians, which states, "I bear on my body the marks of Jesus." The first known case of stigmata, and the first to be accepted by the Roman Catholic Church, was that of St. Francis of Assisi (1182–1226), who the Church claims received stigmata in La Verna, Italy, in 1224.

5. Displaying and garlanding the portraits of deceased relatives is another Tamil tradition related to the veneration of ancestors. See epilogue. In some families, these ancestors are believed to exist as spirits who can also possess people at random or in ritual contexts.
6. Like many Hindus, Vadivambal believes that Mary is just another manifestation, another avatar of the Goddess, the female deity who is everywhere, in all things, both multiple and one.
7. Love marriages are considered by many South Indians to be far from ideal. An ideal marriage, especially from an orthodox Brahmanical point-of-view, is one arranged by the parents of the bride and groom—ideally, a match of cross-cousins with a perfect compatibility of astrological signs, attractiveness, *jāti*, and so on.
8. A pseudonym.
9. Suicide is fairly common in India, and is often a response to perceived humiliation or is used as form of punishment or manipulation. See Sarah Mitter, *Dharma's Daughters: Contemporary Indian Women and Hindu Culture* (New Brunswick, NJ: Rutgers University Press, 1991); Veena Talwar Oldenburg, *Dowry Murder: The Imperial Origins of a Cultural Crime* (New York: Oxford University Press, 2002); Upendra Thakur, *The History of Suicide in India: An Introduction* (Delhi: Munshi Ram Manohar Lal, 1963); and Jocelyn Lim Chua, *In Pursuit of the Good Life: Aspiration and Suicide in Globalizing South India* (Berkeley: University of California Press, 2014).
10. The English word "jolly" is used in Tamil to connote light fun, freedom, openness, and, often, sexuality or flirtation.
11. In India, such play is considered completely inappropriate for a father and daughter of Nancy's age, regardless of caste or class. Men and women from various caste, social, and economic positions told me this.
12. Leela uses the verb *āṭu*, which in Tamil often connotes possession (see the introduction).
13. Note the verb *iraṅku* that Leela uses here, signifying that Mātā descended.
14. Leela is referring here to Rosalind-as-Jecintho, who acts like an old woman while possessed.
15. Note that Leela speaks of Nancy now as if she and Mātā are different people.
16. A. Sivasubramanian, *Uppittavarai* (Palayamkottai: Folklore Research and Resource Center, n.d.).
17. The rite for providing holy water, as written in the Roman Ritual, includes the requirement of mixing salt with water. Holy water is used in the rite of Baptism—itself a rite of exorcism—as well as for many other feast days and blessings. To provide holy water, the priest first exorcises "the demon" from the salt, and then also exorcises the water. Then he pours the salt into the water in the form of a cross.
18. On various readings of *shakti*, see Margaret Egnor, "On the Meaning of Shakti to Women in Tamil Nadu," in Wadley, *Powers of Tamil Women*, 1–34; and Sheryl B. Daniel, "Marriage in Tamil Culture," in Wadley, *Powers of Tamil Women*, 65, 68, 72. Cf. Ram, who critiques any presentation of Tamil femininity as a "timeless cultural essence," *Mukkuvar Women*, 82.

19. On suffering and *shakti* in the Indian Catholic tradition in particular, see Dempsey, *Kerala Christian Sainthood*, 134–137.
20. On Dravidian (or Tamil nationalist) oratory and political speech and the way it employs archaic forms of Tamil (suggesting an ancient and authoritative mode of speech) to move whole publics, specially through "beautiful Tamil," see Bernard Bate, *Tamil Oratory and the Dravidian Aesthetic: Democratic Practice in South India* (New York: Columbia University Press, 2009).
21. Catherine Bell, in her discussion on strategic negotiations that enact change while maintaining the force of authenticity, focuses on the importance of shifting relations between actors, context, and audience in ritual acts. Bell, *Ritual Theory, Ritual Practice*.
22. This is just one famous example that J. L. Austin gives in his discussion of speech act theory and performatives. Austin suggests that the social context of the performative gives rise to numerous possibilities for "firing" or "misfiring" (a felicitous speech act performance versus an infelicitous one). J. L. Austin, *How to Do Things with Words*, ed. J. O. Urmson and M. Sbisa (Cambridge, MA: Harvard University Press, 1994).
23. The popular myth of Shiva as Mother is said to hail from the temple town of Tiruchirappalli (Trichy), where Shiva is known as Maatribhuuteshvara, or Taayumaanavar, "he who became a mother," and who acts as midwife. An even more famous old-woman literary trope, dating from the *Caṅkam* period, is that of Avvaiyar (sometimes referred to as Auvaiyar, on in short, Avvai). In Tamil, the word *avvaiyar* or *auvaiyar* is titular, meaning "elderly lady." An entire body of devotional poetry to Shiva is ascribed to her. Having been abandoned by her husband because of a miraculous power Shiva bestows on her, Avvai reneges her beauty, becoming an old woman, and dedicates herself to Shiva. At least two older films featuring her play repeatedly on Tamil television film channels—the bodily comportment of K. B. Sundarambal, the actor playing the title role of *Avvaiyar* (1953); and the poetess in *ThiruviLaiyaaDal* (1964) is closely akin to that of Jecintho. Most South Indians know of her. See M. S. H. Thompson, "The Avvai of the Sangam Anthologies," *Bulletin of the School of Oriental and African Studies* 12, no. 2 (1948): 399–402; S. S. Iyer, "What We Have Yet to Learn," *Science*, n.s. 185, no. 4149: 400; and Craddock, *Siva's Demon Devotee*.
24. Both Rosalind and Nancy had studied the New Testament and heard sermons referring to all three biblical women; both referred to them without my prompting. St. Anne, patron saint of grandmothers, unmarried women, and women in labor, is particularly famous in Tamil Nadu. The shrine of St. Anne in Arulanandapuram, a tiny, modest village of one hundred and fifty households, about ten miles south of Madurai, attracts devotees drawn to her fertility and healing powers. See Selva J. Raj, "Shared Vows, Shared Space, and Shared Deities: Vow Rituals among Tamil Catholics in South India," in *Dealing with Deities: The Ritual Vow in South Asia*, ed. Selva J. Raj and William P. Harman (Albany: State University of New York Press, 2006), 47.
25. By 1976, a national Charismatic Catholic convention in Bombay attracted 1,500 registered delegates, and another in 1978 attracted 3,500. Thomas Csordas, "Global Religion and the Re-enchantment of the World: The Case of the Catholic Charismatic Renewal," *Anthropological Theory* 7, no. 3 (2007): 295–314.
26. Ibid., 298.
27. Divine Retreat Centre, Muringoor, http://www.drcm.org, accessed August 7, 2014. For previous quotation, see Csordas, "Global Religion," 298.
28. Jesuits disciplined transgressors through public humiliations and often violent punishments as an attempt to turn Tamil converts from wayward, flagrantly pagan

idolaters ("buffalos with human faces") into inwardly focused, moral, Christian individuals. See Mosse, *Saint in the Banyan Tree*, 62.

29. http://www.motherofkanchikode.com. Videos of Rani John's experience went viral on You Tube, as did videos of Julia Kim, a South Korean woman who claimed that the Eucharist had turned to blood on her tongue, in repeated instances beginning in 1996.
30. Mary Elizabeth Hancock, *Womanhood in the Making: Domestic Ritual and Public Culture in Urban South India* (Boulder, CO: Westview, 1999), 16, 171; Wadley, *Powers of Tamil Women*.
31. In the Indian numbering system, a lakh is one hundred thousand units, and is written 1,00,000.
32. For a description of the *shakti karakam*, the pot that is the goddess, see chapter 4. For a reference to the women in Andhra Pradesh who maintain the goddess in their kitchens in the form of two clay pots filled with water poured off cooked rice (called *taravani* in Telugu), see Joyce Flueckiger, *Everyday Hinduism* (West Sussex: Wiley-Blackwell, 2015), 154. While the pots are filled with rice water, not milk, the water is milky *looking*—and the pots aren't pots; they *are* the goddess. Flueckiger, personal communication.
33. This reference is likely out of Isaiah: "sinning with the hands, sinning with the feet, mouth . . . " or from Matthew 18:8: "If your hand or your foot causes you to sin, cut it off and throw it away. It is better for you to enter life maimed or crippled than to have two hands or two feet and be thrown into eternal fire." It could also refer to the Chaplet of Divine Mercy, a prayer ritual in which one says the rosary while focusing on the five wounds of Christ: "Pray each decade while reflecting on the many sins we commit with our head (mind), our hands, our feet etc. For example, we commit the sin of gossip with our mouth and our mind, the sin of assault with our feet and hands, the sin of envy with our eyes etc." See http://www.wikihow.com/Pray-the-Chaplet-of-Divine-Mercy (accessed March 6, 2008).
34. There are various explanations for the alleged blood's appearance, including psychosomatic ones. On stigmata and modernity, the Christian theologian Ivan Illich writes: "Modern philosophy says that no one can actually feel the pain of another; it can only be believed. I do not want to challenge this assertion, nor do I have to in order to explain what is happening at this particular moment in western history. Compassion with Christ, for these late medieval mystics, is faith so strong and so deeply incarnate that it leads to the individual embodiment of the contemplated pain. The Stigmata of St. Francis of Assisi witness to the enfleshment of his faith in the Incarnate God who faces him from the cross." Illich, "Hospitality and Pain" (academic paper presented in Chicago, 1987), 16, http://www.davidtinapple.com/illich/ (accessed May 28, 2017). Blood-related signs of divinity in Hinduism are too numerous to list here, but one example is Caitanya Mahaprabhu, the sixteenth-century ascetic Vaishnava monk from Bengal and a proponent of *bhakti* yoga. Caitanya reportedly experienced blood oozing from his body during intense devotional experiences (*Caitanya Caritamrita*, 2.2.6, 2.13.104, 3.14.93). On Christian incidents of stigmata, see Caroline Walker Bynum, *Holy Feast and Holy Fast: The Religious Significance of Food to Medieval Women* (Berkeley: University of California Press, 1987); and Caroline Walker Bynum, *Fragmentation and Redemption: Essays on Gender and the Human Body in Medieval Religion* (New York: Zone Books, 1992).
35. On the two-facedness and confusion among church hierarchy over un-orthodox expressions of devotion, see Raj, "Shared Vows, Shared Space," 13, 62.
36. *Mehendi* serves not only an ornamental function: it also allows women time off from work. The longer the dye sets, the deeper the red and the longer it stays.

Wearing it, one is unable to do much of anything: no cleaning, no cooking, no handiwork, no tending to children—and in my case, no writing.

CHAPTER 4

1. William Dalrymple shared the information on Mary and Bhagavati, personal communication, April 2008. On Mary and Kaṇṇaki's "sibling" processions, and the leftover blood offerings saved for Mary after sacrifices to her Hindu sister, see Dempsey, *Kerala Christian Sainthood*, 56.
2. Bayly, *Saints, Goddesses and Kings*, 341–347, 375, 378. On caste rivalry during car festivals, see Ballhatchet, *Caste, Class and Catholicism in India*, 115. On the more peaceful relationship between Christian and Hindu festivals, see Dempsey, "Siblings and Other Metaphors for Christian-Hindu Relations," in Dempsey, *Kerala Christian Sainthood*, 52–87; Meibohm, "Past Selves and Present Others"; and Joanna Waghorne, "Chariots of the God/s: Riding the Line Between Hindu and Christian" in Raj and Dempsey, *Popular Christianity in India*, 61–84, 11–38. On festivals as outward expressions of honor, kingship, and patronage in precolonial and colonial South India, see Nicholas Dirks, *The Hollow Crown: Ethnohistory of an Indian Kingdom* (Cambridge: Cambridge University Press, 1987). On festivals and processions as sociopolitical action, markers of territory, assertions of distinction, and negotiations of power, see Mines, *Fierce Gods*. For the roles of women in a North Indian car festival, and a study of the festival's significance in relation to time, see Frédérique Apffel Marglin, "Time Renewed," in *Wives of the God-King: The Rituals of the Devadasis of Puri* (Delhi: Oxford University Press, 1985), 243–281. For a brief description of village processions of the goddess, see Lynn Foulston, *At the Feet of the Goddess: The Divine Feminine in Local Hindu Religion* (Brighton: Sussex Academic Press, 2002), 127–131.
3. Susan Bayly, "Saints' Cults and Warrior Kingdoms in South India," in *Shamanism, History and the State*, ed. Nicholas Thomas and Caroline Humphrey (Ann Arbor: University of Michigan Press, 1994), 117–132. In the fourteenth- and fifteenth-century Hindu empire at Vijayanagar, the military overlordship—and indeed all the "little kings" of the kingdoms and petty states of Malabar and Tamil country—encouraged the embellishment of shrines, the recruitment of ritualists, and the promulgation of car or chariot processions, all of which were "as much as part of statecraft as the creation and financing of armies, the building of alliances and the formation of a revenue system" (48). By the eighteenth century, warrior lords emerged out of the southern *poligar* country, transforming the processions into a state-level culture of kingship and patronage. They did this in part by aligning themselves with ascetic Brahmans who had accumulated power as a result of earlier *bhakti* devotional movements, and by instituting *Navarāttiri* as a lavish state ritual that symbolized their conquest of the new kingdom in the name of its patron goddess. (66; see also Carol Appadurai Breckenridge, "From Protector to Litigant—Changing Relations Between Hindu Temples and the Raja of Ramnad," *IESHR* 14:1 (1977): 75–106.)
4. Bayly, *Saints, Goddesses, and Kings*, 67.
5. Ibid., 343.
6. Ibid.
7. Ibid., 344.
8. The divine orchestration of festivals via a local god or goddess is not unusual in South India. Nicholas Dirks, for example, has written about how the principal village deity in Pudukkottai District, Aiyanar, gave "permission" for all village festivals to begin (after which, the village headmen, *ambalams*, also gave permission, announcing the date of a festival with the help of an astrologer). Dirks, *Hollow Crown*, 298.

Furthermore, I later learned that Dhanam, while possessed by Mātā, had instructed headmen to begin the annual village festival to Our Lady in Mātāpuram.

9. See chapter 2.
10. Rev. Fr. A. Thomas, the parish priest, told me that the parish members were mostly middle-class, "They have at least one job. Very few families are very poor people. Others are middle class and lower middle class. Such is (a) housing board settlement." Personal communication, May 27, 2005. However, Thomas's definition of "at least one job" does not establish middle class status, much as he may have wanted to state such.
11. The lack of an English-language service could suggest a lack of upward mobility and higher education among the parishioners, given the globalized economy.
12. On such a trend in *poligar* Tamil country, see Bayly, "Saints' Cults," in Thomas and Humphrey, *Shamanism, History and the State*, 117–132.
13. Rev. Fr. A. Thomas, Muthamizh Nagar's parish priest, confirmed this oral history. Personal communication, May 27, 2005.
14. "Building a shrine under a thatched hut" fits a larger trope, repeated in many oral and written histories of churches in South India, including the original Velankanni Shrine in Nagapattinam, the Chinna ("Small") Velankanni Church in Besant Nagar, and the Mātā chapel in Mātāpuram.
15. Interview with a founding member of the church, May 2006.
16. When I reported this statement at the prayer house, Robert said that he and his father had indeed approached Thomas, who had said they could have their feast on May 30. "We arranged everything," Robert said. "Then he called in the morning and said, 'Even if you get permission from the Bishop, you may not have a procession.'"
17. Our Lady Jecintho community members said that the council members had approached them in a threatening manner and did not make it clear that they were delivering a message from the bishop. Personal communication, May 27, 2005.
18. Usually, it was Francina, Rosalind's assistant and closest friend, who took notes, in a hardcover notebook, while Rosalind-as-Jecintho was giving messages.
19. The prayer house has published dozens of these songs in a songbook and on two volumes of CDs. Rosalind's speaking voice begins each CD, and professionals sing her songs.
20. In Sanskrit, *garbha* (womb) *griham* (house) is the inner sanctum of the temple. Rosalind-as-Jecintho seemed to be telling people that after the procession, there would be no need to return the Mātā statue to the prayer house. In Brahmanical Hinduism, the iconic form of the god or goddess is often held in the inner sanctum of the temple, the *garbha griham*. It is in that sanctum where Brahmin priests often perform *abhishekam*, the ritual bath in which they rub or pour water, milk, honey, yoghurt, butter and/or sugar on the icon—though *abhishekam* can be done anywhere. Also, recall the *Haranyagarbha* (golden womb) at the start of this chapter.
21. For a description of *abhishekam* being performed on the goddess, see Foulston, *At the Feet of the Goddess*, 125–127.
22. During the September 2005 festival at Velaknanni, on one night, young women—mostly from Goa—carried palanquins.
23. In Hindu temple rituals, *ārati* is usually performed by a priest, or, if the *puja* is a domestic ritual, by the woman of the household. The person performing *ārati* offers a lamp or tray of fire to devotees, who cup one or both hands over the flames and touch their eyes and faces or wave the smoke over their hair, bringing the warmth and light of the deity to themselves. *Puja* also usually comprises the rite of

bathing the icon (*abhishekam*), which is then dressed or adorned with new clothes, gold, jewels and perfume, often receiving a dot of red turmeric on the forehead. Plates of boiled rice and sweets are offered to the deity (*naivedya*) to the accompaniment of ringing bells. After the deity's meal, the curtain is drawn back so that devotees can get *darshan* (vision of and by the deity). They can also see the final stage of ritual, the display of lamps (*dīpārādhana*), in which the priests wave camphor lamps in a circular motion before the icon.

24. In fact, in most Marian apparitions authorized by the Vatican, Mary asks for a church to be built in her name—and Church fathers comply.
25. The rose, indigenous to Asia, is likely to have come to India via busy trade routes with China. Perpetually blooming roses from China burst onto the European scene in the 1800s, at the same time the British Empire was busy colonizing abroad, and cultivating a love for gardens at home. Early Christians identified the rose's five petals with Christ's wounds, though church leaders hesitated to adopt it because of its association with Roman and pagan rituals. The non-elite habits and devotions, however, won out: the red rose was adopted as a symbol for Christian martyrs and eventually came to be associated with the Virgin Mary.
26. The *shakti karakam* is used in goddess festivals throughout Tamil Nadu, across religious lines. Foulston writes that it "is a receptacle for the power of the goddess and, as such, is representative of her." See Foulston, *At the Feet of the Goddess*, 127–131. Foulston also writes that the streets through which the procession occurs are considered a sacred extension of the temple, 130.
27. The Sacred Heart Jesus is a particular icon of Jesus, one in which his heart is visible on his chest, wrapped in thorns and glowing red.
28. Hindu gods and goddesses, too, ride vehicles. Vishnu rides Garuda, a winged bird; Shiva rides the bull Nandi; Ganesh rides Mushika the rat; Murugan, a peacock; Durga, the lion Manashtala.
29. Foulston writes that the Mahā-Shivarātri festival in Cholavandan consists of a series of processions between the river and the temple, around the temple, and finally to the nearby cremation ground. In the Jenaki Mariamman festival, furthermore, she writes, a *pūkapparai* "flower *kapparai*" will be carried to the cremation ground. See Foulston, *At the Feet of the Goddess*, 128, and also plate 18. The *capparams* I saw at Jecintho Prayer House look just like the *pūkapparai* in Foulston's colored plates.
30. On the *linga* as an aniconic image, see Diana Eck, *Darśan: Seeing the Divine Image in India*, 2nd ed. (Chambersburg, PA: Anima Books), 34. On the *linga* as an aniconic representation of the male sexual organ in erection, in particular as the erect phallus of Shiva, and also as an aniconic pillar of light or an abstract symbol of the god, see Wendy Doniger, *The Hindus: An Alternative History* (New York: Penguin Press, 2009), 22–23.
31. Eck, *Darśan*, 38.
32. On people's beliefs about the enlivened Muslim *pir* ("saint") in the metal battle standards (symbols on poles, often dressed to represent a specific *pir*) during Muharram, see Afsar Mohammad, *The Festival of Pirs: Popular Islam and Shared Devotion in India* (New York: Oxford University Press, 2013). On the shared religious sensibilities of Hindus and Catholics regarding car processions in India and beliefs in the real presence of deities in processions, see Waghorne, "Chariots of the God/s." On the goddess being alive in *murtis* in New York, as well as in India, see Corinne Dempsey, *The Goddess Lives in Upstate New York: Breaking Convention*

and Making Home in a North American Hindu Temple (New York: Oxford University Press, 2006). On the shared spaces, beliefs and practices among Hindus and Muslims in Kerala at the temple of Vavar Swami and Ayyappa, and the saint's and god's installations in aniconic form, see Dominique-Sila Khan, "Vavar Swami: A Hindu-Muslim Saint of Kerala," in *Lines in Water: Religious Boundaries in South Asia*, ed. Eliza Kent and Tazim Kassam (Syracuse: Syracuse University Press, 2013).

33. See Foulston, *At the Feet of the Goddess*, 130. Also, for how bio-icons volatize general publics, see Bishnupriya Ghosh, *Global Icons: Apertures to the Popular* (Durham, NC: Duke University Press, 2011). Mary, in this case, would be considered a bio-icon.
34. According to Catholic liturgy and theology, in the sacrament of the Eucharist, the shape of the bread and wine—that which is perceptible to the eye, the "accidents," as they are called philosophically, or the appearance—remains the same. But the essence of the thing—in this case, the (aniconic) bread and wine—is transformed as it becomes the body and blood of Jesus.

INTERLUDE

1. Yama, also known as *lokapala*, or "guardian of the directions," represents the south. He is also regarded as justice, and is sometimes referred to as Dharma, the order, or law, that sustains the order and harmony of the universe. Three hymns in the tenth book of the *Rig Veda* are addressed to him. Two dogs guard the road to his abode, which are said to wander about people as his messengers. A major temple dedicated to him stands about three hours from Mātāpuram, in Sricanchiyam, Thiruvarur District. In accordance with Yama, many Hindus follow the practice of laying dead bodies facing south before cremation. South Indian Christians, who tend to bury their dead rather than burn them, often lay the body facing east, and they often sleep in that direction, too. While these practices (often consciously) oppose Hindu sleep and death rituals, they coincide with another ritual practice: Hindu *murtis*, the icons in which deities reside, also traditionally point east. When I later pointed out this out to Dhanam, she said, "No, Hindu gods and goddesses face everywhere!"—a comment on their multiplicity.
2. The Tamil solar calendar is based on the classical Hindu solar calendar; the new year follows the vernal equinox and generally falls on April 14 of the Gregorian year. Each Tamil month generally begins on the fourteenth or fifteenth day of each Gregorian month, though this shifts with the movement of the planets.
3. The water tank, or *kulam*, next to the temple of the Hindu goddess Kali, is a prominent site in the neighboring village.
4. Ecclesiastes 1:3–4.
5. Ecclesiastes 1:10.
6. *Tiruvayiṟṟiṉ* is the genitive case of the phrase literally translated as "holy stomach/belly." I left it in the literal translation of the formal prayer. Common words for "womb" would be *karuppai* or *sūrappai*, but these are more specific to biomedical discourses, whereas Tamils (or at least the early translators of the "Hail Mary") might colloquially say, "there is a child growing in her belly."
7. A reference to A. K. Ramanujan, "What She Said," *Kuruntokai* 3.
8. The *Mandukya Upanishad*, one of the early scriptures of Hinduism, speaks of four states of consciousness: the first and lowest state is *vaishanavara*, the normal state of being awake and thus open to sense perception and rational thought (this is also called *maya*, or illusion); the second is *taijasa*, the dreaming state, in which the senses are turned inward and consciousness takes flight, leaving the fetters of the

material world to the workings of the person's own mind; the third state is *prajna*, the state of deep sleep, where the person "neither dreams nor desires," and in which there is no separateness, but only a state of unification in which the spirit is not scattered over a profusion of objective and subjective things. What keeps this state from being the highest of all is that the sleeper is not conscious of this unification and bliss. The fourth state, the superconscious state of *turiya*, is a transcendent state of illumination, an elevated state in which the sleeper realizes Brahman, or ultimate reality. These states of consciousness are said to be all contained in the mystical syllable, AUM.

9. This Interlude was partly inspired by James Agee's *Let Us Now Praise Famous Men: Three Tenant Families* (Boston: Houghton Mifflin, 1969), 19–21.

CHAPTER 5

1. See the introduction, note 96.
2. For the history of village catechists in Tamil Nadu, see Mosse, *Saint in the Banyan Tree*, 2012), 121–122.
3. The Feast of Our Lady is the most important of the year, along, perhaps, with All Soul's Day, November 2, when Christians go to the graveyard and pray for the dead.
4. See chapter 4, note 8. This chariot festival (*tēr bavani*) had been performed annually since the 1980s, when Adaikkala Mātā possessed Dhanam for the first time. She had called four village headmen into the chapel and ordered them to hold an annual car procession in her honor. Like the Hindu Pallars' response to higher-caste dominance in Chinna Unjanai (which had resulted in tragedy), Dhanam was facilitating the village's own Mātā chariot festival, separate from that of the dominant parish, and also open to all: Hindus and Christians of all castes. Notably, the Adaikkalam Mātā procession maintained patriarchal hierarchy, allowing only men to pull the car (as did Rosalind-as-Jecintho's procession).
5. See chapter 4.
6. This place figures prominently in the sacred geography of the great Hindu epic, the *Ramayana*, which narrates the story of Rama, an avatar of the god Vishnu. According to legend, Kandadevi, which means "the seen goddess," is the place where the great bird Jatayu, a demigod, saw Rama's wife Sita being abducted by the demon Ravana. Jatayu fought Ravana in the skies, but fell, wounded, and died just after telling Rama what he had seen. Rama, remembrance of Jatayu, installed the Shiva linga on the spot.
7. "Thevar" is an honorific title (lit. "lord") used in the district to refer to relatively dominant people who trace their roots to wealthy feudal landlords or who have economic and political power in the region. It is synonymous with "Mukkulathor," or three groups of people who comprise the Agamudayur, Kallar, and Maravar social groups. Nadars also sometimes take on the title of "Thevar." The Nadar (also "Nattar" or "Shanar") community (historically *palmyra* climbers) is not a single caste, but developed from an assortment of related subcastes and classes, including the Kallar. Historically, among their lower ranks in particular, Nadars faced discrimination, but as a group made their way up in the caste system, claiming *kshatriya* status in part through the aid of Christian missions. See Eliza F. Kent, *Converting Women: Gender and Protestant Christianity in South India* (New York, Oxford University Press, 2004), 51–79; and Robert Hardgrave, *The Nadars of Tamilnad: The Political Culture of a Community in Change* (Berkeley and Los Angeles: University of California Press, 1969).

8. S. Viswanathan, "The Caste Juggernaut," *Frontline*, July 2–15, 2005; "A Temple Car and Caste Tensions," *Frontline*, August 2–15, 2003.
9. Hanging *margosa* leaves over an entrance is a common way to welcome the goddess throughout South India—and to combat heat and heat-inducing illnesses that are also associated with her. See Brenda Beck, "Color and Heat in South Indian Rituals," *Man* 4, no. 4 (1969): 553–572.
10. By August 2016, the car still had not been pulled despite the High Court's orders, because the Hindu Religious and Charitable Endowments Department, which administrated the festivals, claimed that the car was "under repairs." See J. Balasubramaniam and A.R. Venkatachalapathy, "From Kandadevi to Kallimedu," *The Hindu*, August 2016. http://www.thehindu.com/opinion/lead/j-balasubramaniam-from-kandadevi-to-kallimedu/article8975104.ece (accessed August 25, 2016).
11. See *Caṅkam* poetic tropes and the symbolism connected to these landscapes, in the introduction.
12. See the introduction. Also see chapter 7: Dhanam had diagnosed Sahaya Mary as having been possessed by Pandi some years back.
13. Mosse, *Saint in the Banyan Tree*, 46.
14. Dirks, *Hollow Crown*, 373.
15. See A. Pandian, *Crooked Stalks.*
16. Ibid., 4.
17. Catholic Bishops' Conference of India website, http://www.cbci.in/DiocesesofIndiaDisp.aspx, accessed April 26, 2013.
18. Mosse, *Saint in the Banyan Tree*, 36.
19. Sahaya Māta Church had about 850 families as members in 2006, according to the parish priest. That's about 4,200 members—and more than twenty times the population of Mātāpuram.
20. See the introduction.
21. See Nabokov, *Religion against the Self*, 83, 87, 94–95, 99; cf. Ram, *Mukkuvar Women*, 100–101.
22. See chapter 7.
23. Dierdre Sklar, "Unearthing Kinesthesia: Groping among Cross-Cultural Models of the Senses in Performance," in *The Senses in Performance*, ed. Sally Banes and Andre Lepecki (New York: Routledge, 2007), 38–46. On kinesthesia as a literary device, see Liz Bureman, "Kinesthesia: Definitions and Examples for Writers." http://thewritepractice.com/kinesthesia/ accessed June 6, 2017.
24. In 1918, the Rev. L. Besse, S.J. wrote,

> The first church he [Beschi] erected was at Conancoopam Aryanur in the District of Parur (South Arcot), which then belonged to *Moothoosamy Cachiroyan*, a poligar chieftan. After its completion, Fr. Beschi proceeded to Mylapore, and solicited the then Bishop of that diocese [Bishop D. Francis Laynez, S.J. +June 11, 1715] to procure for him, from Manila, an image of the Blessed Virgin Mary in the native dress, with the Child Jesus in her arms, according to a model he had drawn for that purpose. The prelate complied with that request, and on the arrival of the statue to which they gave the name of Periya Nayaguiammal [*sic*] (The Great Lady or the Great Princess) [the same name as that of the Hindu goddess on whom Padma and I had gazed in Kandadevi] he took it to Conamcoopam, and placed it in the church he had built in her honor, after performing a novena of prayers. The novena is still celebrated every year, and the fifteen hymns (*padels*), which are still sung during the feast, were composed by him. He founded another church at Tirucavalur, and dedicated it to the

Blessed Virgin under the title of Mother of Refuge (Adeikalamada) [*sic*]. It was erected on the land granted to the Christian Church situated at Ellacurichy, by Malavarayan, chieftan of Aryalur, in the district of Trichinopoly. (Besse, *Fr. Beschi of the Society of Jesus*, 37)

Many miracles are said to have taken place at the Elakurichi shrine, including the statue of Adaikkala Mātā herself, which is said to smile and blink. (Many videos of this perception have been posted on YouTube, accessed June 5, 2017.)

25. http://www.adaikalamadha.org/index.html (accessed June 5, 2017).
26. On material religion, and the different associations it acquires as it moves from one social context or culture to another, "negotiating differences and carrying with it the veneers of significance," see David Morgan, "The Materiality of Cultural Construction," in *Museum Objects: Experiencing the Properties of Things*, ed. Sandra H. Dudley (New York: Routledge, 2012), 101–102.
27. Practically everyone I interviewed on this question throughout Tamil Nadu—even Hindu devotees to Mary—said this. Hindus added that she was one with all goddesses.
28. Amy Allocco, personal correspondence, June 7, 2013. Ben Williams also told me about a possession he witnessed in North India, at a Mahalakshmi temple in Kolhapur, which he also wrote about on his blog post: "A woman . . . pours some powder into (her hand). She then lights a match, igniting a flame on her hand which remains perfectly cupped as the rest of her body continues to shake. With a loud 'Om Mahalakshmi Namo Namah' and a lightning like movement, she swings her hand to her mouth and swallows the flame, and then proceeds to collapse to the ground in a pile of sari." Personal correspondence, June 7, 2013.
29. Hayes, *Holy Harlots*, 3, 128.

CHAPTER 6

1. Goslinga, "Embodiment and Metaphysics," 201n3.
2. Goslinga notes that Pandi "is known to draw devotees from all castes, high and low, vegetarian and non-vegetarian, and from all religious creeds, though mostly Hindus. . . . Pandi [also] cures 'childlessness' . . . often by becoming a woman's lover" (ibid., 109, 110).
3. *Kalyāṇa puticu maṇam* (the new fragrance of marriage).
4. Sahaya Mary and Aarokkiyam's math does not add up. By her accounts, she would have been thirty-one when we visited in 2005, not twenty-eight, as Aarokkiyam had said. But then, ages are often estimated by people of the lowest classes and castes of Tamil Nadu, and birth records are not readily available.
5. Aarokkiyam later confirmed these events. "I am a man, what do you expect me to do?" he told Thavamani.
6. Goslinga also writes that possessed women report talking to or laughing with Pandi—a euphemism for sex—in "Embodiment and Metaphysics," 110–111.
7. *Maḻai cōru*, literally "rain rice," is made during an annual nine-day festival in late September-October as an offering to Mātā for rain. The entire village gathers in the chapel. On the ninth day, they cook and share food. A small pack of dogs had been fighting over some of this food when Sahaya Mary crossed their path, and one ran up and bit her from behind.
8. Goslinga, "Embodiment and Metaphysics," 109–123.
9. Ibid. Note the interesting (nonincestuous) twist on the Virgin Mary's impregnation by her "Father" (God) via the Holy Spirit.

10. Nabokov, *Religion against the Self*; and Lewis, *Ecstatic Religion*.
11. As we saw in chapter 2, Catherine Bell writes about this process not as "ritual," but as "ritualization," a verbal noun of circularity. Bodies become "ritualized" over time by preexisting bodies (individual and social); these newly ritualized bodies in turn produce practices that ritualize bodies. See Bell, *Ritual Theory, Ritual Practice*, 93.
12. See the introduction for a description of this poetry.
13. Ram, *Mukkuvar Women*, 4–6, and throughout; and Nabokov, *Religion against the Self*, 8–10; 25–29; 73–74; 128, 136, 156. For an analysis of gender and space in a South Indian village near Bangalore, Karnataka, and its relation to *olage* (inside) and *horage* (outside)—Kannada vernacular terms—see Seemanthini Niranjana, *Gender and Space: Femininity, Sexualization, and the Female Body* (New Delhi: Sage, 2001), 47–51, 89–117.
14. For analysis of such boundary crossing in a mid-twelfth-century Tamil devotional story, for example, see David Shulman, *The Hungry God: Hindu Tales of Filicide and Devotion* (Chicago: University of Chicago Press, 1993), 35.
15. Ram, *Mukkuvar Women*, 47.
16. Interview with the company's managing director, S.V. Pethaperumal, April 10, 2006.
17. By 2013, however, there were fifteen bore wells in the village. Even Aarokkiyam and Sahaya Mary had one. Dhanam did not, though her daughter Sofia Mary did, and the two of them shared. Each well cost one lakh. Aarokkiyam said his brother, Fr. Arlappan, helped them get the money to pay for it, and Sofia Mary's husband sent money from Malaysia.
18. Worried that sick people were being given this "holy water" to drink, Padma told villagers they should boil it first—but I do not know that they ever did. This same water was sometimes mixed with neem and turmeric to make "God's medicine." I drank it and did not get sick.
19. Thanks to Leila Ahmed for this insight.
20. Mosse, *Saint in the Banyan Tree*, 44; and Ines Županov, *Disputed Mission: Jesuit Experiments and Brahmanical Knowledge in Seventeenth-Century India* (New York: Oxford University Press, 1999).
21. Many Hindu women told me this. Also see Dempsey, *Kerala Christian Sainthood*, 69–70.
22. See Mines, *Fierce Gods*, 72. Cf. Anthony Good, *The Female Bridegroom* (Oxford: Oxford University Press, 1991), 194–198. For an analysis of purity and pollution in relation to danger, and how context and social history is key to the meanings attached to sacred boundaries and their maintenance, see Mary Douglas, *Purity and Danger: An Analysis of the Concepts of Purity and Taboo* (London: Routledge and Kegan Paul, 1966).
23. Overheating of the female body is believed to occur when there is a concentrated accumulation of blood, especially for women during menstruation and pregnancy. See Ram, *Mukkuvar Women*, 86. The head is often thought to be where heat resides—and the accumulation of that heat can erupt into associations with the angry Goddess. See Brenda Beck, "The Goddess and the Demon: A Local South Indian Festival and Its Wider Context," *Purusartha* 5 (1981): 83–136.
24. For similar uses of these terms among the Roman Catholic coastal Mukkuvar, see Ram, *Mukkuvar Women*, 81.
25. Not all women in Mātāpuram subscribed to the notion that women could move freely in their menstrual state. While a number of women, including Dhanam, said they did not consider menstruation to be polluting, others, like Sahaya Mary, said that menstruating women should not cook or fetch water. These differences may be

partly attributed to women's marrying into Mātāpuram, carrying with them the discourses and practices of their natal homes. There is a wide range of evidence for such differences among South Indian Christians. See Carl Gustav Diehl, *Instrument and Purpose: Studies on Rites and Rituals in South India* (Lund: CWK Gleerup, 1956); Lionel Caplan, "Caste and Castelessness among South Indian Christians," *Contributions to Indian Sociology*, n.s., 14 (1980): 213–238; Caplan, "Class and Christianity in South India: Indigenous Responses to Western Denominationalism," *Modern Asian Studies* 14, no. 4 (1980): 645–671; Caplan, *Class and Culture in Urban India: Fundamentalism in a Christian Community* (Oxford: Clarendon, 1987); Mosse, *Saint and the Banyan Tree*; Christopher Fuller, "Kerala Christians and the Caste System," *Man*, n.s., 11, no. 1 (1976): 53–70; G. Eichinger Ferro-Luzzi, "Women's Pollution Periods in Tamil Nadu (India)," *Anthropos* 69 (1974): 113–161.

26. Not all South Indian Christian women practiced such restrictions.
27. Kenneth David, "Hidden Powers: Cultural and Socio-Economic Accounts of Jaffna Women," in Wadley, *Powers of Tamil Women*, 93–136; Ram, *Mukkuvar Women*, 87–89; Holly Baker-Reynolds, *To Keep the Tali Strong: Women's Rituals in Tamil Nadu*, (PhD thesis, University of Wisconsin-Madison, 1978); Nabokov, *Religion against the Self*.
28. Ram, *Mukkuvar Women*, 88.
29. Baker-Reynolds, *To Keep the Tali Strong*, 230.
30. Aarokkiyam was slapped by a *pēy* once while in hospital being treated for a "twisted vein" (probably varicose) in his leg; he had become close to his hospital roommate, who died after a spinal tap, and he felt the man's *pēy* on him for several days. Sebastian Samy was caught once by the spirit of his dead sister-in-law when he was alone at night, during the period in which Dhanam was possessed by Mātā in the chapel. He fell very sick and ended up staying in the chapel himself for three months.
31. Note that Dhanam does not talk about this land being "our" land. The land "where we do work"—Hindu land—has historically been the land of the "Other," the higher caste landowner.
32. Hindu goddesses are often associated with snakes and *nagas*. See chapter 2.
33. Literally, "'You all come; having done the deed of coming like that, you are going to beat me?' it asked."
34. See chapter 5.
35. This was the same language that Alex had used when describing his visitation by Mātā in the hospital, when she said, referring to the rosary, "Take up your weapon and walk." See chapter 2.
36. See Heidi Hartmann, "The Unhappy Marriage of Marxism and Feminism," in *Women and Revolution: A Discussion of the Unhappy Marriage of Marxism and Feminism*, ed. Lydia Sargent (Boston: South End Press, 1981), 1–41; Nancy Hartsock, "The Feminist Standpoint: Developing the Ground for a Specifically Feminist Historical Materialism," in *Discovering Reality*, ed. Sandra Harding and Merrill B. Hintikka (New York: Kluwer Academic Publishers, 1983), 283–310; Gayle Rubin, "The Traffic in Women," *Toward an Anthropology of Women*, ed. R. Reiter (New York: Monthly Review Press, 1975), 157–210.
37. The Mahatma Gandhi National Rural Employment Guarantee Act (MGNREGA) guaranteed one hundred days of daily wage work per year to any rural household whose members were willing to do unskilled manual labor. It was passed in 2005 and implemented in 2006.
38. She was referring to a *muni* statue.
39. *Kuri* means "sign." Giving or telling *kuri* (*kuri collutal*), akin to "fortune-telling," as we use the term loosely in English, is telling the deeper meaning of things, or discerning the possibly supernatural cause of a problem.

40. This is a common way of giving birth in many Tamil villages.

CHAPTER 7

1. See Kalpana Ram, *Fertile Disorder: Spirit Possession and its Provocation of the Modern* (Honolulu: University of Hawaii Press, 2013), 133–134.
2. I had finished my dissertation in 2008, and had mentioned Dhanam only in the Introduction. The entire extended family, which had gathered a few days after the ordination at Dhanam's house, accepted it graciously. Dhanam's younger brother, the priest from Agra, flipped briefly through the five-hundred-some-page tome and set it down. Dhanam—who did not know how to read, let alone in English—simply laughed.
3. The word "charism," in Catholic theology, means a gift from God, an extraordinary grace given to an individual for the good of others. These extraordinary spiritual gifts include the word of wisdom, the word of knowledge, faith, the gift of healing, the working of miracles, prophecy, the discerning of spirits, diverse kinds of tongues, and interpretation of tongues (1 Corinthians 12:8–10).
4. Father Arul Jeeva, the former Devakottai parish priest whom we had interviewed in 2005 said that that he knew Dhanam but denied any knowledge about her healing practices. Father Aasir Vatham, the next parish priest, told me in 2012 that he knew nothing about Dhanam's practices, and went so far as to call a great deal of popular Marian devotion, including much of what happens at Velankanni, "a virus."
5. Unjanai is one of four *nadus* associated with the Kandadevi temple. Mātāpuram (Dalit Christian) and Chinna Unjanai ("Small Unjanai," which is Dalit Hindu) also belong to the same *panchayat* (village council) as Periya Unjanai ("Large Unjanai"), which is how people also refer to the upper-caste part of Unjanai *nadu*.
6. See Nicholas B. Dirks, *The Hollow Crown: Ethnohistory of an Indian Kingdom* (Cambridge: Cambridge University Press, 1987), 299; and Louis Dumont, "Possession and Priesthood," in *Contributions to Indian Sociology* 3 (1959): 59–74.
7. On concepts of evil in Hinduism, see Wendy Doniger O'Flaherty, *The Origins of Evil in Hindu Mythology* (Berkeley: University of California Press, 1976).
8. On Beschi, see chapter 5.
9. In addition to the *pēy* of the five murdered Hindu Dalit men, Dhanam had also been caught by the *pēy* of a Hindu woman who had died in childbirth (see introduction).
10. I am using the word "interpellated" (to call, cite, appeal to, or summons) to invoke Judith Butler, whose use of the term in *Bodies That Matter* invokes Althusser. In her discussion of gender and the early section of her book in which she talks about "girling" and "being girled," Butler uses "interpellation" to describe how subject positions are given and assumed in the process of "hailing" and "being hailed." See *Bodies That Matter*, 7–8 and throughout. Althusser famously gives the example of a policeman calling out, "Hey, you there!" That person, thus called, turns around—and the minute he does so, becomes that subject. "Why?" Althusser writes. "Because he has recognized that the hail was 'really' addressed to him, that 'it was *really* him who was hailed' (and not someone else) . . . The existence of ideology and the hailing or interpellation of individuals as subjects are really one and the same thing." See Louis Althusser, "Ideology and Ideological States Apparatuses," in *Lenin and Philosophy and Other* Essays, trans. Ben Brewster (London: New Left Books, 1969), 163.
11. For a pioneering theorization of possession as "instrumental" agency, see Keller, *Hammer and the Flute*, especially 75–77. Keller uses the term "instrumental" in

three senses. The first, "serving as an instrument or means," such as a hammer might be used in labor, or in a labor negotiation, Keller cites "as an instrument or means for production or protest in service of ancestors, deities, or spirits who employ them." The second, "that which is performed by instruments," Keller explains as "the flutelike character of a possessed body that is played or played upon." Third, the linguistic case of "instrumental," indicates that "the subject exercises a unique type of agency that is neither autonomous nor passive." Many South Asian languages, such as Tamil as well as Hindi, us the instrumental case to mark differences between subjects that indicate a type within a spectrum of possible degrees of agency. Keller writes, "Semiotically, the possessed woman undergoes the experience neither as a subject (she does not remember) nor as a patient (she is 'gone,' not unconscious)." Keller also notes that this definition of instrumental also answers to a tension in recent arguments about agency made by Ronald Inden and Talal Asad. See Ronald Inden, *Imagining India* (Oxford: Basil Blackwell, 1990), chaps. 1 and 2; and Asad, *Genealogies of Religion*, 4.

12. Such gestures of submission made by women who cover their hair is mentioned in many ethnographies of South Asia. See Bellamy, *Powerful Ephemeral*, 91; and Emma Tarlo, *Clothing Matters: Dress and Identity in India* (Chicago: University of Chicago Press, 1996), who writes, "The cloth is almost in constant motion, being drawn, adjusted, withdrawn and redrawn . . . It becomes in short an extension of the female space and a portable means of maintaining the possibility of shifting from the public to the private sphere at any moment" (160).
13. This reference to *kāṭci* (scene) suggests the theatrical or dramatic aspect of possession in South India—though not in the sense of theater or drama that those of us raised in Europe or America may associate with the term. Rather, as indicated as early as *Tolkāppiyam* and in forms of dance such as *veṟiyāṭṭam* ("sacred dance," today known as *teyyam*), certain kinds of dramatic action on a stage (*kaḷam*) is also understood to be a form of possession. See Nirmal Selvamony, "The Seeds of Drama in *tolkaappiyam*" (paper delivered at the National Seminar on Contemporary Indian Drama, January 19–20, 2014, Bangalore, India). Also see David Shulman and Deborah Thiagarajan, eds., *Masked Ritual and Performance in South India: Dance, Healing, and Possession* (Ann Arbor: University of Michigan Press, 2006).
14. P. Thirumagal, "Religious Conflicts and Hindu Sectarianism," in *History of People and Their Environs: Essays in Honour of Prof. B. S. Chandrababu*, ed. S. Ganeshram and C. Bhanvani (Chennai: Indian Universities Press, 2011), 170.
15. Ibid. Another popular Tamil saying is *Shakti illeṉṉā, Shivaneṉṟu iru* (If there is no Shakti, Shiva remains simply, thinking). This thinking, reclined Shiva is a state of corpus, of nonagency, or potential or latent agency.
16. This ritual of bodily purity was yet another action to welcome Mātā.
17. In interpreting Dhanam's experience, I was influenced by Julia Kristeva's theories on language, subjectivity, abjection, horror, love, and the separations necessary to establish identity. See *The Portable Kristeva*, updated ed., ed. Kelly Oliver (New York: Columbia University Press, 2002). Moreover, I was deeply struck by the ways in which the *akam* and *puṟam* poetry of the *Caṅkam* period communicated much of her thought, so compactly, in poetry.
18. These days correspond to the days that Rosalind holds prayer sessions, and they differ from the Hindu days of worship—Tuesdays and Fridays. Here again was similarity and difference (or, as Jacques Derrida would say, *différance*).
19. These marks of superhuman ability to bear physical suffering also seemed important to the trope of possession. In Rosalind's case, this involved standing for

hours, administering blessings after fasting and even while sick; in Nancy's case, it involved stigmata.

20. Aiyanar is not the only god in India thought to eat fetuses. In the temple of Balaji in Bharatpur, Rajasthan, a spirit named Masan is believed to eat unborn babies in the womb. See Sudhir Kakar, *Shamans, Mystics and Doctors: A Psychological Inquiry into India and Its Healing Traditions* (Boston: Beacon Press, 1982), 71.
21. Recall Sahaya Mary's sexual tussle with Pandi Muni in chapter 6.
22. See Julia Kristeva on mimesis in *Revolution in Poetic Language*, trans. Margaret Waller (New York: Columbia University Press, 1984). On her theory of mimesis as "reverse reactivation of sacrifice," and the poet as scapegoat—in this case, Dhanam would be the poet/scapegoat—see Dennis King Keenan, "Kristeva, Mimesis, and Sacrifice," *Philosophy Today* 47, no. 1 (Spring 2003): 23–33. On the connections between terrors and healing, and on the complex workings of memory and mimesis, see Michael Taussig, *Shamanism, Colonialism, and the Wild Man: A Study in Terror and Healing* (Chicago: University of Chicago Press, 1987), especially 134, and 391–392. On the mimetic faculty and its historical dynamism, see Walter Benjamin, "On the Mimetic Faculty," in *Walter Benjamin: Selected Writings*, Vol. 2, Part 2, 1931–1934, ed. Michael W. Jennings, Howard Eiland, and Gary Smith, trans. Rodney Livingstone and Others (Cambridge, MA: The Belknap Press of Harvard University Press, 1999), 720-722.
23. Other factors contributed to the relative decline of Dhanam's possession and healing practices. The water issues as described in chapter 6 were one: newcomers to the village wanted water access, and threats from one angry newcomer in particular—during a period when Dhanam's husband was away doing migrant labor—frightened her and caused her to withdraw slightly. Another factor was the rise of Charismatic Catholicism in her local parish in Devakottai. Around 2004, the parish had welcomed itinerant preachers who cultivated Charismatic services as well as trainings for parishioners, to teach them about charisms and about how to spread the good news. Dhanam had begun attending the monthly training meetings for women who would go door-to-door to spread the word of God, and to encourage people to come to the church services. She was not, she told me, spreading the word about her own healing practices during these house visits: to the contrary, she was careful not to do so, as the parish priest would not have been pleased. She did, furthermore, experience "possession by the Holy Spirit" during one of these meetings—which she explained to me in full detail and which did not resemble her possession practices by Mātā.
24. Actually, even doctors in India often use the term "abortion" as an umbrella term to mean stillbirth or miscarriage.
25. In physics and many other of the sciences, this is known as the "observer effect."
26. Julia Kristeva, in *Powers of Horror: An Essay on Abjection* (New York: Columbia University Press, 1982), uses the term "abjection" to refer to the embodied disgust toward a particular food, a piece of filth, waste, or dung. Judith Butler extends the term to disgust and rejection of entire populations, both in *Gender Trouble: Feminism and the Subversion of Identity* (New York: Routledge, 1990), ff. 133, and *Bodies That Matter: On the Discursive Limits of Sex* (New York: Routledge, 1993), 3. The notion of an "abject" woman is always implied by her opposite, the "ideal" woman; neither concept can exist without the other. But the world is not one of ideals, no matter how people may continue to treat it as such—and so Dhanam's healing ground is also a forum for integration, what Janice Boddy might call a "cultural therapeutic," in which "a woman is given scope to expand and

regenerate her sense of self and recontextualize her experiences," 4. See Boddy, "Spirits and Selves in Northern Sudan: The Cultural Therapeutics of Possession and Trance," *American Ethnologist* 15, no. 1 (1988): 4–27.

27. Michel Foucault, *History of Sexuality, Vol. 1.* (New York: Vintage, 1990).
28. Eck, Diana. *Darśan: Seeing the Divine in India*, 3rd ed. (New York: Columbia University Press, 1998).
29. On the mutually constitutive exchange between human and non-human worlds, and thus of power flowing in more than one direction, see Christopher Fuller, *The Camphor Flame: Popular Hinduism and Society in India* (Princeton, NJ: Princeton University Press, 1992, 2004).

CHAPTER 8

1. In a *puja* ritual, one honors the god and/or a respected guest by holding a lighted lamp in the right hand and waving it clockwise, vertically, in front of the *murti* or person. At the end of *ārati*, one places one's hands over the flame and then gently touches ones eyes and top of the head. The ritual likely has Brahmanical roots.
2. A round pot filled with water, dabbed with *kumkum*, and topped with a coconut, incarnating *shakti*. See chapter 4.
3. The Order of the Mass is prescribed by the Second Vatican Council (1962–1965), during which Pope Paul VI promulgated an ordinary form of the Mass—a change from the Tridentine Mass. The Second Vatican Council, in its 1963 document *Sacrosanctum Concilium*, promoted the use of local vernacular languages, to be decided by the "competent ecclesiastical authority" of the local episcopal conference of bishops, and as approved by Apostolic See (the Pope). The Conference of Catholic Bishops in India for the Latin Rite have, with the approval of the See, authorized translations of the Order of the Mass into each of the major vernacular languages of India, including Tamil. The Indian Order, in its scripture readings and Liturgy of the Word and the Eucharist, follows quite closely that of the United States Conference of Bishops.
4. Actually, Aananthan announced that he would read through verse 22 but read only through 21. Luke 4:16–22 was not one of the prescribed Gospel readings for an ordination according to the Order of the Mass for the Conferral of Holy Orders, but rather, seemed to be centered around one of the four choices for the verse that comes before the Gospel reading, the Alleluia verse—Luke 4:18. For the Lectionary for the Mass, see "The Catholic Lectionary Website, Second Typical Edition," section 2, "For the Conferral of Holy Orders." http://catholic-resources.org/Lectionary/2002USL-Masses-Rituals.htm (accessed August 22, 2015).
5. The Pope announced this on April 14, 2010 (italics mine), http://w2.vatican.va/content/benedict-xvi/en/audiences/2010/documents/hf_ben-xvi_aud_20100414.html# (accessed August 25, 2015).
6. Violence against women (and/or their natal families) in India by husbands (and/or their natal families) who feel cheated is well documented. There were no women's shelters that I knew of in Sahaya Mary's district, and women I knew in Chennai who chose to go to such shelters remained in very precarious situations.
7. Cf. Victor Turner, who expanded on Arthur van Gennep's threefold structure of rites of passage, which consisted of a preliminal phase (separation), a liminal phase (transition), and a post-liminal phase (reintegration). Turner theorized that the liminal phase was a "betwixt-and-between"—a limbo period characterized

by humility, seclusion, sexual ambiguity, and *communitas*. See Victor Turner, *The Ritual Process: Structure and Anti-structure* (New York: Aldine de Gruyter 1995).

8. His mother, however, would travel to Agra to visit him.
9. While I use the word "peripheral" here to invoke the contrast of "central" versus "peripheral" for which that I. M. Lewis is so famous for distinguishing in *Ecstatic Religion: A Study of Shamanism and Spirit Possession*, 3rd ed. (New York: Routledge, 2003), 27–31, 114–133, and throughout, I am arguing, against Lewis, that "peripheral cults" (as he would have categorized Marian possession cults) can be much more powerful and effect much more change than he admits.
10. On the expectation that every woman will become a *cumaṅkali*, a "docile, husband-worshipping wife," see Hancock, *Womanhood in the Making*; Reynolds, "Auspicious Married Women"; and Sheryl B. Daniel, "Marriage in Tamil Culture," in *The Powers of Tamil Women*, ed. Susan Wadley, Foreign and Comparative Studies/South Asian Series 6 (Syracuse, NY: Maxwell School of Citizenship and Public Affairs, 1980).
11. This is also how men dress when they make pilgrimages to Murugan.
12. Hematologists I consulted with said the term "O-light positive" was meaningless. "Realistically, this is not something that happens," one American specialist told me. One recent study reported that scientists had been able to convert types A and B blood to something closer to O by developing enzymes that cut away the antigens in A and B blood types. See David H. Kwan, Iren Constantinescu, Rafi Chapanian, Melanie A. Higgins, Miriam P. Kötzler, Eric Samain, Alisdair B. Boraston, Jayachandran N. Kizhakkedathu, and Stephen G. Withers, "Toward Efficient Enzymes for the Generation of Universal Blood through Structure-Guided Directed Evolution," *Journal of the American Chemical Society*, 137, no. 17 (2015): 5695. "That's when you put blood into a beaker," the hematologist said. "The only way to make that happen in the human body is through a bone marrow transplant." At the very least, then, Nancy's statement speaks to the willingness of believers to subscribe to phenomena that fly in the face of science.
13. *Iṟaivaṉ* is another old Tamil term for god which means "king" or "lord." Cf. *kaṭavuḷ*, chapter 2.
14. The Eucharistic doxology is usually sung by the presiding priest, concluding the Eucharistic prayer and followed by the Our Father. In English: "Through him, with him, and in him, O God, Almighty Father, in the unity of the Holy Spirit, all glory and honor is yours, forever and ever. Amen." When sung, it follows the same pitch and cadence, no matter what language, though some priests simply speak it.
15. *Catechism of the Catholic Church* online, part II, section 2, chapter 1, article 3. http://www.vatican.va/archive/ENG0015/_INDEX.HTM (accessed August 25, 2015). On October 15, 1976, Pope Paul VI approved the eleven-page "Declaration on the Question of the Admission of Women to the Ministerial Priesthood," which argues against the ordination of women. http://www.vatican.va/roman_curia/congregations/cfaith/documents/rc_con_cfaith_doc_19761015_inter-insigniores_en.html (accessed August 25, 2015). Meanwhile, since 2002, a group called Roman Catholic Womenpriests has ordained women as deacons, priests, and bishops, claiming a line of apostolic succession through an ordained, male, Roman Catholic bishop (who left the church in 1975). The group has been excommunicated and its ordinations deemed invalid. Many Protestant sects, which differentiate themselves from Catholics over many matters including transubstantiation (to Protestants, the act is symbolic), do ordain women priests and bishops.

16. On other fronts, Archbishop Chinnappa had retired by 2010, and a new man was installed. Rev. Fr. A. Thomas, who had first complained to the archbishop about the prayer house, had been promoted to Santhome Cathedral. The most active clerical supporter of the prayer house, Rev. Fr. Pitchaimuuthu, had "been retired" from his post on the outskirts of Pondicherry and had moved somewhere else. Prayer house numbers, however, remained strong, and the core group remained the same.
17. Michel Foucault, *The Order of Things: An Archaeology of the Human Sciences* (New York: Vintage, 1994).
18. Mines, *Fierce Gods*, 17. For an important distinction between the terms "local" and "village" goddesses, and that in India, one should not assume "local" to mean "village," see Foulston, *At the Feet of the Goddess*, 1.
19. For examples of a composite mix of goddesses in a village settlement in Orissa and a town in Tamil Nadu, and how the goddesses' many names, incarnations, and origin stories are linked to a sense of oneness and to the religious individuality of each place, see Foulston, *At the Feet of the Goddess*, 62–83.
20. Two types of exceptions to this statement warrant a long note. Jesus can certainly act and look different, cross-culturally. The "Black Jesus," for example, is for many members of the Black Church a savior who evades the visual symbolism of the white slave master. However, to my knowledge, this Jesus is not associated with a specific place, but rather with a culture, ethnicity, and experience of racism. Another exception, a variation on the theme of Our Lady of One-Name-or-Another, is the Infant Jesus. The "Infant Jesus of Prague," for example, is represented as a child dressed in a long white or red robe and carrying a *globus cruciger*, an orb topped with a cross, symbolizing Christ's dominion over the world. The statue, housed in the Carmelite Church of Our Lady Victorius in Malá Strana, Prague, and venerated around the world, is associated with miraculous healing, especially in regard to fertility (and in Ireland, to weather). This connection to fertility and to the seasons, I would argue, is also key to this icon's particularity in multiplicity. This popular infant statue is pre- and postdated by many other infant Jesus icons around the world, venerated for similar reasons.
21. Mary's first known portrayal as queen appears on the wall of S. Maria Antiqua, the oldest Christian building in the Roman Forum. Historian Marina Warner interprets the multilayered message of this enthroned virgin bride, "[S]he belongs to a classical tradition of personifying cities and institutions as goddesses, as and such, in the heart of Rome, she embodied the New Rome which is the Church just as the *Dea Roma* now on the capitol represented the pagan city. And because she is arrayed in all the pearl-laden, jewel-encrusted regalia of a contemporary secular monarch, she also proclaims, in a brilliantly condensed piece of visual propaganda, the concept that the Church is a theocracy of which the agent and representative is the pope, the ruler of Rome." Warner, *Alone of All Her Sex*, 104.
22. Regarding this timing, Warner writes that "the image of *Regina Caeli* holds up a mirror to the fluctuations of the Church's self-image: in times of stasis and entrenchment, as under the popes Pius XII and to some extent Paul VI, veneration of the Virgin is encouraged, and in times of strong ecumenism and change, when the Church is less self-righteous and assured, devotion to the Virgin, especially under her triumphant aspect, is restrained and declines." Ibid., 103.
23. A quick look at Mary's depictions through history clearly suggests this mix of carnality and queenship. The earliest extant image of Mary, in the Catacomb of S. Priscilla, Rome, shows her with the child at her breast and a male figure pointing

upward to a star. The eighth-century icon of Mary Regina at S. Maria Trastevere, Rome, portrays her as a Byzantine empress, holding a boy Jesus on her lap and Pope John VII kneeling before her. The Latin inscription reads, "As God himself made himself from thy womb, the princes among the angels stand by and marvel at thee, who carried in thy womb the child who is born." She is repeatedly depicted as Bride of Christ, and as such, his queen and consort. See Warner, *Alone of All Her Sex*, 132 and 121–122, which depicts Agnolo Gaddi's late fourteenth-century *Coronation of the Virgin*; a Florentine diptych, likely from that same period, in which Christ coyly clasps Mary's right hand with the formal and legal gesture of nuptial union; and the famous twelfth-century mosaic in S. Maria in Trastevere, Rome, in which Christ as love in the Song of Songs embraces his mother, enthroned on his right as his queen bride.

24. While there is no proof that the full-figured, female figurines unearthed from the ruins of the Indus River Valley Civilization (ca. 2000 BCE) were worshipped as goddesses, many scholars argue that they provide strong evidence of a prehistoric cult of the Mother. See Marija Gimbutas, *The Gods and Goddesses of Old Europe, 7000 to 3500 B.C.* (London: Thames and Hudson, 1973). Debunking this notion are historians, theologians, and paleo-archaeologists alike (including feminist ones), who warn that we should not mistake these finds for evidence of an original matriarchal society. Some say that the notion itself is a product of nineteenth-century European thought, birthed with the feminist movement. See Rosemary Radford Ruether, *Goddesses and the Divine Feminine: A Western Religious History* (Berkeley: University of California Press, 2005), 2–6. In regard to Hinduism, we know that the assimilation of goddesses into the pantheon of major Indian gods occurred long after the acceptance of Shiva and Vishnu. "This assimilation," Wendy Doniger tells us, "came in two distinct phases: first, the Indo-Aryan male gods were given wives. Then, under the influence of Tantric and Shakti movements which had been gaining momentum outside orthodox Hinduism for many centuries, these shadowy female figures emerged as goddesses in their own right, and merged into the Great Goddess." See Wendy Doniger O'Flaherty, trans., *Hindu Myths: A Sourcebook Translated from the Sanskrit* (London: Penguin Classics, 1975), 238. Also see David R. Kinsley, *Hindu Goddesses: Visions of the Divine Feminine in the Hindu Religious Tradition* (Berkeley: University of California Press, 1988), 6–8, and 96.
25. See the introduction.
26. Perhaps the most famous of these defectors was Mary Daly, a radical feminist philosopher and theologian who eventually gave up theology altogether, believing it to be hopelessly patriarchal. According to biblical narration, Daly argued, Mary was raped by her father. See Mary Daly, *Gyn/Ecology: The Metaphysics of Radical Feminism* (Boston: Beacon Press, 1978), 85. The canonical New Testament story shares commonalities with earlier creation myths: Zeus, a serial rapist, had sex with two sisters, Hera and Demeter, and Adonis—herself the offspring of Myrrah and her father, Cinyrus. For an argument that these rapes refer to Hellenistic conquests of goddess's ancient shrines, see Robert Graves, *The Greek Myths* (Baltimore, MD: Penguin, 1975), I, 27, *k*. For Brahmanical Hinduism's earliest sacred texts depicting patriarchal incest, see Doniger O'Flaherty, *Hindu Myths*, 25–34.
27. See Ruether, *Sexism and God-Talk*, especially chap. 5, in which she discusses Mary's free choice and co-creatorship with God and humanity, in which "faith ceases to be heteronomous submission to external authorities and becomes a *free act*" (154; italics mine). "When such faith is absent, Christ can do nothing. This is the radical

dependence of God on humanity. . . . Mary is exalted because, through her, God will work this revolution in history. Or, to be more accurate, she herself is both subject and object of this liberating action" (154–155).

28. See Leonardo Boff and Clodovis Boff, *Introducing Liberation Theology*, trans. Paul Burns (Maryknoll, NY: Orbis, 1987).
29. See the introduction.
30. For an eloquent and piercing analysis of how memory can be used to contest the evil of the "fantastic hegemonic imagination," see Emilie M. Townes, *Womanist Ethics and the Cultural Production of Evil* (New York: Palgrave Macmillan, 2006). Also see Frantz Fanon, *Black Skin, White Masks*, trans. Charles Lam Markmann (New York: Grove Press, 1967), 8. While Fanon calls on the black man to remake himself without necessarily depending on the language or culture of the precolonial order, he does call for invention (229). For an analysis of how Christian Zionists of the Tshidi Baralong of South Africa used ritual and symbols drawn from both precolonial and colonial systems to protest their oppression in the 1960s and 1970s, see Jean Comaroff, *Body of Power, Spirit of Resistance: The Culture and History of a South African People* (Chicago: University of Chicago Press, 1985). Comaroff calls the rituals of Zion "a *bricolage* whose signs appropriate the power both of colonialism and of an objectified Tshidi 'tradition,' welding them into a transcendent synthesis; an integrated order of symbols and practices that seeks to reverse estrangement, to reconstitute the divided self" (12).
31. http://www.thecatholicdioceseofmeerut.com/Default.aspx (accessed Sept. 25, 2016).
32. In 1981, for example, the National Biblical and Catechetical and Liturgical Centre (NBCLC) in Bangalore held a weeklong workshop called "The Indian Church and the Struggle for a New Society." Among its many topics was the role of women. The group set to study this role over the course of a year comprised four women and five men; it concluded, "Women in the Church will continue to be over-dependent on men as long as ordination to priesthood is denied. The New Society calls for a freedom in ministries." See D. S. Amalorpavadass, ed., *The Indian Church in the Struggle for a New Society* (Banglaore: NBCLC, 1981), 1045. Meanwhile, five years later, in an NBCLC book on popular devotions, a paper by Fr. Antonio F.X. Rodrigues, C.Ss.R., entitled "Devotion to Our Lady," aimed "to foster what is healthy and correct, rather to suggest means to overcome what is unhealthy, superstitious and unliturgical [*sic*]" (393). Quoting the 1975 papal encyclical *Evangelii Nuntiandi*, which warned that popular religiosity "is subject to penetration by many distortions of religion and even superstitions," Rodrigues stressed "*proper* catechesis on the role of the Blessed Virgin Mary in the work of salvation of humankind" (398–399; italics mine) and concluded, "[I]t is wrong to interpret devotion to Mary as 'praying to Mary', it is rather praying to God with/and or through Mary: prayers offered to Mary are always meant to secure her intercession with God, her Son" (401). See Antonio F.X. Rodrigues, "Devotion to Our Lady," in *Popular Devotions*, ed. Paul Puthanangady, SDB (Bangalore: NBCLC, 1986), 393–401. On Second Vatican Council debates over Mary, see Hans Küng, *My Struggle for Freedom: Memoirs*, trans John Bowden (Grand Rapids, MI: Eerdmans, 2003), 386; and on his disappointing symposium on "Christian Revelation and non-Christian Religions" in India, 407–408.
33. On policing the Charismatic Movement, see Pope John Paul II's 1992 "Address to the Council of the 'International Catholic Charismatic Renewal Office,'" in which he stressed the importance of obedience: "*there can be no conflict between fidelity*

to the Spirit and fidelity to the Church and her Magisterium [his italics]."https://w2.vatican.va/content/john-paul-ii/en/speeches/1992/march/documents/hf_jp-ii_spe_19920314_charismatic-renewal.html (accessed September 2, 2016).

34. See Michael Bergunder, *The South Indian Pentecostal Movement in the Twentieth Century* (Grand Rapids, MI: Eerdmans, 2008); Allan Heaton Anderson, *To The Ends of the Earth: Pentecostalism and the Transformation of World Christianity* (New York: Oxford University Press, 2013); Todd Hartch, *The Rebirth of Latin American Christianity* (New York: Oxford University Press, 2014); and Lamin Sanneh, *Whose Religion is Christianity: The Gospel Beyond the West*, 4th ed. (Grand Rapids, MI: Eerdmans, 2003).
35. Janet Soskice, *After Eve: Women, Theology, and the Christian Tradition* (Grand Rapids, MI: Zondervan, 1990), 73–88; Elisabeth Schüssler Fiorenza, *Wisdom Ways: Introducing Feminist Biblical Interpretation* (Maryknoll, NY: Orbis, 2001), 22–24.
36. On the debates over contraception during Vatican II, see Küng, *My Struggle for Freedom*, 438–441; Charles Curran, *Loyal Dissent: Memoir of a Catholic Theologian* (Washington, DC: Georgetown University Press, 2006), esp. chap. 3, "The Uproar over Humanae Vitae"; and Robert Blair Kaiser, *The Encyclical That Never Was: The Story of the Pontifical Commission on Population, Family, and Birth, 1964–66* (New York: Sheed and Ward, 1987). On the contemporary Vatican view on sex, see the 2012 "Notification of the Congregation of the Doctrine of the Faith Regarding the Book *Just Love: A Framework for Christian Sexual Ethics* by Sister Margaret A. Farley, RSM," http://www.news.va/en/news/72432#TESTO%20IN%20LINGUA%20ORIGINALE (accessed September 10, 2016). On abortion, see the Phoenix Hospital Case, especially Professor Therese Lysaught's moral analysis that was rejected by Bishop Olmsted, and the USCCB Committee On Doctrine's affirmation of his rejection, in Grant Gallicho, "The Moral Analysis Rejected by Bishop Olmsted," December 21, 2010, *Commonweal*, https://www.commonweal-magazine.org/blog/moral-analysis-rejected-bishop-olmsted (accessed September 10, 2016); and Patricia Miller, *Good Catholics: The Battle over Abortion in the Catholic Church* (Berkeley: University of California Press, 2014).
37. See Vatican II's *Lumen Gentium*, chapter VIII.
38. For example, see Ludwig Feuerbach, *The Essence of Christianity* (New York: Prometheus, 1989); Adolf von Harnack, *What Is Christianity?*, trans. Thomas Bailey Saunders (Eastford, CT: Martino Fine Books, 2011); and Kathryn Tanner, *Theories of Culture: A New Agenda for Theology* (Minneapolis, MN: Fortress, 1997).
39. Bruce Lincoln, *Holy Terror: Thinking about Religion after September 11* (Chicago: University of Chicago Press, 2003), 3.
40. Shri Bhagavati is understood to be an incarnation of the fierce goddess Durga, who herself is the incarnation of Adishakti, or "first Shakti"—feminine, primordial cosmic energy and first cause of all creation, existence, and destruction. For more on Durga's origination among various tribal, mountain, and nomadic peoples and her eventual amalgamation and absorption into Brahmanical myth and philosophy, see June McDaniel, *Offering Flowers, Feeding Skulls: Popular Goddess Worship in West Bengal* (New York: Oxford University Press, 2004), 214.
41. Mahmood, *Politics of Piety*, 10–17. For a nuanced critique of the usefulness of Mahmood's argument in understanding spirit possession, see Ram, *Fertile Disorder*, 268–269.
42. First-wave feminism, which occurred primarily in the nineteenth and early twentieth centuries in Europe, Canada, and the United States, focused mainly on the

rights of women through legal issues such as women's suffrage. Often forgotten are the ways in which many of these women worked with and enabled the conditions for the aforementioned philosophers to work and write at all. Second-wave feminism began roughly in the 1960s in the United States. By the 1970s, this movement had created new waves among feminists of color, who argued that freedom for them meant different things, including to be able to form families—since the history of slavery and racism had torn families apart and continued to create obstacles in this quest. See Patricia Hill Collins, *Black Feminist Thought: Knowledge, Consciousness, and the Politics of Empowerment* (New York: Routledge, 1991); Angela Davis, *Women, Race, and Class* (New York: Vintage, 1983); Audre Lorde, *Sister Outsider: Essays and Speeches* (Berkeley, CA: Crossing Press, 1984); and "A Black Feminist Statement" made by members of the Combahee River Collective. See *The Second Wave: A Reader in Feminist Theory*, ed. Linda Nicholson (New York: Routledge, 1997), 63–70.

43. Mahmood, *Politics of Piety*, 14.
44. On resituating the "romance of resistance," see Ram, *Fertile Disorder*, 270–271.
45. Miriam Cooke, "Saving Brown Women," special issue, *Gender and Cultural Memory*, *Signs* 28, no. 1 (Autumn, 2002): 468–470.

EPILOGUE

1. Catholics and Hindus alike in South India garland portraits of the deceased and may pray to or worship the person before their image. For descriptions of similarities between Hindu and Catholic death rituals in Tamil Nadu, including practices that turn certain deceased persons into local saints, see Mosse, *Saint and the Banyan Tree*, 71–82. On sainthood in South India and the complicated nature of using terms appropriate to one tradition in order to explore the meanings of another, see Dempsey, *Kerala Christian Sainthood*, 115–155. As for the priests' presence at the *tiru uruvappaṭam*-blessing ceremony in May, Fr. G. Pushparaj, one of the two priests, told me he had come to pay his respects to Fredy.
2. While the specific details of death rituals differ across sectarian lines, caste, class, and region in South India, they also bear significant resemblances. In Brahmanical Hinduism, the one-year death rite is known as *shraddha*, translated loosely as "act of faith." Traditionally, Hindus and Catholics alike may perform rites in the days immediately following the death to help the person's soul move on to the next life, or to help them become a *pitṛ*, or "beneficent dead" (though there are many classes of *pitṛs*), as opposed to a *bhut* or a *pēy*. Hindus may also practice *shraddha* on the six-month death anniversary. Rosalind's family, like many Catholics, marked Fredy's six-month death anniversary with a Mass and the unveiling of his portrait; Charles called this Fredy's "first memorial." Tamil Catholics not only visit the graves of the deceased on death anniversaries for at least a year following the person's death; they also observe All Saints' Day—the same day as Fredy's death—by visiting graves with garlands, flowers, incense, candles, and food, often bringing food or snacks they know the deceased person especially liked.
3. South Indians across religious lines often mark the one-year anniversary of a person's death with a visit to their grave, offerings of food, and a communal meal (see note 6, below).
4. By 2016, almost all the devotees had added the moniker "Jecintho" before their own names.
5. I missed the memorial because of my teaching schedule.

6. Family members told me that she had been doing so since November 2, 2015.
7. Hindus often place *pindu* (rice balls) in front of the images of the deceased or with the body before cremation—and Tamil Christians and Hindus of many stripes offer sweets or food they think the person would especially enjoy. Some say such offerings are meant to help the deceased person's transition to the afterlife, and also serve to remind the living of the very real presence of the dead. In explanation of the dinner ritual with Fredy, Charles agreed that this was a common South Asian practice. He added, "It is just remembering."
8. In South India, the practice of *prasādam* (lit. gift) often extends to deified ancestors. Whether offered to an ancestor, deity, avatar, or saint, materially, *prasādam* is created through a system of exchange—the giving and receiving of a substance between a human and a divine being.

GLOSSARY

abhishekam Bathing and decorating the image, or *murti*, of the god or goddess.

Aiyanar Warrior god of village boundaries, usually seated on a horse or depicted as a terra-cotta horse itself.

aiyō A colloquial Tamil expression of surprise and distress, lit. "father!"

akam Inner, internal. *Akam* poetry is the "inner," love poetry of *Caṅkam* literature.

akkā Elder sister; female parallel cousin older than self.

ammā Mother. Also a term of respect for women.

ammaṉ Goddess Parvati. Also a suffix added to the names of goddesses who are fierce or especially powerful (for example, Mariyamman).

aṉbu Love, affection.

aṇṇaṉ Older brother, male parallel cousin older than self.

āṇṭavar God, from the verb *āḷ*, "to rule over." See also ***kaṭavuḷ*** and ***iṟai***.

appā Father.

ārati Part of the *puja* ritual, in which one honors a deity or a respected guest by holding a lighted lamp in the right hand and waving it in a clockwise motion, vertically.

ārōkkiyam Health.

Ārōkkiya Āṉṉai Our Lady of Good Health, lit. "Maiden of Health."

aruḷ Grace, mercy, gift.

aṭaikkalam Shelter.

Aṭaikkala Mātā Our Lady of Refuge (Shelter), commonly spelled "Adaikkala Madha."

attai Father's sister, mother-in-law, father of any cross-cousin.

āṭu To dance, shake.

āvi Spirit of a deceased person.

bhakta Devotee.

bhakti Emotional devotion to a god or goddess. From the Sanskrit *bhaj*, "to join."

brahman The divine substance of the universe, absolute reality. In the Vedic ritual period, power, sacred speech formulation.

Brahmanical Hinduism Hinduism that traces its roots to the Sanskrit Vedas.

brahmin A member of the priestly caste, the highest *varna* or social category.

cāmi A god. Also an honorific title of respect.

cāmiyār God dancer.

Caṅkam Lit. "society." *Caṅkam* literature is the classical literature of South India, dating back to the first to sixth centuries CE.

cantaṉum Sandalwood paste.

capparam A small wooden chariot used in processions.

cāṭci Witness.

chappals Sandals.

churi dar The pajama pant and long blouse (*kurta*) worn mostly by younger or professional women in South India.

citti Aunt. Mother's younger sister or wife of father's younger brother.

cūdam Camphor oil.

Dalit Lit. "ground," "ground-down," "broken," or "downtrodden." An explicitly political term of identification for castes once—and often still—considered "untouchable" in the Hindu caste order.

darśan/darshan Seeing and being seen by the deity.

farangi Foreigner (usually white). Derived from the Persian and Arabic word for Frank.

Ganesh The elephant-headed god; son of Shiva and Parvati; Hindu god of new beginnings and remover of obstacles. Also known as Vinayaka, and more than one hundred other names.

garbha Womb.

iṟaivaṉ Presiding male god, from *iṟai*, "king," and *–aṉ* (indicating male gender).

iṟaivi Presiding female god (*–vi* indicating female gender).

iraṅki The verb "to descend."

Iyēcu Jesus (pronounced Yēsu).

jāti Lit. "birth" in Sanskrit; denotes the hereditary clan or subgroup—usually endogamous—that one is born into.

jebam Prayer.

jebam mālai Prayer beads; rosary, lit. "garland of flowers."

Jecintho The specific name for Mary, "Queen of Roses," as revealed first to Rosalind.

kaḷam Measured space. In *Tolkāppiyam*, a stage.

Kali Fierce Hindu goddess; "she who is black." Often regarded as the Shakti of Shiva.

Kallar A predominant caste in the southern Tamil country, commonly identified as bearing a warrior heritage, along with the Maravars and Agamudaiyars/Agambadiyars (the three Mukkulathor).

kammai A lake or small water body.

kaṉṉi Young unmarried woman, maiden.

karakam A small round pot filled with water, and sometimes a coin, dabbed with *kumkum*, and topped with a coconut, incarnating Shakti.

karmaṉ Karma; a theory of cause and effect; an order of moral consequences in the present and future life as the fruit of past deeds.

kaṟpu Chastity, modesty, fidelity; associated with women.

Karuppar/Karuppan Lit. he who is black. A god usually associated with Muni or one of the twenty-one peons of Aiyanar; patroller of boundaries. Also known as Karuppu Sami.

kaṭavuḷ God, from *kaṭaṉ*, "debt, obligation." The deity to whom one wishes to repay for gifts. Compare ***āṅṭavar*** and ***iṟaivaṉ***.

kāṭu Uncultivated area, thick forest, scrub jungle, barren desert, cemetery or burning ground, fallow open ground, or dry upland field—all considered to be wild and unruly peripheral zones opposed to the order of settled places. See ***nāṭu***.

kolam Geometric pattern made of rice powder, usually drawn by women outside the entrance of their homes to welcome the goddess Lakshmi.

kōyil Temple, from *kō*, "king," and the locutive - *il*, which translates as "place of the king." Also used in Tamil country to mean "church."

kōyilpiḷḷai Village catechist.

Krishna Hindu god of compassion, tenderness, love, and beauty; the eighth incarnation of Vishnu. Featured in the *Bhagavata Purana* and the *Bhagavad Gita*. To some devotees, a supreme god in his own right.

kulam The large water tank, often the size of a small lake, outside a temple.

kumkum/kumkumam Red power made of turmeric and lime, which turns the turmeric red when dried in the sun; often applied to the forehead for auspiciousness.

kuṟi Sign, or prediction.

Lakshmi Sanskritic goddess of hospitality and good fortune; consort of Vishnu.

linga The sign for Shiva, an erect stone (in Sanskrit, lit. "sign").

Lord Swarnamoorti Eshwarar A local form of Shiva in Kandadevi.

lungi A cotton or synthetic printed cloth tied and worn around the waist by men.

Madras Presidency The territory of the southern Indian peninsula under direct British rule between 1857 and 1947, including the modern state of Tamil Nadu and parts of what are now Andhra Pradesh, Karnataka, and Kerala.

Madurai The courtly seat of classical Tamil literary production, the capital of the medieval Pandya and Telugu Nayak kingdoms, the administrative center of the colonial Madura District, and the largest city in southern Tamil Nadu.

makaḷ Daughter.

makaṉ Son.

makimai Power.

malai Mountain, hill, or mountain forest.

mālai Garland (usually of flowers).

māmaṉ Mother's brother, father-in-law, father of any cross-cousin.

***maṉacu* (or *maṉam*)** The heart/mind as a faculty of desire, feeling, thought, and will.

manaivi Wife.

Manikkavacakar A ninth-century Tamil Shaivite, *bhakti* poet-saint.

mantiram Mantra.

Maravar A predominant caste in the southern Tamil country, commonly identified as bearing a warrior heritage, along with Kallars and Agamudaiyars/Agambadiyars.

mariyātai Respect, honors, propriety of conduct.

marutam Countryside, pastoral region; one of the five landscapes of *Caṅkam* poetry, representing a lover's unfaithfulness and sulking scenes.

Mariyē, vāḻka! Hail Mary!, lit. "Long live Mary!."

Mātā Mother. Sanskrit loan-word, often used in Tamil to refer to certain Hindu goddesses, and to Mary.

Mātāmmā An intimate form of *Mātā*.

Meenakshi Temple A temple to the "fish-eyed" goddess Meenakshi, in Madurai.

mehendi The red paste used to decorate women's hands, usually for weddings.

mukkāṭu A veil, usually formed when a woman pulls the long end of the sari over her head.

Mukkulathor A political term identifying Kallars, Maravars, and Agamudaiyars/Agambadiyars as "three families" of a common martial or royal heritage.

Muni Also *Munnēswaran* or *Muniyāndi*. A fierce, meat-eating warrior god. A *muni* can also mean "saint" (though the Christian valence only approximates the Tamil meaning), or a holy sage who has achieved divine status after death. Muni has many forms, one of which is Pandi Muni. He and the others serve Aiyanar. See also **Pandi Muni.**

murti An icon, form, or solid object in which the god or goddess manifests, incarnate; not just an image of the deity, but identical to that deity.

Murugan Patron god of Tamil Nadu, son of Shiva and Parvati; handsome young god of love and war, associated with a bow and arrow, spear, and peacock.

nambikkai Belief.

nāṭu/nādu The settled and cultivated country as opposed to the uncultivated tracts on its periphery. In medieval times, the term identified a local agrarian territory (sometimes "kingdom") and, in modern times, the "country" or "state" of national Tamil belonging (as in Tamil Nadu).

Navarāttiri Nine-night, ten-day festival to the goddess.

nērccai Vow.

paittiyam Crazy person.

pālai Wasteland, desert, or arid tract; one of the five landscapes of Tamil *Caṅkam* poetry, that of anxiety in love, or separation.

paḻakkam Habit; embodied familiarity.

panchayat Village council.

pandal A festive, usually makeshift entrance or gateway.

Pandi Muni A bachelor god, usually fierce; also called *Pandi cāmi*. One of the many *munis*.

paricutta āvi Holy Spirit.

Parvati Brahmanical goddess, consort of Shiva; mother of Murugan and Ganesh.

pēy The spirit of a person who has died an untimely death.

picācu Ghost.

pon tēr Golden chariot.

prasādam From the Sanskrit "gift" (in Tamil transliteration, *piracātam*); usually a material substance such as food or other objects (flowers, garlands, saris) blessed by a deity and distributed back to devotees.

puja Hindu ritual worship; sometimes taken on by Roman Catholics to mean "Mass."

puṟam Outer, external. *Puṟam* poetry is the *Caṅkam* poetry of the "outside," public world, including that of war.

Shaiva Pertaining to the god Shiva.

Shaivism A sect that worships Shiva. Compare Vaishnavism.

shakta A devotee of Shakti.

Shakti The supreme goddess; the divine feminine that activates male gods and the material world.

Shiva One of the three major gods in Brahmanical Hinduism (the others being Vishnu and Brahma); the god of creative destruction, who is both erotic and ascetic; the supreme god of Shaivism.

tāli Marriage thread, a pendant worn by married women.

Tamil land The predominantly Tamil-speaking region of southern India, identified today with the Indian state of Tamil Nadu.

taṅkai/taṅkacci Younger sister.

tāy Mother.

tēr Chariot or, colloquially, a "car," on which a deity or saint rides in procession.

tēr bavani Chariot procession or festival.

tēva God.

tēvi Goddess.

Thevar An honorific title (lit. lord) taken by Kallar, Maravar, and sometimes Nadar men, and used more generally to refer to people of these castes.

tiruppali Roman Catholic Mass.

Tiruvācakam Lit. "sacred utterance." A volume of Tamil hymns written in the ninth century by Manikkavacakar, a Shaivite *bhakti* poet-saint.

Tolkāppiyam The earliest extant Tamil text of grammar and poetics, written sometime between the first and sixth centuries CE.

uḷḷam The heart, as that which is *uḷ*, or inside.

uppu Salt.

ūr Town or village, one's natal place.

urukkam Melting.

utsava murti Festival image.

vahana Vehicle (of a god or goddess), usually an animal; often called the deity's "mount."

Vaishnavism A sect that worships Vishnu.

vaittiyar Healer.

varna In Sanskrit, lit. "color," or "category." One of the four categories of society listed in the *Rig Veda*. These are *brahmins* (priests), *kshatriyas* (warriors), *vaishyas* (agriculturalists and traders), and *shudras* (servants and artisans). In Brahmanical Hinduism the three upper *varnas* were allowed an initiation ritual that made them "twice-born"; the fourth (and the fifth, or outcastes) were not.

varu The Tamil verb "to come."

varu mēl "To come on"; spoken of a deity who comes onto the head of a person.

Velankaṉṉi Mātā Velankanni Mother (*veḷḷai,* "white," and *kaṉṉi*, "young woman" or "maiden"), the Mary residing in Velankanni, Nagapattinam District. Also known as ***Ārōkkiya Mātā***, or Our Lady of Good Health.

Venkateshwara The Lord who destroys all sins, an avatar of Vishnu.

veshti A white cotton or silk cloth tied and worn around the waist by men, especially on formal or auspicious occasions.

vibhuti Sacred ash.

Vinayakar The elephant-headed god, son of Shiva and Parvati. Also known as Ganesh.

Vishnu One of the principle gods of Hinduism, and the supreme god of Vaishnavism.

vīṭu House, household, and domestic or interior space.

Yama God of death.

BIBLIOGRAPHY

SOURCES IN TAMIL

Madurai Anand. *Irai arul̥ ōviyam*. Chennai: Metaku Peeraayar AruLtaas James, 2002.

Rajangam, Stalin. *Sathiyam: Kaikoodatha Neethi*. Nagercoil: Kalachuvadu Publications, 2011.

Sivasubramanian, A. *Uppittavarai*. Palayamkottai: Folklore Research and Resource Center, n.d.

Subramanian, P. R., ed. *Kriyāvin tal̥kālat tamil̲ akarāti*. Dictionary of Contemporary Tamil (Tamil-Tamil-English). 5th ed. Adyar, Chennai: Cre-A, 1992.

PRINTED SOURCES IN WESTERN LANGUAGES

Agee, James. *Let Us Now Praise Famous Men: Three Tenant Families*. Boston: Houghton Mifflin, 1969.

Althusser, Louis. "Ideology and Ideological State Apparatuses." In *Lenin and Philosophy and Other Essays*, translated by Ben Brewster, 123–173. London: New Left Books, 1969.

Amalorpavadass, D.S., ed. *The Indian Church in the Struggle for a New Society*. Banglaore: National, Biblical, Catechetical and Liturgical Centre, 1981.

Appadurai, Arjun. "The Capacity to Aspire: Culture and the Terms of Recognition." In *Culture and Public Action*, edited by Vijayendra Rao and Michael Walton, 59–84. Stanford, CA: Stanford University Press, 2004.

Asad, Talal. *Genealogies of Religion: Disciplines and Reasons of Power in Christianity and Islam*. Baltimore, MD: Johns Hopkins University Press, 1993.

Austin, J. L. *How to Do Things with Words*. Edited by J. O. Urmson and M. Sbisa. Cambridge, MA: Harvard University Press, 1994.

Ayyar, P. V. Jagadisa. *South Indian Customs*. New Delhi: Asian Educational Services, 1992.

Baker Reynolds, Holly. "The Auspicious Married Woman." In *The Powers of Tamil Women*, edited by Susan Wadley, 35–60. Foreign and Comparative Studies / South Asian Series 6. Syracuse, NY: Maxwell School of Citizenship and Public Affairs, 1980.

———. *"To Keep the Tali Strong": Women's Rituals in Tamilnad, India*. PhD diss., University of Wisconsin, Madison, 1978.

Ballhatchet, Kenneth. *Caste, Class and Catholicism in India, 1789–1914*. Surrey, UK: Curzon, 1998.

Bama. *Karukku*. Translated by Lakshmi Holstrom. Chennai: Macmillan India, 2000.

Baron-Cohen, Simon. *The Essential Difference: Male and Female Brains and the Truth about Autism*. New York: Basic, 2004.

———. *Mindblindness: An Essay on Autism and Theory of Mind*. Cambridge, MA: MIT Press, 1995.

Bate, John Bernard. *Tamil Oratory and the Dravidian Aesthetic: Democratic Practice in South India*. New York: Columbia University Press, 2009.

Bayly, Susan. *Caste, Society and Politics in India from the Eighteenth Century to the Modern Age*. Cambridge: Cambridge University Press, 2001.

———. "Saints' Cults and Warrior Kingdoms in South India." In *Shamanism, History and the State*, edited by Nicholas Thomas and Caroline Humphrey, 117–132. Ann Arbor: University of Michigan Press, 1994.

———. *Saints, Goddesses and Kings: Muslims and Christians in South Indian Society, 1700–1900*. Cambridge: Cambridge University Press, 1989.

Beck, Brenda E. F. "Colour and Heat in South Indian Ritual." *Man* 4, no. 4 (1989): 553–572.

———. "The Goddess and the Demon: A Local South Indian Festival and Its Wider Context." *Purusartha* 5 (1981): 83–136.

Behar, Ruth. *The Vulnerable Observer: Anthropology That Breaks Your Heart*. Boston: Beacon, 1996.

———, and Deborah A. Gordon, eds. *Women Writing Culture*. Berkeley: University of California Press, 1995.

Bell, Catherine. *Ritual Theory, Ritual Practice*. Oxford: Oxford University Press, 1992.

Bellamy, Carla. *The Powerful Ephemeral: Everyday Healing in an Ambiguously Islamic Place*. Berkeley: University of California Press, 2011.

Besse, Rev. L., S.J. *Fr. Beschi of the Society of Jesus: His Life and His Writings*. Trichinopoly, India: St. Joseph's Industrial School Press, 1918.

Bhabha, Homi K. *The Location of Culture*. London: Routledge, 1994.

Bloch, Maurice. "The Slaves, the King, and Mary in the Slums of Antananarivo." In *Shamanism, History and the State*, edited by Nicholas Thomas and Caroline Humphrey, 133–145. Ann Arbor: University of Michigan Press, 1994.

Boddy, Janice. "Spirit Possession Revisited: Beyond Instrumentality." *Annual Review of Anthropology* 23 (1994): 407–434.

———. "Spirits and Selves in Northern Sudan: The Cultural Therapeutics of Possession and Trance." *American Ethnologist* 15, no. 1 (1988): 4–27.

———. *Wombs and Alien Spirits: Women, Men, and the Zār Cult in Northern Sudan*. Madison: University of Wisconsin Press, 1989.

Bourdieu, Pierre. *Distinction: A Social Critique of the Judgment of Taste*. Cambridge, MA: Harvard University Press, 1984.

———. "The Forms of Capital." In *Handbook of Theory and Research for the Sociology of Education*, edited by John G. Richardson, 241–258. New York: Greenwood, 1986.

———. *In Other Words: Essays on a Reflexive Sociology*, translated by Matthew Adamson. Stanford, CA: Stanford University Press, 1990.

———. *Outline of a Theory of Practice*. Edited by Richard Nice. Cambridge: Cambridge University Press, 1977.

Bourguignon, Erika. *Possession*. San Francisco: Chandler and Sharp, 1976.

———. "World Distribution and Patterns of Possession States." In *Trance and Possession States*, edited by Raymond Prince. Montreal: R. M. Bucke Memorial Society, 1968.

Bowen, Elenore Smith (aka Laura Bohannon). *Return to Laughter*. New York: Doubleday, 1964.

Breckenridge, Carol Appadurai. "From Protector to Litigant: Changing Relations between Hindu Temples and the Raja of Ramnad." *Indian Economic and Social History Review* 14, no. 1 (1977): 75–106.

Brown, Karen McCarthy. *Mama Lola: A Vodou Priestess in Brooklyn*. Berkeley: University of California Press, 1991.

Butler, Judith. *Bodies That Matter: On the Discursive Limits of "Sex."* New York: Routledge, 1992.

———. *Excitable Speech: A Politics of the Performative.* New York: Routledge, 1997.

———. *Gender Trouble: Feminism and the Subversion of Identity.* New York: Routledge, 1990.

Bynum, Caroline Walker. *Fragmentation and Redemption: Essays on Gender and the Human Body in Medieval Religion.* New York: Zone Books, 1992.

———. *Holy Feast and Holy Fast: The Religious Significance of Food to Medieval Women.* Berkeley: University of California Press, 1987.

Caplan, Lionel. "Caste and Castelessness among South Indian Christians." *Contributions to Indian Sociology*, n.s., 14 (1980): 213–238.

———. "Class and Christianity in South India: Indigenous Responses to Western Denominationalism." *Modern Asian Studies* 14, no. 4 (1980): 645–671.

———. *Class and Culture in Urban India: Fundamentalism in a Christian Community.* Oxford: Clarendon, 1987.

———. "Invitation to a Dialogue." In *Subaltern Studies: Writings on South Asian History and Society*, vol. 4, edited by Ranajit Guha. Oxford: Oxford University Press, 1999.

Chandramouli, C. "Provisional Population Totals: Paper 2 of 2001." Chennai: Census Operations, Tamil Nadu, 2001.

———. "Quality of Living Index in Chennai: An Approach Paper." In *Proceedings of the Third International Conference on Environmental Health, Chennai, India.* Chennai: Department of Geography, University of Madras and Faculty of Environmental Studies, York University, 2003.

Chaudhury, Ajit K. "In Search of a Subaltern Lenin." In *Subaltern Studies: Writings on South Asian History and Society*, vol. 4, edited by Ranajit Guha. Oxford: Oxford University Press, 1999.

Chua, Jocelyn Lim. *In Pursuit of the Good Life: Aspiration and Suicide in Globalizing South India.* Berkeley: University of California Press, 2014.

Clark-Decès, Isabelle. *The Encounter Never Ends: A Return to the Field of Tamil Rituals.* Albany: State University of New York Press, 2007.

Clarke, Sathianathan. *Dalits and Christianity: Subaltern Religion and Liberation Theology in India.* New Delhi: Oxford University Press, 1998.

Clifford, James. *The Predicament of Culture.* Cambridge, MA: Harvard University Press, 1988.

———, and George E. Marcus. *Writing Culture: The Poetics and Politics of Ethnography.* Berkeley: University of California Press, 1986.

Clooney, Francis X. *Fr. Bouchet's India: An 18th Century Jesuit's Encounter with Hinduism.* Chennai: Satya Nilayam Publications, 2005.

Cohen, Emma. *The Mind Possessed: The Cognition of Spirit Possession in an Afro-Brazilian Religious Tradition.* New York: Oxford University Press, 2004.

Cohen, Lawrence. "On Transplant Victims, Wounded Communities, and the Moral Demands of Dreaming." In *Ethical Life in South Asia*, edited by Anand Pandian and Daud Ali, 253–274. Bloomington: Indiana University Press, 2010.

———. "Where It Hurts: Indian Material for an Ethics of Organ Transplantation." *Daedalus*, special issue, *Bioethics and Beyond* 128, no. 4 (Fall 1999): 135–165.

Collins, Patricia Hill. *Black Feminist Thought: Knowledge, Consciousness, and the Politics of Empowerment.* New York: Routledge, 1991.

Comaroff, Jean. *Body of Power, Spirit of Resistance: The Culture and History of a South African People.* Chicago: University of Chicago Press, 1985.

Cone, James H. *A Black Theology of Liberation.* 40th anniversary ed. Maryknoll, NY: Orbis, 1970.

Cooke, Miriam. "Saving Brown Women." *Signs*, special issue, *Gender and Cultural Memory* 28, no. 1 (Autumn, 2002): 468–470.

Craddock, Elaine. *Śiva's Demon Devotee: Kāraikkāl Ammaiyār.* Albany: State University of New York Press, 2010.

Cronin, Vincent. *A Pearl to India: The Life of Roberto de Nobili.* London: R. Hart Davis, 1959.

Csordas, Thomas J. *Body/Meaning/Healing.* New York: Palgrave Macmillan, 2002.

———. "Global Religion and the Re-enchantment of the World: The Case of the Catholic Charismatic Renewal." *Anthropological Theory* 7, no. 3 (2007): 295–314.

Curran, Charles. *Loyal Dissent: Memoir of a Catholic Theologian.* Washington, DC: Georgetown University Press, 2006.

Cutler, Norman. *Songs of Experience: The Poetics of Tamil Devotion.* Bloomington: Indiana University Press, 1987.

Daly, Mary. *Beyond God the Father: Toward a Philosophy of Women's Liberation.* Boston: Beacon, 1973.

———. *Gyn/Ecology: The Metaphysics of Radical Feminism.* Boston: Beacon, 1978.

Daniel, E. Valentine. *Fluid Signs: Being a Person the Tamil Way.* Berkeley: University of California Press, 1984.

David, Kenneth. "Hidden Powers: Cultural and Social-Economic Accounts of Jaffna Women." In *The Powers of Tamil Women*, edited by Susan S. Wadley, 1–34. Foreign and Comparative Studies / South Asian Series 6. Syracuse, NY: Maxwell School of Citizenship and Public Affairs, 1980.

Davis, Angela. *Women, Race, and Class.* New York: Vintage, 1983.

Dempsey, Corinne G. *The Goddess Lives in Upstate New York: Breaking Convention and Making Home at a North American Hindu Temple.* New York: Oxford University Press, 2006.

———. *Kerala Christian Sainthood: Collisions of Culture and World View in South India.* New York: Oxford University Press, 2001.

Diehl, Carl Gustav. *Instrument and Purpose: Studies on Rites and Rituals in South India.* Lund, Sweden: CWK Gleerup, 1956.

Dirks, Nicholas B. *The Hollow Crown: Ethnohistory of an Indian Kingdom.* Cambridge: Cambridge University Press, 1987.

Doniger, Wendy. *The Hindus: An Alternative History.* New York: Penguin, 2009.

———, trans. *The Laws of Manu.* With Brian K. Smith. London: Penguin, 1991.

Douglas, Mary. *Purity and Danger: An Analysis of the Concepts of Purity and Taboo.* London: Routledge and Kegan Paul, 1966.

Dumont, Louis. "Possession and Priesthood." *Contributions to Indian Sociology* 3 (1959): 59–74.

Eck, Diana L. *Darśan: Seeing the Divine Image in India.* 3rd ed. New York: Columbia University Press, 1998.

Egnor, Margaret. "On the Meaning of Shakti to Women in Tamil Nadu." In *The Powers of Tamil Women*, edited by Susan S. Wadley, 1–34. Foreign and Comparative Studies / South Asian Series 6. Syracuse, NY: Maxwell School of Citizenship and Public Affairs, 1980.

Falk, Nancy Auer. *Living Hinduisms: An Explorer's Guide.* Belmont, CA: Thomson Higher Education, 2006.

Fanon, Franz. *Black Skin, White Masks.* Translated by Charles Lam Markmann. New York: Grove Press, 1967.

Ferro-Luzzi, G. Eichinger. "Women's Pollution Periods in Tamil Nadu (India)." *Anthropos* 69 (1974): 113–161.

Feuerbach, Ludwig. *The Essence of Christianity*. New York: Prometheus, 1989.

Flueckiger, Joyce Burkhalter. *Everyday Hinduism*. Lived Religions. West Sussex, UK: Wiley-Blackwell, 2015.

———. *In Amma's Healing Room: Gender and Vernacular Islam in South India*. Bloomington: Indiana University Press, 2006.

Flood, Gavin. *An Introduction to Hinduism*. Cambridge: Cambridge University Press, 1996.

———. *The Tantric Body: The Secret Tradition of Hindu Religion*. London: I. B. Taurus, 2006.

Foucault, Michel. *The History of Sexuality*. Vol. 1: *An Introduction*. New York: Vintage, 1990.

———. *The Order of Things: An Archaeology of the Human Sciences*. New York: Vintage, 1994.

———. *Technologies of the Self: A Seminar with Michel Foucault*. Edited by Luther H. Martin, Huck Gutman, and Patrick H. Hutton. Amherst: University of Massachusetts Press, 1988.

Foulston, Lynn. *At the Feet of the Goddess: The Divine Feminine in Local Hindu Religion*. Brighton, UK: Sussex Academic, 2002.

———, and Stuart Abbott. *Hindu Goddesses: Beliefs and Practices*. Brighton: Sussex Academic, 2009.

Frenz, Matthias. "The Virgin and Her 'Relations': Reflections on Processions at a Catholic Shrine in Southern India," in *South Asian Religions on Display: Religious Processions in South Asia and in the Diaspora*, edited by Knut A. Jacobsen, 92–103. London: Routledge, 2008.

Fuller, C. J. *The Camphor Flame: Popular Hinduism and Society in India*. Princeton, NJ: Princeton University Press, 1992.

———. "Kerala Christians and the Caste System." *Man*, n.s., 11, no. 1 (1976): 53–70.

Ghosh, Bishnupriya. *Global Icons: Apertures to the Popular*. Durham, NC: Duke University Press, 2011.

Gimbutas, Marija. *The Gods and Goddesses of Old Europe, 7000 to 3500 B.C.* London: Thames and Hudson, 1973.

Gonda, Jan. *Notes on "Bráhman."* Utrecht, Netherlands: J. L. Beyers, 1950.

Good, Anthony. *The Female Bridegroom*. Oxford: Oxford University Press, 1991.

Goslinga, Gillian. "Embodiment and the Metaphysics of Virgin Birth in South India: A Case Study." In *Summoning the Spirits: Possession and Invocation in Contemporary Religion*, edited by Andrew Dawson, 109–123. London: I. B. Tauris, 2011.

———. "The Ethnography of a South Indian God: Virgin Birth, Spirit Possession, and the Prose of the Modern World." PhD diss., University of California–Santa Cruz, 2006.

Gramsci, Antonio. *Selections from the Prison Notebooks*. New York: International Publishers, 1971.

Graves, Robert. *The Greek Myths*. Baltimore, MD: Penguin, 1975.

Grosz, Elizabeth. *Volatile Bodies: Towards a Corporeal Feminism*. Bloomington: Indiana University Press, 1994.

Guha, Ranajit. "On Some Aspects of the Historiography of Colonial India." In *Subaltern Studies I: Writings on South Asian History and Society*, edited by Ranajit Guha. Oxford: Oxford University Press, 1982.

Hadot, Pierre. *Philosophy as a Way of Life*. Malden, MA: Blackwell, 1995.

Hancock, Mary Elizabeth. *Womanhood in the Making: Domestic Ritual and Public Culture in Urban South India*. Boulder, CO: Westview, 1999.

Hardgrave, Robert L., Jr. *The Nadars of Tamilnad: The Political Culture of a Community in Change*. Berkeley: University of California Press, 1969.

Hardy, Friedhelm. *Viraha-Bhakti: The Early History of Kṛiṣhṇa Devotion in South India*. Delhi: Oxford University Press, 1983.

Harnack, Adolf von. *What Is Christianity?* Translated by Thomas Bailey Saunders. Eastford, CT: Martino Fine Books, 2011.

Hartmann, Heidi. "The Unhappy Marriage of Marxism and Feminism." In *Women and Revolution: A Discussion of the Unhappy Marriage of Marxism and Feminism*, edited by Lydia Sargent, 1–41. Boston: South End Press, 1981.

Hartsock, Nancy. "The Feminist Standpoint: Developing the Ground for a Specifically Feminist Historical Materialism." In *Discovering Reality*, edited by Sandra Harding and Merrill Hintikka. New York: Kluwer Academic, 1983.

Hayes, Kelly. *Holy Harlots: Femininity, Sexuality, and Black Magic in Brazil*. Berkeley: University of California Press, 2011.

Hiltebeitel, Alf, and Kathleeen Erndl, eds. *Is the Goddess a Feminist? The Politics of South Asian Goddesses*. Sheffield, UK: Sheffield Academic, 2000.

Hinnebusch, W. A., ed. "Rosary." In *The New Catholic Encyclopedia*. 2nd ed. Vol. 12, 373–376. Washington, DC: Catholic University of America, 2003.

Hirschkind, Charles. *The Ethical Soundscape: Cassette Sermons and Islamic Counterpublics*. New York: Columbia University Press, 2006.

Iyer, S. S. "What We Have Yet to Learn." *Science*, n.s. 185, no. 4149 (1974): 400.

Kaiser, Robert Blair. *The Encyclical That Never Was: The Story of the Pontifical Commission on Population, Family, and Birth, 1964–66*. New York: Sheed and Ward, 1987.

Kakar, Sudhir. *Shamans, Mystics and Doctors: A Psychological Inquiry into India and Its Healing Traditions*. Boston: Beacon, 1982.

Khan, Dominique-Sila. "Vavar Swami: A Hindu-Muslim Saint of Kerala." In *Lines in Water: Religious Boundaries in South Asia*, edited by Eliza Kent and Tazim Kassam. Syracuse, NY: Syracuse University Press, 2013.

Kalpagam, U. "Secularism, Religiosity and Popular Culture: Chennai's Roadside Tem-ples." *Economic and Political Weekly* 41, no. 43/44 (Nov. 4–10, 2006): 4595–4600.

Kapadia, Karin. "Pierced by Love: Tamil Possession, Gender, and Caste." In *Invented Identities: The Interplay of Gender, Religion, and Politics in India*, ed. Julia Leslie and Mary McGee. New Delhi: Oxford University Press, 2000.

———. *Siva and Her Sisters: Gender, Caste, and Class in Rural South India*. Boulder, CO: Westview, 1995.

Kapferer, Bruce. *A Celebration of Demons: Exorcism and the Aesthetics of Healing in Sri Lanka*. 2nd ed. Explorations in Anthropology Series. Providence, RI: Berg, 1991.

Keenan, Dennis King. "Kristeva, Mimesis, and Sacrifice." *Philosophy Today* 47, no. 1 (2003): 23–33.

Keller, Mary. *The Hammer and the Flute: Women, Power, and Spirit Possession*. Baltimore, MD: Johns Hopkins University Press, 2002.

Kent, Eliza F. *Converting Women: Gender and Protestant Christianity in Colonial South India*. New York: Oxford University Press, 2004.

———, and Tazim R. Kassam, eds. *Lines in Water: Religious Boundaries in South Asia*. Syracuse, NY: Syracuse University Press, 2013.

Khalid, Amna, and Ryan Johnson, eds. *Public Health in the British Empire: Intermediaries, Subordinates, and the Practice of Public Health, 1850–1960*. New York: Routledge, 2012.

Kinsley, David R. *Hindu Goddesses: Visions of the Divine Feminine in the Hindu Religious Tradition*. Berkeley: University of California Press, 1988.

Klostermaaier, Klaus. *Hinduism: A Short Introduction*. Oxford: OneWorld, 2002.

Kristeva, Julia. *The Portable Kristeva*. Edited by Kelly Oliver. New York: Columbia University Press, 2002.

———. *Powers of Horror: An Essay on Abjection*. New York: Columbia University Press, 1982.

———. *Revolution in Poetic Language*. Translated by Margaret Waller. New York: Columbia University Press, 1984.

Küng, Hans. *My Struggle for Freedom: Memoirs*. Translated by John Bowden. Grand Rapids, MI: Eerdmans, 2003.

Kwan, David H., Iren Constantinescu, Rafi Chapanian, Melanie A. Higgins, Miriam P. Kötzler, Eric Samain, Alisdair B. Boraston, Jayachandran N. Kizhakkedathu, and Stephen G. Withers. "Toward Efficient Enzymes for the Generation of Universal Blood through Structure-Guided Directed Evolution." *Journal of the American Chemical Society* 137, no. 17 (2015): 5695–5705.

Lakshmi, C. S. "Tradition and Modernity of Tamil Women Writers." *Social Scientist* 4, no. 9 (1976): 38–47.

Lambek, Michael. "From Disease to Discourse: Remarks on the Conceptualization of Trance and Spirit Possession." In *Altered States of Consciousness and Mental Health*, edited by Colleen A. Ward. Newbury Park, CA: Sage, 1981.

———. *Knowledge and Practice in Mayotte: Local Discourses of Islam, Sorcery, and Sprit Possession*. Anthropological Horizons. Toronto: University of Toronto Press, 1993.

Lewis, I. M. *Ecstatic Religion: A Study of Shamanism and Spirit Possession*. 3rd ed. New York: Routledge, 2003.

Lincoln, Bruce. *Holy Terror: Thinking about Religion after September 11*. Chicago: University of Chicago Press, 2003.

Lipner, Julius. "The Rise of 'Hinduism': Or, How to Invent a World Religion with Only Moderate Success." *International Journal of Hindu Studies* 10, no. 1 (2006): 91–104.

Lorenzen, David. "Who Invented Hinduism?" *Comparative Studies in Society and History* 41, no. 4 (1999): 630–659.

Lorde, Audre. "The Master's Tools Will Never Dismantle the Master's House" (1984). In *Sister Outsider: Essays and Speeches*, 110–113. Berkeley, CA: Crossing Press, 2007.

Lucia, Amanda. *Reflections of Amma: Devotees in a Global Embrace*. Berkeley: University of California Press, 2014.

Ludden, David. "A Brief History of Subalternity." Introduction to *Reading Subaltern Studies: Critical History, Contested Meaning and the Globalization of South Asia*, edited by David Ludden. New York: Anthem, 2002.

———. *Peasant History in South India*. Delhi: Oxford University Press, 1989.

MacPhail, Richard D. "Finding a Path in Others' Worlds: The Challenge of Exorcism." In *Popular Christianity in India: Riting between the Lines*, edited by Selva J. Raj and Corinne G. Dempsey, 141–162. Albany: State University of New York Press, 2002.

Mahmood, Saba. *Politics of Piety: The Islamic Revival and the Feminist Subject*. Princeton, NJ: Princeton University Press, 2005.

Marglin, Frédérique Apffel. *Wives of the God-King: Rituals of the Devadasis of Puri.* Delhi: Oxford University Press, 1985.

Mauss, Marcel. "A Category of the Human Mind: The Notion of Person, the Notion of Self." In *The Category of the Person: Anthropology, Philosophy, History*, edited by Michael Carrithers, Steven Collins, and Steven Lukes, 1–25. Cambridge: Cambridge University Press, 1985,

———. "Les Techniques du Corps." In *Sociologie et Anthropologie*. Paris: Presses Universitaires du France, 1950.

McDaniel, June. *Offering Flowers, Feeding Skulls: Popular Goddess Worship in West Bengal.* New York: Oxford University Press, 2004.

Meibohm, Margaret. "Past Selves and Present Others: The Ritual Construction of Identity at a Catholic Festival in India." In *Popular Christianity in India: Riting between the Lines*, edited by Selva Raj and Corinne C. Dempsey, 61–83. Albany: State University of New York Press, 2002.

Meyer, Eveline. *Aṅkāḷaparamēcuvari: A Goddess of Tamilnadu, Her Myths and Cult.* Weisbaden: Franz Steiner Verlag, 1986.

Miller, Patricia. *Good Catholics: The Battle over Abortion in the Catholic Church.* Berkeley: University of California Press, 2014.

Mines, Diane P. *Fierce Gods: Inequality, Ritual, and the Politics of Dignity in a South Indian Village.* Bloomington: Indiana University Press, 2005.

Minsheu, John. *Spanish-English Dictionary.* Edited by Richard Perceval. London: Edmund Bollifant, 1599.

Mitter, Sara S. *Dharma's Daughters: Contemporary Indian Women and Hindu Culture.* New Brunswick, NJ: Rutgers University Press, 1991.

Mohammad, Afsar. *The Festival of Pirs: Popular Islam and Shared Devotion in South India.* New York: Oxford University Press, 2013.

Molina, J. Michelle. *To Overcome Oneself: The Jesuit Ethic and Spirit of Global Expansion.* Berkeley: University of California Press, 2013.

Morgan, David. "The Materiality of Cultural Construction." In *Museum Objects: Experiencing the Properties of Things*, edited by Sandra H. Dudley. New York: Routledge, 2012.

Mosse, David. "Catholic Saints and the Hindu Village Pantheon in Rural Tamil Nadu, India." *Man*, n.s., 29 (1994): 301–332.

———. "Possession and Confession: Affliction and Sacred Power in Colonial and Contemporary Catholic South India." In *The Anthropology of Christianity*, edited by Fanella Cannell, 99–133. Durham, NC: Duke University Press, 2006.

———. *The Saint in the Banyan Tree: Christianity and Caste Society in India.* Berkeley: University of California Press, 2012.

Müller, Max. *The Six Systems of Indian Philosophy.* London: Longmans, Green and Co., 1899.

Mundadan, A. Mathias, *History of Christianity in India.* Vol. 1, *From the Beginning up to the Middle of the Sixteenth Century (up to 1542).* Bangalore: Theological Publications in India, 1984.

Nabokov, Isabelle. *Religion against the Self: An Ethnography of Tamil Rituals.* New York: Oxford University Press, 2000.

Nicholson, Linda, ed. *The Second Wave: A Reader in Feminist Theory.* New York: Routledge, 1997.

Niranjana, Seemanthini. *Gender and Space: Femininity, Sexualization, and the Female Body.* New Delhi: Sage, 2001.

O'Flaherty, Wendy Doniger. *Hindu Myths: A Sourcebook Translated from the Sanskrit*. London: Penguin, 1975.

———. *The Origins of Evil in Hindu Mythology*. Berkeley: University of California Press, 1976.

Oldenburg, Veena Talwar. *Dowry Murder: The Imperial Origins of a Cultural Crime*. New York: Oxford University Press, 2002.

Ong, Aihwa. *Spirits of Resistance and Capitalist Discipline: Factory Women in Malaysia*. 2nd ed. Albany: State University of New York Press, 2010.

Ortner, Sherry B. *Making Gender: The Politics and Erotics of Culture*. Boston: Beacon, 1996.

Pandian, Anand. *Crooked Stalks: Cultivating Virtue in South India*. Durham, NC: Duke University Press, 2009.

Pandian, M. S. S. *Brahmin and Non-Brahmin: Genealogies of the Tamil Political Present*. Delhi: Permanent Black, 2007.

Pelikan, Jaroslav. *Mary through the Centuries: Her Place in the History of Culture*. New Haven, CT: Yale University Press, 1996.

Pennington, Brian. *Was Hinduism Invented? Britons, Indians, and the Colonial Construction of Religion*. New York: Oxford University Press, 2005.

Priolkar, Anant Kakba. *The Goan Inquisition: Being a Quatercentenary Commemoration Study of the Inquisition in India*. Bombay: Bombay University Press, 1961.

Raj, Ebe Sundar, Sam Thambusamy, and Ezra Samuel. *Divide to Rule: Communal Attacks on Christians in India During 1997-2000*. Rev. ed. Chennai: Bharat Jyoti, 2000.

Raj, Selva J. "An Ethnographic Encounter with the Wondrous in a South Indian Catholic Shrine." In *Miracle as Modern Condundrum in South Asian Religious Traditions*, edited by Corinne G. Dempsey and Selva J. Raj, 141–165. Albany: State University of New York Press, 2009.

———. "Shared Vows, Shared Space, and Shared Deities: Vow Rituals among Tamil Catholics in South India." In *Dealing with Deities: The Ritual Vow in South Asia* edited by Selva J. Raj and William P. Harman, 43–64. Albany: State University of New York Press, 2006.

———, and Corinne G. Dempsey, eds. *Popular Christianity in India: Riting between the Lines*. Albany: State University of New York Press, 2002.

Ram, Kalpana. *Fertile Disorder: Spirit Possession and Its Provocation of the Modern*. Honolulu: University of Hawaii Press, 2013.

———. *Mukkuvar Women: Gender, Hegemony and Capitalist Transformation in a South Indian Fishing Community*. New Delhi: Kali for Women, 1991.

Ramanujan, A. K. *The Interior Landscape: Love Poems from a Classical Tamil Anthology*. Delhi: Oxford University Press, 1994.

Ramaswamy, Sumathi. *The Goddess and the Nation: Mapping Mother India*. Durham, NC: Duke University Press, 2009.

———. "Maps and Mother Goddesses in Modern India." *Imago Mundi* 53 (2001): 97–114.

———. *Passions of the Tongue: Language Devotion in Tamil India, 1891–1970*. Berkeley: University of California Press, 1997.

Renou, Louis. "Sur la notion de *bráhman*." In *L'Inde fondamentale*, edited by Charles Malamoud, Paris: Hermann, Collection Savoir, 1978).

Robinson, Sandra. "Hindu Paradigms of Women: Images and Values." In *Women, Religion, and Social Change*, edited by Yvonne Yazbeck Haddad and Ellison B. Findly, 181–216. Albany: State University of New York Press, 1985.

Rodrigues, Antonio F. X. "Devotion to Our Lady." In *Popular Devotions,* edited by Paul Puthanangady, 393–401. Bangalore: National Biblical, Catechetical and Liturgical Centre, 1986.

Rubin, Gayle. "The Traffic in Women." In *Toward an Anthropology of Women*, edited by R. Reiter. New York: Monthly Review Press, 1975.

Rubin, Miri. *Mother of God: A History of the Virgin Mary*. New Haven, CT: Yale University Press, 2009.

Ruether, Rosemary Radford. *Goddesses and the Divine Feminine: A Western Religious History*. Berkeley: University of California Press, 2005.

———. *Sexism and God-Talk: Toward a Feminist Theology*. Boston: Beacon, 1983.

Sandness, A. "On *Ritá* and *Bráhman*: Visions of Existence in the Rig Veda." *Annals of the Bhandarkar Oriental Research Institute* 88 (2007): 61–80.

Sanneh, Lamin. *Whose Religion Is Christianity? The Gospel beyond the West*. 4th ed. Grand Rapids, MI: Eerdmans, 2003.

Schuler, Barbara. *Of Death and Birth: Icakkiyamman, a Tamil Goddess in Ritual and Story*. Wiesbaden: Harrassowitz, 2009.

Scott, James. *Weapons of the Weak: Everyday Forms of Peasant Resistance*. New Haven, CT: Yale University Press, 1987.

Selvamony, Nirmal. "The Seeds of Drama in *tolkaappiyam*." A paper delivered at the National Seminar on Contemporary Indian Drama, January 19–20, 2014, Bangalore, India.

———. "Serving *Flesh and Fishblood* as Neopostcolonial Poetics." *Journal of Contemporary Thought* 37 (2013): 105.

———. "Tinai as Our Future Family." In *Moral Ground: Ethical Action for a Planet in Peril*, edited by Kathleen Dean Moore and Michael P. Nelson. San Antonio, TX: Trinity University Press, 2003.

———. "*tiNai* in Primal and Stratified Societies." *Indian Journal of Ecocriticism* I, no. 1, (2008): 38–48.

Shulman, David. *The Hungry God: Hindu Tales of Filicide and Devotion*. Chicago: University of Chicago Press, 1993.

———. *Tamil Temple Myths: Sacrifice and Divine Marriage in the South Indian Śaiva Tradition*. Princeton, NJ: Princeton University Press, 1980.

———, and Deborah Thiagarajan, eds. *Masked Ritual and Performance in South India: Dance, Healing, and Possession*. Ann Arbor: Centers for South and Southeast Asian Studies, University of Michigan, 2006.

Simon, Roger. *Gramsci's Political Thought: An Introduction*. London: Lawrence and Wishart, 1982.

Singh, Paramjit, and Gurpreet Bal. *Strategies of Social Change in India*. New Delhi: MD Publications, 1996.

Sklar, Deirdre. "Unearthing Kinesthesia: Groping Among Cross-cultural Models of the Senses in Performance." In *The Senses in Performance*, edited by Sally Banes and Andre Lepecki, pp. 38–46. New York: Routledge, 2007.

Smith, Frederick M. *The Self Possessed: Deity and Spirit Possession in South Asian Literature and Civilization*. New York: Columbia University Press, 2006.

Spivak, Gayatri Chakravorty. "Introduction: Deconstructing Subaltern Studies." In *Selected Subaltern Studies*, edited by Ranajit Guha and Gayatri Chakravorty Spivak. Oxford: Oxford University Press, 1988.

Springs, Jason. "'Dismantling the Master's House': Freedom and Ethical Practice in Brandom and Foucault." *Journal of Religious Ethics* 37, no. 3 (2009): 419–448.

Srinivas, M. N. "The Cohesive Role of Sanskritization." In M. N. Srinivas, *Collected Essays*, 221–235. New York: Oxford University Press, 2002.

Stoller, Paul. *Sensuous Scholarship*. Philadelphia: University of Pennsylvania Press, 1987.

Sweetman, William. *Mapping Hinduism: "Hinduism" and the Study of Indian Religions*. Halle, GE: Neue Hallesche Berichte, 2003.

Tanner, Kathryn. *Theories of Culture: A New Agenda for Theology*. Minneapolis, MN: Fortress, 1997.

Tarlo, Emma. *Clothing Matters: Dress and Identity in India*. Chicago: University of Chicago Press, 1996.

Thakur, Upendra. *The History of Suicide in India: An Introduction*. Delhi: Munshi Ram Manohar Lal, 1963.

Thapar, Romila. "Syndicated Hinduism." In *Hinduism Reconsidered*, edited by Herman Kulke and Gunther-Dietz Sontheimer, 54–81. New Delhi: Manohar, 2001.

Taussig, Michael. *Shamanism, Colonialism, and the Wild Man: A Study in Terror and Healing*. Chicago: University of Chicago Press, 1987.

Thieme, Paul. *Zeitschrift der Deutschen Morgenländischen Gesellschaft* 102 (n.F. 27), no. 1 (1952): 91–129.

Thirumagal, P. "Religious Conflicts and Hindu Sectarianism." In *History of People and Their Environs: Essays in Honour of Prof. B.S. Chandrababu*, edited by S. Ganeshram and C. Bhanvani, 157–190. Chennai: Indian Universities Press, 2011.

Thompson, M. S. H. "The Avvai of the Sangam Anthologies." *Bulletin of the School of Oriental and African Studies* 12, no. 2 (1948): 399–402.

Torjesen, Karen Jo. *When Women Were Priests: Women's Leadership in the Early Church and the Scandal of Their Subordination in the Rise of Christianity*. San Francisco, CA: HarperSanFrancisco, 1993.

Townes, Emilie M. *Womanist Ethics and the Cultural Production of Evil*. New York: Palgrave Macmillan, 2006.

Trawick, Margaret. *Notes on Love in a Tamil Family*. Berkeley: University of California Press, 1990.

Turner, Victor. *The Ritual Process: Structure and Anti-structure*. New York: Aldine de Gruyter. 1995.

Visweswaran, Kamala. *Fictions of Feminist Ethnography*. Minneapolis: University of Minnesota Press, 1994.

Wadley, Susan Snow, ed. *The Powers of Tamil Women*. Foreign and Comparative Studies / South Asian Series 6. Syracuse, NY: Maxwell School of Citizenship and Public Affairs, 1980.

Waghorne, Joanne Punzo. "Chariots of the God/s: Riding the Line between Hindu and Christian." *History of Religions* 39, no. 2 (1999): 95–116.

Warner, Marina. *Alone of All Her Sex: The Myth and the Cult of the Virgin Mary*. New York: Vintage, 1976.

Williams, Paul, Anthony Tribe, and Alexander Wynne. *Buddhist Thought: A Complete Introduction to the Buddhist Tradition*. New York: Routledge, 2011.

Wilkins, Katharina. "Mary and the Demons: Marian Devotion and Ritual Healing in Tanzania." *Journal of Religion in Africa*, no. 39, fasc. 3 (2019): 295–318.

Young, Iris. *Justice and the Politics of Difference*. Princeton, NJ: Princeton University Press, 1990.

Zelliot, Eleanor. *From Untouchable to Dalit: Essays on the Ambedkar Movement*. New Delhi: Manohar, 1996.

Županov, Ines G. *Disputed Mission: Jesuit Experiments and Brahmanical Knowledge in Seventeenth-Century India.* New York: Oxford University Press, 1999.

———. "La Science et la Demonologie: Les Missions des Jésuits Français en Inde (XVIIIe Siècle)." In *Missions d'évangélisation et circulation des savoirs (XVIe-XVIIIe siècle)*, edited by de Castelnau-L'Estoile, M.-L. Copete, A. Maldavsky and I. G. Županov. Madrid: Collection de la Casa de Velázquez 120, 2011.

———. *Missionary Tropics: The Catholic Frontier in India, 16th–17th Centuries.* Ann Arbor: University of Michigan Press, 2005.

NEWSPAPER AND MAGAZINE SOURCES

Balasubramaniam, J. and A.R. Venkatachalapathy. "From Kandadevi to Kallimedu." *The Hindu,* Opinion. August, 2016. http://www.thehindu.com/opinion/lead/j-balasubramaniam-from-kandadevi-to-kallimedu/article8975104.ece. Accessed August 25, 2016.

Bohannon, Laura. "Shakespeare in the Bush." *Natural History*, August–September, 1966.

Hari, T. S. V. "Special Report: Ramnad Thevars Go Harijan Hunting." *Onlooker*, July 8–22, 1983, 40–44.

Viswanathan, S. "The States: A Temple Car and Caste Tensions." *Frontline*, August 2–15, 2003.

———. "States within a State." *Frontline*, August 2–15, 2003.

———. "The Caste Juggernaut." *Frontline*, July 2–15, 2005.

GOVERNMENT SOURCES

Hemmingway, Fr. "Tanjore." *Imperial Gazetteer*. Vol. 1. Madras: Government Press, 1908.

Thurston, Edward. *Castes and Tribes of Southern India*. Madras: Government Press, 1909.

PUBLIC DOCUMENTS

Affadavits of Witnesses. Aiyvaalar, Kaddupaadu Arai, Devakottai. June 28–30, 1979.

Certified Copy of Counter Affadavit. Court of the Subordinate Judge of Devakottai, I.A No. 363 of 1979 on O.S. No. 86 of 1979.

Forensic report. Tamil Nadu Forensic Science Laboratory. "Forensic House." Kamarajar Salai, Madras. No. T. 6976/79 Biol. B. 495/79. November 3, 1979.

Original Wound Certificates and Post Mortems. Government Hospital, Devakottai, Ramnad District, Aug.–Nov., 1979.

Police Records. Statements of Doctors, Surgeons, and other Medical Workers. Government Hospital, Tiruvadanai and Government Hospital, Devakottai. July–Nov., 1979.

Police Reports. State Inspector of Police, Devakottai Circle, Davakottai, Petitioner. Devakottai, June 6, 1979.

Serology Report. Tamil Nadu Forensic Science Laboratory. "Forensic House." Kamarajar Salai, Madras. No. T. 6976 Ser. 692/79. December 28, 1979.

WEBSITES

"Army of Mary Excommunicated by the Vatican." Catholic News Agency, September 14, 2007. http://www.catholicnewsagency.com/news/army_of_mary_excommunicated_by_the_vatican. Accessed September 29, 2013.

Benedict XVI. General Audience in Saint Peter's Square. Wednesday, April 14, 2010. http://w2.vatican.va/content/benedict-xvi/en/audiences/2010/documents/hf_ben-xvi_aud_20100414.html#. Accessed August 25, 2015.

Bloomer, Kristin. "Notes From the Field: Retrieving the Dead." The Martin Marty Center for Religion and Culture Web Forum. Chicago: University of Chicago, February 2005. http://divinity.uchicago.edu/sites/default/files/imce/pdfs/webforum/022005/commentary.shtml. Accessed June 5, 2017.

Bureman, Liz. "Kinesthesia: Definitions and Examples for Writers." http:// thewritepractice.com/ kinesthesia/. Accessed June 6, 2017.

Catechism of the Catholic Church. http://www.vatican.va/archive/ENG0015/_INDEX.HTM. Accessed August 25, 2015.

Catholic Diocese of Meerut. http://www.thecatholicdioceseofmeerut.com/Default.aspx. Accessed September 25, 2016.

The Catholic Lectionary Website, Second Typical Edition, Section II. "For the Conferral of Holy Orders." http://catholic-resources.org/Lectionary/2002USL-Masses-Rituals.htm. Accessed August 22, 2015.

Census of India, 2011. Office of the Registrar General and Census Commissioner, India. http://www.censusindia.gov.in/. Accessed August 25, 2015.

Divine Retreat Center. http://www.drcm.org. Accessed August 7, 2014.

Gallicho, Grant. "The Moral Analysis Rejected by Bishop Olmsted." *Commonweal*, December 21, 2010. https://www.commonwealmagazine.org/blog/moral-analysis-rejected-bishop-olmsted. Accessed September 10, 2016.

Illich, Ivan. "Hospitality and Pain." Academic paper presented in Chicago, 1987. http://www.davidtinapple.com/illich/. Accessed June 5, 2017.

John Paul II, Pope. "Address to the Council of the 'International Catholic Charismatic Renewal Office.'" Sunday, March 14, 1992. https://w2.vatican.va/content/john-paul-ii/en/speeches/1992/march/documents/hf_jp-ii_spe_19920314_charismatic-renewal.html. Accessed September 2, 2016.

Messages of Our Lady of Kanchikode. http://www.motherofkanchikode.com. Accessed June 5, 2017.

"Notification of the Congregation of the Doctrine of the Faith Regarding the Book *Just Love: A Framework for Christian Sexual Ethics* by Sister Margaret A. Farley, RSM." 2012. http://www.news.va/en/news/72432#TESTO%20IN%20LINGUA%20ORIGINALE. Accessed September 10, 2016.

Our Lady Jecintho. http://www.jecintho.com. Accessed June 5, 2017.

Paul VI, Pope. "Constitution on the Sacred Liturgy: *Sacrosanctum Concilium*." 1963. http://www.vatican.va/archive/hist_councils/ii_vatican_council/documents/vat-ii_const_19631204_sacrosanctum-concilium_en.html. Accessed August 22, 2016.

Paul VI, Pope. *Declaration on the Question of the Admission of Women to the Ministerial Priesthood*. http://www.vatican.va/roman_curia/congregations/cfaith/documents/rc_con_cfaith_doc_19761015_inter-insigniores_en.html. Accessed August 25, 2015.

Saint Mary's Forane Church. www.kuravilangadpally.com. Accessed April 10, 2013.

Shrine of Our Lady of Refuge, Elakurichi. http://www.adaikalamadha.org/index.html. Accessed June 5, 2017.

Stella Maris Mission Statement. http://www.stellamariscollege.org/vision_mission.php. Accessed June 15, 2008.

FILMS

Anand, K. V. *Anegan*. Chennai: AGS Entertainment, 2015.
Palekar, Amol. *Paheli*. DVD. London: Eros International, Ltd., 2005.
Ray, Satyajit. *Devi*. DVD, 1960.
Vasan, S. S., *Avvaiyar*. DVD. Directed by Kothamangalam Subbu, 1953.

INDEX

Aananthan, xiv, 188–191, 203, 209–213, 215, 281n3; Mass celebrated by, 232–233
Aarokkiyam, xiv, 133, 137–138, 161, 164, 170, 179–180, 189, 275nn4–5, 276n17; children of, 160; life story of, 158–159; marriage of (*see* Sahaya Mary: marriage of); *pēy* catches, 174, 277n30; spirit of dead father of, 160, 173
abhishekam, 116–117, 270n20, 271n23. *See also* statues: bathed
Adaikkala Mātā (~Adaikkala Madha; Our Lady of Refuge), 30, 134, 273n4; as *Aṭaikkala Mātā*, 26, 258n90; Beschi introduces, 27, 149–150, 274–275n24; church or *kōyil*, 194; Dhanam and, 30, 148, 175, 177, 194–195, 198–199, 202–203, 212, 214; in ordination invitation, 191, 213; statue of (*see under* statues)
Adaikkala Raj, xiv, 203
agency, 10, 17, 55, 230–231; of deities, spirits, or Mary, 21–22, 229; Dhanam's, 188, 195–199, 231; emotions and, 58, 88; Enlightenment ideas of, 229–230; feminism and, 230; forms of, 20; habits or habituation and, 188; instrumental, 196–197, 278–279n11; Nancy's, 97–98, 188; possession and, 141, 150, 188, 195, 278n11; priests and, 97; Rosalind's, 55, 188
Aiyanar, 4, 110, 208, 250n17, 269n8; boundaries patrolled by, 155, 192–194, 248n4; in Chinna Unjanai, 1–2, 134–136, 192; clashes over festival for, 1, 134, 248n4, 249nn6–7; Dhanam and, 155, 192, 194–195, 197–204; fetuses eaten by, 202, 279n20; horses for, 1, 185, 192, 249nn5–6; Pandi Muni and, 156; possession by, 9, 155; water tank by temple of, 183, 185
akam. *See* Caṅkam poetry: *akam*
Alangara Mātā Church, 134
Alex, xiii, 32–35, 67, 70, 82, 224–225, 235, 242, 259n5, 277n35; at festival or procession, 116–117, 126; illness of, 32–33, 69, 76; interviewed, 76–78; possession of, 37, 63, 68, 69, 76–77; Rosalind and (*see under* Rosalind); vision of, 33–34
Alphonsa Mary, 11, 252n37
Ambrose, Rev. Fr., xiv, 104–105
amman. *See* goddesses
anbu, 42, 44, 63, 77, 80–82
Ankaḷaparameswari, 261n26
Anna Francis, xiii, 123, 127, 242
Annai Velankanni Church. *See* Velankanni Mātā churches
Anne, St., 95, 267n24
āṇṭavar, 80–81, 100, 102, 211, 262n2. *See also* gods
Anthony, St., 8, 146
Antony (Nancy's brother), xiv, 85, 92–93
Antony, Rev. Fr. Michael (Dhanam's brother), xiv, 146, 210, 232
apparitions of Mary, 15, 16, 17, 22, 120, 214, 237, 271n24; Alex sees, 33; of Fatima, 104, 260n20; of Kanchikode, 97; in Kuravilangad, Kerala, 256n79; Rosalind sees, 67–68; of Velankanni, 14, 67

ārati, 119, 210–211, 270n23, 280n1
Arlappan, Rev. Fr., xiv, 133–135, 137–138, 158, 173, 179, 191, 215, 276n17
Ārōkkiya Aṉṉai. *See* Our Lady of Good Health
Arokkiya Mary, 158–159
Ārōkkiya Mātā. *See* Our Lady of Good Health
aruḷ, 37, 44, 50, 82, 86, 107, 116, 131, 191
Austin, J. L., 267n22
authenticity, 16, 54, 205–206, 228, 264n21, 267n22; church authorities and, 108, 228; of Dhanam, 185, 199, 200, 203, 206; of Nancy, 85, 87, 94, 96–97, 104–105, 199, 206; of Rosalind or Jecintho Prayer House, 59, 63, 67, 69, 74, 85, 87, 199, 206; "similar-but-different" practices mark, 94, 155, 203
āvi, 9, 64, 82, 147, 160, 174
Avvaiyar, 95, 267n23

Bayly, Susan, 253n53, 261n32, 269n3
belief. *See* nambikkai
Bell, Catherine, 20, 264n26, 267n21, 275n11
Benjamin, xiii, 34–35, 62, 67, 124, 259n9
Besant Nagar, 11, 15, 29, 56, 120, 270n14
Beschi, Constantine Joseph, 27, 149–150, 169, 195, 274n24
Bhabha, Homi, 79
Bhagavati, 109, 229, 286n40
bhakti, 268n33, 269n3; Catholics use term, 44, 50, 58, 80, 82, 91, 96, 107, 199; defined, 6; poetry, 12, 50, 252n47, 261n29; Shakta, 198
Bhārat Mātā ("Mother India"), 41, 200, 260n19
Bible, 76, 80, 97, 101, 229; Hebrew, 102, 254n67; Rosalind or Jecintho Prayer House and, 115–116, 128, 237, 242; Mary in, 16, 120, 254n67, 267n24, 284n26; Nancy and, 101, 105–107, 219, 267n24; New Testament, 16, 72, 102, 191, 228, 254n67, 266n4, 267n24, 268n32, 284n26; ordination readings from, 211–212, 281n4; Tamil translation of, 131; women in, 95, 267n24
black magic, 66, 98, 147, 158–160, 177, 193
blood, 87, 97–100, 268n33, 281–282n12
bodies: abject, 207, 280n26; consciousness or mind and, 20, 58–59, 272–273n8; disciplined, 73, 164, 264n29; female, 21, 141, 164, 207, 276n23; healing of, 23, 63; as homes for Mary or Mātā, 57, 73, 79, 83; hot or cold, 261n28; making space for Other in, 206; Mary's, 16–17, 227–229; pierced, etc. during possession, 153; possession's changes to, 9, 44, 94, 196; relations between, 141; restrictions on, 172; ritualized, 73, 275n11; touching of, 37, 44, 46–48, 59
boundaries: Aiyanar patrols, 155, 192–194, 248n4; Hindu gods or goddesses patrol, 173, 175; Mātā patrols, 172, 175; processions mark, 134; of religions, 206, 228; of self, 9, 163; temple, 8, 160; transgressions of physical, 154, 172, 174, 192, 197
Bourdieu, Pierre, 20, 262nn3–4
Brahmanical Hinduism, 6, 17, 215–216, 250n19; Catholicism and, 72, 152, 192, 213, 287n2; defined, 256n78; gods or goddesses of, 225, 248n4, 261n26, 270n20, 286n40; hegemonic, 21; marriage in, 266n7; purity or pollution in, 87; rituals or temples in, 152, 192, 225, 270n20, 287n2
British, 22, 140, 187, 221, 248n2, 250n19, 253n59, 271n25
brooms, 4, 28, 174, 184, 258n93
Butler, Judith, 278n10, 280n26

cāmis, 155, 174, 202; Jesus, 91, 144; Mary or Mātā, 86, 144; *pēy* and, 204, 205; possession by, 9, 153, 194, 197–198; stone baby, 183–185. *See also* gods
cāmiyārs, 9, 12
Canada, 11, 48, 286n42

candles, 153–154
Caṅkam poetry, 179, 258n91, 267n23, 279n17; *akam*, 5, 24, 163–164, 181–182, 279n17; contemporary Tamil views and, 163; landscapes of, 24, 26, 141, 193–194, 257n86 (*see also* pālai; marutam); possession in, 24; *puṟam*, 5, 24–26, 163, 179, 181–182, 200, 279n17
car festivals (*tēr bavaṉi*), 6, 90, 109–110, 131, 134–137, 192, 269nn2–3, 273n4, 274n10
caste, 6, 13, 21, 187, 192, 207, 273n7, 275n2; in Christianity, 57, 169; clothing marking, 135, 136; in colonial era, 248n2; impact on spatial freedom of, 164; *jāti*, *varna*, and, 247n2; labor and, 163; violence, 1, 134, 200, 208, 248n4, 273n4
casteism, 141
catechists (*kōyilpiḷḷai*), 80, 133, 144, 145
Celina, xiii, 62, 221, 236, 241–242
Chalakudy, 96–98, 102, 105
chapels: in Chennai, 15, 60, 111; homes renovated into, 37; in Manapunjai, 3, 231–233; in Mātāpuram (*see* Mātāpuram chapels); Rosalind's in Kodungaiyur (*see* Our Lady Jecintho Prayer House); spread of, 14; thatched hut, 14, 111, 143, 257n89, 270n14; Velankanni (*see* Velankanni Mātā churches)
Charismatic Catholics: in Devakottai, 280n23; as global movement, 96, 227, 285n33; in India, 267n25; in Kerala, 96–97; Nancy and, 95–99, 154, 219; priests, 52, 113; Rosalind and, 222; in U.S., 4–5, 9. *See also* Roman Catholics: charismatic
charisms, 191, 215, 277–278n3, 280n23
Charles, M., xiii, 39, 44–46, 50–52, 84, 151, 221, 260n15; as family patriarch, 61–62; at festival, 114, 125; Fredy and, 62, 234–238, 287n2, 287n7, at Lata interview, 64, 66; on Prayer House finances, 78–79, 224; priests and, 49, 114
Chennai: archdiocese (*see* Madras-Mylapore Archdiocese); churches or chapels in, 15, 60, 104, 111, 120 (*see also* Santhome Cathedral; *see also under* Velankanni Mātā churches); city arrest in, 29; colonial-era, 253n59; gendered labor in, 163; hospitals in, 32–35, 64, 70, 258n2; Mary in, 52, 60; migrants to, 54, 55, 64; population in, 263n15; Portuguese in, 253n59; possession in rural areas vs., 67, 151; religiosity in, 6; slums in, 60; St. Thomas Mount, 30, 50; tsunami or flooding in, 237, 258n95; women's shelters in, 281n6
Chettiars, 25, 27, 135, 163
childbirth, 3, 141, 144, 147, 161–163, 169, 182, 252n36, 278n9; of stone baby, 182–185
Chinna Unjanai, 1–2, 26, 130, 135–136, 178, 192, 200, 248n4, 249nn6–8, 273n4, 278n5
Chinnadurai, Rev. Fr. Vincent, xiii, 50–53, 236
Chinnappa, Most Rev. Dr. A. M., xiii, 112, 227, 282n16; in Muthamizh Nagar Velankanni festival, 118–119; prayers for, 128; on Rosalind and prayer house, 120–122, 215
Church of South India, 95
Clarke, Santhianathan, 18
colonialism, 17, 55, 79, 207
Comaroff, Jean, 284–285n30
converts: caste of, 21, 187, 251n22; to Danish Lutheranism, 150; Jesuits and, 13, 109–110, 267n27; Mary and, 14, 105–106, 120; to Roman Catholicism, 13, 14, 21, 89, 90, 110, 112, 140, 143, 187, 217, 242, 267n27; St. John de Britto's, 140, 143; St. Thomas's, 13; witnessing by, 54

Dalits: Catholic or Christian, 57, 119, 133, 142, 178, 187, 212, 247n1 (*see also under* priests, Roman Catholic); census figures of, 247n1; in Chinna Unjanai, Mātāpuram, or Ramnad, 133–137, 142, 143, 163, 178, 249nn6–7; double rupture for female, 208; in festivals or

Dalits: Catholic or Christian (*Cont.*)
processions, 137, 185, 192; Gandhi and, 135; higher castes and, 19, 135–137, 140, 193; murdered, 1–4, 140, 141, 179, 185, 187, 192, 195, 200, 249n8, 278n9; name for, 1, 247n1; politics, 134, 136; villages or hamlets of, 1–2, 4, 130, 134, 137, 140, 143, 187, 192, 200, 257n89. *See also* Scheduled Castes; Untouchables; names of specific castes
Daly, Mary, 284n26
darshan, 72, 125, 127, 201, 208, 210, 271n23
de Britto, St. João (John), 22, 140, 143
de Proença, Antão, 143
Dempsey, Corinne, 14, 269n1, 271n32, 287n1
Devakottai, 27, 147, 178, 179, 190, 209; Charismatic Catholicism in, 280n23; history of, 135; parish of, 26, 280n23; priests of, 26, 191, 209; Sahaya Mātā Church in, 144, 213
Dhanam: Adaikkala or Velankanni Mātā and, 148, 150, 194–195, 198–199, 202–203, 214, 273n4; Aiyanar and (*see under* Aiyanar); *akam/puṟam* discussed by, 181–182; boundaries patrolled or transgressed by, 172, 194; as Dalit, 247n1; early life of, 145–146; family of, 27, 142, 144–146, 165, 191, 203, 249n11, 276n17; fasting by, 191; gifts to, 148, 176–177; healing by, 23, 27, 31, 139, 142, 144, 146–153, 157, 159–162, 170, 173, 177, 178, 188, 203, 205, 207; hegemony and, 19–21; Hindu deities and, 204, 272n1; Hindu practices and, 154–155; Holy Spirit possesses, 280n23; interviewed, 27–28, 144–152, 153–154, 165, 174–177, 192, 204–206; in Manapunjai, 3, 145–146, 231–233; mantras said by, 147, 174; Mātā appears to, 3–4, 27, 148, 151–152, 192, 200–201, 203; Mātā diagnoses or "sees" through, 27–28, 147, 149, 150, 159, 192, 203; Mātā gives child to, 202; Mātā possesses, 10, 27, 75, 134–135, 144, 146–152, 155, 159–160, 172, 176–177, 187–188, 192, 194, 196–200, 203, 269n8, 273n4, 277n30; Mātā talks to or through, 146–148, 150, 176–177, 194, 198, 202–203, 269n8; as midwife, 144, 161, 182–185; *mukkāṭu* gesture of, 197, 202, 279n12; Nancy and/or Rosalind compared to, 9–10, 19, 23, 31, 66, 75, 141, 148, 155, 188, 199, 200, 203, 206, 216, 227, 230–231; oppression and, 186, 196; ordination of son of, 188–191, 203, 209–213, 215, 224, 277n2; patients of, 27, 146–152, 170, 176–177, 203; *pēy* discussed by, 146, 150–151, 160, 174, 204; *pēy* exorcised by, 23, 28, 146–147, 150–151, 154, 176–177, 183, 203, 231; *pēy* or *muni* possess, 4, 28, 30, 65, 137, 155, 187, 192, 194–198, 200–203, 278n9; practices reduced by, 191, 203, 280n23; prays, 27, 131, 146, 148, 152, 153, 177, 198–199, 203; priests or Church hierarchy and, 135, 191, 213–214, 227, 278n4, 280n23; "sees" for patients, 149; story of, 1–4, 9, 28, 133, 145–146, 154, 192–193, 205; village of (*see* Mātāpuram); villagers' views of, 135, 144, 172, 175–179, 181, 196, 206; on Wednesdays and Saturdays, 146, 202, 279n18
domination, 18–20, 214, 227, 262n4
Doniger, Wendy, 252n46, 256n78, 271n30, 284n24
dowry, 21, 89, 159, 249n11
drums, 2, 124, 136, 147, 209, 249n9
Durga, 225, 229, 271n28, 286n40

Elakurichi, 150, 195, 274–275n24
Eucharist: bloody, 97–98, 268n28; bun as, 222–223, 240, 242–244; doxology, 223, 282n14; Fredy and, 237, 239, 240, 245; liturgy for, 114, 233, 281n3; menstruating women can (not) receive, 169–170; as possession, 128–129; at prayer house (*see* Our Lady Jecintho

Prayer House: Mass at); priests control, 72, 97, 223 (*see also* priests, Roman Catholic: Mass performed by); transubstantiation of, 128, 213, 223, 272n34, 282n15; women's performance of, 73, 223, 231, 282n15
evil eye, 8, 39, 61, 169, 259–260n14
exorcisms, 11–12, 95, 162, 173, 266n17; in America, 9, 207; brooms used in, 28, 258n93; candles used in, 153–154; by Dhanam, 4, 148, 154–155, 157, 170, 177; Hindu, 28, 96, 153, 154; at Marian churches and shrines, 10, 252n36; of *pēy*, 96, 153, 154, 214; by priests (*see under* priests); by women, 21, 213
Ezili, 11, 17

faith. *See* nambikkai
Fanon, Franz, 284n30
Fatima, 45, 150; apparition at, 15, 113; churches, 90, 104, 216, 219; pilgrimage to, 7; prayer ("O My Jesus"), 41, 260n20; statues (*see under* statues)
Feast of Our Lady, 14, 134, 261n32, 273n3
feminism, 19, 55, 168, 181, 230, 231, 283–284n24, 284n26, 286n42
festivals: controversies over, 110–115, 117, 120–122, 131, 135, 274n10; dates of, 14, 110, 253n64; flags at, 52, 110, 113, 114, 126, 261n32; gendered roles or tasks in, 118, 123, 134, 270n22, 273n4; Hindu, 1, 14, 25, 109, 110, 122, 130, 134–137, 249nn5–6, 261n32, 269n8, 271n26, 271n29; Hindus or Muslims at Marian, 90, 109, 110, 128, 134, 273n4; history of, 6, 109–110; honors at, 136, 145; for Jecintho (*see under* Our Lady Jecintho Prayer House); *karakam* at (*see* karakam); Marian, 6, 109–110, 134, 145, 275n7; Mātāpuram (*see under* Mātāpuram); patronage of, 79, 109, 110; scholarship on, 269n2, 271n32; Velankanni, 6, 14, 90, 106, 253n63, 261n32, 270n22; village, 134, 269n8; violence at or over, 1, 25, 130, 134, 137, 140, 249n6. *See also* car festivals; processions
Florine Monis, Sr., xiii, 70–71, 126, 128–129
flowers, 35–36; prayers as, 80. *See also* rose petals
Foucault, Michel, 54, 208
Foulston, Lynn, 269n2, 271n26, 271n29
Francina, xiii, 48, 78, 83, 116, 222–223, 239–240; festival preparations by, 122; as note taker, 81, 270n18; in procession, 125–126
Fredy (Frederick Aswin), xiii, 30, 34, 61–62, 73; as altar boy, 129; death of, 234–237; as Jesus, 237–240, 242–243, 245; pictures or portrait of, 237, 238, 240, 242, 243, 287nn1–2; witnesses to, 238

Gandhi, Mahatma, 60, 135
gender, 10, 15, 254n66, 278n10; boundaries or spaces and, 172–173, 175, 182, 185, 194, 276n13; labor or work and, 139, 157, 163; norms, 21, 37, 40, 49, 87, 98, 141, 175, 193, 214; possession and norms of, 154, 157, 164; possession that crosses, 68, 78; roles, 22, 73, 77, 214; story patterns shaped by, 63
ghosts. *See* pēy; picācu
globalization, 12, 22, 56, 264n24, 270n11
glossolalia, 5, 6, 8, 95, 244, 278n3; Nancy's, 92; Rosalind's, 43, 47, 115–117, 222–223
Goa, 251n24, 253n59, 257n81, 270n22
God, 26, 56–57, 69, 74, 80, 97, 114, 152, 165, 209, 212, 226, 239, 244, 262n2, 265n36; agency and, 97; blessings, grace, or miracles of, 46, 82, 96, 106, 113, 116, 161, 177, 191, 277n3; in heart, 83; Jesus as, 90, 100, 102, 129; Mary or Mātā and, 90, 105, 107, 120, 128, 191, 203, 218, 229, 275n9, 284n27, 285n32; sacrifice for or service to, 95, 105; surrender to, 46, 83,

God (*Cont.*)
120, 128; Tamil names for (*see* Tamil: words for God or deities in); in Trinity, 32, 81, 82, 90, 222, 225, 237
"god-dancers," 9, 12
goddesses: Adishakti or Devi, 150, 198, 225, 284n24, 286n40; agency or autonomy of, 21–22, 231; Brahmanical, 225, 261n26, 261n28, 270n20; Dhanam's view of, 174–175, 193; domestic rites for, 6, 225, 268n31; family, 12; festivals for, 14, 109, 122, 127, 269n3, 271n26; fierce, 12, 26, 28, 44, 173, 229, 248n4, 261n26; heal and afflict, 9, 13, 193; Mary and or as, 11–15, 19, 22, 28, 94, 102, 208, 253n65, 266n6, 283n21; multiplicity of, 225, 272n1; in pantheon, 5, 284n24; possession by, 8, 9, 12, 15, 22, 43, 44, 89, 128, 264n21; pots as, 268n31 (*see also* karakam); prehistoric, 283n24; *shakti* of (*see* shakti); Tamil or South Indian, 12, 15, 28, 56, 208; temples for, 135, 136, 270n20; vehicles for, 271n28; village and/or local, 192, 207, 225, 248n4, 261n26, 261n28, 282n18
gods, 56, 194, 197–198; bachelor, 174; family (*kulatēvam*), 12; Hindu vs. Christian, 174–175; Jesus as, 91; Mary or Mātā as, 86, 144; number of, 13, 253n49; possession by, 9, 153, 155, 160, 173, 185 (*see also* "god-dancers"); vehicles of, 271n28; village or local, 173, 192, 248n4; warrior, 12, 250n17 (*see also* Aiyanar); words for, 56–57, 204, 282n13. *See also* āṇṭavar; cāmis; iṟaivaṉ; kaṭavuḷ
Goslinga, Gillian, 4, 275n2, 275n6
Gounders, 216, 251n33, 265n2
Guadalupe, 7, 15, 17, 113
Guha, Ranajit, 255n73, 256n77

habitus, 20, 80, 262nn3–4
"Hail Mary," 41, 42, 95, 126, 131, 148, 260n20; in Tamil, 131, 229, 272n6. *See also* rosary; Virgin Mary: *Mariyē vāḻka* expression for
hair, 171; loosened during possession, 4, 8, 171, 194; tonsured, 7
Haiti, 11, 17
healing: affliction and, 193, 205; of black magic, 66, 159; of bodily problems, 27, 54, 63, 141, 148, 261n28; in Charismatic Catholicism, 5, 96; by Dhanam (*see under* Dhanam); of economic problems, 23, 54, 63; of family problems, 23; of fertility problems, 7, 23, 144, 147, 207, 283n20; by Hindu deities, 9, 12, 193; by Hindu healers, 147, 148, 149, 155; by laying on of hands, 95; by Marian-possessed women, 10–11, 21, 23, 27, 45–46, 67, 71, 114, 144, 188; of marital problems, 23; by Mary, 4, 34, 59, 67, 148, 188, 230; in Mary chapels, 3, 27, 147, 149, 177, 206; of *pēy* problems, 27–28, 54, 66, 96; rituals or services for, 36; by saints, 8, 95, 267n24; of sick cattle, 11; vows for, 7, 159; witnesses to, 53–54, 205–206
health (*ārōkkiyam*), 59, 63
heart/mind (*maṉacu*), 58–59, 79, 83, 188, 199, 206
hegemony, 10, 17–21, 141, 213, 216, 231, 284n30; colonial, 79; defined, 18, 255n73; gender and, 208; types of, 21
Hindu nationalism, 21, 23
Hinduism: blood in, 268n33 (*see also* pollution); boundaries of, 228–229; Brahmanical (*see* Brahmanical Hinduism); caste, 207, 215; Christianity as seen in, 13; definition of, 5, 250n19; inclusivity of, 12–13; local or popular forms of, 57, 208, 225; non-Brahmanical, 8, 21, 192, 213, 256n78, 261n28; pantheon of, 248n4, 253n49, 284n24; possession in, 10; tools or tropes from, 63, 214
Holy Spirit, 82, 104, 106, 212, 240, 242; feather from, 47; gender of, 228; Mary sent, 107, 275n9; Nancy and, 90, 97–98, 106–107; *paricutta āvi*, 107; people "slain" by, 7, 8, 9; possession by, 43, 107, 227, 239,

280n23; Rosalind and, 47, 82, 222; Second Vatican Council on, 227; in Trinity, 32, 90, 222, 225, 237, 244
holy water, 28, 89, 92, 112, 122, 123, 166, 266n17, 276n18
honor. *See* mariyātai

Icakki Amman, 9, 26, 28
inclusivity, 12–13, 70, 175
India: Christians or Christianity in, 5, 13–14, 23, 250n22; colonial, 5, 13, 140, 248nn2–3, 250n19; "Mother" (*see* Bharat Mātā); North, 5, 146, 269n2, 275n28; Order of the Mass in, 281n3; soul or "self" in (*see* "self"); South (*see* South India)
interpellation, 196, 199, 278n10
iṟaivaṉ, 191, 222, 262n2, 282n13. *See also* gods

jātis, 27, 247–248n2. *See also* caste
jebam (*mālai*), 79–80, 148–149, 160, 177, 198, 199; as *mantiram*, 160
jebuvīṭu, 259n13. *See also* Our Lady Jecintho Prayer House
Jecintho Mātā: age or bent posture of, 43, 44, 75, 78, 92, 95, 265n36, 267n23; books about, 58, 63, 75, 81, 238, 264n31; bread or bun demanded by, 221, 239; as bride, 127; crowned, 124, 129; devotees adopt name of, 237, 287n4; fierce, 66, 78; flags, 125, 126, 237; God or Jesus and, 81, 90, 222, 223; messages given by Alex- or Rosalind-as-, 75–76, 81, 237, 244; as model, 82–83; as mother, 222, 224; name of, 45, 68–69; Nancy-as- (*see under* Nancy Browna, S); *pēy* driven out by, 54, 66; prayer house (*see* Our Lady Jecintho Prayer House); Prayer or prayers to, 41, 55, 65, 69, 73, 79–80, 111, 260n21; Rosalind-as- (*see* Rosalind-as-Jecintho); seal on vestments, 128, 129; statue or iconography of, 45, 54, 59, 67–69, 72, 117, 123–126, 128–129, 222, 238, 242; Velankanni and, 67; vision of, 68–69
Jesuits, 22, 27, 96, 143, 169; converts of, 13, 109–110, 267n27; Marys brought by, 14, 109, 149; rosary and, 79
Jesus, 13, 16, 57, 102, 212; as baby or infant, 36, 89, 129, 242, 243, 283n20; in bun, 221; bleeding poster of, 85–86, 88, 100; as *cāmi*, 91, 144; forms of, 282–283n20; Nancy and, 90, 96, 102, 105–107; path of, 81; prayers to, 80; Rosalind and, 72; Sacred Heart of, 89, 123, 126, 271n27; statues of, 36, 40, 60, 89; stigmata of, 265–266n4
Jews, 13, 16, 212, 228, 254n67
Julie, xiii, 34, 62, 73, 84, 122, 221, 224, 242

Kadiapatti, 158–159
Kali (Amman), 9, 12, 28, 60, 174–175, 184, 229, 272n3
Kalist, Rt. Rev. Bishop Francis, 210–211, 227
Kallars, 1, 135–136, 140, 163, 232, 248n3, 249n6, 273n7
Kandadevi, 1, 110, 131, 134–135, 140, 150, 192, 248n4, 273n6, 274n24, 278n5
kaṉṉi, 14, 203, 229
Kanniyakumari (goddess), 229
Kanyakumari District, 31, 75
Karaikkal Ammaiyar, 95
Karaikkudi, 26, 175, 178, 188
karakam, 122, 128, 210–211, 271n26
Karuppar, 192
kaṭavuḷ, 57, 102, 262n2. *See also* gods
kāṭu, 8, 137, 160
Kerala: Catholics in, 5, 118; Charismatic Catholics in, 96–97; Christians in, 13–14, 251n24, 253n54; Dhanam's husband in, 142, 146, 165, 176; Mary in, 256–257n79; priest from, 143, 257n89; Syrian Christians in, 109, 251n24
kinesthetic knowledge, 141, 149
Kodambakkam, xiv, 10, 85, 87, 98, 102, 104, 217, 219
Kodungaiyur: car festival in, 110–111, 122, 124–125; as neighborhood, 32, 59–60, 263n13; prayer house in (*see* Our Lady

Kodungaiyur: car festival in (*Cont.*)
Jecintho Prayer House); Velankanni shrines in, 259n9
Kodungaiyur Mātā, 99, 102
kolams, 6, 189
kōyil: defined, 257n89; east-facing, 210; Mātā, 26, 188, 193, 194, 198, 200, 208; prayer house as, 259n13
Krishna, 88
Kristeva, Julia, 279n17, 279n22, 280n26
kumkum, 2, 122, 280n2
kuṟi, 8, 97, 183, 265n4, 277n39
Kutram, 84–87

Lakshmi, 6, 88, 123, 225, 275n28
Lata, xiii, 64–67, 82, 147, 154, 242
Lawrence (Charles's son), xiii, 62, 117, 129, 224, 241–242
Lawrence Pius, Rev. Dr., xiii, 112, 114, 120, 128; Jecintho Prayer approved by, 55, 69
Leela, xiv, 85–86, 88–89, 91–94, 98–102, 108, 218, 266nn12–15
Lourdes, 7, 14, 15, 45, 68, 113

Maatavan Shanthakumar, xiv, 85, 89–90, 217, 220, 265
MacPhail, Richard, 10
Madhavaram, 33, 60, 111
Madras-Mylapore Archdiocese, 50, 69, 108, 120, 124
Madurai, 5, 143; Meenakshi temple, 4, 43, 109; Pandi Muni temple, 8, 157, 160, 162, 183, 261n26
makimai, 93, 195, 197–198, 201, 203
Manapunjai, 3, 145–146, 231–232
Manikkavacakar, 50, 261n29
mantras, 3, 146–147, 160, 174, 176, 177, 231, 256n78
mantravādis, 21, 147, 155
Maria Auxilia, xiii, 62, 242
Mariamman, 8–9, 28, 44, 89
mariyātai, 58, 63, 81, 263n6
marutam, 26, 137, 257n86
Mary Magdalene, 16, 239
Mātā: affliction and healing by, 193; Alex and, 33–35, 37, 68–69, 76–77, 259n5, 277n35; benevolent or compassionate, 23, 174, 188, 252n36; boundaries patrolled by, 172, 175; as *cāmi*, 86, 144; candles and, 153–154; deterritorializing of, 200; Dhanam and (*see under* Dhanam); festivals or processions for, 110, 117, 123–129, 134, 273n4, 275n7; fierce or threatening, 23, 28, 66, 88, 92–93, 187, 203, 207; forms of, 68, 142, 148, 150; grace or blessings of, 45, 54, 59, 77, 82, 110; Hindu deities and, 197, 199, 202–203, 208; Hindus worship, 89, 128, 175; Jesus, God, and/or, 81, 90, 105, 144, 152, 191, 203, 218, 222, 227; Lata and, 65–66; *mantiram* said in name of, 176; Mary called, 3, 33; meaning of, 259n4; Nancy and (*see under* Nancy Browna, S); offers ways to renegotiate, 162; performance of, 63, 78; *pēy* vs., 23, 28, 144, 147, 150, 154, 187, 195; reciprocal or mimetic relations with, 201–203, 208; Rosalind and (*see under* Rosalind); Sahaya Mary sent to Pandi by, 160; *shakti*, 13, 122, 148; songs to, 43, 115, 244, 270n19; statue, 45, 90, 130, 270n20; tsunami survivors and, 30–31; witnesses to, 54, 195. *See also* Virgin Mary
Mātāmma, 239, 259n4
Mātāpuram: agricultural work in, 26, 137, 163–167; Aiyanar's importance to, 155, 192–193; *akam/puṟam* discussed in, 181–182; as alias, 25; as Catholic village, 1, 143–145, 155, 170, 171, 191, 208; clothing in, 171; cotton mill in, 23, 26, 137, 142, 146, 158, 164; described, 25–26, 130–131, 137, 142–143, 152; festival in, 134, 269n8, 273n4; healthcare in, 161; Hindu temples in or near, 166, 178, 192; history of, 140, 143; menstruation or pollution in, 169–170, 172; migrant laborers from, 142, 165; newcomers to, 178; people or population of, xiv, 26, 141, 144, 274n19; possession in, 141, 151, 193; priest from,

133–134; Unjanai and, 248n4, 278n5; water problems of, 166, 178–179, 181, 276n17, 280n23; widows in, 170
Mātāpuram chapels: candles in, 153–154; in center of town, 3, 4; description and history of, 26–27, 143, 257n89; Dhanam in, 3–4, 27, 151–153, 175–177, 183–184, 188, 194–195, 198, 200–203, 206, 224, 273n4, 277n30; holy water in, 166; ordination at, 210–211, 224; patient bound to tree next to, 168; patients stay in, 147, 149, 159–160, 162, 167–168; "rain rice" festival in, 275n7; small, roadside, 210; statues in, 26, 130, 148, 150, 152, 198, 210
Medjugorje, 7, 15
Meenakshi, 4, 109
mehendi, 105, 107, 217, 268n35
memory, 25, 33, 188, 205–206; cultural, 227; of dead, 208, 209, 241; embodied or muscle, 73, 141; lost during possession, 9, 49, 73, 101, 157, 200; of pain, 208; retained during visions, 151; shared or social, 24, 214
menstruation, 21, 99, 146, 163, 276n23; Eucharist during, 169, 170; Hindu vs. Catholic rituals for, 169; healing of problems with, 23; pollution of, 168, 169, 172; Tamil expressions for, 169; women's movements circumscribed during, 170, 174–175, 183, 185–186
messages: from Jecintho, 11, 49, 50, 68, 72, 75–77, 81, 115, 222, 237, 243, 261n24, 270n18; from other forms of Mary, 67–68, 97, 113; sermons vs., 114; from St. Anthony, 8. *See also* kuṟi
Michael, St., 39, 123, 126
middle class, 10, 22–23, 32, 39, 54, 60, 61, 63, 78, 87, 94, 224, 270n10
mimesis, 53, 149, 188, 195, 196, 200, 203, 205, 279n22
miracles, 7, 35, 97, 113, 126, 177, 214, 275n24, 278n3; bun, 221, 239; Nancy and, 85, 96, 98–99, 106–107
missionaries, 5, 140, 200, 204, 227; colonialism and, 21, 149, 200, 256n77; indigenous customs used by, 6, 169; Jesuit, 13, 96, 149, 169; Mary introduced by, 149–150, 195; Roman Catholic, 6, 14, 21
modernity, 22–23, 56, 63, 141, 263n16, 268n33
Mosse, David, 251–252n36, 287n1
mukkāṭu, 175, 197–198, 202
Mukkuvars, 10, 75, 163, 169
Mundadan, Mathias, 13, 253n54
munis, 4, 155, 156, 160, 170, 192–194, 250n17
murtis, 72, 109, 127, 136, 223, 260n18, 270n20, 272n1, 280n1. *See also* statues
Murugan, 88, 257n86, 271n28, 281n11
Muslims, 5, 15, 43, 61, 109, 134, 247n1, 250n22, 259n13, 271–272n32; Mary and, 10, 16, 71, 81, 110, 112, 124, 127–128; as rulers, 140
Muthamizh Nagar, xiv, 35, 69, 114, 270n13; new parish of, 111; procession for Annai Velankanni Church in, 117–120
Mylapore, 13–14, 253n59, 274n24

Nadars, 135, 163, 232, 249n6, 273n7
nadus, 192, 278n5
Nagapattinam, 7, 14, 35, 89–90, 229, 270n14
nagas, 12, 277n32
Nagercoil, 50, 54, 64, 67
nambikkai, 45, 58, 63, 106–107, 148, 201, 229
Nancy Browna, S., xiv, 10; benefits of Mātā or possession for, 93–94, 220, 231; caste or class of, 10, 265n2; Charismatic Catholics and, 95–96, 154; considers becoming nun, 95–96, 98, 101, 102, 106, 216, 220; Dhanam compared to (*see* Dhanam: Nancy and/or Rosalind compared to); early influences on, 95–97; Eucharist bloody for, 97–98; family of, 10, 93, 106,

Nancy Browna, S. (*Cont.*)
217–218, 231, 251n33, 265n1, 266n11; hegemony and, 19–21, 227; interviewed, 87–93, 95, 101–104, 105–107, 217–220; Jecintho possesses, xiv, 84–94, 96, 101–103, 216, 217, 219, 220, 265n3; Jecintho Prayer House and, 85, 91–92, 99–100, 108; Jecintho threatens, 88, 92–94, 216; Jecintho visions of, 216; Jesus and, 90, 96, 102, 105–107; *māman* of, 89, 101, 105, 107; marriage of, 88–94, 96, 98, 101, 103, 107, 141, 216; Mātā and, 105–107, 142, 203, 219, 220, 230; parish views of, 104–105; Pentecostals and (*see under* Pentecostals); "power" comes to, 93, 98; prays, 90, 101, 102, 107; Rosalind and, 10, 23, 85, 87, 94, 99, 101–102, 151 (*see also* Dhanam: Nancy and/or Rosalind compared to); stigmata or blood of, 10, 85, 87–88, 90, 99–100, 102–103, 217, 279n19, 282–283n12; television program on, 25, 84–86, 103, 108

Narendiran, 115–116

Navarāttiri, 14, 109, 269n3

nuns: Alex, Rosalind, or prayer house and, 33, 35, 38–39, 45–46, 70–72, 125, 127, 128, 129, 222, 224; Dhanam and, 3, 146, 191, 211; Franciscan Missionaries of Mary, 62, 71; Nancy considers becoming, 95–96, 98, 101, 102, 106, 216, 220; possessed by Mary, 11, 252n44; *shakti karakam* carried by, 128

offerings, 23, 27, 37

Our Lady Jecintho Prayer House: archbishop bans attendance at, 111, 112, 114; archbishop on, 120–122; bodily practices at, 59; brochures or pamphlets about, 30, 54, 259n9; church officials' conflict with, 110–114, 120–122, 270n16; core group at, xiii–xiv, 25, 55, 61, 71, 78, 80–81, 114, 115, 122, 126, 224, 282n16; crowds at, 36–37, 39, 78, 114, 124, 129, 282n16; described, 37–48, 242–243; devotional book published by (*see* Turning toward the Dawn); donations to, 37, 78–79, 108, 114, 224; festival or function at, 50–53, 71, 79, 110–117, 122–129; festival patrons at, 79, 110; festival procession or cars at, 110, 112, 117, 123–128, 134, 270n23; Fredy's portrait in, 237, 242, 287nn1–2; Hindus or Muslims at, 45, 52, 71, 81, 110, 124; as home or home's importance for, 57, 66, 79, 81, 83, 141; hospitality committee in, 122–123; important words or themes for, 57–58, 82; in Kodungaiyur, 10, 29–30, 37, 38, 46, 51, 56, 83, 87, 91–92, 98, 117, 120; Mass at, 52, 72, 79, 110–114, 124, 128–129, 237; monstrance in, 222–224, 243; murals in, 224, 243; name of, 259n13; Nancy and (*see* Nancy Browna, S: Jecintho Prayer House and); parish or parish priest of, xiv, 69, 111–114; possession cured at, 54, 65–67; priests or nuns at, 46, 50–53, 69, 70–72, 110, 117, 124–129, 227; reasons for attending, 45, 63; sermons vs. messages at, 114; social or cultural capital of, 70, 263n4; statues in, 40, 41, 42, 44, 45, 69, 124, 236, 237, 242; television show on, 84–85, 87; threatened, 113–114, 270n17; website, 75; witnesses at (*see* witnesses)

Our Lady of Fatima. *See* Fatima

Our Lady of Fatima Church (Kodambakkam), xiv, 104

Our Lady of Good Health, 7, 14, 111, 159

Our Lady of Lourdes. *See* Lourdes

Our Lady of Refuge. *See* Adaikkala Mātā

Our Lady of Succor. *See* Sahaya Mātā

Our Lady of the Snows, 14, 109–110

Our Lady of Velankanni. *See* Velankanni Mātā

Padma Balaji, S., xiv, 87; at Ambrose interview, 104; as Hindu, 136, 204, 274n24; at Mātāpuram interviews, 133–134, 138, 142, 146, 151–154, 156, 159–160, 170, 175, 185, 204, 276n18; at Nancy interview, 87–89, 101–103, 216
pain: Alex's, 32–33; Dhanam's, 2–3, 28; different types of, 141; economic, 64; Illich on, 268n33; Mātā's, 188; possession enabled by, 208; of stigmata, 102, 258n33; transferred to healer, 28, 149, 161, 203; as trope of possession, 279n19
pālai, 26, 137, 167, 187, 232, 233, 257n86
Palayamkottai, 5
Pallars, 1, 27, 136, 248n3, 249n6, 273n4
Pandi Muni or Munisvarar, 4, 44; as bachelor god, 174; children given by, 160–161, 203, 274n12; devotees of, 275n2; hair offerings to, 138; possession by, 4, 8–9, 44, 156–157, 159–162, 173, 261n26, 274n12, 275n6; temple of, 8, 160–162, 173, 261n25; virgins and, 156–157, 160, 203
Paraiyars, 2, 136, 158, 164, 249n9, 251
Paramakudi, 133–134
Paravas, 109–110
Parvati, 88, 136, 192, 225, 261n26
patriarchy, 215, 230; Marian possession as challenge to or refuge from, 10, 18, 19, 98, 141, 207, 214, 216, 220; Marian possession's confirmation of, 10, 19, 55; in Roman Catholic Church, 5, 18, 19, 21, 55, 214, 273n4, 284n26; subalterns vs., 256n77; in Tamil Nadu, 21
Paul, M., xiii, 33, 61–62, 242
Pentecostals, 18, 23, 121, 227, 261n25; Nancy and, 89, 93, 95, 105–106, 193, 217, 219
Perambur, 59–60, 64, 239
Periyanayaki Amman: Hindu goddess, 136, 150; Mary statue called, 150, 274n24
Peter Raj, xiv, 145, 165
pēy: *aṭṭam* or dance of (*see* possession: dance of); Dhanam and (*see under* Dhanam); films about, 12; general beliefs about, 2, 9–10, 15, 28, 147, 154, 157, 160, 193–194, 287n2; Hindu gods as, 193, 204; Mātā or Mary vs., 23, 28, 54, 106, 144, 147, 150, 154, 176, 181, 193–195, 200–201, 208, 214; Nancy and, 87, 96, 103, 106; possession by, 4, 9, 15, 44, 54, 65–66, 96–97, 153, 160, 167–169, 174, 176–177, 181, 258n92, 261n26, 277n30; pregnancy prevented by, 2, 202; spaces or boundaries and, 167, 172, 181, 185; stone baby and, 183–186
Philip, Rev. Sr. Dr. Mother Annamma, xiii, 71–73, 126, 128
picācu, 9, 12, 146, 169, 198, 204–205, 258n92
pilgrimage: to goddess sites, 12; Marian, 6, 7, 13, 30, 34, 46, 89, 259n13; to Murugan sites, 281n11; to Potta, 96
Pitchaimuuthu, Rev. Fr., xiii, 113–115, 124–126, 128–129, 282n16
pollution, 87, 157, 163, 168–170, 172, 194; Hindu vs. Catholic views of, 169, 172
Pondicherry, 8, 113, 114, 282n16
Poondi Mātā, 195
Portuguese, 5–6, 14, 16, 22, 187, 247–248n2, 253n57, 253n59, 265n38; missionaries, 140, 143, 200; Velankanni and, 14, 17
possession: affliction and, 193; in America vs. India, 8–9, 11; catches, grabs, or plucks, 9, 28, 64, 66, 146, 156, 164, 167, 175, 204, 259n12; dance of, 4, 8–9, 92, 96, 147, 157, 159, 160, 177, 181, 194–195, 198, 202, 261n26, 266n12; by demons, evil spirits, or Satan, 9, 95, 96, 100, 106, 192, 252n47; divination of agent of, 96–97, 153, 194; everyday practices and, 139; eyeglasses and, 42, 72; films about, 12; gender and, 15, 77, 157, 162, 173–174; by goddess, 9, 11, 44, 89; hair during (*see under* hair); hegemony and,

possession: affliction and (*Cont.*) 19–21, 141; history of, 11–12, 22, 252n47; invited vs. uninvited, 12, 23; by Mary or Mātā, 10–12, 22, 63, 75, 105, 144, 151, 162, 225–226; mimetic, 200, 205; by muni, 4, 9, 170; oppression and, 162; by Pandi Muni (*see under* Pandi Muni); as performance, 63, 78, 279n13; by *pēy* (see under *pēy*); protest as, 181; rural vs. urban practices, 151; self-awareness lost in, 9, 49, 55, 73, 91, 151, 200–201, 227, 230; by spirit or deity, 7, 9, 11–12, 15, 94, 160, 266n5, 279n13; in Sri Lanka, 11; Tamil for (see Tamil: words for possession in)

Potta, 96–97

power, 7, 15, 18–21, 93–94, 97–98, 109, 127, 140, 162, 207–208, 213. *See also* makimai; shakti

prasādam, 82, 91, 110, 249n12, 265n42, 287n8

pregnancy: boundaries of, 154, 155, 167, 170, 185, 186; *munis* and, 170; Pandi Muni and, 160; *pēys* and, 2–4, 194, 202; stone baby, 182–185; in Tamil Nadu, 250n14, 276n23; Virgin Mary's, 105, 107, 226

priests, brahmin, 21, 23, 247n2, 250n19, 256n78, 270–271n20

priests, Hindu, 6, 72, 136, 248n4, 270n23

priests, Roman Catholic: authority of, 108, 213, 227; caste and or of, 57, 133; Dalit or low-caste, 133–134, 212, 215, 258n93; from Divine Retreat Center in Potta, 96–98; exorcisms performed by, 9, 21, 22, 28, 96, 258n93, 266n17; heresy identified by, 227, 257n81; honors or garlands for, 53, 116, 119, 124, 129, 210; Jecintho Prayer House and, 30, 49–53, 55, 69, 71–73, 110–111, 113–116, 120–122, 124–126, 129, 222–223, 235, 237, 287n1; as Jesus, 212–213, 223–224; Marian possession as viewed by, 22, 105, 108, 113, 135, 191, 215–216, 227, 257n83; Mass performed by, 26, 52, 69, 72, 110–113, 118, 144, 223, 232, 237, 240, 282n14 (*see also* Eucharist); Nancy and, 96–98, 103–105; ordination of, 188–191, 209–215, 282n15; ordination of women as, 18, 73, 282n15, 285n32; parish, 35, 49, 69, 103, 111, 120, 144, 208, 209, 240, 259n8, 270n10, 278n4, 280n23; practices appropriated, 155

processions: Hindu, 43, 109, 135–136, 249n5, 271n29; history of, 109–110; Jecintho Prayer House's, 110–112, 114–115, 124–128, 235, 237, 270n16, 270n20, 273n4; Marian, 6, 90, 110, 117–118, 134, 145, 269n1, 273n4; in Mātāpuram, 134, 191, 273n4; power of, 127; small, 117–119. *See also* car festivals

Protestants, 8, 150, 193, 282n15. *See also* Church of South India; Pentecostals

puja, 88, 225, 270n23, 280n1

Puliyal, 3, 145

purity, ritual, 6, 157, 163, 168–169, 172, 194. *See also* pollution

Ram, Kalpana, 10, 171, 266n18

Ramanathapuram (Ramnad) District, 134, 135, 140, 143

Rani John, 97

rape, 229, 284n26

resistance, 17–19, 230–231

respectability. See *mariyātai*

resurrection, 58, 239

Rex, xiii, 80, 126, 242

Robert, xiii, 34, 76, 221, 224, 241, 265n36, 270n16; crowd control by, 78; in festival or procession, 122, 124–125; Fredy and, 235, 238–239; math lecturer, 62, 79; on prayer, 82; touching explained by, 37, 77

Roman Catholics: candle dousing by, 153–154, 202; caste and, 21, 57, 142, 169; charismatic, 22, 63, 191 (*see also* Charismatic Catholics); converts (*see under* converts); demographics, 5; doctrines or theology of, 16–17, 19–20, 90,

116, 128, 202, 214, 222, 223, 272n34, 277n3; festivals of (*see under* festivals); foot washing by, 72; garlands or flowers used by, 53, 110, 287n1; as hegemonic, 21, 213; Hinduism or Hindu practices and, 13, 50, 72, 88, 152, 155, 158, 169, 171, 206, 213–214, 258n90, 261n32, 271n32, 287nn1–2; history in India, 14–15, 18, 253n59, 265n38, 281n3; "local" vs. "universal," 10, 17, 193, 214, 228; Mary's or Mātā's importance to, 105, 144, 158, 226; materiality of worship of, 7, 80; "new," 63; nuns (*see* nuns); organizations, 134; orthodox, 8, 15, 17, 18, 21, 63, 141, 191, 202, 207, 214, 216, 222, 228; Pentecostal practices and, 42, 44, 63, 95, 227; priests (*see* priests, Roman Catholic); "rain rice" (*maḻai cōru*) of, 159, 275n7; schools, 70, 95, 142, 145 (*see also* Stella Maris); Tamil or South Indian, 20, 50, 79–80, 93, 95, 171, 193, 229–230, 259n7, 287n2; upward mobility of, 57–58; villages of (*see under* villages)

Rosalind, xiii, 10, 25; agency of, 55, 188; Alex and, 34–37, 63, 67, 69, 76–77, 200, 224; authenticity of (*see under* authenticity); authority of, 72; body of, 57, 73, 223; conceives son, 240; daily routine of, 73–74; death of son of, 235–243; Dhanam and/or Nancy and, 10, 23, 75, 87, 94, 95, 141, 142, 148, 149, 151, 155, 188, 200, 227, 231; education of, 62, 70, 222; Eucharist and, 222–224, 239–240; family of, 10, 39, 53, 61–63, 74, 78, 108, 224, 236, 238, 241, 263n4; fasting by, 39, 47, 48–49, 74, 236, 264n30, 279n19; followers of, 36–37, 44, 50, 55, 57, 64–65, 71, 87; gender norms and, 77–78; health of, 39, 49, 74; hegemony and, 19–21, 55; husband of, 62, 63, 224, 241; interviewed, 30, 48, 67–69, 73–75, 220–222, 259n12; Jecintho and, 35–37, 45 (*see also* Rosalind-as-Jecintho); messages given to, 49, 68–69; mother of, 74, 127; nuns and, 70–72, 224; other Marys and, 68; prayer house of (*see* Our Lady Jecintho Prayer House); prays, 37, 46, 48, 73–74, 82, 241, 243; president of trust, 79, 224; priests and, 49–51, 53, 55, 72, 113–115, 120–121, 129, 215, 227, 236; in procession, 125–127; songs written by, 115–116, 244–245, 270n19; status of, 49, 55, 224; television show about, 84–85, 87, 108; visions of, 45, 67–68, 224; on Wednesdays and Saturdays, 10, 37, 39, 74, 146, 236, 237, 279n18

Rosalind-as-Jecintho, xiv, 10, 37, 42–49, 68–69: bent posture of, 44, 75, 78, 87, 92, 95, 222, 265n36, 266n14; blessings or grace of, 47, 54, 65, 68, 77, 82, 91, 115, 222, 236; eyeglasses of, 42, 48, 72, 115; feet washed by, 72; festival or procession ordered by, 111, 115–117, 122, 237, 270n20; glossolalia of, 43, 115–117, 222–223, 244; messages or predictions, 49, 50, 75–76, 81–83, 113, 115–116, 270n18; Nancy and, 85, 87, 91, 94, 99, 101; "occupied," 36, 115, 259n12; on prayer, 82, 115, 222; as priest, 222–224, 231, 243; rosary beads given or used by, 81, 83, 223; roses or petals used by, 43, 91, 115, 122, 222, 244; salt water used by, 93, 222, 244; on salvation, 58; touch of, 37, 77, 115, 116, 265n34

rosary: beads, 7, 33, 40, 81, 83, 100, 129, 131, 223, 277n35, 260n18; as garland, 79–80 (see also *jebam* [*mālai*]; history of, 260n20, 265n38; Jecintho Prayer added to, 41–42, 80, 111, 115; prayed, 73, 79–82, 112, 115, 126, 131, 148, 160, 222, 242, 243, 268n32; prayed by family, 34, 74, 259n7

rose oil, 91–92

rose petals: congregation given, 43, 91, 122–123, 222, 244; in festivals or processions, 110, 119, 126, 128, 129; in Jecintho iconography, 243; miraculous appearance of, 34–35, 200, 201; Nancy uses, 87; photo of, 30, 35, 41, 42, 67, 259n9; Rosalind given or uses, 69, 115, 222, 244; as symbol, 34, 271n25
Ruby Mary, xiii, 62, 122
Ruether, Rosemary Radford, 284n24, 284n27

Sahaya Mary, xiv, 137–139, 144, 170, 186, 190, 275n4, 275n7, 276n17; childbirth of, 161, 172; interviewed, 154–161, 172; marriage of, 157–159, 162, 173, 214; Pandi Muni possesses, 156–157, 159–160, 162, 173, 274n12; Pandi Muni temple visited by, 160–162, 173; on pollution, 169, 172; possessed by *āvi*, 160
Sahaya Mātā (Our Lady of Succor), 60, 118; Devakottai church, 144, 274n19
salt, 42–43, 67, 92–93, 122, 123, 222, 243, 244, 266n17
salvation, 57–58
sandalwood paste, 119, 122, 123, 125, 169
Santhome Cathedral (Chennai), 13, 45, 50, 55, 104, 120, 282n16
Sauri Rajan, Rev. Fr., 124, 125, 128
Scheduled Castes, 10, 85, 247n1, 248n2, 251n22, 265n2. *See also* Dalits; Untouchables
Scott, James C., 18
Sebastiammal, xiv, 138, 158
Sebastian Samy, xiv, 144–146, 152, 190, 202–203; on Dhanam's possession, 175; in Kerala, 142, 146, 165, 176; Mary saves, 176; at ordination, 190, 210–211; *pēy* catches, 174, 176, 277n30
Second Vatican Council, 227, 228, 281n3, 285n36
"self," 9, 54, 163, 188
Shaktas, 198, 250n19
shakti, 12, 128, 150, 208, 250n19, 284n24, 286n40; *karakam*, 122, 271n26, 280n2; Mary, Mātā, or Jecintho as or possessing, 13, 45, 122, 144, 148; of mothers or women, 94, 171; related terms, 93; "Shiva without . . .," 199, 279n15
Shiva, 88, 127, 248n3, 250n19, 271n28; devotional poetry for, 261n29, 267n23; festivals for, 1, 109, 134–136, 192; in Hindu pantheon, 248n4, 284n24; *linga* of, 127, 136, 271n30, 273n6; as mother, 95, 267n23; Pandi Muni and, 156–157; possession by, 4; Shakti and, 199, 208, 279n15, 284n24; *Shivaṉē* expression about, 198; as Sundareshwara, 109; as Swarnamoorthi Eswarar, 130, 135
shrines: defined, 259n13; in Elakurichi, 150, 195, 274–275n24; festivals at, 261n32; Hindu, 6, 12, 263n16, 269n3; in homes or homes as, 7, 8, 73, 110, 126; for Jecintho, 14, 29, 259n13 (*see also* Our Lady Jecintho Prayer House); for Mary, 11, 14, 15, 60, 113; roadside, 6, 15, 60, 143, 259n9, 263n16; for St. Anne, 95, 267n24; thatched-hut, 111, 143, 270n14; for Velankanni, 89, 111, 259n9, 270n14
signs. *See* kuri
sins, 16, 54, 102, 213, 260n20, 268n32
Sivagangai Diocese, 143
Sivagangai District, 25–26, 54, 75, 133, 178
snakes, 65, 66, 130, 174, 264nn21–22, 277n32
Sofia Mary, xiv, 145–146, 165, 212, 276n17
soul, 9, 287n2. *See also* "self"
South India, 6, 67, 73, 102, 111, 128, 150, 213, 237; Christians in, 251n24, 253n54, 259n7, 272n1, 276n26; churches in, 260n21, 270n14; death or funeral rituals in, 287nn1–3; festivals or processions in, 109–110, 134, 269n2, 269n8; goddess worship in, 273n9; Hindus in, 287nn1–3, 287n8; Marian

possession in, 11–13, 15, 22, 94, 216, 228; marriage in, 158, 249n11, 266n7; Mary in, 229; medicine (Western or Siddha) in, 249n13, 261n28; modernity in, 22–23; oppressive regimes in, 17–18; Pentecostal growth in, 227–228; rural, 186, 190; spirit or deity possession in, 9, 11–12, 15, 94, 279n13; television or film in, 267n23; temples or *kōvil/kōyil* in, 210, 257n89, 259n13, 260n21, 261n32; urban, 59; women in, 34, 36, 62, 197, 207, 229, 249n11, 251n28, 276n26

speech acts, 230, 167n22

spirit possession. *See* possession

statues: of Adaikkalam Mātā, 26–27, 148, 150, 152, 175, 195, 202, 210, 275n24; of Aiyanar, 155; of angels, 242; bathed, 45, 54, 59, 116–117, 271n23; brought to India, 14, 274n24; crowned, 40, 60, 67, 68, 69, 124, 129, 150, 242; dressed, 7, 45, 54, 59, 111, 123, 150, 152, 242, 271n23; face east, 130; of Fatima, 26, 104, 150, 152; in festivals (*see* car festivals); garlanded, 7, 39, 40, 124, 150, 210, 238, 260n18; Hindu (*see* murtis); in home shrines, 61; of Jecintho, 45, 54, 59, 69, 123–127, 222, 237, 238, 270n20; of Jesus, 36, 40, 41, 89, 236, 242, 243, 283n20; living, 127; of Lourdes, 68; from Manila, 14, 109, 274n24; of Mary, 7, 26–27, 39–42, 44, 60, 72, 89, 100, 111, 116–117, 145, 238; of Our Lady of Snows, 14, 109; of Poondi Mātā, 195; processions with (*see* car festivals; processions); of saints, 39, 89, 152; of Velankanni, 35–36, 40, 89, 242, 259n9

status: caste or class and, 6, 135, 248n3, 270n10, 273n7; education and, 143; foreigner's presence improves, 51, 217; of Mary, 17, 226, 229; possession improves, 15, 19, 20, 23, 49, 55, 224; in prayer house, 63, 81, 110; temple honors and, 140; of women, 19

Stella Maris Women's College, 114, 264n31; faculty, staff, or nuns of, xiii, 70–72, 126, 224; Rosalind as graduate of, 62, 70, 222

stigmata, 17, 265–266n4, 268n33; Nancy receives, 10, 85, 87–88, 95, 103–104, 142, 201, 217, 279n19; Rani John receives, 97, 268n28

subalterns, 18, 149, 214, 255n73, 256n77

submission, 73, 121, 173, 197, 199, 215, 230, 279n12, 284n27. *See also* surrendering

suicide, 9, 66, 82, 90, 249n10, 266n9

surrendering, 46, 82–83, 120, 128, 194, 244

Syrian Christians, 14, 18, 109, 251n24

Tamil: formal vs. colloquial, 86–87, 94, 117, 259n5; glossolalia in, 43; grammar, 11–12, 24, 88, 278n11; liturgy, Mass, or prayers in, 41, 50, 80, 111, 152, 211, 229, 233, 281n3; poetry, 150, 258n90 (*see also* Caṅkam poetry; *bhakti*: poetry); translation from, 204–205; verb tenses in, 198, 258n3; word *farangi* in, 39, 56, 260n15; word *kaḻḻar* in, 140; word *kaṉṉi* in, 229; word *kōyil* in, 257n89, 259n13; word *matam* in, 262n1; word *urukkam* in, 199; words for emotions in, 58, 82, 88, 258n92; words for God or deities in, 56–57, 222, 262n2, 282n13; words for mind in, 58, 263n10 (*see also* heart/mind [*maṉacu*]); words for possession in, 8–9, 36, 96, 204, 251n31, 259n12, 265n3, 266nn12–13; words for power in, 93

Tamil Nadu: binding in, 171; bodies' heat or coolness in, 261n28; calendar in, 272n2; Christians in, 5–6, 22, 27, 57, 261n25, 267n24, 267n27 (*see also* Roman Catholics: Tamil); churches or altars in, 26, 152; colonial-era, 140, 265n38; families

Tamil Nadu: binding in (*Cont.*)
or familial relations in, 61, 249n11, 250n14, 258n1, 266n11; garlands or honors in, 260n18, 266n5; gender norms in, 21, 37, 40, 49, 87, 98, 139, 141, 214, 216, 249n11, 250n14; gods or goddesses in, 28, 56–57, 88, 193, 208, 250n17, 257n86, 282n19; Hinduism or Shaivism in, 95, 261n29, 267n23; kingship in, 269n3; Mary in, 19, 28, 67, 150, 258n90, 259n4, 259n9; names in, 265n1; possession in, 9–10, 15, 18, 28, 44, 55, 114, 199, 224, 252n47; rituals in, 260n18, 287nn1–3, 287n7; soteriology in, 57; southern, 1, 140, 248n3; statistics about, 247n1; Tanjore (Thanjur/Thanjavore) District, 11; tsunami's impact on, 30, 134, 258n95; view of inside vs. outside spaces in, 163, 181
television, 84–87
Thavamani, M., xiv; at Mātāpuram interviews, 179–181, 183, 185, 198, 204, 275n5; at Nancy interviews, 217–219; at ordination, 188, 190, 192
Thevars, 136, 232, 248n7
Thomas, Rev. Fr. A., xiv, 69, 111, 118–119, 122, 227, 270n16, 282n16; interviewed, 112–114, 270n10
Thomas, St. ("doubting Thomas"), 13–14, 16, 251n24, 253nn53–54
Tiruchirappalli, 267n23
Tiruvācakam, 12, 50, 261n29
Tolkāppiyam, 11–12, 24
Trinity, 41, 82, 90, 115, 116, 222, 225, 239
Tsunami of 2004, 30, 75, 133, 134, 222, 258n95
turmeric, 28, 174, 271n23, 276n18
Turner, Victor, 281n7
Turning toward the Dawn, 58, 63, 75, 81, 264n31
Tuticorin, 14, 109–110

Ubakaram, xiv, 138
Unjanai, 192, 248n4, 278n5
"Untouchables," 1, 247n1. *See also* Dalits; Scheduled Castes

Vadivambal, xiv, 88–89, 93, 101, 216–218, 266n6
Vaigai River, 8, 135
Vatham, Rev. Fr. Aasir, xiv, 209–210, 278n4
Vatican, 72, 215, 223, 253n57, 285n33; apparitions authorized by, 271n24; doctrines of (*see* Roman Catholics: doctrines or theology of); Fredy and, 238; local practices and, 17, 227–228; on Mary or Marian possession, 11, 13, 223, 226–229, 252n44; on "messages" vs. "sermons," 114; patriarchal hegemony of, 18; Two (*see* Second Vatican Council)
Vedas, 11, 247n2, 248n4, 252n46, 253n49, 256n78, 272n1
Velankanni Mātā, 35, 278n4; apparition of, 14, 17, 113; bottles shaped like, 100; calendar art, 130; Dhanam and, 148, 150; festival, 90, 106, 261n32; healing by, 7, 159; Hindu devotion to, 89; history and popularity of, 14; iconography or statues of, 30, 35–36, 40, 60, 89, 242, 259n9; pilgrimage to, 6, 30, 34, 46, 89, 159, 217; popularity of, 259n9; as prototype, 67; as unmarried maiden, 229
Velankanni Mātā churches: Besant Nagar, 15, 57, 120, 270n14; Chennai, 15, 60; Nagapattinam, 7, 217, 270n14; Mutamizh Nagar, 35–36, 111–112, 117–119
vibhuti, 2, 119
villages: caste tensions or violence in, 110, 136; Dalit (*see under* Dalits); exorcisms in, 28; festivals (*see under* festivals); globalization or modernity's impact on, 23; healthcare in, 186; migration from, 47, 54, 142; possession in, 67, 141, 151; Roman Catholic, 1, 4, 25, 131, 134, 143, 145, 169 (*see also* Manapunjai; Mātāpuram); temples' relation to, 135–137, 192; tsunami's destruction of, 30, 134; women change at marriage, 157, 165, 169

Virgin Mary: agency or choices of, 229, 284n27; apparitions or visions of (*see* apparitions); Bharat Mātā or Mother India and, 14, 41; body of, 16–17; in Europe or Americas, 7, 19, 229, 253n65; forms or images of, 68, 69, 150, 283nn21–23; Hindu devotion to, 6, 13, 275n27; as Hindu goddess's "sister," 109, 269n1; history of, 16, 22, 253n65, 254n67, 283nn21–23; in India, 13–15, 22; as liberating figure, 19; local or multiple forms of, 15, 17, 19, 225–226, 258n90; *Mariyē vāḻka* expression for, 42, 126, 128, 131, 243, 260n23; messages to bishop from, 113; as mother, 203, 229; as old woman, 95, 113; orthodox version or views of, 16–17, 19, 214, 285n32; possession by (*see* possession: by Mary); pot/milk imagery for, 102, 107; in Tamil or South Indian Catholicism, 6, 13, 229; virginity of, 16, 203, 229, 254n67. *See also* Mātā
Vishnu, 52, 109, 198, 248n4, 250n19, 271n28, 273n6, 284n24
Vodou, 11, 17
vows, 7, 159, 230

Warner, Marina, 253n65, 283nn21–22
witnesses, 87, 195, 261n33, 268n33; defined, 53; to Fredy, 238–239; at Jecintho Prayer House, 47, 53–55, 63; to Nancy, 86; to stories, 205
women: abject vs. ideal, 206, 228, 280n26; clothing, hair, or jewelry of, 171; *cumankali*, 216, 281; dangerous spaces for, 164, 167; importance for Church of, 213; "improper" behavior by, 215; *kolams* drawn by, 6, 189; modesty or propriety of, 40, 59, 98, 260n17; old, 78, 86, 88, 94–95; ordination of, 18, 73, 282n15, 285n32; possessed more often, 15, 154, 174, 254n66; rolling to shrines by, 7; touching of or by, 37, 77; traditional virtues of, 77; Velankanni's popularity with, 7; violence against, 159, 162, 281n6; widows, 170; work by, 157, 162–166, 181–182

Županov, Ines, 13

CPSIA information can be obtained
at www.ICGtesting.com
Printed in the USA
BVHW032016061019
560372BV00002B/3/P

9 780190 067809